DOMESTIC CAPTIVITY AND THE
BRITISH SUBJECT, 1660–1750

Domestic Captivity and the British Subject, 1660–1750

CATHERINE INGRASSIA

UNIVERSITY OF VIRGINIA PRESS

Charlottesville and London

University of Virginia Press
© 2022 by the Rector and Visitors of the University of Virginia
All rights reserved
Printed in the United States of America on acid-free paper

First published 2022

9 8 7 6 5 4 3 2 1

Library of Congress Cataloging-in-Publication Data

Names: Ingrassia, Catherine, author.
Title: Domestic captivity and the British subject, 1660–1750 / Catherine
 Ingrassia.
Description: Charlottesville : University of Virginia Press, 2022. | Includes
 bibliographical references and index.
Identifiers: LCCN 2022008343 (print) | LCCN 2022008344 (ebook) |
 ISBN 9780813948089 (hardcover) | ISBN 9780813948096 (paperback) |
 ISBN 9780813948102 (ebook)
Subjects: LCSH: English fiction—Early modern, 1500–1700—History
 and criticism. | English fiction—18th century—History and criticism. |
 Captivity in literature. | Master and servant in literature. | Women in
 literature. | Authority in literature.
Classification: LCC PR769 .I54 2022 (print) | LCC PR769 (ebook) |
 DDC 823.4/09—dc23/eng/20220318
LC record available at https://lccn.loc.gov/2022008343
LC ebook record available at https://lccn.loc.gov/2022008344

Cover art: Marriage A-la-Mode: 1, The Marriage Settlement, William
Hogarth, ca. 1743. (The National Gallery, London, NG1130)

For my parents

· CONTENTS ·

· ACKNOWLEDGMENTS ·

The initial drafting of this book took place during a residential fellowship at Virginia Commonwealth University's Humanities Research Center. The semester of that fellowship enabled weekly meetings with my co-fellows Shermaine Jones, Brooke Newman, and Oliver Speck; their suggestions and insights formatively shaped this book at an early stage. Additionally, I appreciate the support and comments from then-HRC director Richard Godbeer. A semester of research leave from VCU also helped advance the progress of the manuscript and I value the support of then-dean of the College of Humanities and Sciences Montse Fuentes.

At Virginia Commonwealth University, I am fortunate to have many colleagues who work in the early modern period and participate in our longstanding working group. I have benefitted from lively discussions with Carolyn Eastman, Eric Garberson, David Latané, Mary Caton Lingold, Sarah Meacham, Bernardo Piciché, Catherine Roach, Sachi Shimomura, Ryan Smith, and Rivka Swenson. I am also thankful for the generous readings of individual chapters by colleagues including Paula R. Backscheider, Lance Bertelsen, Sean Moore, Laura Rosenthal, Jonathan Silverman, and Manushag Powell. Julian Neuhauser offered essential assistance at the British Library at a crucial moment. Wayne Bodle's capacious knowledge of Colonel William Cosby and all things colonial remain an invaluable resource. Madge Dresser provided a wonderful tour of Bristol and insights into the city's amazing M Shed Museum. The intellectual support of Jennifer Keith and Laura Runge (who have probably read the entire manuscript in some form) during our biweekly meetings has been, and continues to be, a lifeline. I treasure their wisdom, friendship, and careful reading of my work. The project was enriched by interactions with colleagues at ISECS and regional and national ASECS conferences. Working in such an invigorating, vital field is to be reminded of the persistent relevance of work on race, gender, and power. Similarly, the students at Virginia Commonwealth University with whom I have explored these ideas have sharpened my thinking. I finished this book while chair of the Department of English at Virginia Commonwealth University. The extraordinary skill, generosity, and high level of performance of the department's core staff make that job a daily pleasure and also made balancing administration and research possible. The entire staff—Kelsey Cappiello, Thom Didato, Gregory Patterson, and Margret Schluer—has my deep gratitude and affection. Equally important, the amazing people at VCU Libraries make everything possible and VCU Libraries remains the sine qua non for all of us in the humanities at this institution. Although I rarely get to meet the wonderful individuals in interlibrary loan who regularly help me get the books and articles I need, they have my boundless thanks. Earlier versions of chapters 1 and 5 were published in *Restoration: Studies in English Literary Culture, 1660–1700*.

At University of Virginia Press, Angie Hogan has been a fantastic and supportive editor to work with every step of the way. The comments, suggestions, and insights of the two anonymous readers of the manuscript definitely strengthened the book. Marilyn Campbell was a valuable copyeditor. Closer to home, I always cherish the good humor, boundless support, and camaraderie of my life partner, Miles, and our children Sophia and Pablo, but particularly during the completion of this book.

DOMESTIC CAPTIVITY AND THE
BRITISH SUBJECT, 1660–1750

Reading Captivity

What happens when scholars read literary texts from the early eighteenth century through the lens of captivity? If we better understand how the language of confinement, restraint, and subjection operates not (just) as metaphor but as a representation of material practices and cultural attitudes, might we interpret popular literary texts of the period differently? The short answer is yes.

When we recognize the often-coded markers and shared references to what I term "domestic captivity"—the captivity of white British subjects— we gain an enriched understanding of the anxieties of the period and their manifestation in literary texts. Domestic captivity's intimate connection to Britain's investment in the enslavement of Africans and their use as unfree labor in colonial sites is undeniable. Emergent and escalating concerns about the limitations placed on the British subject or about the consolidation of power by agents of control also become clear. And, once legible, these representations of captivity, these expressions of anxiety and fascination, complicity and fear, change how we read the texts in which they appear. As this book argues, these representations reveal such texts—many of them among the most popular of the era—emerge foundationally from a culture defined by diverse forms of captivity.

This book considers fictional texts by British authors from the Restoration and first half of the eighteenth century in which captivity informs identity, actions, or human relationships for white British subjects. During the period this book explores, the exercise of power on both an institutional and personal level could create conditions in which those least empowered—the poor and the dispossessed, the young and unprotected, and women both married and single—perceived themselves to be captive subjects. "Domestic captives" might include individuals held in indentured servitude or British subjects restrained by other forms of power (and the people manifesting that power) emanating from institutional, economic, social, or legal structures and their agents—a workhouse warden, a parish official, the military, a press gang, a landlord, a plantation owner, or even a spouse. The inequities institutionalized within England's socioeconomic structure created asymmetrical power relationships, assumptions of privilege, and the objectification of entire categories of people. These factors contributed to a "culture of captivity"—a culture with a persistent awareness of and anxiety about the presence and possibility of captivity and confinement in various forms.[1] Individuals across different ranks and genders lived in a world in which their identities were shaped by their connection to domestic captivity—a captivity that shaped those in a position of subjection but also those holding the power to constrain others.

My book focuses primarily on white subjects whose captivity originated or occurred in England; I give particular attention to forms of domestic captivity affecting women. To be clear, those I discuss as "domestic captives" did not occupy the permanent and inheritable status of people who endured a system of racially based enslavement. To use the term "captivity" in connection with the confinement of Irish, English, or European subjects is in no way to equate their captive condition to the bondage of enslaved Africans in a colonial site. The captivity of Britons and Europeans was a contingent not a perpetual state, a temporary not inheritable condition. But forms of domestic captivity and colonial enslavement are mutually reinforcing, reflecting the worst assumptions and possibilities about power and subjugation.

Domestic captivity cannot be understood separately from England's substantial involvement in the systematic enslavement of kidnapped Africans or the wealth accumulation realized from those actions, even as early fictional narratives elide or ignore the experience of enslaved people. These texts largely deny Black subjects humanity, voice, or sustained examination; their presence, though alluded to or assumed, is counterintuitively marked by their absence. The erasure of Black subjectivity in texts from the period explored in this book denies access to the interiority of nonwhite fictional subjects even as those texts and characters within them implicitly (and at times explicitly) summon the experience of the enslaved. This narrative pattern replicates a cultural pattern wherein enslaved people are "seldom represented as possessing personhood or subjectivity," an observation Felicity Nussbaum makes about silenced women of color from this same period.[2] Thus to focus on the domestic captivity of the British subject is to consider how the absence and inaccessibility of Black domesticity and, in turn, Black captivity, centrally shape (if in a kind of negative relief) the culture of captivity in England. It is impossible to separate an understanding of domestic captivity as enacted on a British subject from the actions and structures of enslavement in colonial locations. Even individuals not participating directly in the economy of enslavement would nevertheless register its presence domestically in the broadest sense of that term—domestic within England and domestic within the household—whether in the physical presence of enslaved people, the products of their labor, or the economic profits realized from West Indian plantations. Further, the expanding carceral punishments upon British subjects including transportation to the colonies were among the emergent cultural practices that intensified existing tendencies of England's dehumanization across class, race, and, at times, gender. The worldview that had so quickly naturalized enslavement simultaneously created a horizon of behavior, language, and beliefs that permeated culture and facilitated, indeed authorized, the continuation (or creation) of domestic forms of oppression, subjection, and captivity.

States of Confinement

To understand Britain's culture of captivity requires an understanding of how institutionalized, state-authorized, and financially lucrative forms of captivity altered the conceptions of personhood in England in fundamental ways. By beginning my study in 1660, I don't mean to suggest that British subjects somehow lived without constraint in earlier periods. A subsistence laborer, a restricted wife, a political prisoner, or a devout Christian who would perceive himself to be held in a "bondage . . . out of which none but the Lord alone can deliver"—these are a few among the many individuals who might have felt themselves to be constrained, confined, or otherwise held captive by the situations in which they found themselves.[3] Yet, a sequence of actions by the state following the Restoration and continuing into the early eighteenth century—including the establishment in 1663 of the

Company of Royal Adventurers Trading to Africa (which would become the Royal African Company) and the escalating practice of the transportation of individuals deemed criminal, institutionalized in 1718—created categories for humans that conceptualized them purely as property or captive labor. Such categorization simply hadn't existed before. These changes, while most directly affecting enslaved Africans, also reconceptualized the relationship between the British subject and the state, shifting the way individuals thought of themselves and those around them. The state's commitment to captivity as a concept, as a means of wealth acquisition, and as an empowering structural mechanism necessarily redounds to domestic manifestations of personal interaction and understanding. The concurrent practices of enslavement and human commodification foundational to England's colonial expansion and global ascent fostered a naturalized attitude toward the condition of captivity—including domestic captivity—that permeated British culture.

The narrative of England's involvement in the Atlantic slave economy is increasingly well known, but some important details merit reiteration because the country's intimate engagement with the global trade in enslaved Africans is central to understanding a domestic culture of captivity. By royal charter in January 1663, Charles II created the corporation initially known as the Company of Royal Adventurers Trading to Africa. Further, the legal codifying of enslavement, what Peter Linebaugh describes as the moment "that human beings become 'real chattels,'" began almost simultaneously with the passage of the Barbados Slave Code by the colonial legislature in 1661.[4] The state-authorized engagement in global enslavement created what Elizabeth Bohls terms the "captive spaces of the Atlantic" that profoundly shaped Restoration and early eighteenth-century culture.[5] Certainly England had engaged in the enslavement of Africans previously. One of the "arresting features of British colonial enterprises" between 1603 and 1638, notes Arthur H. Williamson, was "their ubiquity."[6] As early as 1562, John Hawkins brought the first enslaved African to England. The Senegal Adventurers received a charter in 1588 for a ten-year monopoly on trade with Senegal and Gambia.[7] Charles I issued a charter in 1631 for the English Guinea Company and then, in 1634, for what was known as "the Guinea Company of Scotland." Both Guinea companies pursued the "African trade" with a focus primarily on gold.[8] In the aftermath of the restoration of the monarchy, however, a more coherent practice of colonial exploration emerged as Charles II recognized the opportunity for financial expansion in the Americas.

The Company of Royal Adventurers was reconstituted with a new charter as the Royal African Company on September 27, 1672, with James, Duke of York, as its director. Ostensibly the Royal African Company (RAC) traded in a range of commodities with a particular focus on ivory and gold. Indeed, the twenty-one-shilling gold coin known as the guinea came into circulation in February 1663, a month after the company's original chartering.[9] As Holly Brewer observes, "Charles II not only pledged his body and his sword to slavery; he pledged the coin of the realm."[10] The coin, which included an image of an elephant to symbolize the corporation's association with Africa, derived its name from the Guinea Coast of Africa, the source of the coin's gold. But the coin's iconic representation of an elephant could not obscure the fact that the primary trade of the Royal African Company was in enslaved Africans. As the 1667 document seeking additional RAC subscribers details, the company was committed to providing "the *English* Plantations in *America*" with "a competent and a constant supply of *Negro-servants* for their own use" and to selling "all Blacks that are found in Lotts (as hath been *customary*) at £.17. sterling p. head in money . . . or Bills of Exchange for *England* with good assurance of payment."[11] Between 1662 and 1689, the Royal African Company tightly held monopoly control on the trade; between 1680 and 1689, it transported an average of 5,000 enslaved Africans annually, sponsoring 249 voyages to Africa.[12]

In the middle of the seventeenth century, indentured servants and enslaved Africans in initially nearly equal numbers were used on West Indian plantations. Richard Ligon in *A True and Exact History of the Island of Barbados* (1657) refers to "servants, both Christian and slaves," often interchangeably. However, the escalating labor needs demanded by the cultivation of sugar coupled with the increasing dependence on the labor of enslaved people changed patterns of unfree labor in the West Indies. Planters quickly recognized the economic advantage of purchasing the enslaved, subject to a life of captivity, rather than the indentured, owned only for a set period of time. The transition from the use of indentured servants to primarily enslaved Africans marks not only their shared origin in meeting the demands for a labor source but also how the categories of unfree labor initially were not as well delineated as they would later become. The RAC cast the use of the enslaved rather than the indentured as beneficial to England (simultaneously distinguishing between and leveling those two categories of labor). *Certain Considerations Relating to the Royal African Company of England* (1680), a pamphlet commissioned by the company to advocate for itself, posits that its trade in enslaved Africans will prevent "exhausting the Nation of its natural born subjects,"[13] figuring British subjects as the other labor source. While the RAC would lose its monopoly on the trade in enslaved Africans by 1698, the public narrative that the transatlantic slave trade was in the national interest would persist, gaining renewed momentum after 1713 with the *asiento* and the establishment of the South Sea Company—another example of a state-sponsored commitment to enslavement.[14]

With James the Duke of York serving as the RAC's governor, the crown was inextricably connected with the global trade in enslaved Africans.[15] (That connection would have been visually underscored by the branding of enslaved individuals with the letters "DY" for the Duke of York.)[16] People with significant holdings in the West Indies constituted a network of sorts and, certainly during Charles II's reign, relatively few families in the gentry and aristocracy were without some connection to the economic engine of the West Indies. Although the financial investment in the so-called "African trade" was initially led by the crown and the court, it increasingly attracted a much wider range of participants in the decades that followed. The important work by the Centre for the Study of the Legacies of British Slavery, led by Catherine Hall, has exploded the idea that slave ownership in England was concentrated only among a few wealthy families possessing large numbers of enslaved individuals.[17] Financial participants in some element of slave ownership constituted a diverse group of people in terms of geography, gender, and class. In the early part of the eighteenth century the investment in West Indian properties was an aspirational act, an opportunity to potentially improve one's situation. Individuals regarded investment in the West Indies much as they did any other form of speculative investment—as an opportunity to accumulate and retain wealth quickly and with relative ease. By the end of the eighteenth century (well beyond the scope of this book), that pattern of investment became so normalized that, as Hall and her colleagues document, purchasing "shares" in enslaved people was seen as a "safe" investment for widows and members of the clergy.

During the Restoration, the Duke of York's investment in enslavement both financially and psychologically created what Holly Brewer terms "a fashion for slavery" within the court.[18] As Peter Fryer observes, in the latter part of the seventeenth century "[h]aving a black slave or two in one's household soon became a craze for all who could afford it."[19] Elite Britons incorporated "African servants into their households," details Catherine Molineux, "because their rarity, expense, and imperial origin elevated their master or mistress."[20] British portraiture from the period regularly includes representations of young, liveried African boys in postures of submission and adoration, evidence of the sitter's wealth and status; such paintings also worked to "obscure the violent origins of imperial wealth."[21] As with narratives of the same period, these images invoke but ultimately deny the experience of Black domesticity.[22] The satiric pamphlet *The Character of a Town Miss* (1675) describes the "Town Miss" of the pamphlet's title as always having "two necessary Implements about her, A *Blackmoor,* and a little Dog,"[23] a chilling characterization that levels the two "Implements." (The word "implement" itself is telling, meaning both "something necessary to make a thing complete" and something that serves as an outfit or a piece of equipment.) Such a text, like others from the same period, situates enslaved Africans within representations of the domestic as a kind of narrative accessory that simultaneously contributes to Black erasure and reiterates its connection with urban fashion.

The widespread involvement in imperial actions in the West Indies meant that domestic evidence of enslavement and England's participation in Atlantic commerce was everywhere. For example, the presence of enslaved people on English soil was increasingly visible. "Once the lens through which we view the eighteenth century is refocused," notes Gretchen Gerzina, "[it] becomes occupied by a parallel world of Africans and their descendants working alongside the English."[24] They are undeniably part of British domestic culture even as their presence and their own capacity to realize a domestic existence is elided. Enslaved Africans would have been a familiar sight in London and many other cities in England. Madge Dresser and Andrew Hann detail both the presence of the enslaved in the British country house as well as the degree to which the wealth derived from "the trade and labour of enslaved Africans" shaped the "erection, renovation, and occupation of a significant number of Britain's stately homes."[25] Even individuals who did not have a direct personal economic investment in or connection with the colonies (although that was in fact a smaller number of people than perhaps originally imagined) could not escape the effects of the British involvement in the West Indies and the system of unfree labor on which it depended, or the evidence of those colonial ventures in England.

Additionally, notices of enslaved individuals who have run away operated as repeated visual reminders both of the presence of enslaved Africans in England (even when absent) and of their colonial origins.[26] "A Negro Woman short but thick," recognizable by her "Stuff" petticoat and jacket and "marked with a P and B on her back" had "run away from her Mistress on Friday night."[27] Like the woman, "marked" with initials branded on her back, many enslaved people bear the physical signs of their bondage. "A Negro 18 years old, of middle stature" who "speaks very little English" "is about London" and will be known by "a bare place on his Head of the bigness of a shilling." "Champion, about 14 years of Age, very black and handsome" is distinguished by "A scar on his forehead over his nose."[28] "Benjamin, . . . Aged about 20" has "Both Ears cut or clipped" and is "Branded on both Shoulders."[29] While the notices foreground the physical appearance of the absent enslaved, they do not construct the narratives those bodies implicitly invoke or infuse the individuals with the humanity they are due.

Such postings often sat adjacent to both other notices of lost property ("a young Grey Mare," "a white Spaniel Bitch," "a Gold Pendulum Watch with a Shagreen-Case,"[30] "a Petticoat of Musk Coloured Silk, shot with Silver on the right side"[31]) and evidence of the parallel restraint and control of white British subjects on domestic soil. The fifteen-year-old "Thomas Parker apprentice to Mr. Thomas Moody" "went away from him the second Instant." "Summerset Robins, aged about 20, down look'd, lank Hair'd, having a blemish in one of his Eyes, went away . . . from his Master Ralph Aguter."[32] "A Soldier in Captain Cornwal's Troop" not only "went away the first instant at night from the Golden Lyon," but also took valuable property: "a black Gelding near 15 hands."[33] Elizabeth "the Wife of Tho. Byfeld. . . . Eloped from her said Husband," "pick'd his Locks, rifl'd his House, and took and convey'd away divers Good and Chattels, to the value of 330 *l.* and upwards."[34] Newspapers also mark various kinds of confinement. Notices of bankruptcy demanded that the individual "Being declar'd a Bankrupt" "is hereby requir'd to surrender himself to the Commissioners," moving into a state of confinement beyond the restraint of debt alone. The incarceration and public punishment of those convicted of crimes is also described. William Westwood was "committed to Newgate" for breaking into a warehouse and "stealing from thence a large Quantity of new Nails." For "stealing Checque Linnen to a considerable Value," Mary Butts, alias Fleming, was committed to Newgate, tried at the Old Bailey, and then "whipt at the Cart's Tail last Saturday."[35]

The newspapers also chart another significant development in the culture of captivity—the practice of transporting prisoners to labor in the West Indian colonies, a form of punishment used with increasing frequency after 1660 and institutionalized in 1718 with the Transportation Act.[36] Traditionally, the punishment for crimes for which an individual could escape execution by demonstrating their literacy or "pleading the clergy" included branding on the thumb, pillorying, or public whipping. Yet, as James Beattie details, after 1660 the use of transportation as an alternative form of punishment gained increasing popularity; judges during the period viewed it, as stated in a 1663 royal warrant, as a policy that "might become . . . an advantage to the public."[37] (It is useful to remember that during this period, crimes of petty larceny that could result in transportation included theft under one shilling.) In 1718, the House passed the Transportation Act, which had the twin benefits of ridding England of those deemed "criminal" and providing the colonies with another supply of able-bodied laborers for what Peter Linebaugh terms "a period of slave labour."[38] Abigail Swingen similarly insists that transportation, or "coerced colonial labor," must be considered "part of a larger imperial project, intimately connected to both indentured servitude and slavery,"[39] a connection that further fuels a culture of captivity.

The nightmares experienced by Corinna of Jonathan Swift's A Beautiful Young Nymph Going to Bed (1734) span the forms of domestic captivity to which the dispossessed of London might be subject. "[I]f she chance to close her eyes," Corinna initially dreams of being whipped (she "feels the lash, and faintly screams") or being sent to a House of Corrections like Bridewell where inmates were required to labor during their term of service, a punishment formalized by the Workhouse Act of 1723. Corinna's nightmare also includes the fear of transportation as she imagines that she might "to Jamaica" be "transported, / Alone, and by no planter courted."[40] Rather than be imprisoned domestically she could be transported to labor for a period of time in a colonial site. Captivity remained in the consciousness (or in Corinna's case, unconsciousness) of early modern Britons, suggests George Boulukas, in part because all around them existed reminders of the various ways in which they "imagined that they themselves could become enslaved."[41]

Newspapers began including the "ship news" or information on "home ports" that relayed the arrival and departure of ships, heading to or returning from the American colonies or the West Indies. Following the Transportation Act of 1718, which allowed the state to transport subjects deemed "criminal," newspaper listings of the transportation of those identified as "convicts" bound for the West Indies sit adjacent to notices of ships transporting enslaved Africans or consumer products resulting from their labor.[42] The "Plantation News" kept a rapt London readership apprised of the events and expectations in the colonies. Advertisements featured descriptions of goods from colonial locations. Notices for exotic pets regularly appeared, detailing the sale of "a large Muccow, Scarlet Nightingales from the West Indies, both Cocks and Hens of the sort for Breeding as well as Singing; . . . common Coloured Pea Cocks and Pea Hens, several sorts of fine Pigeons, Turtle Doves, two Musk Cats from the West Indies" "with other Rarities."[43] William Turner sold imported rum and "Madera Wine from the West Indies."[44] Books detailing "the Spanish-Rule of Trade to the West-Indies" complete with an account of "who may go to the Indies, Slaves carry'd over, . . . the Ports in the Indies &c." could be purchased.[45] The mobility of Londoners—and the goods they acquire—is also implicit in the notices. "The Incomparable Powder for Cleaning Teeth" "is sent for in large Quantities to the Plantations beyond the Seas . . . and is as effectual in the East or West Indies as at London."[46] The newspapers embody in print what Richard Steele experiences in person at the Royal Exchange as he describes in *Spectator* No. 69. It represents the degree to which London the "Metropolis" is "a kind of Emporium for the whole Earth."[47] Consumers had the capacity to buy items from distant and exotic locales to bring into their domestic spaces.

As British imperial expansion developed, its distant locations engaged the cultural imagination due, in part, to what Emma Rothschild describes as "the multiplier effects of empire, in which individuals at home were connected by information and expectations to events."[48] Rothschild suggests that individuals living at this time had "a more intimate proximity to the domesticity of empires" than may previously have been recognized. As the anonymous author of a 1698 pamphlet objecting to taxes on sugar explains, "the Plantations are a Part of Ourselves, tho' they are plac'd

Remote."[49] Catherine Molineux remarks upon "the seemingly irresistible desire to break down the distance to the colonies." Kathleen Wilson observes that empire had an "immediacy" to those in England. Elizabeth Maddox Dillon has demonstrated how substantially empire shaped theatrical representations in London and, later, throughout the Atlantic world.[50] Individuals did not have to be investors in plantations to have a connection with that imperial enterprise. Similarly, individuals did not have to be slaveholders to have ample evidence of England's participation in Atlantic commerce generally and enslavement specifically. Slavery, as John Richardson notes, was "a visibly important part of English trade" present throughout "ordinary public discourse." It "permeated the fabric of English life," adds Simon Gikandi.[51]

Beyond British imperial expansion's pervasive presence in everyday discourse, it also engendered a certain emotional or imaginative investment— not unlike the excitement aroused by opportunities offered from the new financial instruments and speculative investments, which also capitalized on the colonial opportunities. To invest in West Indian plantations constituted an aspirational act. This sense of opportunity expanded following the Treaty of Utrecht in 1713, when England entered into the *asiento*, which gave the "Subjects of Great Britain . . . the Liberty of Importing Negroes into Spanish America."[52] This agreement led to the creation of the South Sea Company, granted the trading rights by Queen Anne; its success depended in no small part "on the public favorably imagining the prospects of the Atlantic slave trade," as Carl Wennerlind describes. The very name of the South Sea Company invoked the West Indies and the slave trade in which it promised to participate. The *asiento*, the South Sea Company, and the centrality of the Atlantic slave trade to English political and economic life forged what Wennerlind terms a "closer mental association" between London, slave forts in Africa, and colonial towns.[53] Herman Moll's map of "the Coasts, Countries, and Islands within the Limits of the South-Sea Company" acknowledges that the prospect of "the Company newly Establish'd to carry on a Trade to the South Seas, cou'd not but excite the Curiosity of all wish it well."[54] These financial opportunities, the presence of enslaved people and the products of their labor, and the economic profits realized from West Indian plantations, coupled with expanding domestic forms of restraint (including transportation to the colonies) constructed a world marked by confinement and control. The literary texts of the Restoration and early eighteenth century this book explores simultaneously reflect and reinforce the emergent culture of captivity.

Reading Captivity

The first chapter of this book describes how captivity was a powerful lens through which many Britons read the world and their position within it. Drawing on diverse literary texts and co-texts, familiar and more obscure, chapter 1 demonstrates how forms of confinement were woven into material practice and cultural discourse. This chapter first draws on the unpublished correspondence of poet Judith Cowper Madan and her Nevis-born, plantation-owning husband Colonel Martin Madan, to suggest how personal conceptions of self, even among the privileged, draw on the language of captivity. That sense of limitation was perhaps felt more profoundly by those less empowered such as the working poor and, especially, women. As the chapter details, poems by working-class poets such as Mary Barber and Mary Collier, like the creative work of Madan herself, reflect upon the captive conditions they witness or experience. Building on the work of Moira Ferguson and others, this orienting chapter also closely considers how women especially recognize, experience, and articulate the threat of domestic captivity.

The next four chapters then turn to works by five authors in which captivity is either the direct subject of discussion or the structural basis for the narrative. Chapter 2 reconsiders the presence of captivity in three dramatic texts by Aphra Behn. Behn represented the effects of patriarchal-imperial powers throughout her oeuvre, explicitly linking the kinds of enslavement instituted by colonial dominance with the domesticated subjugation of women. Although *Oroonoko* (1688) is often read as Behn's primary examination of the colonial practice of enslavement, that familiar text is actually the culmination of a sustained and nuanced interrogation of captivity that accelerates during her career, informed by her increasing understanding of the colonial enterprise. A constellation of Behn's earlier dramatic texts including *The Young King* (partially written in Surinam) and *The Younger Brother* (which specifically references her Surinam experience) share a focus on the imperial project, human commodification, and the consequences of a culture of captivity. Her London-produced dramatic works invoke the instruments of control fundamental to a culture of captivity and, consequently, remind Behn's readers and viewers of the long reach of colonial power and its enduring, inescapable domestic manifestations.

Even more strikingly, *The Emperor of the Moon*, among her most frequently produced plays with 133 performances between its first production in 1687 and 1748, offers a sustained and explicit critique of the process of colonization—a process that results in the captivity of indigenous people, which Behn witnessed firsthand. The text's genre—farce—intentionally obscures its deep criticism of the mechanisms of colonial power and allows Behn to safely—if absurdly—represent the state powers she sees shaping human lives. The text reflects on class- and race-based power structures and demonstrates how imperial control in a colonial setting necessarily shapes other domestic forms of subjection vividly present in her dramatic texts. Behn also regularly uses the colonial situation to meditate on what, in many of her texts, is the ultimate condition of confinement: the institution of marriage.

Like Behn, Richard Steele was extremely savvy about the effects of Britain's colonial efforts (as well as its cost to women), even while he endorsed—and participated in—those activities, and understood their connection to captivity, confinement, and human commodification. He generally supported the state's imperial energies, and in his writing frequently uses representations of individuals in subjected states not as an object for critique but as a mechanism for prompting a "sentimental" reaction from his fictive male figures. Steele's well-known representation of enslavement in *Spectator* No. 11 recounts the narrative of Yarico, a text whose brevity belies its complexity. Just as *Oroonoko* is often considered as Behn's primary exploration of enslavement, so too Steele's 1711 retelling of Richard Ligon's abbreviated story of Inkle and Yarico is often considered the text most informed by Steele's material engagement in the West Indies as the owner of a Barbadian sugar plantation. Yet his most popular play, *The Conscious Lovers*, written nearly contemporaneously with the narrative of Inkle and Yarico, also substantially draws on that experience of ownership in previously unremarked ways.

As chapter 3 discusses, *The Conscious Lovers* (1722) sits within a rich web of connections with sites and cultural practices of enslavement that unquestionably coded a culture of captivity to an eighteenth-century audience. However, the text's innovative dramatic form, "sentimental comedy," obscures its fundamental grounding in the exploitative Atlantic economy of captivity, indentured servitude, and plantation slavery. The generic force of "sentimental comedy," like the play's persistence within eighteenth-century performance history, distracted from the text's representations of female domestic captivity, as well as characters' engagement with, and naturalization of, the business of enslavement in the British Atlantic. Because the play foregrounds its attempts to engender an emotional response from the viewer (as well as display the sensibility of its main male characters), the language of captivity and control seems only metaphorical. Consequently the heroine Indiana's laments about her own status as "an Infant Captive!" and her fear of debtors' prison or other forms of confinement have been explained as simply part of the extravagance of the genre. The discourse of confinement and subjection operates upon audiences on the level of dramatic trope even as it references material practice. In fact, Indiana's situation vividly anticipates the restricted movement and dangerous options for any unprotected, impoverished woman. The harsh material mechanisms of captivity underpinning much of the wealth enjoyed by the play's characters remain obscured by both the play's telling popularity and the scaffolding of genre. At base, *The Conscious Lovers* illustrates the interwoven subjectivity of the captive and the agent of that captivity, a dynamic of privilege and oppression that shapes each of the texts in this study.

In the same way Steele's *The Conscious Lovers* has been read through the generic prism of sentimental comedy, so too Penelope Aubin's work has long been understood and underestimated as primarily conventional, highly didactic prose fiction, draining her texts of their subversive quality. Her 1720s prose fictions, second in popularity to only Eliza Haywood's, have traditionally been read as a pious alternative to amatory fiction. Actually, Aubin presents graphic accounts of physical and sexual violence punctuated by relatively perfunctory professions of Christian faith. Her most frequently republished book from the 1720s, *The Noble Slaves*, appearing in 1722 like *The Conscious Lovers*, represents a kind of captivity about which British subjects remained particularly anxious: Barbary captivity, the enslavement of a British subject in the Barbary Coast of North Africa, which affected thousands of British subjects between 1660 and the 1730s. Popular accounts across multiple genres detailed the conditions for enslaved British subjects, campaigned for ransom funds, and celebrated the infrequent release of captives. Aubin draws on this recognizable narrative in her prose fiction, but uses it to her own ends. Although *The Noble Slaves* presents a world of abduction, confinement, and enslavement at the hands of Barbary captors, Aubin's real focus is the threatening domestic dangers that women regularly confront. As detailed in chapter 4, Aubin's treatment of Barbary captivity actually serves as a strategic vehicle to covertly comment upon the oppression and exploitation of women in England. The received understanding of Aubin's work as a "virtuous" alternative to scandalous prose fiction overshadows her texts' deep engagement with and explicit representation of specific forms of domestic captivity.

The final chapter looks at narratives by Eliza Haywood and Edward Kimber: *Memoirs of an Unfortunate Young Nobleman* (1743) and *The History of the Life and Adventures of Mr. Anderson* (1754) respectively. These authors' tremendously popular books, based on historical events, depict the captivity of British subjects in colonial America in the form of indentured servitude resulting from abduction while still a youth. In both texts, young boys—destined for inheritance or lives in the gentry—are kidnapped on English soil and relegated to life as what the text terms "indentured slaves" in an American colony. Their elevated status in England cannot protect them from kidnapping. These two novels vividly represent the boys' experience of captivity, the brutality of their American masters, and the abuse of the other unfree laborers around them. Neither text questions the oppressive system in which the boys find themselves. Indeed, the captive state acts as a crucible that refines their "innate" qualities of mastery and superiority. During their captivity, the boys, largely through the tutelage of captive women, receive education commensurate with their status in England, preparing them for their freedom and return to England. The novels' representation of the boys' captivity, rather than revealing the horrors of a slave economy, affirms the idealized model of British masculinity found in members of the ruling classes (and these two young men) who prove to be the most "appropriate" masters. The novels ultimately endorse a culture of captivity, in both the West Indian colonial space and the British domestic one, especially when governed by appropriately prepared men. The texts also detail other states of domestic captivity regularized within England—indentured servitude, the workhouse, apprenticeship—and elaborate upon the particularly threatening conditions for women held captive within a colonial space.

The texts this book explores provide perspectives on diverse forms of domestic captivity. They each offer insights into the emergent attitudes toward captivity as authors grappled with shifting cultural practices and attitudes while also attempting to satisfy the literary marketplace's abiding fascination with captivity. In some texts, fictional British subjects appropriate the language of enslavement to characterize their own condition. Others, although representing captivity at a geographic distance from England, directly reflect upon the domestic captivity of the British subject. All these texts have domestic captivity as a defining element, even when the captivity is initially illegible.

These chapters are representative not exhaustive in their scope, and three factors informed my selection of texts. First, these works were among if not *the* most popular and culturally persistent by the authors. I argue that a work's popularity often stemmed directly from its representation of captivity that tapped into the persistent anxiety about and fascination with captivity; the representation of captivity arguably increased a text's wide appeal. Britons' perception of themselves as potentially confined or unfree did not deter their interest in reading about the captive state of others (for some it may have intensified that interest). Yet even texts not overtly focused on captivity draw significantly on the language, shared references, or structural relationships that mimic the captive state, something that an eighteenth-century reader understood. The language of captivity infuses the period. Second, the authors discussed in this book each, in some way, had a connection in the material workings of the British colonial presence in the West Indies whether through geographic proximity, plantation ownership, personal relationships, or business interests. That shared connection speaks less to the unusual nature of the writers and more to the widespread, intricate network of influences and relationships between colonial and domestic sites. Indeed, few individuals were not implicated in some element of imperial endeavors. Finally, each text represents some form of domestic captivity imposed upon a female subject. The culture of captivity pressed most forcefully on women: limited in their earning capacity, vulnerable to assault, and, if married, essentially invisible legally, women most keenly felt the pressures of confinement and control.

Such literary works provide the opportunity to consider what Raymond Williams terms the "structures of feeling" for the cultural moment of a text's production. The creation of texts, as Williams notes, is "always a formative process within a specific present." The text displays the "specific feelings" and "specific rhythm" unique to a particular cultural moment.[55]

Because captivity (domestic and colonial) was incremental, yet pervasive, foundational yet progressive, its presence in literary texts during the period this book studies reveals a culture coming to terms with itself. The texts in this study, ranging from roughly 1670 to 1755, variously interrogate, affirm, or resist domestic forms of confinement. They emerge during a period of actions by the state—from the creation of the RAC to the *asiento* to the Transportation Act—that not only normalize but also institutionalize the commodification and dehumanization of entire categories of people. The attitudes, language, and representations of captivity in these texts differ starkly from those produced in the latter quarter of the eighteenth century. Felicity Nussbaum describes the slippage of the very term "'slavery' in common parlance" largely undistinguished "from other kinds of captivity" until the creation of the Society for Effecting the Abolition of the Slave Trade (1787).[56] Following the Mansfield decision (1772), the creation of the society, and the visible and concerted efforts of abolitionists such as Thomas Clarkson (1760–1846) and William Wilberforce (1759–1833), representations of the enslaved and the strategic use of captivity within literary texts accelerated. As numerous scholars have discussed, during that period the discourse of captivity and enslavement, like literary representations of the same, were generally legible, often foregrounded. Such texts are not my focus. Rather, I am concerned with texts and writers of this earlier period, a time when the categories of captivity were more fluid, provisional, emergent, and inchoate, but a period nevertheless when captivity shaped constructions of identity and conceptions of agency within the popular imagination.

Because captivity in diverse forms was so deeply engrained within the culture, its literary representation, like the lived experience, was naturalized. References to the locations, instruments, and mechanisms of captivity, frequently oblique, invisible, or illegible to modern readers, would have been quite obvious if unremarkable to an eighteenth-century subject. The topical references (to places, people, cultural practices) reveal how deeply enmeshed British subjects were with both colonial slavery and domestic captivity. Sometimes, because this shared language so often lies outside the twenty-first-century reader's own frame of reference, the literal is read as only metaphorical, as a kind of cultural shorthand or emotional trigger. Consequently, the imagery of captivity became familiar, unacknowledged, and unremarkable within a textual space—a discursive and literary legacy of British slaveholding and the mechanisms of captivity. The language of captivity became a narrative accessory for those wishing to invoke a specific—albeit distilled—emotion. Scholars risk unwittingly reproducing the layer of oppressions when such language is ignored or not fully unpacked. The details of place, labor, clothing, expectations, and personal interactions reference specific cultural practices related to captivity. That language codes variously a character's involvement as a financial actor in the economy of the enslaved or as a subject within a state of domestic captivity. These situations, like the words that describe them, are mutually reinforcing. Imagery of restraint, confinement, or control seamlessly and unquestioningly became part of the literary landscape, emerging from a material condition.

Implications for Reading Captivity

Once legible, domestic captivity is revealed to be a persistent, naturalized, indeed "normative" presence, a cultural shorthand that infuses eighteenth-century literary texts. The texts I discuss are formative in terms of creating the language and expectations for subsequent, traditionally canonical prose fiction of the eighteenth century, where characters easily, almost casually draw upon the shared references of captivity to represent their own situation. Those texts domesticate captivity within that most domestic of genres—the eighteenth-century novel. In *Humphry Clinker* (1771), Tobias Smollett's Tabitha Bramble refers to her life as that of an "indented slave" (the same term used within Haywood's and Kimber's texts). Yorick of Laurence Sterne's *Sentimental Journey* (1768) gives "full scope" to his "imagination" to consider "the miseries of confinement." While he begins trying to envisage the "multitude," "the millions of my fellow-creatures born to no inheritance but slavery," he seeks his emotional release in a "single captive" and "burst into tears" at "the picture of confinement which my fancy had drawn.—" Captivity and enslavement strategically operate as nothing more than emotional triggers or narrative aids within a culture of sensibility. When Sophia Western in Henry Fielding's *Tom Jones* (1749) begs her aunt not to force her to marry Blifil, she is like a "wretched captive" who attempts "to raise compassion"; unmoved, her aunt remains "determined . . . to deliver over the trembling maid into the arms of the gaoler Blifil." The language and comparisons continue.

Canonical texts are not the focus of this study; however, it is useful to consider how even a cursory examination of eighteenth-century prose fiction with the lens of captivity unveils the degree to which novels traditionally taught as part of the "canon" represent—indeed often hinge upon—characters who live as captive subjects or operate as agents of control. The central questions my book asks—how have representations of domestic captivity been obscured and what are the implications of restoring their legibility—prompt reconsiderations of such eighteenth-century texts. Once we recognize the presence of domestic captivity, it becomes an inescapable if overwritten world that shapes literary texts in both profound and imperceptible ways.

Daniel Defoe produced fiction that abounds with characters subject to or agents in indentured servitude, enslavement, confinement, and restraint. As Defoe's biographer Paula Backscheider notes, Defoe himself actually engaged in the practice of selling people who were destined for transportation, making a £8.5s profit on just one man in 1688.[57] His experience helped him understand and include quite accurate details about the complicated status of indentured servants and transported convicts, situations he recounts in texts like *Colonel Jack* (1722) and *Moll Flanders* (1722). Captivity also foundationally informs *Robinson Crusoe* (1719), a text predicated on travel prompted by Crusoe's eager participation in the slave trade. His ownership of the enslaved frames the novel. Crusoe's early stint as a Barbary captive does not preclude his investment in the captivity of others as a means to his own economic success. (Indeed, he promptly sells the young boy Xury who aided his Barbary escape.) Early in the text, to secure the "advancement of [his] plantation" in Brazil, the "first thing" Crusoe does is buy "me a negro slave, and an European servant also—I mean another besides that which the captain brought me from Lisbon." When he returns to Brazil (the country that used more enslaved Africans than any other during the eighteenth century) at the end of the novel after decades away, he is given a strict accounting of "how the estate was improved, and . . . how many slaves there were upon it." The central experience of the novel, Crusoe's time alone upon the island, is similarly defined by his creation, in microcosm, of a domestic slave economy. Crusoe fantasizes about his ability to enslave the "savages" with whom he believes he shares the island: "I was now eager to be upon . . . these savages. . . . I fancied myself able to manage one, nay, two or three savages, if I had them, so as to make them entirely slaves to me, to do whatever I should direct them." Crusoe reads the world through a lens of captivity in which he is now the captor. The central relationship of the text, of course, depends on Friday's enslavement. Crusoe interprets

Friday's initial reaction to him upon their first encounter as a "token of swearing to be my slave for ever."[58] If, as Lynn Festa suggests, Crusoe is "the epitome of novelistic individualism," a model for British male identity, then that identity is undeniably founded upon mastery within a culture of captivity.[59] It is also dependent upon advancing the financial gains of white Britons at the expense of persons of color.

Like Defoe, Jonathan Swift recognized the commodification of human subjects on a global scale as well as the forms of domestic captivity around him in Ireland; he too represented that complicated dynamic within his literary work. Just as Crusoe's travels stem from his engagement in the slave trade, so too Swift's iconic character Gulliver earns his living as a surgeon on ships making voyages to the West Indies, ships unquestionably connected with the slave trade. Back in England, Gulliver attempts to get "some addition to my fortune" by establishing himself on "Fetter Lane" "hoping to get business among the sailors," but fails to "turn to account." Thus, he, instead, "accepted an advantageous offer from Captain William Prichard, master of the Antelope, who was making a voyage to the South Sea. We set sail from Bristol, May 4, 1699, and our voyage was at first very prosperous." An eighteenth-century reader would know a ship sailing from Bristol to the South Seas was connected with West Indian plantation slavery, transporting either the products of slave-labor or the enslaved people themselves. Notably, it is Gulliver's Bristol crew on the *Antelope* (the name of a slaving vessel that actually sailed three voyages—including one from Bristol—between 1720 and 1726, the year *Gulliver's Travels* was published)[60] that subjects him to the worst forms of captivity. The Bristolian sailors' treatment of Gulliver anticipates abolitionist Thomas Clarkson's use of Bristol as an example of the corrupting effects of slaving upon all connected with it. Over the course of his journeys in four books, Gulliver experiences loss of liberty, transportation, confinement, discipline, displacement, and exploitation. Swift reveals the degree to which the commodification of human capital—human flesh—had been naturalized in the countries Gulliver visits just as that commodification has been naturalized in the British Isles for the Irish and for enslaved Africans.[61]

Two undeniably iconic male characters, arguably the most well known from early prose fiction—Crusoe and Gulliver—secure their resources through a connection with slaving (while failing to reflect fully on their own experiences of captivity). Similarly, two novels often regarded as helping solidify the ascendance of the domestic novel, *Pamela* (1740) and *Clarissa* (1748), structurally depend upon domestic captivity—literally the repeated physical confinement of unmarried young women (who both carefully narrate their own captivity). Nancy Armstrong has written about the influence of North American captivity narratives on *Pamela,* an influence she suggests shapes "a whole range of novels throughout the Victorian period."[62] But the domestic captivity described in my book, witnessed and effected in Britain, proves an equally potent context. Pamela's experience marks the novel's foundational engagement with captivity as a normative state. Pamela understands that Mr. B will render her a "kept slave" whether she accedes to his proposals and becomes his mistress, or remains in what she terms "captivity" through her refusal. Her "bondage," a term invoking both biblical and plantation slavery, is literal. A single, unprotected young woman's imprisonment foundationally reiterates the male privilege and power that shape the text (and the nation) in both the domestic and colonial space. She avers that she is not "a sordid slave, who is to be threatened and frightened into a compliance with measures." "My restraint is indeed hard upon me: I am very uneasy under it." She claims her need to be a "free person," affirming an inextricable link between "The meanest slaves, or those who hedge and ditch," and the "rich" fed "by their sweat." "Nor let the rich the lowest slave disdain: / He's equally a link of Nature's chain." These connections reinscribe the culture of captivity. While the quoted verse asserts that "king and slave" are "levell'd . . . in the silent grave," the text does not evince such leveling. Like Indiana upon her union with Bevil in Steele's *The Conscious Lovers,* Pamela enters a state of legal subordination when she marries Mr. B; just as Indiana exclaims her devotion to Bevil as her "lord" and "master," so too Pamela happily names B in the same way.

Samuel Richardson's novel does not critique marriage itself, but it reminds us of the fate of unmarried, unclaimed, or discarded women who similarly occupy a subordinated place within a culture of captivity. The removal of Sally Godfrey to Jamaica, a common destination for fictional women who cannot be recuperated within narratives because of their behavior, reiterates the dominance of colonial captivity within and beyond the confines of England, just as sending "a little negro boy, of about ten years old, as a present" naturalizes the commodification of enslaved people (and the gifting of humans as though only property devoid of humanity) within Britain's domestic sites.[63] The brevity of the child's narrative and

the absence of his name, like the denial of further insight into Sally Godfrey, marks the novel's inability or unwillingness to represent Black domestic captivity. It elides its very existence. More profoundly, the child's
unknown and unknowable experience of captivity marks the narrative erasure and silencing of marginalized voices (both the young boy's and Sally
Godfrey's) that characterizes early canonical fiction. Pamela has precious
little geographic movement within the novel, but markers of enslavement
and the colonial enterprise nevertheless impinge upon her constricted
domestic world.

Clarissa Harlowe's experience similarly demonstrates how fully domesticated captivity had become with the British novel and within eighteenth-
century British culture. As with Pamela, Clarissa's captivity is quite startling
when considered in the simplest possible terms: confined, kidnapped,
imprisoned, raped, jailed. Her experiences of extremity share much with
Aubin heroines caught in Barbary captivity; yet, unlike a Barbary captive
held abroad, Clarissa cannot be ransomed or rescued.[64] Her experience is
thoroughly British. Whether held at the hands of her avaricious family or
the predatory Lovelace, the manifestations of Clarissa's confinement are
numerous, well-documented, and unfailingly domestic. Like Aubin, Richardson demonstrates that most intense threats to women are too often from
those with whom they are most intimate. Clarissa laments she is "treated
by my brother, and, through his instigations, by my father, as a slave." From
the earliest letters Clarissa mourns "what a poor prisoner I am" (Letter 25),
"a poor prisoner, in her hard confinement" (Letter 45). That her uncle Anthony Harlowe, like her proposed fiancé Solmes, has significant investments
in the West Indies where he "had acquired great fortune" underscores the
family's unquestioning acceptance of human mastery over the subjugated,
especially as a strategy for wealth accumulation. Clarissa understands their
acquisitive brutality when she begs to be sent "any-whither: let me be sent
a slave to the Indies; any-whither of these I will consent to" rather than give
"vows to a man I cannot endure!—." Those two conditions exist in parallel
states for her, the domestic captivity cast as the most intolerable of the two.

The literature and popular discourses of the period demonstrate that many
British subjects perceived their lives to be defined by a form or threat of
confinement or by their capacity to place or hold someone else in a captive

state. However, it is not simply the dispossessed or disempowered who understood themselves as somehow captive or who appropriated the language of captivity to express their personal condition. Perhaps surprisingly, the language of captivity—of characterizing oneself as existing in a captive state—emerges as an available (if inaccurate) mode for other kinds of expression at multiple point of the social hierarchy. By connecting diverse forms of domestic captivity and exploring the implications of that connection, I mean to accentuate, not elide the difference between and among these discrete conditions while asserting captivity's significance for understanding Restoration and eighteenth-century culture. As the first chapter reveals, even those who, by any measure, occupied a position of privilege still perceived themselves as living within a culture of captivity.

· CHAPTER 1 ·

Cultures of Captivity

Captive Subjects

Martin Madan, husband of poet Judith Cowper Madan (1702–81), was by any measure a man of privilege. The son of a West Indian plantation-owner, the Cambridge-educated Martin (1700–56) rose to the rank of colonel in the King's Dragoon Guards, was appointed as a member of the household of Frederick, the Prince of Wales, and, near the end of his life, served as a member of Parliament.[1] Perpetually insolvent and something of a spendthrift, Martin pinned his financial aspirations on the potential profits to be realized from sugar plantations he owned in Nevis and Antigua, operations dependent on the labor of enslaved people. Like many gentlemen of his class and generation, Martin recognized how the West Indies could make a man rich; his father had "made his fortune there," his maternal grandfather had been governor of Nevis, and Martin himself held the unrealized aspiration to be governor of the Leeward Islands.[2] Martin had an intimate understanding of the colonial enterprise.

Despite Martin's self-described role as "a Proprietor in the Land of Canaan" (February 12, 1732), a reference to the land and human property that comprised his West Indian holdings, Martin perceived *himself* to be unfree. He "repines" his condition as an "unhappy dependent" and desires to be "releas'd" from "this Disagreeble confinement." He laments that "I have not a minute I can call my own." He repeatedly uses the language common to the institutionalized system of colonial enslavement—a system in which he is an agent of control—as a metaphor for his own life. Explicitly comparing himself to an enslaved laborer on his own plantation, Martin asks "when shall I be free?"[3] Martin introjects a paradigm of captivity into the narrative of his own life.[4] He conceives of his situation as one of subjection—to the demands of his commanders, to the Prince and his entourage ("my fate is in the Hand of Courtiers"), and to domestic pressures from afar. Most keenly, perhaps, he feels constrained by an economic instability exacerbated by the failure to realize financial gains from his West Indian holdings.[5] A man with connections to some of the most powerful people in the empire nevertheless believes he lives a life of confinement, a life characterized by restraint rather than liberty. Martin's expressions of frustration provide a glimpse of the complex, interdependent web of power and powerlessness, liberty and restraint, shaping all but the most rarified existence during this period. He is most certainly not enslaved, yet he believes himself to be not fully free. He understands himself to be a captive subject.

The irony of such an attitude from a slave-owning white man like Martin is not lost on the twenty-first-century reader. Martin, attempting to profit from the labor of enslaved humans commodified on a global scale, remains enured to the institutionalized violence he enables, and focuses instead on easing the social and financial strictures he believes limit his own life. Like other absentee landlords of the West Indies, he seems, in Simon Gikandi's words, "oblivious to the lived experience of slavery." Gikandi observes how the brutal reality of slavery "could be strictly quarantined" from the "consciousness and everyday existence" of those owning plantations and estates.[6] While such a lack of consciousness could result from geographic distance (Martin left Nevis by the time he was eight years old), it also stemmed from attitudes that naturalized the condition of captivity. The perpetual bondage of enslaved people is never questioned or commented upon; their condition detailed only in connection to their capacity for labor. Every element of the situation is normalized. Surrounded by the scaffolding of captivity, Martin remains completely unreflective about the vast divide between his situation and that of the human property he owns and to whom he so readily compares himself.[7]

Martin's indifference to the foundational and institutional inequalities that structure eighteenth-century culture extends, unsurprisingly, to his marriage.[8] Despite his expressed affection for his wife, Judith, Martin, like many men of his time, never questions (and at times embraces) the legal power he has over her. Judith, as a married woman in eighteenth-century

England, exists in a subordinate state. When William Congreve's Millamant in *The Way of the World* (1700) laments she must "dwindle into a wife," she articulates a legal reality later codified by William Blackstone who asserted that married women do not have a separate "legal existence." Judith bristles at the limitations placed upon her as a wife within a union that she rightly believes confines her. The Madans' extensive correspondence, the result of prolonged absences demanded by Martin's thirty-year military career, reveals Judith's complicated relationship with the forms of confinement she experiences and observes.

Their correspondence—more than 350 letters between 1723 and 1750—exemplifies the collision of the emotional intimacy and the legal realities of marriage most acutely felt by women. (Judith's sentiments anticipate Eliza Haywood's description of marriage as an institution that binds women by the "irrevocable ties of love and law.")[9] In the same letter in which Judith characterizes Martin as "the most desirable of your sex," she acknowledges that marriage inevitably forces her to "give up my liberty."[10] The emotion she has for Martin, "an endless source of undiminished Fondness, a Love no Language can Express," will be "Proof against the very Bondage of marriage" she knows to be inescapable.[11] She draws on the financial and colonial language of the public sphere to characterize her dominated condition. Martin maintains an "Empire so Firmly Establish'd" over her that nothing "can ever have power to dispossess you."[12] However, she also feels his affections to have a volatility comparable to the new financial instruments; "Like Publick credit or The Stocks," she writes, "I Rise or fall in value according to . . . the Reputation I maintain with you."[13] She can only hope that the sympathetic distress she experiences—"my heart is opprest wth ye Difficulties you Labour under, & I am Seiz'd & Perplext to ye last Degree wth your Disappointments"—will be reciprocated. Despite her confinement, she characterizes her devotion to Martin as liberating, signaling the complex situation for wives: "it is not Life to me worth Having that is not Imployed in y^r Service, wch ever was, & ever will be to me *Perfect Freedom*." Her service to him is a form of freedom. "'Tis in vain to Struggle," she writes, "we can only Sooth our Fate by an absolute submission, wch will reward us by Giving the most Abject Slavery all the Charms of the most unbounded Liberty."[14] Her expressions of affection to Martin that convey her emotional devotion—"I put myself into your power"—simultaneously reiterate the legal status of a married woman. Marriage gives Martin complete control—indeed ownership—over everything that "belongs" to Judith (and, technically, over Judith herself). Like all wives of her time, Judith lives in what might be considered a form of domestic captivity. She more intimately experiences a condition of confinement that Martin believes he endures; she too can be seen as a captive subject.

Over the course of their marriage Judith assumed increasing domestic responsibilities because of Martin's prolonged absences. But she did not enjoy commensurately increased authority or unfettered access to their financial resources, and she was acutely aware of the discrepancy between the responsibilities that devolved to her and the limited power she actually held. A consistent source of tension in the Madans' marriage was their financial situation. When Martin describes "the many anxieties I feel" and "the disappointments I have met with," he refers to his finances.[15] Perpetually low on household funds, Judith had to consult with him about which debts or servants to pay, where more economical housing for the family can be found, and when to sell livestock. Martin apologizes that her "occasions for money have been so pressing," implicitly acknowledging his own carelessness in reducing her to that level.[16] She chides him when he repeatedly fails to "Remember my Finances wch indeed were very Low,"[17] while he simultaneously admonishes her to be careful with his money: "I need not recommend frugality to you, you too well know the necessity there is for it."[18] She loses their cook because of unpaid back wages ("I am extreamly distress'd"),[19] but does not have the power to change the situation.

More profoundly than the quotidian irritations, Judith keenly felt the withholding of the independent funds that had been negotiated specifically for her upon the occasion of their nuptials. In her will, written twenty years after the 1756 death of her husband, Judith reveals that throughout their thirty-three-year marriage Martin diverted the money expressly stipulated in their marriage contract as her pin money to compensate for the lackluster return on the investments in his Caribbean estates. As she tells her daughter Maria: "I had the Best & Dearest of Fathers—he always had given me £100 Gineas per year & insisted on ye same for me from your Dear Father—wch was readily agreed to, & the Settlements to the Effect be made accordingly: I rec^d *one half year* from y^r Father of this, in Money, & *only once—*." She explicitly attributed his failure to honor this agreement primarily to the fact Martin was "Disapointd in his Estate, (then only y^t at Nevis)." That Martin diverted money owed to Judith toward his West Indian holdings created a situation in which his repeated, annual investments in the purchase of enslaved Africans and the mechanisms of their bondage exacerbate Judith's own sense of confinement (at times desperation) within the marriage. She lacks any means to compel Martin to provide her negotiated "Allowance," as she termed it. She "in a slight, trifling way, would remind him, how much he was Running on, in my Debt" only to have him "smile, & Say 'very True.'"[20] His passivity exacerbated her frustration over a withholding she felt quite sharply (and a frustration she clearly still felt twenty years after his death). Not only did Judith express her dissatisfaction in writing, she also created a financial narrative "in a book w^t became due to me, from year to year on Acct of My allowance." She calculates his nonpayment over the years "as nearly as I could Compute it" as "about 12 or 13" hundred pounds. Such a narrative accounting, written expressions of a persistent anger, becomes her only means to articulate her resistance to the strictures her role as wife places upon her—the kind of domestic captivity inevitable for married women.

Judith's resentment about Martin's withholding of the money owed her and his redirection of those funds to his Caribbean investments increased commensurately with her intimate knowledge of the plantations' struggling operations. Martin's status as an absentee landlord was, in a sense, twofold; neither did he live in the West Indies and have direct oversight of his holdings, nor was he present in England to receive the regular correspondence regarding plantation affairs or to monitor the sale or shipment of sugar from the colonies. Those responsibilities fell to Judith.

Even as Judith resists Martin's preoccupation with the minutiae of their holdings and bristles at its continued presence in their written exchanges (particularly in light of her knowledge that he has diverted money owed to her to finance these endeavors), she accepts the responsibility as yet another moment of necessary self-abnegation. In a particularly pointed letter, she carefully delineates between information she must share with him and the subjects she actually wishes to discuss: "I have been as Particular as I can in relation to y^r Affairs abroad wch take as a Proof that I always Prefer w^{tt} I imagine may be acceptable to you to w^t is agreeable to myself.—indeed whilst I have been writing this long heap of stuff, Love has several times attempted to Turn my Pen to a more Pleasing Subject; but I have resisted all his importunities, being well assur'd tho you can't tell w^t is doing at St. Kitts unless I tell you you well know w^t is Passing in my Heart."[21]

His "affairs abroad" are a "long heap of stuff" keeping her from writing about "a more Pleasing Subject." She does not suggest that the news from Saint Kitts is not pleasant because of the nature of information—the commodification and enslavement of humans—although she might at some level have some knowledge of the true working of a culture of captivity. Rather it is unpleasant because it is not about their love relationship. Judith defers what is "agreeable" to herself and anticipates what she knows will be "acceptable" to him. While she realizes that she is his only means to know "what is doing at St. Kitts," she never threatens to withhold the valuable information. Certainly she expresses fatigue with his persistent preoccupation with their holdings and regularly signals her desire to pivot with the phrase "and so much for business." For her, business is something "to wch tis with Difficulty I can attend at anytime, much more at this—when my whole Soul is Engross'd with Cares of a more Touching nature."[22] She describes it as "ever *Disagreeable* to me who have a heart and Head so Little Turn'd for it." It is "doubly" disagreeable when "it Interrupts" what she considers the true, "the Darling Business" of her life—"The conversing wth my ever Dearest Madan!"[23] That business, unlike the plantations and the sugar trade, is one that her "Soul alone Dictates." That business also enables her to create a kind of alternative economy within their exchanges.

Despite her stated resistance, Judith dutifully receives, transcribes, and summarizes for Martin letters from various functionaries connected to these Caribbean operations. In doing so, she essentially documents a narrative of failure. The letters bring nothing but bad news and do not offer much "Pleasure from their Contents." Martin writes of his fear he "shall be told I am involv'd in the common calamity & must expect no Sugar from thence this year, hard tidings! but I am wise enough to arm my Self against the worst."[24] The vicissitudes of Caribbean weather diminish the value of his investment; some years his sugar "was Burnt up," other years, "storms have done damage" and "pretty many canes yet to take off tho not very good."[25] Martin lacks the ability to expand his holdings, telling Judith how he was "much disappointed when I read Capt Pyms letter, not finding any encouragement from him to expect the purchasing of Land at St. Xtopher's."[26] Judith carefully notes the arrival of ships from the West Indies, and monitors the price of sugar, although in her letters to Martin she pointedly refers to it as "your" sugar (and he, in turn, calls it "mine"). Martin alerts her to expect "20 hghd [hogshead] of sugar on board the Dispatch Captain Burroughs who was to sail in 5 weeks from the 4th of April."[27] Later he instructs her to "send Mr Butler the names of the 7 ships on which Mr Ward has ship'd my Sugars. I cannot say what the value of Sugar is at present therefore cannot direct what the value of the whole may be, but I should think £15 p^r Hhd sufficient."[28]

She expresses relief that their manager Butler has "sold all y^r Sugars, wch I am very glad of, there being 30 sail of sugar ships expected every hour, wch would sink their Price greatly."[29] Their timing is not always so fortunate, however. Judith recounts how "Butler has sold in all 45 h^{hds} of your sugar, ye last . . . 'tis a pity they came so late, & more are yet to come so fear they will come to a worse market but hope ye Quantity will make you amends."[30] This unfortunate timing happens repeatedly. "Butler was here the beginning of the week," writes Judith, " & has sold ye sugars you left wth him, but not so well as ye other, having no very good ones to help them off wth such as ye first . . . & says he believes you will have a good deal more sugar this year, but coming so late fears it will not come to such a market as ye first."[31] As the subsequent letters reveal, Butler proved to be not merely an incompetent manager, but a dishonest one as well, incurring debt, misdirecting funds, and failing to maintain the basic operations of the plantations. Mr. Wilson, Martin's agent in Saint Kitts, ominously describes Butler as "a Gentleman of Pleasure" who has kept the estate "very Backward."[32] He fails to improve the soil, maintain the equipment, or process the sugar correctly. Martin lamented that he suffered from "ye Villiany of an Unjust Manager" and threatened to "make use of the Law to bring him to Account."[33]

The most chilling element of the correspondence between Martin and Judith is their discussion of the enslaved people on the plantation. Like Martin, Judith remains enured to the cruel irony at the center of their written exchange. She recounts details about the management of the plantation with Martin's same indifference to the unfree labor on which the operation depends. Martin consistently hopes to increase the number of enslaved laborers, a desire woven throughout their correspondence. Judith, the conduit for his aspirational plans, serves as the one who must attempt to follow his set of instructions. Martin directs her to "write to Mr Wilson by first opportunity & return him thanks for his care, and repeat my request to him to buy 4 or 5 young negroes for the plantation wch number I will purchase every year for some time, & likewise desire He will hire 25 Slaves for the present by the years 'till my Gang is sufficient for the Land."[34] Subsequently,

Judith recounts how "Mr. Wilson has bought you 6 Negro's 4 men & 2 women & advises me of a bill he shall draw for their Pay^t."[35] They both write of the purchase of enslaved Africans in hopes of improving their financial situation with absolutely no reflection upon the connection between the labor of the unfree and their own domestic existence. Inoculated by their own sense of privilege, they displace the humanity of the enslaved who function only as property to be acquired on an annual basis.

A sustained exchange about the deteriorating state of the plantation provides a disturbing glimpse into the harrowing lives of the enslaved people owned by the Madans. Without comment, Judith transcribes an entire letter of August 18, 1743, from their agent Mr. Wilson who ominously describes the living conditions under the feckless Mr. Butler: "y^r Negro's or Stock don't Thrive Under Mr. B w^t is ye reason of it I can't tell; he assures me he takes care to feed Negro's & Stock Well, but whether he has ye care to see it done himself I can't answer for." The possible causes for this state—Butler's failure to make sure the enslaved people are adequately fed—marks the utter disregard for their well-being, a disregard underscored by the equating of enslaved humans and the "stock" or animals on the plantation. A subsequent letter from Wilson, which Judith paraphrases rather than transcribing verbatim, offers further insight into the conditions on Martin's plantations. While at this point Mr. Butler has been replaced as manager by a Mr. Ward, the "improvements" under his new management mark the full degree of the previous deprivation. Judith writes that "Mr. Wilson says he can with Great Pleasure assure you, y^r Stock & Negro's begin to Thrive since Mr. Ward had ye care of them,"[36] the jarring terms "care" and "thrive" used without a trace of irony.

More revealing are the unspecified but inescapable markers of the oppression and brutality endemic to the system of plantation slavery. Judith writes that "5 of Ten Runaway negro's are Return'd Since he [Mr. Ward] came on ye estate, where he Says he found ye stock Poor & Low & nothing in any order or repair: wch I really Believe True, one negro is Dead Yonca Cuamino if you know him by y^t Name, I fancy an old one."[37] The juxtaposition of these pieces of information—the death of one named enslaved man (who Judith, perhaps in an act of self-rationalization, "fancies" to have died of old age) alongside the capture (under unspecified conditions of physical brutality) of five other enslaved people marks how dislocated and nonspecific it all is to Judith, who writes of enslavement and the cost of human life in only the most abstract manner. She fails to account for the structures of violence, surveillance, and enforcement on which the plantation economy is founded.

This utter lack of connection or perhaps willful ignorance about the material realities of life for enslaved workers reaches its apex with a prose piece Judith writes on the occasion of Martin's possible appointment as governor of the Leeward Islands. Martin's West Indian ambitions go beyond acquiring additional land, increasing the number of enslaved Africans on his plantations, or making his fortune from sugar. He harbors the hope that he may get a colonial governorship. When Martin learns that Colonel William Cosby (ca. 1690–1736), originally tapped for the Leeward Islands governorship, was instead "to be made Governor of New York," Martin writes "to Mr. Schults to know the truth & to desire if He wou'd assist me getting the Government of the Leeward Islands."[38] The Leeward Islands are part of the Lesser Antilles and include Nevis and Saint Kitts, the locations of Martin's plantation holdings. During this period when the governorship remained a possibility, Judith writes a letter to Martin in the style of Giovanni Paolo Marana's popular *Letters Writ by a Turkish Spy*, a narrative published in English in 1687.[39] Marana's *Turkish Spy* "Mahmut" is an "Arabian" sent by the Turkish sultan to spy on the French court. In her letter, Judith assumes the persona of "Mahmut the Slave of the Grand Seignor" as she writes to Martin, whom she names "Captain Bashaw."[40] She fashions herself as the "first" of Bashaw's slaves.[41] Judith racializes "Mahmut" as enslaved other, conflating Turkish and African identity.

The letter embraces—indeed invites—the asymmetrical power dynamic inherent in the relationship between an enslaved person and a colonial governor as a metaphor for the Madans' own marriage and a vehicle to create intimacy and increase their physical proximity, at least narratively. While the letter uncomfortably invokes the exploitation of enslaved women that commonly occurred (perhaps summoned by the description of the Madans' plantation manager as a "Man of Pleasure"), it also vividly demonstrates how normalized the institution of enslavement had become in Judith's mind. Whether through willful ignorance, a lack of interest, or profound insensitivity to the realities of colonial life for the enslaved, Judith uses "Mahmut" not just as a narrative accessory. She actually adopts it as a narrative persona within a creative piece by a fawning wife trying to bolster her insecure, and frequently inattentive, husband. That Judith believes this narrative approach will effectively demonstrate her support and devotion bespeaks the subsuming of her identity within their relationship.

Judith begins with a stance of utter abjection: "I prostrate myself at the Feet of thy Benignity & Kiss with the most profound Reverence, the Hem of thy Scarlet Robe" (a reference to the red coats worn by members of the British military).[42] After a description of the "Dominions of Friendship," she moves to the subject that "at present seems to demand thy most serious attention": Martin's possible appointment as the governor of the Leeward Islands. Judith as "Mahmut" first praises the qualities that make Martin/Bashaw ideal for the governorship ("Experience," "Knowledge," and "natural Justice & Goodness of thy Disposition" all "season'd with Age"); he will be "the Father of a People, who I doubt not, will live Happy under thy Wise & Grave Administration." The term "a People" refers to those people in a community without rank or position, those who would, in Judith's words, "live Happy under" Martin's control. While the term "people" certainly includes the British colonists, it must also encompass the island's enslaved and indigenous; all these "people" fall away in the narrative, however, as Judith focuses on the position of her narrative surrogate "Mahmut."

More important than the praise of Martin's qualifications is the way Judith specifically figures herself into the narrative. As "the Slave Mahmut, the Faithfull Follower of thy Fortunes, & as much as possible, Imitator of thy Virtues,"[43] Judith imagines a kind of domesticity unavailable, of course, to an enslaved woman. Eschewing gold, diamonds, and pearls, she is "inflam'd with an insatiable avarice" to receive a "more rare & durable Treasure": "the Distinction of being nam'd amongst the first of thy slaves, who have found Favour in thy Sight." Her "avarice" exists only in her own self-commodification, as she seeks to move from being enslaved by "the Grand Seignor" to being enslaved by "Bashaw." "Mahmut" secondarily asks that "Bashaw" find a small home for her, "allot a Retirement for the Humblest of thy Vassals, in that Part of thy Dominion wch thou shall judge nearest Thee; & farthest from all Deceit, an asylum in which I may conclude the Remnant of my Days in Peace."[44] This idealized notion of a domestic space for retirement envisages a life for "Mahmut" completely at odds with a system of plantation labor that denies domesticity, humanity, and personhood to the enslaved.

Judith's wishful vision of a domestic space ignores the material conditions of plantation enslavement; it also seems particularly poignant within the dynamic of the Madans' marriage. As his "vassal" Judith seeks only a spot "nearest" Martin, a desire that echoes wishes expressed in her poems prior to her marriage where she hopes only for a "humble cottage" or a "silent grotto." Also, after years of separation due to Martin's career and the unstable, often peripatetic domestic situation she endured in his absence, Judith seeks a measure of stability. Perhaps one could attribute Judith's self-representation as "the first of thy slaves" to an exaggerated manifestation of the metaphorical language of romance commonly found in early sonnets (although as scholars have frequently noted, the self-identified "slave" more often is the man presenting himself as subject during the period of courtship). Perhaps it is an extension of her claim that she finds "perfect freedom" in her service to him. But within the context of Martin's role as a slaveholder, his potential (if ultimately unrealized) governorship of a colony populated with nearly 500,000 enslaved Africans by 1757, and the familiarity with which the Madans discuss the purchase of enslaved laborers in their personal correspondence, Judith's language seems more than just metaphor. Figuring herself as "first of thy slaves" ironically literalizes many of the constraints already present in her marriage and gives (perhaps knowing) voice to the nature of their relationship. If, as Mahmut/Judith's wish to be in a physical space "nearest" Bashaw/Martin might suggest, she had wearied of Martin's prolonged absence and possible inattention, situating herself as a laborer necessarily under constant surveillance solves that problem (albeit uncomfortably). This striking prose piece evinces how fully the Madans inhabited a culture of captivity that infected their language as well as their conception of their personal relationships and the world as they know it. As the same time, it marks how unreflective and unaware they were about the actual material manifestations of enslavement, the production of sugar, or the operations of a plantation. For Judith to use enslavement as a performative prop in a cheery letter to her husband is a narrative form of racial appropriation that marks the subordinate position Judith naturalizes within her own marriage.

The Madans' correspondence, like Judith's creative work, illustrates how the incongruities of power foundational within a culture of captivity inhere in their marriage. In this most intimate of domestic relationships, Martin and Judith each express frustration and anxiety that mark their sense of themselves as (differently) captive. Slaveholder Madan, unable to secure the financial success he desires, perceives himself as subject to forces beyond his control: "the malice of our ill fortune,"[45] "the constant succession of unhappy accidents that have befallen us abroad and at home," the inexorable power of his superiors, the court, and the demands of his military career. Simultaneously, he exploits the financial opportunities his status as husband provides and his ability to appropriate, with impunity, monies earmarked for Judith. He uses his personal dominance within the marriage to advance his public holdings. Further, he uses his rhetorical skills within their correspondence to artfully maintain her emotional commitment to the relationship. Writing of £25 owed but still unpaid, Martin opines, "I wish my Dear it was in my power to bestow all the good of this Life on thee, but alas! I've nought to give but Love, if that's a Treasure, thou are wond'rous rich."[46] Throughout he considers only the restraints or limitations to his own situation, likening his own condition to the state of captivity he perpetuates in others. With his appropriation of the language of captivity, Martin, with a questionable level of awareness, uses a significant, visible metaphor he, although a privileged white man, finds compelling—a gesture that suggests the degree to which many subjects in eighteenth-century England perceived themselves as not entirely free. His occlusion of the suffering of the enslaved people under his (distant) control does not seem a strategy to repress his discomfort within a system he knew to be morally abhorrent. Raised in Nevis, committed to increasing his fortune, and implicated within other structures (most obviously, the military) also defined by hierarchies of (often brutal) power, Martin seems to accommodate the state of the enslaved within a naturalized worldview.

Similarly, in Judith, we find a woman bound by her deep affection for her husband and restricted by her status as a wife. That her creative prose letter figures her as "the Slave Mahmut, the Faithfull Follower of thy Fortunes" reveals how normalized her subordinate position truly is. If Martin's conception of himself as enslaved seems wildly inappropriate, Judith's self-representation seems a cruel irony in an act of narrative racial appropriation. Their correspondence manifests a dynamic unique to this particular moment in British culture—as agents of the colonial enterprise, with Martin's holdings of land, sugar works, and enslaved Africans, they participate (although at a distance) in a mechanism of dominance and exploitation. (Although Judith does not legally own any of these holdings, her role as correspondent and conduit of information make her an active, if at times unwilling, participant in the enterprise.) They perpetuate a condition of enslavement for an unknown and, for them, unknowable population. Simultaneously they unironically characterize the real and perceived limitations of their own existence as a kind of inescapable confinement. They believe themselves to live in a culture defined by manifestations of captivity in their personal lives, even as they are immediately surrounded in England and distantly connected (on their plantations) to others far more captive than they.

Writing Captivity

Contemporaneous with the Madans' correspondence filled with self-descriptions of domestic captivity, published literary discourse (including Judith's) invoked similar images. Prior to her marriage and the subsequent birth of her nine children, Judith wrote verse that attracted the attention of Alexander Pope, who praised the "softer Wonder" her poetry inspired in his "pleasd soul" and corresponded with her in a dozen letters between 1722 and 1723, sending her "poetical amusements" or challenges for her.[47] Her early poetry, preserved in her brother Ashley Cowper's "Family Miscellany," included occasional verse, expressions of love for Martin ("Lysander"), and commentary on contemporaneous authors and their work. Although Judith Madan wrote less poetry after the birth of her children, her published and manuscript verse abounds with imagery of captivity, intricate power relations, and persistent expressions of confinement without release. "Mahmut the Slave" is not the only text in which Judith engages in a first-person persona. Her verse epistle and perhaps best-known poem *Abelard to Eloisa* (a response to Pope's *Eloisa to Abelard* [1717]) assumes the voice of the cloistered, castrated Abelard who writes to Eloisa from his "dark Cell, low prostrate on the Ground."[48] The poem amplifies Abelard's confining environment ("this awful Cave" [l. 15], "these gloomy Cloister's solemn Walls" [l. 17]), and newly limited physical condition shaped by "Lean Abstinence, pale Grief, and haggard Care" (l. 43). Abelard's true captor, however, is not the monastery but his "voluptuous Love" (l. 72) for Eloisa. Her form "Still wanders" in his "lost, . . . guilty Mind" (l. 101); even as he knows he should seek repentance, still "thy Charms I view, / Yet my Sighs break, and my Tears flow for you / Each weak Resistance stronger knits my Chain" (ll. 131–33). The subtle, near oxymoronic sequence—"weak Resistance stronger"—conveys the convoluted nature of the emotion Abelard expresses, one echoed by Judith Madan's articulation of her own fraught attitude toward her husband Martin. Interestingly, in *Abelard and Eloisa,* Abelard attempts to transfer the responsibility for his spiritual rehabilitation onto Eloisa, burdening her with that emotional labor. Urging her to "labour, strive, thy Love, thy self-controul," he asserts that only her "Change" will affect his "kindred Soul" (ll. 139–40); "let me Mine, from thy Repentance find" (l. 138). The repetition of the first-person pronoun ("me Mine") suggests the solipsism Judith attributes to Abelard. In Judith's nuanced rendering of that relationship, Eloisa is as captive as Abelard because of his demands, even as she (not unlike Judith) must maintain the relationship at a distance.

Liberty and captivity also inflect the work of Dublin poet Mary Barber (ca. 1685–1755), but from a distinctly different cultural perspective and to a very different end. Unlike the Madans' personal correspondence, which documents the subtle negotiation of marital power, social navigation, and colonial investments, Barber's published poems overtly address her concerns about an urban space in which individuals live daily under increasingly onerous restrictions. She records the domestic captivity of victims of the structural inequities of poverty, unemployment, and debt inherent in the economic and political system. Certainly, Barber shared the Madans' sense of economic insecurity, although she in no way possessed their status or means.[49] The wife of a Dublin woolen-draper, Barber witnessed scenes of indigence—the poverty of veterans' widows denied a pension, hungry children, and individuals dispossessed for other reasons. She explicitly lays responsibility for these conditions on "a thankless State" (4) that should not "wonder at *Complainings in Your Streets.*"[50] Threats of confinement loom large; the specter of imprisonment for debt or "crime" haunts the "Wretched" "ev'ry Hour."[51] Barber tells of "Off-spring" who "pine for Bread" and "See their lov'd Mothers into Prisons thrown; / And, unreliev'd in iron Bondage groan" ("Officer's Widow," 24–26). Barber sees captive subjects all around her. Like Madan, she also writes of the psychological experiences of captivity, recording how, even when ostensibly ended, captivity has a persistent, residual effect on an individual. Barber reflects upon her own brief imprisonment for seditious libel in a 1736 poem, observing that liberty granted is not necessarily liberty enjoyed. During their confinement, "wretched captives, long in prison bound, / Where iron bands at once confine and wound" imagine the time when they will be "free to tread the verdant plain." Even when "time unbinds their chains," however, "The fatal weakness which they cause remains."[52] Although a prisoner's bonds are removed, the residual memory of those bonds remains a defining part of the captive subject. One may be no longer literally confined, but one can never be fully free.

Attentive to the individual experience of captivity, Barber also probes structural inequities that restrain and control greater numbers of unnamed people on a national scale. Her poem "On Seeing the Captives, Lately Redeem'd from Barbary by His Majesty" reflects on the situation for 131 Barbary captives, English subjects enslaved in North Africa as a result of kidnapping at sea. She recounts the November 11, 1734, London celebration for these "liberated" men, predominately from the laboring classes, whom Barber pointedly describes as "English Captives."[53] As newspaper accounts detail, after they are "taken out" of the man of war ships *Blandford* and *Sheerness*, placed into "several large Boats in Long-Reach, and carried through Bridge to Whitehall," the men, still in "their Slavish Habits," parade to St. James "to return his Majesty Thanks for delivering them"[54] from their enslaved state. Barber explicitly characterizes the men as "freed Captives" (l. 3), an oxymoron that illuminates the compromised position of the redeemed men (an unstable state literalized by their "Slavish Habits," the clothing of their captivity), and, indeed, the problematic notion of "freedom" for those previously enslaved.

The "freed Captives" return home and "hail their native Shore," apparently to "tread the Land of LIBERTY once more" (ll. 4–5). Yet Barber's Britain, the "land of liberty," is a site of lack, dislocation, and confinement. Britain itself represents a form of domestic captivity nearly as limiting as the global captivity the men just experienced. Within a poem of apparent exultation lies the contested status of the "freed Captives," a term that signals the unrealized promise of the "land of liberty" for all but the most elite. Although "redeemed," liberated from enslavement in North Africa, the Barbary captives return to their homeland only to be held captive by their own country: "The bitter Cup of Slavery is past; / But pining Penury approaches fast" (ll. 36–37). "Slavery" and "Penury," internal rhymes, become metrically equal terms and culturally equal conditions. The men, on domestic soil, remain prisoners to poverty, hunger, and homelessness. "The Joy of Liberty" is fleeting. The act of liberation the crown performs by ransoming the men only reiterates the unalloyed power of the state, which does nothing to alleviate the men's real captor—their debilitating impecuniousness. While Barber urges the newly freed subjects to bless "the Hand, that has unbound thy Chains" (ll. 25–26)—that is, the king—implicit in the statement is the potential for them—or anyone—to be bound again.

The ambiguity of the poem's final lines underscores the freed captives' liminal status. The poet urges "*Albion . . . To break the Bonds, and set the Pris'ners free.*" Containing another sly oxymoron with the juxtaposition of the words "Pris'ners free," this concluding statement might seem to exhort England (Albion) to redeem additional subjects held in North Africa. However, the poem as a whole suggests that freedom comes not from ransoming Barbary captives or other subjects confined by forces outside of the British Isles—that is, in "foreign" places—but rather by fundamentally improving the quality of the life to which the "freed captives" return: easing or removing the kinds of domestic captivity to which they are subject. In these poems, Barber destabilizes the concept of "freedom" for both specific individuals and the collective group. She articulates the pervasive forms of captivity British subjects regularly confront.[55] Consequently, Barber reconfigures the understanding of England as the ostensible "land of liberty" to reveal it instead be a site of domestic captivity.[56]

The anxiety about different forms of captivity also underscores one of the most familiar poems of the period. James Thomson's *Rule Britannia* (1740) expresses the twin, contradictory impulses of power and subjection that shape this period.[57] Like Barber's verse on the Barbary captives, Thomson's poem ostensibly celebrates liberty and power; "Rule Britannia, Britannia rule the waves" seems to be an unambiguous exhortation to British sailors and subjects to maintain maritime ascendance in the British Atlantic and other parts of the globe, a power essential to imperial expansion. The personified Britannia's dominance seems uncontested. Yet, the very next line, "Britons never will be slaves," exposes the persistent anxiety about the possible enslavement of British subjects, one of the realities to which Barber's poem refers. Captivity at home or abroad always remains a risk. However, unlike Barber's direct acknowledgment that "penury" binds the poor or that forms of bondage exist on British soil, Thomson's words elide the kinds of domestic confinement or involuntary servitude to which Britons themselves might be subject (and on which British colonial and maritime expansion depend). Ironically, the naval context with which this song is most closely associated—British sailing vessels—relied upon the impressment of men into service, one of the many authorized and institutionalized forms of confinement that existed as a potential reality for many non-elite Britons.

These published and manuscript texts by Thomson, Barber, and the Madans reveal the degree to which anxiety, fascination, and preoccupation with domestic captivity shaped white eighteenth-century British subjects' understanding of their world and their place within it. Many popular literary texts by British authors reflect and represent the diverse forms of domestic captivity to which individuals—particularly women—could become subject. Further, the language of captivity infuses expressions of self-conceptualization.[58] These texts, like those throughout this book, reveal the degree to which individuals perceived themselves to live in a culture of captivity. The undeniable yet unremarkable cultural presence of enslaved people shaped attitudes toward forms of domestic captivity that emerged simultaneously—a domestic captivity that rendered itself invisible, unquestioned, and often unnoticed through its very pervasiveness. The structural dependence on the labor of the enslaved became a normalized part of eighteenth-century culture and permitted—indeed generated—at this early point a similar accommodation of confinement, restraint, and subjection for domestic subjects. "Domestic captivity" became a naturalized condition for many who existed in a structurally subjected state such as women, the poor, or members of the laboring classes.

A shared language, with the introjection and the explicit comparisons of diverse forms of captivity, describes domestic captivity and reveals a continuity of thought among Restoration and eighteenth-century subjects. Similarly the continuity of language gives a linguistic underpinning to the cultural idea of the time that these forms of captivity—although starkly different in terms of cause, nature, and degree—contribute fundamentally to the understanding of British identity. Twentieth-first-century scholars resist the comparison easily made by late seventeenth- and early eighteenth-century writers; how can the human bondage experienced by an enslaved African be credibly likened to the restrictions experienced by the indentured, the laboring poor, or married women? The enslavement and forced servitude of others was the landscape for contemporaneous forms of subjugation also imposed upon British subjects. It proved a potent if imprecise point of comparison. England's engagement in the slave economy and the not-yet-codified divisions among forms of unfree labor contributed to the continuity of understanding at the time, coupling colonial captivity with forms of domestic captivity increasingly normalized and naturalized for British subjects. As the prologue explains in detail, the patriarchal-imperial impulse that drove Britain's colonizing efforts simultaneously, and perhaps inevitably, contributed to the creation and perpetuation of authorized (often institutionalized) forms of domestic captivity—indentured servitude, impressment into military service, or transportation for any number of minor "crimes." These were mutually reinforcing and mutually informing cultural practices. Similarly, conditions for the laboring poor, the terms of domestic service for many, and restrictions imposed upon wives and daughters—restrictions variously imposed, contingent on class, geography, and individual behavior—contributed to a culture of captivity in which many individuals understood themselves to live as captive subjects.

For example, the abduction and captivity of British subjects in service of the colonial enterprise remained a material reality for many dispossessed people in the Restoration and early eighteenth century beyond the use of transportation as a strategy for simultaneously providing a labor supply and removing low-level criminals. Daniel J. Vitkus details "common forms" of captivity practiced during this period contemporaneous with "the English commitment to the African-Caribbean slave trade": "impressment, the spiriting away of children, the selling of children and of young men and women into apprenticeship or indentured servitude." Some of the first British imperial captives, observes Elizabeth Foyster, were taken by their fellow citizens, not by foreigners. Robert Darby notes how "forms of forced labor remained common." Denver Brunsman estimates that approximately 250,000 British seamen were impressed during the long eighteenth century.[59] The notoriously harsh conditions for those men in army or naval service—corporal punishment including flogging, relentlessly hierarchical structures, and often perilous conditions—created a nearly untenable situation of restraint, one in which "freedom" was deeply contested.

While many men were pressed into service as soldiers or sailors, other men pursued naval or military service to escape the grinding conditions of abject poverty. As the "thresher poet" Stephen Duck (1705–56) describes. "[T]he Sailor terrify'd" with "Thoughts" of "Poverty" "Boldly attempts the Dangers of the Sea." "[T]he Soldier too . . . To fly from Poverty . . . runs on Death."[60] Such a state of deprivation (akin to Barber's "pining penury"), coupled with the exploding labor needs of the British colonies, fueled an

increase in the number of individuals *voluntarily* transported to the colonies. John Wareing asserts that between 1618 and 1718, more than 400,000
people were transported to the colonies as indentured servants to supply the labor needs of the British colonies in the West Indies and North
America.[61]

The conditions for the working poor who remained in England were
profoundly limiting and constricting. Like Mary Barber, many laboring-
class poets question the popular affirmations of British "liberty." Writers
such "washerwoman poet" Mary Collier (1688–1762) like Robert Dodsley
(1704–64) repeatedly describe the laborer's condition as an "abject State."[62]
(While Dodsley would emerge as one of the most important and innovative
printers of the early eighteenth century, he began in domestic service and
his early poems recount that experience.) These poets explicitly compare
their domestically performed "slavish Toil" (domestic both in the sense
that it occurs within a household and within Britain) with the labor performed by the enslaved abroad. In "The Thresher's Labour" (1730) Duck,
who likens his "tedious Labor" (l. 50) to the repetitive "Toils" of Sisyphus,
marks his temporary visual transformation—wrought by the "sooty Peese"
of his labor—to an "Ethiopian." The "imbrication" of the British laboring
classes and slavery, what Roxanne Wheeler characterizes as their "inter-
twined cultural histories," creates a tendency in the eighteenth century "to
think simultaneously about West Indian slaves and British workers."[63]

"The Woman's Labour" (1739), Collier's rebuttal to Duck's poem, acknowledges the thresher's "tedious Hours" of labor and the "Toilsome" life
to which he is subject. However, Collier vividly illustrates how that situation intensifies for women who also confront "domestic Toils incessant"
(l. 76); after they work all day outside the home, they return to "find again
our Work but just begun" (l. 106). Collier uses the word "slave" five times
within the text. Further, Collier suggests that women's lot resembles that
of the "Turks" for none but they "that ever I could find, / Have Mutes to
serve them, or did e'er deny / Their Slaves, at Work to chat it merrily" (ll.
66–68). Responding to Duck's charge that women's talking distracts from
their work, she asserts women's right to "enjoy that pleasing Liberty" the
"only Privilege our Sex enjoy" (ll. 72, 74). The experience of a laboring-
class woman included excessive domestic work within her home coupled
with taxing paid employment outside the household, a situation that intensifies Collier's self-comparison to the enslaved. She characterizes herself

as one "who ever was, and's still a Slave" (l. 5). Although she writes from the perspective a laboring woman, her sentiment is echoed by women of all classes.

Women and Captivity

The limitations upon women were not unique to members of the laboring classes, even if that group most fully bore the onerous burden of physical labor. Legal and financial restrictions perpetuated women's subordination, prompting many women writers of the middling classes, gentry, and aristocracy to explicitly compare their existence to a form of enslavement, fueled by their perception that women lacked agency and control. Many women vociferously articulated their belief that they existed within a state of domestic captivity. Sarah Fyge Egerton (1670–1723) characterizes the totality of women's existence as one of servitude and confinement; "From the first dawn of Life, unto the Grave," she writes in *The Emulation* (1703), "Poor Womankind's in every State, a Slave."[64] These comparisons take on additional urgency during a period in which economic growth was increasingly defined by either the trade in enslaved Africans or the products of their unfree labor.

The social resistance to women's education formed its own kind of captivity. Mary Astell (1666–1731) asserts that women are kept in "ignorance and slavery," inextricably linking the two conditions. Egerton represents the perceived commitment to withhold education and "the Sciences and Arts" from women as a strategy of self-preservation by men who anticipate that women "should excel" their male counterparts if provided with a chance at education. Consequently, men would "our Thoughts controul, / And lay restraints on the impassive Soul" (ll. 17–19) to maintain their dominion over women. Collier describes how the lack of learning also defines the lives of women in the laboring classes: "No Learning ever was bestow'd on me; / My Life was always spent in Drudgery: / And not alone; alas! with Grief I find, / It is the portion of poor Woman-kind" (ll. 8–10). "Poor" here is multiply directed; it refers to both the economically disfranchised—the financially "poor"—and to women as a gender, "poor" in the sense they are unfortunate or to be pitied. The consequences of this lack of education, asserts Lady Mary Chudleigh (1656–1710), is women who, refusing "Wisdom's Aid," become "Slaves to themselves" or "worst of Servitudes in

Love." Driven by "Vices" and "inslav'd by Interest," "their Chains they hug" unwittingly complicit in their own subjugation.[65]

Poet Elizabeth Thomas (1675–1731), lamenting she is "By Customs Tyranny confin'd," similarly likens woman's condition to that of a "Slave" because of opportunities denied her.[66] The dominant attitude of men, she suggests, is that women should "humbly in *Subjection* live." In *An Essay in Defence of the Female Sex* (1721), Judith Drake (*fl.* 1696–1723) cites women's lack of access to education as a concerted effort by men to "train [women] up altogether to ease and Ignorance," and to make them "tamely give up their liberty, and . . . submitt their Necks to a slavish Yoke."[67] Mary Barber satirically ventriloquizes men's negative criticism of women engaged in literary activity. In "The Conclusion of a Letter to the Rev. Mr. C—" (1734), she mimics the voice of the archbishop of Saint Patrick's Cathedral who "thinks it a Crime in a Woman, to read" (l. 7). A sobering image of confinement is at the center of the poem. "Reading the Poets" will "turn" a woman's "Head"; accordingly, she should be in Bedlam, provided with "a dark Room, and a Straw Bed."[68] The consequence of non-normative behavior or pursuit of education is physical restraint. When Eliza Haywood's female subject Annilia in *The Distressed Orphan; or, Love in a Madhouse* (1726) rebels against the premarital restrictions imposed upon her, her guardian confines her to the madhouse of the novel's subtitle. She simultaneously resists her confinement while acknowledging "Subjection" as the inevitable (and unenviable) condition for women: "whatever Subjection I may be destined after Marriage, I take it ill that my Liberty should be restrain'd till then."[69] She is confined not only by law and custom but literally by the very space she inhabits. Annilia's captivity in a madhouse mirrors the 1726 advertisements in London newspapers offering "good Accommodations, at an easy Rate, for such Women as are deem'd or thought Incurable" of their "Lunacy" or "Melancholy."[70]

The legal and financial restrictions placed upon women after they married exacerbated the confinement of their already circumscribed condition. While certainly many women expressed joy about the intimacy of marital unions, the institution of marriage as juridically and socially constructed foundationally confined married women. These limitations are well known. Women completely lost their legal existence upon marrying. A married woman no longer operated as a *feme sole*, a woman able to act legally on her own behalf; she became, instead, a *feme covert*—a woman "covered" legally by her husband. As William Blackstone (1723–80) famously details in his *Commentaries on the Laws of England* (1765–69), "By marriage the husband and wife are one person in law. . . . [T]he very being or legal existence of the woman is suspended during the marriage, or at least is incorporated and consolidated into that of the husband. . . . For this reason, a man cannot grant his wife anything, . . . for the grant would be to suppose her separate existence."[71] George Savile (1633–95) reminds his daughter that "the Laws of Marriage run in a harsher Stile toward your Sex."[72] Women did not have access to divorce (in all but the most unusual circumstances);[73] Mary Chudleigh observes, "when that fatal Knot is ty'd / . . . nothing, nothing can divide."[74] Within marriage women even lost control over their own bodies. In *The History of the Pleas of the Crown* (1736), Matthew Hale (1609–76) details how "the husband cannot be guilty of a rape committed by himself upon his lawful wife, for by their mutual matrimonial consent and contract the wife hath given herself up in this kind unto her husband, which she cannot retract."[75] "The institution of marriage" during this period, suggests Elizabeth Foyster, "was intended to be the bedrock of the patriarchal ideal where women were subordinated to men, and husbands ruled over and dominated their wives."[76] Part of what is different about this particular moment is the juridical and legal infrastructure newly codifying these relationships and limitations.

Consequently, many seventeenth- and eighteenth-century women writing about the experience and legal condition of marriage drew an explicit comparison with the condition of the enslaved, invoking the legal, economic, and cultural strictures of a patriarchal-imperial power structure that affected both women and the enslaved, albeit in very different ways. As Moira Ferguson asserts in her foundational study, "denied education as well as access to law and allied deprivations, feminists of all classes were prone to refer loosely to themselves as slaves."[77] Sarah Fyge Egerton asserts marriage is "the last, the fatal Slavery" (l. 7).

During courtship, armed with the power of refusal, women retain a semblance of control. Astell describes how, prior to marriage, a man "may call himself her Slave a few days, but it is only in order to make her his all the rest of his life."[78] In Samuel Richardson's *Clarissa*, Anna Howe reminds Clarissa that women risk being "courted as princesses for a few weeks, in order to be treated as slaves for the rest of our lives." Describing marriage without love, Richard Allestree writes that "without this [love] 'tis only a Bargain and Compact, a Tyranny perhaps on the Man's part, and a Slavery on the Woman's." Tellingly, he also recommends that widows refrain from remarrying, cautioning them not "to relinquish both Liberty and Property"; in doing so, they may experience "at the best a Subjection, but perhaps a slavery."[79] Once married, women, writes Egerton in "The Emulation," live like "vanquish'd Kings whom Fetters bind."[80]

The specific image of chains or fetters appears throughout poetic descriptions of marriage in the period. Anne Finch (1661–1720) describes women as "close Pris'ners" of marriage, "the larger Slaves of Hymen" who cannot escape "their chain," a reference to the poem's title "The Unequal Fetters."[81] Allestree also uses that imagery, suggesting that on women who adorn themselves with "exquisite deckings," such items are "the chains not of their ornament, but slavery" (26). Laetitia Pilkington (ca. 1709–50), describing her relationship with husband Matthew, characterizes hers as "That heart to you so fondly ty'd / With pleasure wore its chain."[82] In "The Monkey Dance," Elizabeth Thomas characterizes marriage as a condition that reduces spouses to pet monkeys who, in captivity, come to "hug the Chain" of their oppression.[83] In "Epistle from Mrs. Yonge to Her Husband," Lady Mary Wortley Montagu (1689–1762) laments that women are "To daily Racks condemn'd, and to eternal Chains." Montagu further observes that while "A wounded Slave regains his Liberty. / For Wives ill us'd no remedy remains."[84] "Is this the state of wedlock?" asks Eliza Haywood's Betsy Thoughtless, unhappily married to the abusive Munden. "Call it rather Egyptian bondage."[85] In George Farquhar's *The Beaux' Stratagem* (1707), the unhappily married Mrs. Sullen explicitly, and repeatedly, bemoans an Englishman's ability to "enslave his wife" (II.i). She believes the bondage of married women to be inevitable: "a woman must wear chains" (II.i). But she explicitly points to the inappropriateness of that condition for women in England. "Were I born a humble Turk, where women have no soul nor property," she observes, "there I must sit contented. But in England . . . must women be enslaved . . . cheated into slavery[?]" (IV.i). These lines embody the doubly confined position Egerton details in "The Emulation." A husband's "insulting Tyranny" not only accords socially with the dominant, condoned behavior that diminishes the significance of women, but such "ill Manners" are also "justify'd by Law" (8–9). Certainly, twenty-first-century readers recognize the vast, significant, and demonstrable difference in the status, experience, and condition of a married white woman in England and an enslaved African of either gender, a difference that must not be elided or ignored. Yet the language used by writers of the period points to specific elements of the perceived commonality of the experience. While the comparisons may seem predominately metaphorical, they serve to invoke the common foundational legal, economic, and cultural strictures of a patriarchal system that also fuels systemic racism and institutionalized misogyny. At this particular cultural moment, when the awareness, visibility, and reliance upon the labor of enslaved Africans increased, the shared imagery marks an understanding of a continuity between the two conditions. When Judith Drake expresses concern that England will soon emulate the "Eastern Parts of the World, where the Women, like our Negroes in our Western Plantations, are born Slaves, and live Prisoners all their Lives" (19), her comparison functions as more than merely metaphor in a world defined by the *asiento,* the South Sea Company, and the undeniable national investment in enslavement in the "Western Plantations."

That kind of cultural and institutional attitude fuels Mary Astell's pointed question: "If all Men are born free, how is it that all Women are born slaves? As they must be if the being subjected to the inconstant, uncertain, unknown, arbitrary will of Men be the perfect Condition of Slavery."[86] Just as Mary Barber demonstrates inconsistency across a class divide—asking how "liberty" was limited to the few—so too Astell, and others, points to the inconsistency across the gender divide. Women's pleas for liberty, like the conditions of the poor, the impressed, or the indentured, had a particularly poignant resonance within the context of England's reputation as a land of liberty, a country distinct from the oppressive despotism that characterized many European countries. The resonant effects of the Revolution of 1688 included a renewed commitment to, and sense of, England as a county in which liberty—both religious liberty and civil liberty—triumphed over tyranny. Blackstone, for example, denounced James II who, in his words, "attempted to enslave the nation."[87] As Stephen Pincus recounts, in the period following the events of 1688, many Britons "saw the revolution as inaugurating a new age of liberty."[88] This wider perception intensified the dismay of many women writers who recognized the vast divide between a country's ostensible commitment to liberty and their own, constrained state. Elizabeth Thomas concludes her poem "To Sir J—— S——," which details the myriad ways women's actions, thoughts, and movements are limited, with an ironic note of gratitude: "Then thanks to *Heav'n,* we're *English* born and free, / And thank our gracious *Laws* that give such *Liberty.*"[89]

Although the dominant narrative of British identity might appear to be a celebration of liberty, literary representations suggest that narrative became contested with expanding forms of domestic captivity and accelerating resistance to the same. If, as Bruce McLeod suggests, England was "an empire that stood for liberty and commerce,"[90] how could so many people feel anxiety about the threats to that liberty? And how could so much of that commerce depend on the loss of liberty of so many individuals? Captivity functioned as an accessible and persistent narrative trope, but one founded on a material reality. While the disparity between the apparent discourse of liberty and the reality of a confined life pressed most profoundly on women, the laboring poor, the impressed, and the geographically isolated, many English subjects experienced their lives as ones shaped by a state of captivity or confinement. Simultaneously, a persistent fascination with those white, British subjects held in a state of domestic captivity made narratives chronicling that experience popular and saleable. The next chapter situates the work of Aphra Behn within this complex milieu. A writer skilled at subversively representing the limitations marriage places on women, Behn consistently connects such constraints with the patriarchal-imperial impulse and the culture of captivity that shape human interactions in domestic and colonial sites.

CHAPTER 2

Captivating Farce

Aphra Behn's The Emperor of the Moon

Aphra Behn (1640?–89) personally witnessed manifestations of New World slavery during her time in Surinam in 1663 and, upon her return to England, saw evidence of Britain's West Indian investment within the culture of Restoration London. The two worlds impinged upon each other just as Behn's past and present repeatedly intersect in *Oroonoko* (1688). *Oroonoko* arguably constitutes Behn's most extensive—and most frequently discussed—examination of enslavement, human exploitation, and commodification in the West Indies.[1] Written near the end of her life, that rich prose fiction provides a culminating representation of hierarchical power structures shaped by race, class, and gender. That text obviously depicts captivity; Behn directs her attentions to the condition of enslaved Africans, and also points to other, less horrific but no less onerous kinds of confinement or restraint affecting indentured servants, indigenous peoples, and her own female narrative persona. Behn's narrator operates as someone complicit in yet also confined by a colonial power structure. The white patriarchal and imperial forces weigh upon her; yet, unlike Oroonoko, "Behn" has the capacity to escape their most brutal elements.

Written at a temporal distance from Behn's time in Surinam twenty-five years earlier, the fictional text simultaneously draws upon memory and the late Restoration perceptions of that colony present in the contemporary popular press. The successive rebellions of both the indigenous and the enslaved in Surinam produced graphic newspaper accounts of colonists killed and plantations destroyed. Details published in the *London Gazette* in 1678 about a Dutch ensign flayed and put on "a stake, burning the body," find echoes in Behn's lament that the "Indians" "cut a footman, I left behind me, all in joints, and nailed him to trees" or that "they cut in pieces all they could take . . . hanging up the mother and all her children about her."[2] She not only documents the atrocities upon the bodies of the enslaved but, with the benefit of hindsight, she also presages the savagery visited upon vulnerable colonists. Less grimly, Behn marks the transportation of exotic commodities from Surinam to London, like the "unimitable" dress she donated to the King's Theater that appeared in *The Indian Queen*, or her own imaginative depiction of "Colonel Martin . . . celebrated in a character of my new comedy." Newspaper advertisements in England also reference another kind of transport with notices like the one seeking an enslaved boy who had escaped that describes him as someone who "speaks pretty good English, having been from Surinam almost 3 years."[3]

The impact of Behn's time in the then-British colony of Surinam between summer 1663 and February 1664 extends well beyond *Oroonoko*, however; Behn represents patriarchal-imperial power, and resultant domestic forms of oppression, commodification, and confinement in her other works. (In fact, a powerful argument could be made that Behn rarely strays far from that persistent preoccupation; she simply foregrounds or obscures the focus as audience, genre, and style dictate.) That such a brief colonial experience had such a profound effect on her work bespeaks its intensity. Important to my discussion here are *The Young King, The Younger Brother,* and *The Emperor of the Moon,* texts where Behn explicitly flags her own colonial past to frame her work specifically within the lens of captivity. Reading these three plays in concert, situated within a culture brimming with domestic and colonial manifestations of power, reveals the degree to which Behn's time as what she termed an "American" shaped her literary representations and formed her understanding of asymmetries of power within the domestic space of England. Further, these texts also illustrate how fully (and how quickly) the financial, cultural, and imaginative investment in British slave-ownership was naturalized and institutionalized. Behn's dramatic work resonates with heightened cultural anxiety about the possibility and consequences of captivity and offers a sustained critique of the forces that enable such confinement.

This chapter begins by situating Behn's life experience—to the degree that can be reconstructed—within a world marked by real and symbolic forms of confinement that she both observed and endured. In Surinam Behn saw firsthand the formation of a colonial infrastructure dependent on the unfree labor of enslaved Africans and indentured servants; she arrived in Surinam just months after Charles II created what would become the Royal African Company. A careful observer of the Stuart court, Behn understood the intimate connection between the court and the West Indian colonies, two complicated, constraining, and often confusing worlds. She documented how the two environments mirrored each other in central, structuring ways with the exertion of power and enforcement of hierarchies. In London, Behn lived in a world imbued with signs of colonial wealth, persistent threats of incarceration or transportation, and various manifestations of captivity. Of course, as is well known, Behn understood some of these situations personally. While as an author she may have enjoyed certain freedom in her literary representations (although not without risk), she simultaneously navigated threats of debtors' prison, professional relationships constrained by unequal power relationships, and the limitations imposed upon her by persistent impecuniousness and gender. She also recognized—and vividly wrote about—the domestic captivity that legally and economically confined married women of all ranks.

The chapter, then, looks at those texts connected to Behn's time as what she terms an "American." *The Young King* and *The Younger Brother* briefly but significantly incorporate language, imagery, and localized references specific to the discourse used by organizations (such as the Royal African Company) or individuals advancing the slave trade. The appearance of this language within texts Behn explicitly connects to Surinam—within plots representing the abuse of arbitrary power in personal or political governance—subtly but assuredly signals the brutalizing effects of captivity. I then offer a more sustained and detailed examination of *The Emperor of the Moon,* a play that warns of the dangers of spectacle and deceptive language used in the calculated consolidation of colonial and domestic power.

Dismissed as "nothing more than a farce" by Charles Dibdin (1745–1814) in his *Complete History of the English Stage* (1800), *The Emperor of the Moon,* in fact, interrogates state mechanisms and public displays designed to dazzle and subdue the political subject.[4] Behn urges viewers (domestic and colonial) to be aware of the instruments of power acting upon them daily. Farce as a genre offers Behn plausible deniability from any allegation that her candid, if coded, representation cast aspersions on actions by the state. The play shows the pervasive forms of domestic captivity created to confine and contain women, reiterating the connection between the forces of patriarchal and imperial power—a persistent theme throughout Behn's work. *The Emperor of the Moon,* like *The Young King* and *The Younger Brother,* constructs a longer arc of Behn's representation of the conditions of confinement and articulates the dangers of the growing, and to Behn seemingly inevitable, power of the state that shapes the lives of domestic and colonial subjects. These texts of captivity remind Behn's readers and viewers of the long reach of empire, and, equally important, the persistent domestic presence of other forms of captivity. They also demonstrate Behn's sophisticated understanding of the contradictory cultural space she occupied.

Situating Behn: Surinam

British imperial expansion accelerated dramatically during the Restoration with strategic colonization in the West Indies, particularly Barbados and Jamaica.[5] (As Behn notes in *Oroonoko,* British control of Surinam proved a bit more inconsistent.) Equally important, Behn lived in a world that exposed her to the royally sanctioned trade in enslaved Africans monopolized during her lifetime by the Royal African Company (RAC) headed by James II (as discussed in the prologue). The political backing of the newly restored Stuart court accelerated the company's engagement in the trade following its royal charter in January 1663.[6] During its period of incorporation, the RAC, known as the Royal Adventurers until 1672, sponsored 97 voyages between 1663 and 1668 (with the bulk concentrated in 1664–65), transporting 27,110 enslaved people.[7] During Behn's lifetime, 624 ships sailing under the British flag conducted voyages transporting enslaved Africans in the British Atlantic, and, obviously, Surinam or Dutch Guiana was one of the destinations. Initially, however, the exploits of the Royal African Company were "more reminiscent of an aristocratic treasure-hunt than an organized business."[8] Nevertheless, the economic impact of the West Indian plantations and what Gary Puckrein terms the "sugar revolution," and the captivity-based labor on which they depended, made them an integral and present part of British culture.[9] The Royal African Company's importance to the plantations, to the economy, and to the advancing of England's imperial goals was unparalleled. Catherine Hall cites the "state complicity in the Royal African Company" and subsequently, the "navy's

sugar revolution

protection of the trade," as essential factors in the company's success.[10] The RAC, as William Pettigrew details, "transformed the contours and capacity of Britain's slave trade" and shipped more enslaved Africans "to the Americas than any other single institution during the entire period of the transatlantic slave trade."[11] The wealth generated by the RAC, and in turn the planters in West Indian plantations who depended on the steady supply of unfree labor, was tremendous.

Behn knew firsthand the crown's involvement in the transporting of enslaved Africans and recognized them as "royal" property. (Indeed, Oroonoko is a "royal slave" as the subtitle denotes not simply because of his position as a prince in Coramantien but also because an agent of the king kidnaps him and claims him as the king's property, making him a "royal slave.") Behn explicitly marks the vessel that has kidnapped Oroonoko as one that sailed for the Royal Adventurers. When the ship captain deliberates on his treatment of Oroonoko during the passage, he is apprehensive that Oronooko "might commit some Outrage fatal to himself, and the King his Master, *to whom the Vessel did belong*" (84; emphasis mine).[12] Oroonoko, an experienced slave-trader himself, similarly focuses on the ship's connection with the crown: Oroonoko asserts he would "obey the Command of the Captain, as he was Lord of the *King's* Vessel, and General of those Men under his Command" (84).

While in England Behn witnessed how the highest ranks invested in the organization of the slave trade; in Surinam she lived within and observed firsthand the establishment of a slave-based economy. Her close connections with individuals deeply engaged in the colonial enterprise and the trade in enslaved Africans doubtless contributed to what Paula Backscheider terms Behn's "unusual knowledge of British colonial slavery."[13] Jane Jones suggests that Behn may have actually married a man who was, himself, a slave trader; at the very least, Jones offers compelling evidence that connects Behn with a Danish slaving ship, the *King David*, seized at Barbados. Jones posits that this slaving ship, with crewman Johan Behn, transported Behn and her family from the West Indies back to England.[14] Behn straddled the world of individuals directly involved in the transport of the enslaved, as well as individuals who comprised the "complex networks of interconnected social and economic relationships" with higher-level interests in West Indies trade.[15] She personally saw the human cost those efforts exacted from all involved.

Behn's time in Surinam would also have specifically exposed her to what, in many ways, was the most hierarchically oriented of all the British colonies—scattered sites that already tended to be dominated by what Puckrein characterizes as "a planter-patriarch" model.[16] British West Indian planters, suggests Michael Craton, gravitated toward "an aristocratic norm or ideal" with vestiges of "royalist structures," frequently establishing a "patriarchal family household."[17] They tried to replicate British social norms in microcosm, creating a veneer of order and respectability that obscured the violence and oppression inherent to the enterprise. Francis Willoughby, fifth Baron Willoughby of Parham (1614–66), who began settling Surinam in 1651, proves a perhaps extreme example of this model. So dominant was his influence that the colony was often referred to as Willoughby-land.[18] The investment of his personal resources—more than £26,000 by some accounts—populated the colony with more than 300 colonists.[19] The financial incentives he offered individuals to either settle or serve in Surinam made the colony a "viable limb of empire" rather than "a small autonomous outpost."[20] *A Letter Sent from Syrranam* (1664), written by Henry Adis, an early settler to the colony, extols the "Benefits" available through Willoughby's largesse; he praises "your Lordships Promises," as someone now "experimentally sensible of Fames truth in this particular." Although "we have not plenty of that which formerly we have enjoyed in English food," continues Adis, between the "Country and Climate" and "meat and drink," he remains satisfied, believing he fares "Well with the Countreys provisions."[21]

Such financial arrangements centralized control in Willoughby and his surrogates, giving them what Sarah Barber describes as "an unprecedented degree of autonomous action."[22] Willoughby, through his profound financial investment and exacting demands for personal loyalty, had essentially created "a fiefdom."[23] In a 1665 pamphlet, William Byam underscores this deference with his references to Willoughby as "his Excellency" or "the Lord *Willoughby* our Proprietour."[24] He describes the jubilant reaction of Surinam's (unspecified) inhabitants to Willoughby's return: "His Excellency arrived in this River, to the unexpressible Joy of all the Inhabitants, His Excellency under God being the foundation and essence of this Colony."[25] Behn recounts similar moments of deference-tinged celebration in the colonies. As she writes in the dedication to *The City-Heiress* (1682), she has been "an Eye and Ear-witness, with what Transports of Joy, with what unusual Respect and Ceremony, above what we pay to Mankind," men of power "have been celebrated on Forein Shores!"[26] While Willoughby may have had grand aspirations and instituted a firm hierarchical structure, the colony was populated by a disparate group of people (perhaps increasing the need, in Willoughby's mind, for a more rigorous enforcement of one's differential status). After Adis complained of "meeting with some gross incivilities" by residents, Willoughby concedes that in "all new colonies you know of what sort of People generally they are made up of."[27] In *Oroonoko*, Behn also notes the "rude and wild . . . Rabble" she observes in Surinam (118). As Janet Todd details, "Aphra judged Surinam as if it were . . . full of free men." Yet, it was filled with "the few who arrived as planters with capital to invest" and "transported convicts or indentured servants."[28]

This heterogenous population with control over large numbers of enslaved people accelerated the brutality of Behn's Surinam.[29] Planters found that the English social structure they desired was difficult to replicate in the colonies, leading to what Susan Dwyer Amussen describes as "new and increasingly violent ways to maintain social order."[30] In addition to the extreme punishment of Oroonoko himself, Behn graphically describes the material reality of enslavement. For example, Behn references the practice of "*Black Friday*"—the public abuse of the enslaved at the end of every week: "then, whether they work'd or not, whether they were faulty or meriting, they, promiscuously, the Innocent with the Guilty, suffer'd the infamous Whip, the sordid Stripes, from their Fellow-Slaves, 'till their Blood trickled from all Parts of their Body" (105). This kind of ritualistic violence constituted the kinds of "public displays of colonial power" Marisa Fuentes sees as fundamental to the maintenance of the imperial hierarchy.[31] Behn's detail about the symbolic use of horrific punishment resonates throughout the text and within the popular imagination of British readers.

Behn also records the oppressive treatment of the indigenous people by colonists in pursuit of financial gain. She asserts at the beginning of the narrative that the British, from necessity, treated the indigenous people gently, yet she also betrays the ways in which the indigenous have been dispossessed, overpowered, or oppressed. Behn casually documents transgressions on the part of the colonists. In her own trip up the river, she describes how her brother kisses the "very young Wife" of a "young Peeie" or priest, a small but not insignificant gesture of possession (102). Similarly, when the group rowing upstream meets "some Indians of strange Aspects," she reveals they "brought along with 'em Bags of Gold-Dust" (104). This information results in the men—and their gold—being taken "up to *Parham*, where they were kept till the Lord-Governor came." Upon receiving the gold, Willoughby commanded that "a Guard should be set at the Mouth of the River of the *Amazons* . . . and prohibited all People from going up that River, it conducting to those Mountains of Gold." He restricts mobility and enforces confinement (104).

If Behn illustrates the betrayal of indigenous people and brutalization of enslaved Africans, she also references those moments in which she herself is forced into compliance born of obligations arising from an intersection of her gender, dependent condition, and liminal status. In Surinam, she recognizes the limits of her own power. Although Todd's suggestion that Behn might have been sent to Surinam as a spy may be speculative, Behn's narrative persona certainly acts in that capacity. Like a double agent, her female narrator fulfills her obligations to a colonial power structure by distracting and spying on Oroonoko while simultaneously earning his confidence. "I was oblig'd," she writes, "by some Persons who fear'd a Mutiny (which is very Fatal sometimes in those Colonies, that abound so with Slaves, that they exceed the Whites in vast Numbers), to discourse with *Caesar*, and to give him all the Satisfaction I possibly cou'd" (141). The repeated word "obliged," with its etymological roots in the concept of binding, underscores Behn's situation. Moira Ferguson suggests that "Behn's alliance with the colonial ruling class overrides her friendship with Oroonoko," but that assertion may suggest a higher degree of agency than Behn (or her persona) in fact possessed.[32] As a woman "obliged" to fulfill a request from the minority white colonial male rulers ("Persons who fear'd a Mutiny" and the threat to their power), Behn has little choice but to acquiesce. She is compelled to be complicit to a larger atrocity. Her slippage in naming—shifting between his own name Oroonoko and his enslaved name Caesar—marks her unsettled position. Behn must have left Surinam with a sharp awareness of how power, concentrated among a small group of people within a confined geographic space, could easily be abused.

Situating Behn: London

In Surinam, Behn witnessed the brutal effects of a colonial government on the enslaved, the indigenous, and the indentured. Her own relationship with the power structure would likely have been uneasy, requiring compliance—indeed

a kind of complicity—within an exacting environment. Behn personally experienced the state's indifference during her brief stint as a spy for
Charles II's government in the Low Counties from July through December 1666. The kinds of compliance demanded of her in Surinam, like the
often arbitrary exercise of control by those in power, also informed her
time in Antwerp. The crown and her spymasters expressed little concern
for her personally or for any individual they used in that capacity. As Alan
Marshall persuasively demonstrates, the relationship between Behn as a
spy agent and her so-called "spy master" thrust her into another situation
in which she was sharply confined by the conventions of the Restoration intelligence world. The relationship between spy and spy master, as Marshall
explains, can be best understood as one based on "reciprocal need" akin to
those within "a culture of client-patron relationships": "the spy . . . was thus
a suppliant, eagerly seeking a master's praise" and, ideally, remuneration.[33]
The inherent reciprocity—spies gathering information through which they
hope to gain compensation and their spy masters who use that material to
their advantage—embedded a "dynamic of textual debt and credit" into the
written relationship, a debt that was all too real for the impecunious Behn.
Behn suffered from the notorious parsimony of England toward its agents
in the field and her spying left her profoundly in debt. It essentially held her
captive in that position because, as Janet Todd and Francis McKee observe,
Behn was "so much in debt that she could not have left the country if she
had wanted to."[34] A job of monotony and subservience rather than intrigue
and excitement (and a job costing Behn money), operating as spy revealed
her to be expendable. "To the spymasters," writes Marshall, "she was merely
'Mrs Affora' of the 'Memorialls', to be used and discarded like many another
secret agent of the day."[35]

When Behn returned to London in 1667 she would have encountered a
domestic world that reiterated the racialized power dynamic she saw in Surinam. Enslaved Africans lived in London as well.[36] The crown's economic
investment in the trade in enslaved people increased their visibility. "People of African descent were part of the rural and urban landscape of late
Stuart England," writes Amussen. "[T]hey were highly visible in London,
Bristol, and other ports and present in smaller numbers through the rest
of the country."[37] But the presence of enslaved people was also marked by
their absence, moments of escape and resistance. The September 12, 1678,
issue of the London Gazette features a typical advertisement for an enslaved
youth who has run away from his master:

> A Negro Boy, his name *Africa*, by his growth seeming to be about 12 years old, he had a gray cloth Livery, the Lace mixed with black, white, and orange colors, somewhat torn . . . a Silver Ring in one of his ears, his hair newly clipped very close, speaks some English, Dutch, and Blacks. Run away from his Master the first instant Whosoever shall secure him, and give notice to Mr. *Arnold Pidgeon* Barber in *James Street, Covent-Garden*, shall have 20 s. Reward.

Detailing the twelve-year-old male's distinguishing characteristics, the notice captures the imbrication of domestic and global captivity as displayed on the young boy's body. He wears a "gray cloth livery," "the Lace mixed with black, white, and orange colors." It was fashionable among London elite to have enslaved Africans as servants, and "young black males of the period" were particularly "prized for their youth."[38] The twelve-year-old's livery likely marks his labor as a footman or personal attendant. Livery worn by any servant—Black or white—designated the individual's household and functioned to preserve the distinction of rank and erase the attendant's identity. The condition of this young boy's livery, "somewhat torn," might suggest its intense use (perhaps by its previous wearer) or a moment of harshness upon the clothing or the youth himself.

The uniformity of his livery sits a bit uneasily with the child's more exotic details like the "Silver Ring in one of his ears." His hair "newly clipped very close" could indicate that, in accordance with the style of the time, a wig was part of his required attire; or, perhaps, as contemporaneous paintings suggest, the closely cut hair was the preferred mode for enslaved young boys.[39] The note that his hair is "newly" clipped may suggest his recent arrival to London or a change in his status. His polylingual skills, for he "speaks some English, Dutch, and Blacks," echo the languages circulating in the Surinam of *Oroonoko*. While distinguishing the two languages of the dominant colonial powers—English and Dutch—the description erases the complexity of multiple African languages, conflating them simply as "Blacks." The youth's very name, "Africa," summons a place at once partner in and subject to British imperial power. The reward for the young boy's recovery can be collected at a location in James Street, Covent Garden, just blocks from where Behn's *Sir Patient Fancy* had debuted at the Dorset Theatre a few months before.

Such notices seeking to recapture enslaved individuals reveal a culture regularly marked by the intersection of the imperial and the domestic, the

foreign and the familiar in a way that illuminates Behn's relationship to empire, power, and captivity. It also suggests that enslavement, like other forms
of captivity, had already been normalized. The proliferation of newspaper
advertisements in the decades after Behn's return to London for other enslaved men who had "went away" provided a domestic reminder of the
captivity she witnessed in Surinam, an extension of the power dynamic.
The individuals most commonly appearing in advertisement were young
men. The notices typically include detailed descriptions of their clothing, its value often second only to that of the person themselves. Robert
Moore was wearing a "Fawn-coloured" livery, while Fortune, his enslaver
recently deceased, was last seen "in a Mourning Cloth suit."[40] Yet the distinguishing markers were not only the fabric that covered them, but bodily
evidence of physical assault. Moore "lost his thumb from his left hand." A
twenty-one-year-old bears "a scar on his temple, many scars on his neck."[41]
A fifteen-year-old who "went away on Christmas Day" has "a Scar on the
left-side of his forehead, and a Scratch between his eye-brows."[42] "[A] black
Boy well-favour'd, call'd Peter . . . has a small Scar on his upper Lip on his
left side."[43] Such listings are a reminder of the degree to which, as Fuentes
notes, the scars function as a kind of "body memory" of a larger system of
abuse and oppression.[44] For a Restoration reader, these listings would have
been utterly unremarkable.

Notices that implicitly reinforced the categories of captivity in which
British subjects could be held also fill the advertising section of the newspapers. Those subject to other kinds of confinement—those apprenticed, indentured, pressed into military service, or, if women, married—frequently
sought escape and anonymity. Behn additionally points to types of domestic confinement. For example, *The Adventure of the Black Lady* describes
"the Overseers of the poor (justly so call'd from their over-looking 'em)"
who enforce specific, constricting norms. In that text, the pregnant unmarried Bellamora worries about incarceration because of her condition. If she
cannot "give Security to the Parish of twenty or thirty Pound," she will "be
sent to the House of Correction, and her Child to a Parish-Nurse."[45]

While London's urban space presented risks of enforcement and confinement, it also offered the opportunity for concealment, disguise, and re-
invention, opportunities Behn herself pursued. Behn's experience upon her
return to London in 1667 revealed the limits of power for a woman without independent means. Immediately upon her arrival in the city, Behn,

impecunious as a result of her work as a spy, actually had to petition the court to avoid debtors' prison. Her writing became her means to survival. Prolific, Behn produced at least eighteen plays, five short fictions, two collections of poetry, translations, and scores of other poems, prologues, and epilogues that appeared separately or were published posthumously. She was the most prolific and popular playwright of the Restoration (second only to John Dryden). Derek Hughes observes that "Behn had twenty-five percent more plays put on than any *male* competitor."[46]

In the preface to *Sir Patient Fancy* (1678) she casts the position of an author as, to some degree, one of captivity—she is "forced to write for Bread."[47] To write professionally, what Behn describes as a "mean and mercenary Art," demands one regularly produce publishable work that sold. The struggle to maintain financial solvency (or even subsistence) in a marketplace where writers were often the least well compensated individuals in the print trade required what Montague Summers terms "a continual round of work."[48] Playwrights were affected by external factors beyond their control. The economy, public disturbances, or events in the royal family might require theaters to suspend performances, losing ticket sales. In the epilogue to *The Feign'd Curtizans* (1679), Behn laments those moments when "So hard the Times are, and so thin the Town" that fewer people come to the theater.[49] After the death of Charles II in 1685, London's two theatrical companies—the Duke's Company and the King's Company—merged, causing a steep decline in productions, proportionally diminishing both the demand for and the number of playwrights.[50] As she details in the dedication to *The Emperor of the Moon*, political events distract people for whom *"the only Diversion of the Town now, is high Dispute, and publick Controversies in Taverns, Coffee-houses, &c."* (414, ll. 67–71). Consequently, "The scanted Tribute is so slowly paid, / Our Poets must find out another Trade."[51] *"The wiser Wits have now new Measures set, / And taken up new Trades, that they may Eat"* (*Emperor*, 528, ll. 10–11). Behn's repeated use of the term "trade" underscores the commercial environment of the theater and the literary marketplace. Although Behn published consistently throughout the 1670s, she remained in a precarious financial condition; a shrinking theater audience, shifting political alliances, and continuing debt repeatedly placed Behn in increasing economic need. That depressed financial state threatened to expose her to other forms of captivity. She wrote determinedly, "I will not perish in a Prison."[52]

A letter to her publisher Jacob Tonson seeking an additional "5 pound more" as payment for *Poems upon Several Occasions* (1684) reveals her diminished situation: "I have been without getting so long that I am just on the poynt of breaking, especially since a body has no creditt at the Playhouse as we used to have. . . . I want extreamly or I wo'd not urge this."[53] Beyond her financial straits, her brushes with debtors' prison, and her constraining relationships such as the one with her spy master, Behn also lived with a keen awareness of the degree to which she was held captive by her gender. Very few of her texts fail to directly confront or represent asymmetrical power relations—between men and women, free and enslaved, or two sovereign nations. She lived with a cultural awareness of the many authorized (often institutionalized) forms of domestic captivity that shaped her own life and the condition for her fellow subjects in Restoration England.

Reflections on Surinam: *The Young King* and *The Younger Brother*

At first glance, *The Young King* and *The Younger Brother* may seem unlikely candidates for texts that extend Behn's reflections on Surinam. However, the paratexts of both plays explicitly reference Behn's brief but formative time in Surinam and frame the plays with a colonial marker that specifically draws attention to their connection with West Indian captivity. Within the texts themselves, Behn represents the dangers of unchecked, unquestioned power deployed in service of personal gain. An accomplished and sophisticated playwright, Behn assuredly uses details to point to injustices, irregularities, or practices undergirding the culture of captivity, patterns she wants the reader to notice. We cannot underestimate her command over the subtleties of language. *The Young King* has a small but significant representation of personal domination on the part of the tyrannical ruler Orsames that draws on language appearing in contemporaneous pamphlets advertising the Royal African Company. Similarly, *The Younger Brother* (the play Behn references in *Oroonoko*), focuses on Behn's Surinam acquaintance George Marten, and structurally reproduces the human commodification central to the British colonial efforts, transplanting it into a domestic environment. Using the colloquial language of the slave trade, the text shows parents willing to essentially sell their children, privileging financial gain over familial connections. Together the plays directly and dramatically present the power relationships foundational to colonial dominance and to domestic forms of captivity. Although Behn does not focus on the colonial experience per se, she explicitly draws on the audience's knowledge (and her own experience) of the imperial enterprise, ties it to domestic patterns, and situates both within a culture of captivity.

Behn claims in the dedication to have written *The Young King; or, The Mistake* (1679) while still in Surinam in 1663–64.[54] Although she fears "the reproach of being an *American*," she identifies the play as "this youthful sally of my Pen, this first Essay of my Infant-Poetry."[55] She specifically marks her geographic distance from England during the period of this text's composition—"Three thousand Leagues of spacious Ocean"—and her own extensive travel in the intervening years: "she has measured, visited many and distant Shores" since her original time on "that vast tract of Sea & Land" (83) of Surinam. While stylometric research suggests that Behn may actually have significantly revised (or even written) the text in the 1670s, Behn cites the colonial location as the place of composition and draws it into the text's interpretative frame. The play is typically read as evidence of Behn's royalist views; its 1679 production, on the eve of the Exclusion Crisis, certainly aligns with Todd's claim that the revised play specifically offered Behn's "support for legitimacy in the person of the heir to the throne, James Duke of York" (81). Support for James was also tacitly support for the RAC, of which he was the director and largest shareholder. Similarly, by invoking Surinam in the dedication, Behn also reminds us to consider the play's connection with the colonial enterprise, and urges us to read it through a lens of captivity.[56]

The title character Orsames, "the young king," articulates a worldview that linguistically and ideologically aligns with the ethos of the Royal African Company and the plantocracy it serves. The son of the Dacian queen, Orsames has been imprisoned his entire life. His mother had a prophecy that her son, if allowed to reign, would be "fierce and bloudy, a Ravisher, a Tyrant o're his People" (88, ll. 46–47). Thus, she has held him in captivity in what the setting describes as a "*A Castle or Prison on the Sea*" (97). While his sister Cleomena has been trained in the military arts to compensate for his absence,[57] Orsames has "never . . . seen any Humane thing save onely his old Tutor" (84). When Orsames's tutor Geron asks him how he would have created the world, the young king vividly details a world where men like himself "with mighty Souls" wield godlike power and maintain "dominion o're the lesser world," those with "low submissive Souls" (97, ll.

29–35). (The language anticipates Oroonoko's statement of dominion over others.) Living as a king, Orsames would, he details, command

> . . . fear, and awe, as thou hast of the Gods;
> And those I wou'd have made as numberless
> As Curls upon the face of yonder Sea,
> Of which each blast drives Millions to the Shore,
> Which vanishing, make room for Millions more. (98, ll. 37–41)[58]

Total domination is not enough; Orsames demands a "numberless" supply of the subjugated, as "Millions" upon millions are driven "to the Shore."

Language used in contemporaneous texts representing the arrival of the enslaved in the British West Indian colonies resonates within this passage. Richard Ligon (ca. 1585–1662) records activities in the early days of the British presence in Barbados and depicts a place seized by the "fear, and awe" Orsames seeks in his suppliants. Kidnapped Africans arriving in Barbados, writes Ligon, "are held in such awe and slavery, as they are fearfull to appear in any daring act . . . their spirits are subjugated to such a low condition, as they dare not look up to any bold attempt."[59] To Ligon, the growing population of Barbados—enslaved and indentured—seems nearly incalculable or, in Orsames's words, "numberless." "It were somewhat difficult to give you an exact account of the numbers of persons upon the land," writes Ligon, "there being such store of shipping that brings passengers dayly to the place."[60] West Indian planters, legislators, and slave traders wanted the supply of unfree labor to, in Ramesh Mallipeddi's words, "continue without interruption."[61]

Promotional material for the Royal African Company advertises the company's ability to supply enslaved Africans at a constant level. A pamphlet seeking additional subscribers to the company in 1667 includes a letter from company secretary Ellis Leighton to Francis Willoughby. Leighton describes "how necessary it is that the English plantations in America should have a competent and a *constant* supply of Negro-servants for their own use in Planting." To that end, they will "dispatch so many ships" to "furnish . . . a *constant* and *sufficient succession* of them, so as the Planter shall have no just cause to complain of any want" (emphasis mine).[62] The image of nameless people moving, as "numberless" as the waves across an ocean, "Millions" who "vanishing, make room for Millions more," unquestionably invokes the fundamental elements of the nascent transatlantic trade in enslaved Africans.[63] (Rather more ominously, it also points perhaps unwittingly to the high mortality rate among the West Indian enslaved, requiring the "*constant*" arrival of ships bearing newly captured individuals.) Ironically, in a text imagining the forced movement of countless people, Behn's dedication includes a description of her own more independent movement across a "Spacious Ocean" to "many and distant Shores."

Not only does Orsames echo the language found in Royal African Company promotional materials, but he also articulates a vision of draconian punishment that resembles common, brutal plantation practices. When asked by Geron what he would do should any one of these "millions" of people "Refuse obedience," Orsames vividly replies: "I would destroy them, and create anew" (98, l. 44). Orsames describes his subjects as ultimately disposable and replaceable. Using the image of the ocean, the inevitable means of transport for human commodities, he asks, "Hast not observ'd the Sea?" As "ev'ry Wave that hastens to the Bank . . . it overtake[s] a thousand petty ones." He, too, indifferent to the "petty ones," will remain completely "unconcern'd" if his "triumph" results in the "ruine" of others (98, ll. 45–48). The "men with low submissive Souls" would be replaceable, destroyed and created anew (97, l. 34).

Orsames expresses these views while still imprisoned, isolated, and unaware of his royal status. They remain, for him, purely theoretical (even as they document material practices in Behn's world). However, "drest in Royal Robes," Orsames (in an inversion of Oroonoko's fate) is transported, asleep, from his prison (113). He awakes, "The Crown and Scepter lying by on a Table," "and gazes round about him and on himself with wonder" (113). He is transformed from a prisoner to a king. Exalting in his newfound power, "Power [by which] I may do any thing" (114, l. 48), Orsames proves as arbitrary a ruler as his worldview would predict. Like a West Indian planter, he, with impunity, orders those who contradict him be taken "away to death immediately" or sent "Into the Sea" (115, ll. 92, 103). George Warren's *An Impartial Description of Surinam* (1667) details how in that colonial space the enslaved were regularly subject to "the most exquisite tortures."[64] While such behavior could continue unchecked in colonies such as Surinam, within Behn's dramatic text a queen can reverse the male cycle of power (unlike the ultimately ineffectual female narrator in *Oroonoko* who cannot alter his fate). Observing Orsames's actions, his mother the queen pronounces him "a Tyrant in his Nature" (116, l. 157); drugging him, she has him returned to his prison and plans to "still continue to impose upon him" (116, l. 161).

The Young King invokes common colonial and economic practices only to imagine a world in which those baser impulses can be contained and controlled by a female monarch. This closely discussed episode, although brief, aligns with the play's abiding focus on power, authority, and domination. Orsames is not unique among Behn's male figures in his abundant display of what Todd terms an "abuse of power and hereditary privilege."[65] The text's connection with Surinam—especially in light of the actions and attitude of Willoughby, with his apparent sense of privilege and might—like its explicit representation of the dangers of absolute power, demonstrate its powerful resonance with a colonial context.

If *The Young King* demonstrates the dangers of absolute power in a colonial space, *The Younger Brother; or, The Amorous Jilt* (1696) shows the disastrous consequences when those impulses shape personal relationships in England's domestic space. Like *The Young King*, *The Younger Brother* has a specific Surinam connection. The "younger brother" of the play's title is George Marten, the name shared by a man, "George Marten," Behn "so much admired in Surinam two decades before."[66] In *Oroonoko*, Behn refers to this play, noting that the "Colonel Martin" she met in Surinam, "a Man of great Gallantry, Wit, and Goodness," is someone she has "celebrated in a Character of my New Comedy, by his own Name, in memory of so brave a Man" (111). In *Oronooko*, Behn describes Marten as a man of substance and power. "He was wise and eloquent, and, from the fineness of his parts, bore a great sway over the hearts of all the colony" (111). Throughout the novel, Behn positions him at a geographic and ideological distance from the white power structure that brutalizes Oroonoko. When the female narrator learns "that *Cæsar* was taken and whipped liked a common Slave," she fled "down the River, to be secured," meeting the character "Martin" there (78). Behn cites his implicit moral authority or "sway," documenting how he returned "back to *Parham*, thinking to have made an Accommodation" that could change the treatment of Oroonoko (111).

Of course, as Behn well knew, the historical figure George Marten himself participated fully in the plantation system, owning estates in Barbados and Surinam, where he was "an establishment name."[67] A "shrewd operator" by one account, Marten may actually have served as something of an enforcer in Surinam's hierarchical society.[68] Marten's connection with Behn and Surinam is highlighted in the "Epistolary Dedication" to *The Younger Brother* written by Behn's friend and fellow playwright Charles Gildon (1665–1724) who also revised and produced the play, which appeared at the Theatre Royal Drury Lane in February 1696. Gildon dedicates the play to Christopher Codrington (1668–1710), absolutely one of the wealthiest West Indian planters of the time, a man who "combined imperial ambition with private greed."[69] Few men would be as recognizably associated with the plantocracy of the West Indies as Codrington. Todd speculates that Behn may have possibly known the younger Codrington when she was alive.[70] Friendly with the Oxford wits, Codrington had been a classmate of Thomas Creech and, like Behn, praised Creech's translation of Lucretius. Behn certainly had observed the literary and social milieu in which Codrington circulated. He, like his father, also Christopher Codrington (1639/40–98), was part of an intricate West Indian network to which Behn was also connected, albeit without the same wealth or power. The elder Codrington had fought with Willoughby in the Anglo-Dutch War, and had sold George Marten the land on which he built his (unsuccessful) Barbados plantation before he moved on to Surinam where he met Behn. The web of connections is intricate and telling. Dedicating the play to Codrington, Gildon specifically situates it within the socioeconomic colonial network in which Behn, in some measure, formerly circulated.

The dedication to Codrington was followed by Gildon's brief "Account of the Life" of Behn, which further highlights the play's West Indian connection. Gildon specifically places Behn and her family in Surinam, a "Voyage" that resulted "in nothing so considerable as the Admirable History of *Oroonoko.*"[71] He therefore authenticates her authorship of *The Younger Brother* as well as *Oroonoko*, linking the composition of the two. Echoing the claim to truth Behn herself makes at the beginning of that prose fiction ("I was myself an eyewitness"), Gildon writes "I saw her my self write *Oroonoko*, and keep her turn in Discoursing with several then present in the Room. Among several Pieces that I saw of hers, in her own hand-writing, this following Play was one" (749). He offers visual evidence of the act of writing along with verification of her handwriting. The mention of *Oroonoko*, like the timing of *The Younger Brother*, may have been designed to capitalize on the popularity of Thomas Southerne's *Oroonoko*, also appearing at the Theatre Royal Drury Lane in November and December 1695.[72] *The Younger Brother* bears vestiges of an older style of comedy with its lascivious older woman, casual cuckolds, and titillating display of the female body. (Todd goes so far as to call it "morally lax").[73] The preoccupation with genre and theatrical type, however, has caused readers to ignore this text's clear colonial connections. While the play may be the "comic allusion" to Behn's "own obscure past" that Todd claims, it is also dead serious in its representation of the commodification of human beings.[74] Further, while it may be difficult to extract specifically which sections of the play were written by Behn and which by Gildon, the appearance of George Marten within the text, Behn's discussion of him in *Oroonoko,* and her explicit reference to this play in that text makes the play's treatment of him firmly connected with her imagination.

Within *The Younger Brother,* in a reversal of Marten's own life, the fictional character of the slaveholder "George Marteen" is figured as a human body circulating for the profit of others as an apprentice and as a potential husband.[75] Behn first casts "Marteen" as the victim of a specific form of confinement—an apprenticeship—explicitly comparing his treatment as a younger son and apprentice to "slavery." In act I, "Marteen" complains that he, an "out-cast of my Family," is "born to that Curse of our Old *English* Custom: Whereas in other Countries, Younger Brothers are train'd up to the Exercise of Arms, where Honour and Renown attend the Brave: we basely bind our Youngest out to Slavery, to Lazy Trades, idly confin'd to Shops or Merchants Books, debasing of the Spirit to the mean Cunning, how to Cheat and Chaffer" (761–62, ll. 171–76). This passage likens the state of the younger son as a distinctly "English" problem, specifically locating it as a domestic kind of limitation. That "Old *English* Custom" of primogeniture displaces sons from their family estate—"Marteen" is an "outcast"—forcing them into forms of labor. While Michael Jarvis notes that, actually, younger sons often "fanned out across the wider Atlantic world" seeking their fortune in a colonial space, here Behn presents "Marteen" as confined to a specifically English form of constraint,[76] a binding out of youngest sons to "Lazy Trades" in a state where they are "idly confin'd." The imagery presents apprenticeship specifically and a trade generally as another form of domestic captivity.

Not only does Marteen's father Sir Rowlandson wish to apprentice him out, but he also seeks to marry him off, using him as a form of property for his own financial gain. Lady Youthly, the widowed eighty-year-old, wants to marry Marteen and negotiates with his father, himself eager to marry Youthly's granddaughter Teresia. Sir Rowlandson is willing to make "a fair Swap" (783, l. 23). But when Lady Youthly hesitates, seeking time to "consider, and take Advice of my Friends," Sir Rowlandson threatens to sell George in a public auction open to "all the Widows in Town" (783, l. 34): "I shall get more by shewing him, than the *Rhinoceros.* Gad, I'll sell the young Rogue by Inch of Candle, before he's Debauch't and Spoil'd in this lew'd Town" (783, ll. 34–36). The shock value of a privileged white male subjected to a public auction suits this play's broadly comic ends. Rowlandson's claim to profit more from "shewing" George than was earned by showing the rhinoceros (a reference used to mark the play's date of composition), refers to the captured animal shipped from India and exhibited in a tavern in Ludgate Hill. The following advertisement ran in the *London Gazette* for an entire month in October 1684: "A Very strange Beast called a Rhynoceros, lately brought from the East-Indies, being the first that ever was in England, is daily to be seen at the Bell Savage Inn on Ludgate-Hill, from Nine a Clock in the Morning till Eight at Night" (*London Gazette,* October 9, 1684). The owner, seeking to profit from the "complementary processes of exoticism and commodification," exhibits an item as unique as any Behn describes in *Oroonoko.*[77] "The proprietor was said to take in £15 a day at the price of 12 d. for a look and 2 s. for a ride."[78] Transplanted, the captive animal's value lay in what Richard Altick describes as its "sheer size, ugliness, and, of course, rarity." Such animals possessed "the glamor of distance, tangible living evidence of the still largely mysterious regions to which English explorers and traders were now penetrating."[79] Rowlandson's commodification of his son, and comparison with the rhino, places Marteen into a cycle of consumer desire and financial exchange. Commodities, whether humans, objects, or animals, exist for trade, exchange, and profit.

Threatening to sell George Marteen "by Inch of Candle" or in what was known as a "candle auction," Rowlandson plans to use the same form of public auction the Royal African Company explicitly instructed its agents to employ in the sale of the enslaved.[80] In a candle auction, the burning of a candle flame rather than the auctioneer's hammer determines when the bidding concludes. "A pin is placed in the wick of a tallow candle," explains E. Carleton Williams, "about an inch or less from the top, and when the candle is lighted, the bidding opens and continues, until the melting tallow dislodges the pin. The last bid made before the pin falls, secures the lot."[81] Auctions of this sort were commonly used to sell items that were imported by ship. In November 1690, the Royal African Company mandated its agents in Barbados and Jamaica to conduct auctions exclusively "by inch of candle": "We do hereby order and direct you, that such Ships as shall arrive with Negroes for our Accots. after receipt hereof that they be sold by the Inch of Candle each negro apart. & to this purpose you must publish a day of sale for them, giveing such convenient time as shall be necessary for all Buyers to come in."[82] By limiting the time for bidding, sales "by the inch" streamlined the process for selling the enslaved, enabling a greater volume within a shorter period of time. (The practice advances the "numberless waves" Orsames envisages.) This detail about the manner of sale for George Marteen is significant. In December 1662 the Royal Adventurers told Willoughby that all enslaved Africans "imported into the island [Barbados] should be sold by lots, as had been the custom, at the average rate of seventeen pounds per head or for commodities of the island rated at that price."[83] Behn herself details how in Surinam, sale of the enslaved was by lot. Writing with intimate knowledge, she charts how "[t]hose who want Slaves, make a Bargain with a Master, or a Captain of a Ship, and contract to pay him so much a-piece, a matter of twenty Pound a Head . . . So that when there arrives a Ship laden with Slaves, they who have so contracted, go a-board, and receive their Number by Lot" (*Oroonoko*, 60). The move from sale by lot to sale by auction points to what Kenneth Morgan terms a "market efficiency" that demonstrates how increasingly sophisticated mechanisms for selling the enslaved "matured along with the plantation systems."[84] This subtle shift marks a difference that would have been legible to Behn and her audience.

While Behn, of course, was not still alive when the RAC mandated sale by candle, she would have been aware of its common use by the slaving company that monopolized the market. Certainly, a 1696 audience watching *The Younger Brother* would have known its common use.[85] For Rowlandson to threaten to auction off his son in such a manner among eager female bidders not only inverts the typical gendered structure of the marriage market but also displays in the starkest possible terms the normalized commodification of human flesh. Behn slyly effects an inversion of gender, class, and race: she takes a character based on a slaveholding, well-connected, West Indian planter and threatens to subject him to sale by public auction with a technique employed by the RAC. Although at the heart of the comic nature of the play, the auction points to a much darker view of human relations, familial connections, and the commodification of others.[86] The play bears the vestiges of its origins in Behn's colonial experience.

Captivating Farce: *The Emperor of the Moon*

The Young King and *The Younger Brother* invoke the complex intersection of human commodification and colonial power. They present diverse manifestations of captivity, and also deploy contemporaneous language from documents describing the trade in and treatment of the enslaved. *The Emperor of the Moon* similarly presents a culture marked by forms of confinement and constraint, and demonstrates how imperial power depends, in part, upon holding the colonial subject captive through the use of overpowering spectacle. Although written for farce-loving Charles II in 1684, *The Emperor of the Moon* was not produced until the reign of James II in 1687. One of "a series of productions known as the 'Dorset Garden spectaculars' staged under the direction of Thomas Betterton between 1673 and 1692," it debuted in March 1687 at the Dorset Garden Theatre and was immediately, and persistently, popular—second in popularity to only *The Rover* (1675) among Behn's theatrical works.[87] *The Emperor of the Moon* was performed in every decade until the 1740s for more than 130 performances.

Frequently discussed in connection with Behn's parodic treatment of the Royal Academy of Science, *The Emperor of the Moon* has received limited attention in terms of its connection with empire generally or a culture of captivity specifically.[88] The text's status as a "farce"—as the title page categorizes it—makes some critics reluctant to regard it as doing the same kind of cultural work as Behn's other plays. Dibdin concludes his entry on Behn in *The Complete History of the English Stage* (1800) with his only mention of *The Emperor of the Moon* by describing it as "nothing more than a farce. . . . It was whimsical, and had some success" (203). Similarly, Derek Hughes, while acknowledging that *The Emperor of the Moon* shares characteristics with Behn's more "serious" texts, warns that "the play must not be overinterpreted"; he thinks its "significance diminishes in proportion to the lightness of the work."[89] I would suggest the exact opposite is true. Farce enables Behn to safely include pointed commentary about power relations, captivity, and the British imperial efforts in a genre that (as Dibdin and Hughes demonstrate) did not invite excessive scrutiny. The colonization, mastery, and subjugation central to the play mimic actions Behn witnessed in Surinam and in London. The farce, like much of her work, expresses her concerns about the commodification of humans—the paramount being, of course, the enslavement of kidnapped Africans. However, Behn also saw a state that disregards its agents, ignores its authors, and uses its subjects as unfree labor. *The Emperor of the Moon*, as a farce, deploys elements of physical action, disguise, and trickery—elements that contribute to the genre's broader popularity. Those characteristics may obscure but do not eliminate the intensity of Behn's message; indeed, they function almost as a kind of meta-spectacle, diverting attention from the real mechanisms of power Behn wants to highlight. Behn manipulates the components of genre to create a dramatic work that was simultaneously extremely popular and brutally honest in its observations about the dynamics of domination and the dangers of captivity in the broadest conception of that term.

Behn dedicates the play to Charles Somerset, Lord Marquess of Worcester (1660–98), a man with colonial interests. A member of the Committee of the Honorable East India Company (1683–91), Somerset married Rebecca Child, the daughter of the merchant and economic writer Sir Josiah Child, a founding director of the Royal African Company and shareholder in the East India Company (in fact Rebecca's dowry included a large portion of East India stock).[90] Like Christopher Codrington, Somerset was part of the West Indian colonial infrastructure with which Behn was familiar. Behn applauds Somerset's *"illustrious Birth and equal Parts"* in the dedication, describing those attributes as *"of the Glories of your Race,"* language that anticipates the play's preoccupation with breeding and reproduction (411, ll. 15–17). Indeed, Behn attributes the strength of Somerset's *"race"* to his *"illustrious Father"* Henry Somerset, the first Duke of Beaufort (1629–1700), whose title was created to reward his instrumental role in the Exclusion Crisis. Much of the dedicatee Charles Somerset's worth stems directly from *"that Noble Blood he boasts,"* blood from his father Henry who is *"deserving a whole Volume"* of praise (412, l. 27, 24). Todd attributes Behn's mention of Henry to his reputation as "a staunch Tory and ardent royalist," something that would certainly excite Behn's sympathetic admiration.[91] Equally important, perhaps, was his incredible wealth, which was valued at more than £100,000 when he died in 1700; Behn never lost the opportunity to cultivate a potentially generous patron.

In the dedication, Behn singles out viewers like Somerset who possess a *"refin'd Sence, and Delicacy of Judgment"* (413, ll. 45–46). They will see, *"thro' all the humble Actions and trivialness of Business"* of the play, *"Nature . . . and that Diversion which was not meant for the Numbers, who comprehend nothing beyond the Show and Buffoonry"* (413, ll. 45–48). Behn's claim here is two-fold. On the one hand, she flatters her potential patron with praise of the "Sence" and "Judgment" he brings to the text. Unlike "the Numbers" who will respond viscerally to the play's visual stimulation, Somerset's refinement and delicacy endow him with a higher level of thinking. The "Show and Buffoonry," "Actions," and bits of theatrical "Business" are designed to please—indeed distract—the general population or "the Numbers." Simultaneously, the play becomes an object lesson in how the ruling class can continue to effectively maintain power. As Backscheider observes, Behn "knew well the part art played in sustaining an ideology."[92] Somerset can laugh with a knowing recognition at the absurdities imposed upon the aspirational virtuoso Dr. Baliardo. *"Plays and publick Diversions* [are] . . . *one of the most essential Parts of good Government,"* as Behn writes in the dedication to *The Luckey Chance.*[93]

The dedication to *The Emperor of the Moon* sounds a second register, however. Behn specifically invites her reader to regard the play's events as something *"within the compass of Possibility and Nature"* (413, ll. 55–56). At first glance, that seems to remind readers not to become infatuated with speculative ideals like Baliardo, who believes the Moon to be populated. However, those two carefully chosen words—"Possibility" and "Nature" (the latter used twice)—reject the notion that this farce lacks an engagement with deeper issues. The rather dark "Nature" and "Possibility" of *The Emperor of the Moon* ultimately lie within its representations of captivity, power, and race. Farce, Behn suggests, can in fact reflect the world, perhaps even more accurately than serious drama.

While Behn's dedication might initially seem to be privileging the implied powers of perception held by Somerset (and rewarding the power he imposes on others), her simultaneously dismissive characterization of his milieu, whose *"Titles of Honour, a Knack in dressing, or . . . Art in writing a Billet Deux"* had been their *"chiefest Talent,"* begs the question of who best will recognize what her text foretells (412–13, ll. 39–40). The "Numbers," those members of the audience too easily swayed by the superficial aspects of farce and spectacle, risk becoming the very subjects she warns of—those too easily seduced and subdued by language, diversion, and the symbolic use of power. Yet, those wielding the instruments of power may or may not recognize themselves in the representations (or may find affirmation in the techniques successfully used to advance a colonialist ideology).

Behn is particularly concerned here with the power of spectacle, something that also plays an important role in *Oroonoko*, as critics such as Ramesh Mallipeddi and Laura Brown remind us.[94] Although the word itself appears only twice in Behn's novel, the concept resonates with her descriptions of the physical violation of the nonwhite body. Behn details how the governor's council thought that Oroonoko, renamed Caesar, "ought to be made an Example to all the *Negroes*, to fright 'em from daring to threaten their Betters, their Lords and Masters" (112). Fuentes observes how "punishments on enslaved bodies" inevitably involved "public displays of colonial power," and a keen desire to "make the spectacle visible to the greatest number of enslaved people."[95] Behn describes the "frightful Spectacles of a mangl'd King" and prompts a similarly emotional response (in part because, as scholars have suggested, Behn also implicitly references the execution of Charles I).

While Behn regards the dismembered body of Oroonoko as an object for sympathy, as Mallipeddi discusses in detail, Surinam's colonial powers regard it as a tool for social control. As described in the penultimate sentence of the novel, Oroonoko's quartered body is sent "to several of the chief *Plantations*" (118). When "One Quarter" is sent to "Colonel *Martin*," he refuses to have it on his plantation, stating that "he could govern his *Negroes* without Terrifying and Grieving them with frightful Spectacles of a mangl'd King" (118). Marten's rejection actually affirms the strategic purpose of the "frightful Spectacles"—to enhance plantation owners' ability to "govern" in the colonial space. Ligon's *A True and Exact History of the Island of Barbados* documents contemporaneous use of spectacle as a tool for the consolidation of power. Describing a "Collonell Walrond's" frustration with the repeated suicides of enslaved men on his plantation, Ligon details how Walrond severed the head of one dead man and "set upon a pole a dozen foot high."[96] He then forced "all his Negroes to come forth, and march round about this head, and bid them look on it." He created "this sad, yet lively *spectacle*" to deter suicides, and maintain control. His is just one of many examples of disciplinary spectacle within a colonial space used to maintain control and to enhance the ability to "govern."

The power of spectacle extends to its potential use within a domestic space as a means of social control, something about which Behn was keenly aware. Coppola rightly asserts, despite its appearance as an "all-in-good-fun farce," that *The Emperor of the Moon* really operates as a "highly so-phisticated satire" targeting "spectacle itself." Behn, he suggests, wants to "retrain a troubling appetite for uncritical wonder in her audience."[97] However, I would extend the object of Coppola's observations. Behn is concerned not only with an audience's "uncritical wonder" at a theatrical spectacle but also with its susceptibility to the use of spectacle by the state to secure and maintain dominance in colonial and domestic realms. She wants to do more than "retrain" her audience's appetite. She wants to instill an awareness, perhaps sound an alarm, compelling them to more carefully scrutinize their nation's actions abroad, its tools of imperial power, and the domestic deployment of the same. Behn wants to engender increased per-ception and a new sensitivity to the contours of control. Farce—or satire "in masquerade"—covers Behn's incisive critique not of theatrical spectacle per se, but of the deployment of spectacle in the service of state power. By attempting to lay bare the mechanisms by which colonizers gain and consolidate power—justifying the enterprise to both those in the domestic space of England and those in the colonial space—Behn asks readers to be newly attentive to the calculated operations of imperial power. Behn's spec-tacular finale, like the play's paratextual elements, demonstrates her keen awareness of the strategic manufacture and consolidation of power by the state, at home and abroad.

In the face of her concern for the use (and abuse) of power on a national and global scale, Behn does not stray from a persistent theme in much of her drama: the domestic captivity of women and the threat of a forced mar-riage, the most common form of domestic captivity to which women are subject. The captivity of women is a central element of *The Emperor of the Moon*. Indeed, the public subjugation and de facto colonization of the main character Dr. Baliardo, infatuated by all things lunar, occurs because of his dogged confinement of his two female charges—as a result, the women must subdue him if they are to marry the men of their choice (eliding the kind of captivity marriage itself represents). Consequently, Behn structurally, the-matically, and linguistically reiterates the inextricable connection between the patriarchal power that confines women and the imperial power that seduces and subdues colonial subjects.

Drawing on the *commedia dell'arte* tradition and loosely based on the French *Arlequin, empereur dans la lune*, a farce first staged in Paris in March

1684, *The Emperor of the Moon* uses song, dance, and spectacle to present the story of the gullible, moonstruck, and inattentive Dr. Baliardo. Baliardo lives in Naples with his daughter Elaria and niece Bellemante, whom he keeps confined while he seeks appropriate suitors for the two women. However, the women, in league with their lovers, dupe Baliardo into believing those lovers actually come from the Moon—that lunar space with which Baliardo is obsessed. Enlisting the help of Baliardo's servant Scaramouch, the couples work collaboratively to stage the "descent" of nobility from the Moon into Baliardo's backyard. In the elaborate performance designed to bamboozle Baliardo, the two young women under his control appear to "marry" the newly ascended Emperor and Prince of the Moon; in truth, they marry their lovers Cinthio and Charmante right before Baliardo's eyes. "[I]nfected" by his reading about the cosmos, Baliardo readily believes the farce *within* the farce to be real. The play concludes with a spectacular finale that humiliates Baliardo and affirms the union of the two couples.

That plot seems purely farcical—duped virtuoso falls for prank advancing the comic romp with its broad visual humor. Yet Behn's specific details of language, plot, and staging reveal the text's thorough engagement with the ideological and discursive tools of power. The play is set in the colonial space of Naples (also the setting for *The Rover*). Part of the Spanish empire, the Neapolitan setting already makes Baliardo a colonial subject, even before the arrival of the "ambassadors" from the Moon. Similarly the women's lovers, Don Cinthio and Don Charmante, nephews to the (unseen) viceroy, who would have been chosen by the monarch from among the Spanish nobility for his position of colonial authority, also serve as a colonizing force. As a result, the kind of colonizing Baliardo thinks the lunar beings initiate has actually already been imposed upon him by the Spanish powers in Naples.

The ease with which Baliardo is "imposed upon" by the lunar beings foregrounds the deteriorating agency of those subject to imperial control. Consequently, the actions within the farce—although appearing ridiculous— remain within that "compass of Possibility" Behn describes in her dedication. The very title of the farce within the farce—"The World in the Moon"—underscores the parallels between the two texts. The "world" evident within the play—a world of (doubly) colonized subjects susceptible to spectacle and distraction, "Show and Buffonry"—differs little from the London theater in which the play itself appears.[98] The farce *within* the farce foregrounds how that genre can destabilize the very possibility of meaning and present as ridiculous what is, at the conclusion of the play, true: Elaria and Bellemante marry their lovers. Similarly, the imposition and consolidation of state power in domestic and colonial spaces that Behn theatrically represents as ridiculous within the text do, in fact, she reveals, shape the world around her and her audience. The play's three central themes demonstrate the devastating consequences of colonial force: the domestic captivity of women, the colonial preoccupation with race and breeding, and the use of spectacle as an instrument of social control.

Structurally, the play depends on the domestic captivity of women. Baliardo literally imprisons his daughter Elaria and her cousin Bellemante within his house. In the opening moments of the play, Elaria sings about the women's captivity. Lamenting her own confinement, she curses "that faithless Maid, / Who first her Sexes Liberty betrayed" (423, ll. 1–2). She charts a movement from liberty, when women were "Born free as Man to Love and Range," to confinement. She describes how "Nobler Nature did to Custom change" (423, l. 4). Through the imposition of social expectations and the constructed notion of gender, "Custom" strips women of their freedom, imposes restrictions upon them, and confines them to "a restless Slavery" (423, l. 10). In Elaria's song, women move from a state of "Liberty" to a condition of "slavery" in eight lines. The alacrity of the change in status reiterates in terms of dramatic form the change that happens to women in human history. Consequently, women must devise strategies for subversive behavior that might yield some form of liberation. Embracing the inconstancy that Hellena proclaims at the end of *The Rover,* Elaria praises a woman who, though "Constancy Profest," operates as a "well dissembler" (424, ll. 13–14). Deception alone—"seeming to obey" or "feign[ing] to give" that "imaginary sway"—enables the women to survive and perhaps escape (albeit briefly) their confinement (424, ll. 15–16). As a playwright, Behn's use of farce arguably proves a similar act of deception or dissembling. Her apparent conformity to the demands of genre screens her subversive critical message.

Unaware of the women's powers of dissembling, Baliardo focuses on physically containing his female charges, having them "more strictly guarded than usual" (424, ll. 23–24). He falsely believes that kind of domination to be the most important. Held in "Captivity," the women are "mew'd up" and no "Human thing is suffer'd to come near [them], without [their]

Governante and Keeper" (432, ll. 172–74). Elaira is "[C]onfin'd a Prisoner to [her] Apartment, without the hope or almost possibility" of getting out (426, ll. 71–72). Every time Baliardo leaves the house, he insists that "not a Door be open'd till my Return" (451, l. 86). He instructs his servants to "Bar up the Doors, and upon Life or Death let no man enter" (456, ll. 174–75). For these women, home does not provide comfort or domestic tranquility, only confinement and surveillance.

But the possibility for the women's escape lies not in the physical pene-tration or breach of a material structure. Rather psychological penetration, distraction, or seduction will open the door. Because of Baliardo's credulity, the women's lovers can "hatch" a "rare design . . . to relieve [them] from this Captivity" (432, ll. 171–72). They do not need to scale a wall, only dupe a gullible man. With the help of Harlequin, the men easily persuade the moonstruck Baliardo that "the mighty Emperor *Iredonozor*—the Monarch of the Moon" and the Prince of Thunderland are in love with his captive niece and daughter (484, ll. 141–42). Smitten with the prospect of such an advantageous alliance, Baliardo sets aside reason and resistance, letting desire and sensation take over. He is willing to sacrifice the women for anticipated personal gain. When Bellemante's lover Charmante appears to Baliardo as an ambassador from the Moon, Charmante seduces him with the promise that his daughter will mix with the inhabitants of the Moon to "beget Immortal Races" (436, l. 45) and stock "the World with Demy Gods" (437, l. 52). Baliardo believes a superior race of beings lives on the lunar surface, a race with whom he now has the opportunity to breed his female charges and improve his bloodline. Baliardo muses he "would fain have a Hero to my Grandson" (440, l. 117).[99] Todd connects this language purely with alchemy, which "routinely used the language of breeding."[100] In light of Behn's preoccupation with colonial intervention, however, the im-agery also meaningfully aligns with the text's exploration of race, class, and identity. This exchange completes the dedication's language of breeding and its explicit distinction between the "glories" of Charles Somerset's "Race" and other less-refined "Numbers."[101] Because Baliardo remains an object of ridicule, his aspirations seem foolish, misplaced, and ultimately unachievable. Although this kind of discourse expresses Behn's attempt to document the dangers of a hierarchically structured world segregated by bloodlines, she simultaneously concedes that blood does matter.

Eager to secure their liberation, Bellemante and Elaria—as the stage di-rections detail—"*put themselves in Postures of Sleeping*" (474) and pretend to have "the softest Dream that ever a Maid was blest with" so that Baliardo thinks they are entranced with the Emperor of the Moon (475, ll. 23–24). Their language mimics Baliardo's race-based language of breeding, continuing the process of psychological penetration. Pretending to talk in her sleep, Bellemante advances her freedom by claiming hers will be a happy submission to her "glorious Lover," who ties "a Diamond Chain about [her] Arm" (475, ll. 30–31). Bellemante welcomes a man "of a Coelestial Race," who

> . . . easily can penetrate
> Into the utmost limits of the Thought,
> Why shou'd I fear to tell you of your Conquest?
> —And thus implore your Aid. (474, ll. 10–13)

"[T]ake me with you to the World above," she asks (475, l. 17). This fabricated conversation is staged only for Baliardo's benefit, making it artificial, something to be discounted by the knowing audience. Yet, this delivery becomes *Behn's* form of dissembling. Bellemante's words encapsulate the dynamics of domination the farce authentically warns against. The "Coelestial Race" can too easily secure a "Conquest." (The idea of a celestial or godlike race replicates Orsames's vision of having godlike power.) The visual image of a diamond chain embodies the act of colonial conquest. A "diamond chain" appears to be an object of adornment encrusted with precious jewels, but the chain is actually a tool of compliance that transforms Bellemante into an object of male desire. The celestial race's ability to "easily penetrate / Into the utmost limits of the Thought" (a double entendre to be sure) articulates what has in fact just happened to Baliardo.[102] His thoughts have been as penetrated as handily as the garden wall he erected to debar eager male suitors. Once subject to conquest, the colonized, in Behn's configuration, embrace their emergent dependence as they "implore" the colonizer's "Aid" (474, l. 13). The problematic transition to a state of subjection or conquest as a colonized subject is amplified by Bellemante's imminent status as a wife—a condition of double subjection. Although Baliardo remains the intended target of this elaborate plot, Bellemante speaks the words of her own, new, captivity. The "dream" articulates the effective consolidation of power by a colonizing force through physical and mental control. After overhearing Bellemante's dream and the possibilities for union with a lunar being, Baliardo figures himself as the one violated: "I am Ravish'd!" he exclaims (475, l. 14).

The third and final act of the play stages the arrival of the "Emperor" and his prince in a visual expression of their political authority and the symbolic consolidation of power. The finale imitates the ultimate urban spectacle—the Lord Mayor's progressions—an annual public event in London designed to centrally contribute to the building of empire. Such progressions or pageants provided a domesticated version of a global phenomenon.[103] Held October 29 of every year, the Lord Mayor's Show was a day-long ritual of pageants displaying the civic and global power held by the various merchants, guilds, and companies. After 1671, when "Charles II began attending the Lord Mayor's Show regularly," the pageants began to "promote government propaganda directly," as noted by John Patrick Montaño.[104] Montaño connects this ideological use of pageant to the need to "consolidate belief in a national consensus supporting the restored monarchy," and an integral part of that consensus rested on the imperial expansion and the prosperity it created.[105] Published descriptions of the events reveal the careful and elaborate planning of each element of the program with the goal of exhibiting global and domestic command.[106] In the dedicatory letter to Lord Mayor James Edward prefacing the publication of his 1678 pageant, Thomas Jordan (ca. 1614–85), city poet after 1671 and man responsible for the pageants from 1671 to 1684, describes how he has brought "all Exotick Commodities from every Part of the World" into a concentrated space to demonstrate how English commercial efforts have transformed "very brutish Nations, with barbarous Natures" into subjects displaying only "Meekness, Order, and Civility."[107]

The display of global mastery in these shows relied, in part, on the incorporation of African youths into the pageants. As Anthony Gerard Barthelemy details, at least nineteen pageants between 1585 and 1692 featured African characters who functioned as "visible reminders of British success in trade and exploration."[108] Africans were considered "exotics" as Diana Henderson discusses, and were regularly "used in entertainments and pageants as signs of new English wealth and grandeur."[109] The frequency of such appearances accelerated in the decades after the Restoration when the British presence in imperial spaces intensified. Just as African youths appear as visual accessories in portraiture during this period, so too they function as human ornament in a kind of tableau vivant. The examples are numerous (and go a long way toward explaining the incorporation of Africans into *The Emperor of the Moon*). The 1672 pageant *London Triumphant* featured "two *Negroes* attired properly in diverse colour'd Silks, with Silver or Gold Wreaths or Coronets upon their Heads, as Princes of *West-India*," in an ironic inversion of power.[110] In the First Pageant of the 1678 show, sponsored by the Company of Grocers, "a young Negro-Boy" sits atop a carved camel "betwixt two Silver Hampers plentifully stored with all sorts of Fruits and fragrant Spices." After the first speech is given, "the Negro with a Prodigal hand, scatereth abroad in the Tumult, where you might see an hundred persons confusedly scrambling in the dirt for the Frail Achievement of a Bunch of Raisins, or a handful of Dates, Almonds, Nutmegs."[111] The Second Pageant sponsored by the Company of Drapers in the 1675 pageant has the figure of Victory in a chariot drawn by two carved Lions "which are mounted by two Negro's [*sic*] in Robes of Silver, . . . the one representing *Strength*, the other *Concord*."[112] While there were enslaved Africans in London, the city also was home to many free Africans who could have participated both in such pageants and, potentially, in the finale of Behn's production.[113]

Behn's detailed stage directions for "scene the last" invoke the visual iconography of empire as it would be presented in such a pageant and incorporates these common elements of a Lord Mayor's Show. As Cinthio and Charmante descend from "the Moon," a curtain is drawn to reveal "the Hill of *Parnassus*" with "a noble large Walk of Trees leading to it, with eight or ten Negroes upon Pedestals, rang'd on each of the Walks" (515).[114] As with the pageants, so too here Africans, initially situated like statues on pedestals, adorn but cannot be said to fully inhabit the space. With "a Symphony playing all the while," "the Zodiack descends" from above and, upon landing, "delivers the twelve Signs" in the form of twelve Singers (516). As "the Negroes Dance and mingle in the *Chorus*," the song ostensibly describes the signs of the zodiac but in fact reiterates, in miniature, various narratives of submission and captivity (517). Love's "Slavery / in *Taurus* is expres'd," although the bull in turn demonstrates his willing subjection: "Tho' o're the Plains he Conqueror be, / The Generous Beast / Does to the Yoak submit his Noble Breast" (518–19, ll. 81–84). The presence of "Negroes" upon pedestals frames the stage with evidence of England's global conquest and constructs a visual narrative of captivity.

Following the song of the Zodiac, the "Globick World" descends "to show Obedience to its proper Monarch" (520, ll. 111–13); "the Cloud of Foreigners appears, *French, English, Spaniards, Danes, Turks, Russians, Indians*, and the nearer Climes of Christendom" (522, ll. 137–40). The specific delineation of national representatives—a combination of trade rivals (French, Spanish) and colonial subjects (Indians)—highlights the full scope of the text and the differences in identity immediately apparent through the scene's visual metonymy. The personification of nations also replicates a living map of the world, another frequent component of Lord Mayor's Pageants. That the "Globick World" can be contained within a stage in a London theater marks the familiarity of this imperial scope, while also demonstrating the power of spectacle to obscure the violent force inherent in such conquest. Spectacle, observes Paula Backscheider, serves as a "means of subordinating and controlling people," displaying power "and its ways of maintaining itself."[115] Behn reminds us that imperial power, although often rooted in physical violence, relies on the "Show" she describes in the preface for its effective maintenance. The visual presence of Africans on the pedestals surrounding the stage, a reminder of the wealth they literally embody, glorifies English imperial power yet perhaps reminds the least empowered in the audience of the full reach and range of state authority.

That Behn saw meaning in this finale beyond satisfying the generic demands of farce becomes apparent with the reception she poetically imagines the Duke of Albemarle will receive upon his arrival in Jamaica in her Pindaric ode *To the Most Illustrious Prince Christopher Duke of Albemarle on His Voyage to His Government of Jamaica.* Published as a broadside pamphlet the same year *The Emperor of the Moon* was produced, *To Albemarle* celebrates the appointment of Christopher Monck, the second duke of Albemarle (1653–88), as governor of Jamaica. His father, George Monck, the first duke of Albemarle (1608–70), had been a founding director of the Company of Royal Adventurers. Both men were deeply implicated in the imperial network. Despite his father's achievements, Albemarle's youth was less than impressive, characterized by drinking, fighting, and gambling.[116] Further, despite his elevated birth, he suffered a significantly diminished reputation after a lackluster performance defending James II during the Monmouth Rebellion. Surprisingly, Albemarle "begged and received the governorship of Jamaica," which had become vacant in 1686.[117] As was well known by Behn (and presumably her readers), Albemarle had mercenary rather than civic motives. Burdened by mounting gambling debts that compelled him to sell his London home, Albemarle invested in a salvage venture "to retrieve gold from a sunken Spanish ship in the Caribbean" prior to his governorship in Jamaica.[118] That investment resulted in £40,000 of colonial gold that restored Albemarle's wealth and also made him an ideal potential patron for Behn.[119]

The poem's initially laudatory language (that reads as ironic in light of Albemarle's personal history) describes him as a *"Heroe"* whose "Soul by Nature Bravely Rough and Great, / Scorns the Confinement of a Home-Retreat."[120] The domestic soil of England cannot contain him. Ignoring the enslavement that undergirds the Jamaican colonial economy, Behn characterizes only Albemarle himself as someone subject to any captivity or confinement, and that on domestic soil: "Bravely Resolv'd" to leave England, he "breaks the Lazy Chains" (3, l. 35) that hold him there. He must leave "This Scanty Isle He long has Serv'd and Grac't, / And distant Worlds expect Him now" (1, ll. 3–4). Behn figures this movement from England to Jamaica as an opportunity for improvement, a chance to find a location expansive enough for his capacious soul. The poem inverts the more common characterization of Jamaica as site of vice and sin. (Edward Ward's final sentence of *A Trip to Jamaica* [1698] characterizes the colony as a place where "virtue is so Despis'd, and all sorts of Vice Encourag'd, by both Sexes, that . . . [it] is the very Sodom of the Universe.")[121] Instead, Behn casts England as the enervating location. Although "Born for Great Action," Albemarle, indulging in "soft Repose" that "Charm'd Him with her Pleasures long," has been "compell'd to Sloth" in a domestic site (2, ll. 14–17). In the West Indies, however, he has managed to perform a "miracle of alchemy," turning "the Wonders of the Deep" into "the Miracle in Gold" (6, ll. 66–69). Behn presumably also anticipates a miracle of self-improvement.

The poem celebrates the British colonists, "the Brave Inhabitants of the Place, / Who have by Conquest made it all your own" (7, ll. 86–87). The term "conquest" marks the asymmetrical power relationship between the colonists and the "Sun-scorch'd Natives of the Shore" (7, l. 83).[122] That dynamic organizes Albemarle's imagined reception in Jamaica when "that Wondring World . . . on their Shores (*Great Prince*) they Welcom Thee" (5, ll. 50–52):

> What Homage must Your Ravisht Subjects pay
> For the vast Condescention You have shewn?
> What Treasures offer, how enough Obey,
> > Their Humble Gratitude to own,
> > When they behold a Prince so Great
> > From an Illustrious Court retreat,
> To render all their Happiness compleat? (5, ll. 55–61)

Albemarle's arrival in Jamaica repeats key elements of the final arrival of the lunar monarchs at the end of *The Emperor of the Moon*. Like Baliardo who is "Ravish'd" by the arrival of the Emperor, the unnamed "Ravisht Subjects" in Jamaica pay "Homage" to Albemarle (5, l. 57). No offering or "obedience" is "enough" (5, l. 57). They present "humble gratitude" at Albemarle's arrival just as Baliardo demonstrates submission by appearing "modest . . . and humble" (488, l. 197) when receiving the imperial lunar power. What appears restrained and dignified in Behn's poem to Albemarle appears ridiculous in the farce; the stage directions describe how, in his attempt at a low bow, Baliardo *"falls on his Face"* (522).

Albemarle's subjects never speak in the poem as they silently "behold a Prince so Great" (5), just as Baliardo silently surrenders himself and his female charges to the Emperor. In Behn's play, the Emperor uses only gestures and "commands by signs" (523 ll. 151–52); the colonizers "never speak to any Subject" (523, ll. 147).[123] Baliardo's own silence allows a new narrative, a narrative of colonial determination, to fill the void. When Baliardo learns he has been duped and submits to the "Alliance" with the "Noble Youths" (527, ll. 230–31), he happily recants his own previous beliefs and replaces his story with *"your* Story," as he says to the Emperor (527, l. 234; emphasis mine). Captivated, ravished, and overmastered, Baliardo willingly allows the imperial narrative to become dominant as he silences himself.

As the play's epilogue explicitly states, because the narrative of empire has the power to subsume and contain dissenting or resistant voices, the poet necessarily plays a crucial role in the dissemination of the state's message. Yet Behn laments the lack of recognition for the poet in that larger project of ideological maintenance (perhaps a motivation for her critique within the play). The state powers have *"let your Poets starve. / They long in vain, for better Usage"* (528, ll. 13–14). In the absence of support, the poet is compelled either to go rogue as *"desperate Pickeroons"* or pirates, or become one of *"The Drudging Slaves, who for your Pleasure write"* (529, ll. 17, 21). To write "for pleasure" (in some ways anticipating the Beggar's complaint about writing for the "Taste of the Town" in John Gay's *The Beggar's Opera*) points back to the sensual response to the power of spectacle. Yet Restoration poets do not benefit from the appreciative compensation available to authors during the Roman Empire, despite their central role in the consolidation of colonial power. *"[F]lourishing* Rome" treated *"her thriving Poets"* well, notes Behn. *"Wisely she priz'd 'em at the noblest Rate / As necessary Ministers of State"* (529, ll. 22–24). They are *"as useful in a City held, / As formidable Armies in the Field"* (529, ll. 29–30). As powerful as "ministers" or "armies," poets complete *"a Conquest over Men"* by *"gentler force the Soul subdu'd"* (529, ll. 31–32). They can "penetrate" thoughts. This "gentler force," a near oxymoron, exemplifies the skills writers—particularly playwrights—use to "subdue" the colonized subjects and the kinds of "gentler force" used on Baliardo within the text. But in Behn's estimate, British poets, poorly paid, are themselves as captive as the colonized subject, forced, uncompensated, to labor like "Drudging Slaves."

The eighteenth-century performance history of *The Emperor of the Moon* might suggest the prescience of Behn's comments about the role of the poet in advancing and publicly displaying the consolidation of colonial power. As newspaper notices reveal, performances of *The Emperor of the Moon* in the early decades of the eighteenth century frequently coincide with a military victory advancing colonial interests such as "the Great Victory gain'd over the French and Bavarians, by his Grace the Duke of Marlborough" in 1704 or "the Entertainment of an African Prince lately arrived here, being Nephew to the King Bauday."[124] The *Daily Post Boy* from October 2, 1730, notes that the previous night, before "they set out for Portsmouth, in order to embarque for South Carolina," the governor of South Carolina and an accompanying group of "Indian Chiefs" attended a performance of "the Celebrated Comedy of the Emperor of the Moon" at "the Theatre Royal in Lincoln's Inn Fields . . . at which they express'd a great Satisfaction."[125] The *British Journal* provides the additional detail that the previous day the same group had seen "the Play of Oroonoko, or the Royal Slave" (Southerne's adaptation of Behn's novel).[126]

It is, of course, impossible to know whether the colonial party's attendance at the performance of two texts so specifically engaged with delineating imperial power was strategic on the part of either the governor of South Carolina or the state authority to whom he might have been obliged. It is also impossible to reconstruct how such performances might have been received either by the agent of colonial power or those "Indian chiefs," simultaneously honored guests and colonial subjects. The performances of those plays on those successive nights, likely coincidental, may have been nothing more than simply an evening's amusement. The play's visual humor and spectacular finale would have translated across both culture and language.

It is possible, however, to recognize the persistence of *The Emperor of the Moon* as a text that English subjects and ministers understood as relevant to both the colonized and the colonizer. Reframing the context of *The Emperor of the Moon* to foreground its engagement with issues of empire and captivity enriches an understanding of a play that, too frequently discussed as "just a farce," fundamentally contributes to Behn's nuanced treatment of British colonial actions and the role of the author in advancing an ideological agenda through discursive and performative means. That potentially fraught bifurcated position for the playwright—as a complicit enabler and obliged subservient—returns to a problematic contradiction that frames *Oroonoko*. Behn (and "Behn") participates in and depends upon a system that destroys Oroonoko. Yet she simultaneously serves as the only point of entry into the operations of that economic and social structure. In that text too she acts as both "picaroon" and "drudging" writer, held captive by a different but no less powerful set of competing forces.

Just as *The Emperor of the Moon*'s genre of farce has obscured, to some degree, a recognition of its intimate connection with captivity, so too scholars' understanding of the role of captivity in Richard Steele's *The Conscious Lovers* has traditionally been diminished because of that text's status as an originating "sentimental comedy." As the next chapter suggests, however, Steele draws on his own experience as a plantation owner to imbue that text with inescapable ties to the culture of captivity in which it appeared.

CHAPTER 3

Domesticating Captivity

Richard Steele's The Conscious Lovers

Aphra Behn's time in Surinam, her keen observations on the accelerating centrality of the trade in human commodities, and her reflections on her own self-commodification shaped her fiction and dramatic texts. Her determination to critique the exploitation of the colonial subject as well as the subordinated status of women (both ensured by the assertion of patriarchal-imperial power) defines much of her work, as the previous chapter demonstrates. And, as discussed, her own financial precarity heightened her sensitivity to the paralyzing weight of impecuniousness and the persistent threat of debtors' prison. She understood well the diverse range of possibilities for domestic captivity.

If Behn observed the foundational origins of colonial slavery, Richard Steele, writing more than forty years later, inhabited a landscape with far more established—and far more normalized—colonial practices of enslavement as well as expanded and similarly normalized forms of domestic captivity. The Treaty of Utrecht, drawn up at the end of the War of Spanish Succession, included the *asiento*, which essentially gave England the monopoly rights for selling enslaved people in the Spanish South Seas. This proviso led to the creation of the South Sea Company in 1711, intended to provide 4,800 enslaved Africans annually to the Spanish West Indies. Later in the decade, as is perhaps more well known, the South Sea Company also persuaded the British government to allow the company to assume increasing amounts of the national debt. This combination moved the Atlantic slave trade "into the orbit of the state even more thoroughly than the Royal African Company had done," as John O'Brien notes.[1] In the same decade, the Transportation Act of 1718 institutionalized the use of British subjects as moveable, unfree labor in colonial sites. The structures central to captivity still emergent in the Restoration became dominant, a defining part of the financial and social infrastructure in the second and third decades of the eighteenth century.

Steele was intimately familiar with the institution of slavery, like many of his contemporaries. Indeed, the "culture of taste" made so fashionable by the *Spectator* (1711–12) depended on the labor of enslaved Africans in the West Indies, even if that connection was largely invisible or unobserved.[2] Steele himself was a slaveholder, acquiring enslaved people through his possession of an inherited sugar plantation in Barbados. In his personal correspondence during his period of ownership, he wrote frankly and extensively about that experience, revealing its formative effect. He read deeply about the activities in Barbados. He collaborated with other plantation owners seeking to gain more favorable terms on the price of enslaved Africans. Like Martin Madan, he seemed inured to the human cost the plantation system exacted, compartmentalizing his spheres of activity and influence. Dogged by his own problematic debts—which encumbered him essentially all his life—Steele also experienced a persistent anxiety about the kind of captivity emerging from his own impecuniousness (a captivity literalized with his stints in a sponging-house).

At the same time, even as he participated as an economic agent in a system of enslavement, Steele presents ostensibly sympathetic views on the plight of the captive and the enslaved. His well-known *Spectator* No. 11, published March 13, 1711—written at the height of his Barbados involvement—includes his narrative of Inkle and Yarico, prompted by a page in Richard Ligon's *A True and Exact History of the Island of Barbados* (1657).[3] A frame story, the essay's seemingly simple exposition belies its layers of meaning.[4] Mr. Spectator recounts hearing his hostess Arietta tell the story of the English trader Thomas Inkle, who sells into Barbadian slavery his pregnant Amerindian lover Yarico (who had previously saved his life). Her pleas for sympathy because of her pregnancy fall on deaf ears; indeed, her pregnancy only makes her more valuable and enables Inkle to extract a higher price when he sells her in a "Market of *Indians* and other Slaves, as with us of Horses and Oxen." The concise, weighted language of *Spectator* No. 11 intensifies the implications of each textual detail, making it, as Peter Craft notes, "full of ambivalent material."[5] The essay masterfully invests specific descriptions about Inkle and Yarico with resonant cultural markers well-known to Steele's London readership. Yarico's adornment of Inkle's "Cave," "to make his Confinement more tolerable," introduces all the valuable items "which *that* world afforded," like a microcosm of the rare commodities in the Royal Exchange. The essay succinctly provides a tale of human commodification, financial self-interest, and, ultimately, captivity (ironically eliding Inkle's own "confinement").

While the essay records Mr. Spectator's emotional reaction to the fate of Yarico as he "left the Room with Tears in my Eyes," it neither offers a solution for nor a question about Inkle's mercenary motivations as he calculated "his loss of Time." The essay narratively withholds Inkle's emotion or the pain of Yarico. Nor does it explicitly condemn the enslaving and sale of one's lover, or the global trade in enslaved people in which Inkle participates and profits.[6] The only sentiment it offers is Mr. Spectator's self-congratulatory capacity for tears in the face of raw economic interest (although the tears are meant as much a compliment to the hostess Arietta as a comment directly upon the tale she tells). In form (a frame story), genre (a periodical essay), and geography (colonial action embedded in a London domestic space), the piece manifests the compartmentalization of taste and transgression, of sentiment and savagery, so essential to Steele and his contemporaries. The same compartmentalization and distancing characterize Steele's approach in *The Conscious Lovers*.

Nearly simultaneous with the publication of *Spectator* No. 11, Steele began to think about *The Conscious Lovers*. Although the publication of the two texts is separated by more than a decade, Steele's initial conception of the play was almost synchronous with No. 11. Steele "was probably planning [*The Conscious Lovers*] as early as 1710," asserts John Loftis, and he engaged in what Nathalie Wolfram terms a process of "ideological threshing" during the "fourteen-year composition process."[7] It "incubated a long time," adds Peter Hynes.[8] Steele closeted himself away, writing in 1716 of his plan to "Leave the Town, and Turn all my thoughts to finish my Comedy."[9] Steele's protracted method of composition, the meticulous planning of the details for each character, and the published advance notice of the play reiterate the care with which Steele prepared the text during a decade bracketed by the *asiento* and the Transportation Act. He saw the play as a way to restore his always tenuous financial solvency. As he wrote in July 1717, "I must keep my self to my self and have my Play ready this ensuing Winter, in Order to be quite out of Debt."[10] Like Thomas Inkle who knew time was money, Steele felt an urgency to finish a play he believed would repair his financial situation. He circulated the play in manuscript, and, allegedly, saw the first act performed in the garden at his home in Ty-Gwyn. He also strategically publicized and worked through the specific details of each character in his short-lived periodical *The Theatre* (1720).

Despite the temporal gap between *Spectator* No. 11 and *The Conscious Lovers*, both squarely focus on captivity and commodification. In *The Conscious Lovers* Steele clearly drew on Ligon's *History of Barbados* just as he did for *Spectator* No. 11. The play contains extensive specific, coded details about the transatlantic trade in enslaved Africans that, like the language of *Spectator* No. 11, would have been transparent to a 1722 London theatergoer, particularly given the intensity in which it was discussed in the decade following the *asiento*.[11] The layered, dense language that makes *Spectator* No. 11 such a rich, complicated, and ultimately ambivalent text similarly resonates in *The Conscious Lovers*. The more prolix dramatic form and the high emotion that characterize the genre subsume, but cannot erase, the significance of those words and their amplified meaning within the text.

With *The Conscious Lovers*, Steele created what he considered a new genre, sentimental comedy. The play represents Steele's efforts to depict the merchant class, what he described in *The Theatre* as a kind of "third Gentry,"[12] as moral exemplars within a strategically constructed (and publicized) genre that functioned both to demonstrate that class's sympathetic tendencies and to elicit a sympathetic response *toward* them from audiences and readers. The play's emphasis on virtue and morality rejects the more "scandalous" aspects of Restoration comedy and responds to Jeremy Collier's criticisms in *A Short View of the Immorality and Profaneness of the English Stage* (1698). That morality and sentiment serve another function, however. The highly self-conscious genre—with its hyperbole and emotional language—cloaks (and ultimately naturalizes) the brutal economic foundation of the wealth within the text: money derived from an economy dependent on the labor of enslaved workers. The sentimental theatrical form elides that obvious connection, using the emotional labor of its affected male characters to obscure the unacknowledged unfree physical labor that funds their privileged condition within the play. It valorizes sentiment and sympathetic reactions while distancing wealth from its ruthless origins, erasing the reality of African enslavement, and using the female figures in the play as domestic surrogates for the captivity undergirding the text.

Many scholars have argued for the text's connection to the emergent values of the merchant class and Steele's attempt to address the thornier issues connected with race, trade, and empire. Nicole Horejsi suggests the play processes a "mercantilist guilt" over "placing economic prosperity above family," and responds to a "contemporary concern over the potentially ill-gotten fruits of the emerging empire."[13] Similarly, Jennifer Donahue, who shares Horejsi's identification of Indiana as a subject with unstable national identity, sees the play as offering contrasting models of reception for an English subject returning from the West Indies.[14] While this scholarship, like other recent studies of the play, recognizes the essential role of empire and the West Indies, no one discusses how slavery itself figures directly within the text. The "mercantilist guilt" Horejsi identifies within the play stems not from privileging money above family (unless one considers the ruptured families of the enslaved or Inkle's sale of his own posterity) but rather from realizing economic gain from the enslavement and captivity of the unknown and unnamed. In his discussion of Steele's writing on the South Sea Company during the composition of *The Conscious Lovers,* John O'Brien rightly contends that the play exposes the degree to which "the slave trade had become part of the era's unconscious life."[15] The genre functions to obscure the centrality of enslavement and other forms of captivity underpinning the economic system and commercial structures Steele's writing celebrates. Steele displaces, indeed erases the enslavement, captivity, and subjugation inherent in the play's structure and wealth acquisition to advance his idealized construction of the sentimental merchant whose trade depends on human commodification.

This chapter first explores Steele's personal financial stake in the Barbadian plantation system. By closely examining his correspondence, I argue that Steele's stint of plantation ownership, not unlike Behn's time in Surinam, centrally informs his subsequent creative work. *The Conscious Lovers* resonates with codes of captivity and enslavement in a profound though previously underdiscussed way. The chapter then situates that play within this enriched context, carefully unpacking Steele's strategic and long-planned details for each character to highlight his direct involvement in and subsequent representation of the culture(s) of captivity.[16] The text pointedly invokes British commercial interests dependent on the labor of

enslaved Africans and the fate of indentured servants and transported convicts. It also directly incorporates language from Ligon's *History of Barbados*
to highlight the commodification of unmarried women within the play (and
eighteenth-century society as a whole). The persistent pattern of representation simultaneously obscures and foregrounds the domestic captivity the
play represents. Generic concessions to sentiment, sensibility, and normative "moral" behavior strategically ameliorate the text's deep engagement
with different forms of human subjugation. Finally, I suggest the implications of this kind of reading not only for Steele and the representation
of captivity, but for constructions of gender within a culture of captivity.
The captivity from which Bevil rescues Indiana—what she describes as her
future "in chains"—is replaced by her role as his wife, another kind of confinement. The chapter shows how personal and national financial interest,
both dependent on the slave trade, dynamically inhere in *The Conscious
Lovers* and reveal Britain's commercial network in enslaved humans to be
foundational to nearly every element of culture.

Steele and the West Indies

Richard Steele (1672–1729) owned a sugar plantation in Barbados that he
inherited from his first wife Margaret Ford Stretch,[17] a widow formerly
of Barbados who received the estate from her late brother, Major Robert
Ford.[18] Steele's ownership of an economic endeavor dependent on the labor
of enslaved people did not make him unique among men of his time. Some
men like Christopher Codrington had vast holdings in the West Indies,
amassing previously unimaginable wealth. Others, like Martin Madan,
viewed the opportunities more aspirationally, as a possible way to repair
a diminished financial situation or increase wealth more modestly. Steele,
always pursuing the next great financial venture, fell into the latter category.
Like Madan, he was an absentee landlord whose correspondence reveals
how all-consuming his West Indian affairs became but who showed a similar tendency for compartmentalization. While Steele may not have been
unique in his role as a slaveholder pursuing profit from West Indian investments, he was unique in being someone drawing on that experience of
slaveholding to pen a popular periodical geared for the man of taste and to
author one of the most successful plays of the eighteenth century.

The holdings Steele inherited, "call'd the Content plantation," included "Severall Buildings Sugar Works Negro's [sic] Cattle and other Appurtenances

thereunto."[19] The irony of the name "Content" seems to have been lost on Steele. The total was valued at £9,300. "Steele had married a considerable fortune," Calhoun Winton notes, "which he immediately, and characteristically, began entangling in his own indebtedness."[20] Indeed, within months of the Steeles' marriage, the first registered deed for the plantation in September 1705 "made the property chargeable with the debts of Richard or Margaret up to the amount of £2000."[21] The ability to borrow against the value of the plantation—immediately—was ill-suited to Steele's seeming inability to remain financially solvent. As early as October 1700 Steele faced what his nineteenth-century biographer George Aiken describes as the "first of a long series of actions for debt."[22] Like many of his debts, the one brought to action in October 1700 was for a relatively small amount (£42), but between 1700 and the death of Stretch in December 1706 Steele had four more actions for debt brought against him. This pattern of borrowing, and failing to repay loans, continued throughout Steele's life. It also made him keenly aware of the onus of being financially beholden to another.

At the funeral for his first wife Margaret Stretch, Steele met Mary Scurlock (1678–1718) who would become his second wife on September 9, 1707, at Saint Mary Somerset in the City.[23] Despite (or perhaps because of) his continuing indebtedness, Steele's letters to Scurlock during their courtship eschew any real discussion of money. Anticipating Bevil's words that obscure his economic dominance over Indiana in *The Conscious Lovers* (1722), Steele overwrites his pressing financial concerns with the language of sentiment: "There is a dirty Croud of Busie faces all around me talking of *money;* while all my Ambition, all my wealth is Love!"[24] He creates a fluid economy of money and emotion. Just as Inkle "promised [Yarico] the enjoyment" of items and experiences when "he should . . . have her in his Country," so too Steele offers promises of an emotional future with Scurlock (whom he called "Prue") when he lacks the ability to provide any real basis for a stable financial future.[25] "When I have not money," he writes, "I have given promises to keep up y^r spirits and keep you in good humour."[26] Promises became as valuable a specie as gold.

However, Scurlock's mother, perhaps aware of Steele's reputation for financial irresponsibility, wrote her daughter to express her "anxiety for Her Welfare in relation to" Steele.[27] Mary Scurlock's mother was concerned enough to settle "an hundred & sixty pounds a Year liable to certain Debts" upon Steele and Scurlock in 1708. She understood the dangers of her daughter's marriage to a perpetually insolvent man. Upon learning of this letter, Steele details to his future mother-in-law his "Main prospect . . . of Fortune" and promises to "very candidly give you an account of myself to that particular."[28] The primary evidence he provides of his "prospect . . . of Fortune" is his inheritance in the West Indies. "My Late Wife had so extreme a Value for Me," writes Steele, "that she by Fine Convey'd to Me Her whole estate Situate in Barbados, which, with the Stock and Slaves . . . is Lett for Eight hundred and fifty pounds per Annum at Half yearly payments."[29] Steele specifically flags this financial asset as the result of or in compensation for an emotional connection: his first wife left him the plantation because she "had so extreme a Value for me." Here, the meaning of the word "value" vacillates between its emotionally charged sense—value as worth based on esteem—and its financially oriented meaning—the monetary value of something. Even the world of emotions collapses into the language of wealth.

Deeds on the property reveal Steele's holdings included "mansions, windmills, boyling houses, copper still &c," other materials used to process sugar cane, as well as what Rae Blanchard describes as "white servants . . . mentioned as chattels as well as two hundred" enslaved Africans.[30] By way of context, it is useful to remember that Martin Madan lacked the resources to sufficiently meet the labor demands on his own plantation; Steele, however, owned ten times as many enslaved people as Madan. Steele, like his contemporaries, naturalizes his ownership of humans—both the enslaved and the indentured. The indentured, although owned for a contracted period and not a lifetime, are also considered a form of "chattel" property, another commodity. The human cost of this enterprise goes entirely unmentioned. Steele's only concern is his own financial situation.

From the time he inherited the plantation in 1706 and became administrator in January 1707, Steele's letters detail his efforts to maintain or enhance the value of the plantation while simultaneously trying to extricate himself from its ownership, collect the rents owed, and realize some financial gain. Throughout the process he depends upon his well-networked position to advance his interests. He trades on his status as a gentleman with all the assumptions about mastery, masculinity, and privilege inherent for him in that term in order to increase his influence over the administration of his holdings. Within days of assuming administrative control over the Barbados plantation, Steele used his political connections and relationship with Joseph Addison to prompt the new secretary of state, Charles Spencer, the third Earl of Sunderland (1675–1722), to write a note on his behalf to Governor Mitford Crowe (1669–1719) of Barbados: "Being informed that Mr. Steele, a gentleman belonging to His Royal Highnesses' family, has an estate in Barbadoes [sic] legally conveyed to him by his late wife, I desire you will not let him suffer by his absence from the said island, and his little acquaintance with the people, but that you will give him your coun- tenance and assistance in the asserting of his right as far as he has law and justice on his side."[31] The note betrays how much a successful planter de- pended upon presence on-site at his plantation as well as connections at home in England. Without the cover and credibility of Steele's status as a gentleman, his investment might suffer "by his absences" and "little ac- quaintance" with the people (as Martin Madan's surely did).

The note also suggests the degree to which Steele was driven by aspirational—and emulative—behavior. Steele had long known Christo- pher Codrington (1668–1710), one of the wealthiest West Indian planters of the era whose holdings at the time of his death were estimated at more than £100,000. Classmates at Christ Church, Oxford, fellow poets, and soldiers in the Life Guards, Steele and Codrington shared certain qual- ities associated with the man of fashion (even if those qualities were perhaps aspirational rather than fully realized on Steele's part). Thomas Tickell's poem Oxford (1707) explicitly links the two men, joining their names as poets, soldiers, and fellow Oxford alumni:

> When Codrington, and Steele their Verse unrein,
> And form an easie, unaffected Strain,
> A double Wreath of Laurel binds their Brow,
> As they are Poets, and are Warriors too.[32]

Although Steele did not correspond with Codrington during this period (perhaps because both men were in London, Blanchard even suggests they met during this period), Codrington's visibility as what Simon Gikandi terms "a person of taste" makes it quite possible that he remained a role model for Steele (whose wealth never actually materialized), perhaps even influencing his fictional representation of Sealand in The Conscious Lovers. Codrington occupied a personal situation that Gikandi describes as "on one side . . . a distinguished English gentleman, the quintessential man of taste; on the other side . . . the seasoned West Indian slave master."[33] Whether Steele really understood how that fundamental dichotomy was relevant to his own situation, he nonetheless processed the points of connection and difference between gentleman and owner of the enslaved in *The Conscious Lovers.*

Like his friend and patron Codrington, Steele sought to leverage his (much more modest) plantation ownership to his own social and financial advantage. Although Steele obviously lacked Codrington's financial means, his association with someone like him marks the degree to which the resources enabled by West Indian wealth could facilitate the kind of lifestyle Steele sought. That association required a strategic compartmentalization of his London life and his West Indian role. The utter lack of reflection in his correspondence about the human cost of his Barbados plantation suggests that Steele ignored the material reality of enslavement; instead, as Gikandi describes it, he and other absentee landlords of the West Indies "could immerse themselves into a culture of taste" rather than consider the labor that funded those pursuits.[34] Of course, Steele didn't merely immerse himself in a culture of taste; he helped to create it through writings like the *Tatler* and *Spectator.*[35]

Typical of his political nature, during this period Steele also allied himself with a group of other Barbados plantation owners living in London who consistently tried to exert influence in order to protect their financial interests in the colony. Most frequently, their interests revolved around the price of enslaved Africans. For example, Steele was one of eleven owners who signed a petition to Queen Anne seeking greater oversight, participation, and military support in Barbados.[36] "'The Humble Petitions of Severall Gentlemen in England who are Proprietors of very considerable Plantations of yr Majesties Island of Barbados,'" as James Alsop details, "complained that a lack of administration on Barbados was having serious repercussions on the island's trade, prosperity, and ability to defend itself against the French during the current war."[37] More immediately, the plantation owners were concerned that new legislation being passed by those living in Barbados limited the strength of the governor and the ability of absent owners to collect debts, causing the profitability to be "exceedingly diminished."[38] Tellingly the petition presents men's perception of the economic threat with language that likens them to besieged captives. The petitioners cast themselves as victims who have "suffered. . . . great abuses." Their tenants live with perpetual anxiety, "under constant fears and at great charge in being perpetually allarm'd" by potential external enemies or local insurrections.[39] Similarly, in January 1709, Steele and fourteen other plantation owners signed a deposition seeking the continuation of the current secretary of Barbados, recognizing the importance of strong personal relationships, especially for an absentee landlord.[40] Around the same time as this petition, another group of "seventy-six gentlemen with interests in Barbados" wrote the House of Commons on "the necessity for the establishment of a joint-stock company for the African trade with Barbados." The August 1709 document complains about both the inflated price and the depressed supply of enslaved laborers since ending the monopoly rights of the Royal African Company.[41]

Steele's pattern of engagement in the governance and administration of the colony, even as he tried to dispose of his plantation, demonstrates his focus on maintaining the salability of (and revenue stream from) his Barbadian property. It also indicates his intimate knowledge of the politics, economics, and conditions of production in the colony. Ownership and administration, even from afar, depended on current information, an assertive, albeit distant, presence, and personal relationships within a network made up of other like-minded plantation owners and agents. Of course, Steele also exploited these relationships personally. For example, in May 1709, Steele borrowed £140 from George Tilden, agent to the governor of Barbados, an unpaid debt that would lead to his first imprisonment.[42]

The Barbadian plantation also occupied a large space within Steele's marital correspondence and influenced the emotional tenor of the couple's interactions and activities. Like the characters he creates in *The Conscious Lovers*, Steele manifests the near seamless mixture of sentiment and finance, establishing dual economies in his personal discourse. Steele regularly updates his wife about his attempts to make progress with the plantation's "business." While he withholds specific details, he integrates professions of affection with accounts of his energies in connection with the property. "I could not forbear letting you know, that I have received letters this moment from Barbados which will facilitate my businesse."[43] The remaining line of the one-sentence letter ascribes an almost talismanic effect to Prue: "so natural is it that all things must grow better by y^r Condescending to be partner to y^r Most Obliged Husband, and Most Humble Ser^{nt}." A week later, October 16, he is delayed returning home, "having met a schoolfellow from India, by whome I am to be inform'd in things this night which extreamly concern y^r Obedient Husband." Blanchard, editor of Steele's correspondence, hypothesizes this friend to be Codrington, who would have been in London at the time.[44]

An urgency drives Steele's desire to send off letters in a timely manner despite the great geographical distance; he is bound by the schedule of the West Indian Post, which regularly transported packets to Barbados. "I can't Wait upon you to-day to Hampton-Court," he writes Prue. "I have the West-Indian businesse on my hands and find very much to be done before Thursday's post."[45] A few months later, Steele again cancels a trip with his wife to Hampton Court because he is "forced to prepare my letters" for "the West Indian Post going on Saturday."[46] The business simultaneously depends upon and interferes with his social and personal relationships. He consults often with friend and counsel Stephen Clay about "dispatches I am making for the West-Indies," a process of review that indicates the importance he places on the communications.[47] Willard Connely suggests that Steele actually persuaded Clay "to draft for him notices to his tenants in the Barbados" to accelerate the collection of "the island rents."[48] The business's intrusion into the marital correspondence, the attendant interruption to the couple's personal plans, and, most palpably, its real consequences for their financial future suggest on a microlevel the "domesticity of empire" Emma Rothschild describes.[49] The "West Indies" becomes another character in the Steeles' marital exchange.

That Steele placed emphasis on cordial personal relations with other plantation owners is also evident in his suggestion to Prue that "It would not be amisse if [she] visited Mrs. Tryon in Lime-Street," likely the wife of Rowland Tryon, the principal trustee for the sale of Steele's plantation.[50] Steele admonishes Prue to "[b]e in good Humour if you go."[51] His financial interests require Prue to adhere to a high standard for feminine charm and compliance, although she clearly found his insolvency trying. "I wish I knew how to Court you into Good-Humour," writes Steele, reminding Prue "I am always pursuing our Mutuall Good."[52] Steele himself met frequently with Tryon throughout 1709, working with him on February 1 "to make a finall end" to the sale of the plantation.[53] On March 2, 1709, he lacked closure; "I am resolv'd to do something effectually to-day with Tryon,"[54] he writes Prue. The situation still remained unresolved on April 19: "I have been with Tryon. He owns some effects which will be of assistance to Me."[55] But rents are not forthcoming. The expected payment "of my 800l. which I ought to have receiv'd yesterday" is "putt off" by Tryon "till further time," making Steele "very much out of Humour."[56] He cannot extricate himself from the emotional or economic weight of the situation (although this indefinite state of deferral mirrors the unstable situation in which Indiana finds herself in *The Conscious Lovers*).

During this period Steele carried considerable unpaid financial obligations both to individual creditors and to his landlord; by Hilary term 1711, Steele had had twenty-one actions of debt brought against him and had been imprisoned at least twice as a result.[57] Like the fictional Inkle, Steele understood the penalty of lost time and money. While Steele "regretted the inconvenience of debt," notes Winton, "his thoughts of future fortune did not include paying off all debts and settling down to a restricted, frugal life."[58] Nevertheless, Steele worked hard to project a consistent sense of optimism to his wife about their financial future. "Within a day or Two, I doubt not but We shall have our Money," he writes, an event he anticipates "will be the introduction into that life we both pant after with so much earnestnesse."[59] However, the financial future they "pant for" remains perpetually postponed. A few months later, the situation still unresolved, he reassures Prue, "There is no doubt but We shall be easy and happy in a few days."[60] As Winton describes, Steele's letters "glitter with forecasts of impending wealth, of higher place"; he possessed a "*futurus* sense."[61] Steele was very much engaged in the spirit of the age, an age in which wealth increasingly stemmed from the labors of enslaved people.

Throughout his life Steele's repeated investments in speculative schemes contributed to his failure to achieve any sustained financial stability. He was always one for a get-rich-quick scheme, no matter how far-fetched. As early as 1697, while serving in the Life Guards (at the same time as Codrington), Steele "involved himself in alchemical experiments, with the hope of a quick financial return but the reality of lost money and credit."[62] In 1713, he began a decade-long involvement with a project designed to deliver live fish to the London market, the Fish Pool Project, around which he attempted to create a joint-stock company in 1720.[63] However, despite his efforts, his profits there proved as elusive as his previous alchemical endeavors and, ultimately, as his plantation in Barbados.

Steele's inability to manage his investments or control his spending, coupled with the delayed disposition of the estate and "loans sought from one and another of the trustees" diminished the amount Steele ultimately received from the estate.[64] He laments to Prue that although "My little fortune is to [be] settled this month . . . I have inadvertently made my self Liable to Impatient People who take all advantages."⁶⁵ However, Steele refuses to take any personal responsibility for the loss; his indebtedness happened "inadvertently." The disappointment haunted him. "[R]eflection upon what vast sums of money I have lett slip through my hands since I have had opportunityes of mending my fortune in the world," writes Steele, "have made me very anxious for the future."⁶⁶ Reflection begets anxiety, as it does for Inkle in *Spectator* No. 11, whose calculation of lost "Days Interest of his Mony" made him "very pensive."⁶⁷ That Steele's financial woes intrude into his personal correspondence and daily movements marks the stark difference in scale between himself and someone like Codrington. Steele can neither inoculate himself from the concerns of finance nor achieve any sustained economic success.

Despite the disappointment it ultimately represented, and the relatively brief time he owned the plantation, Steele's Barbados experience preoccupied his literary imagination just as it had his personal correspondence. He circulated in a cultural space where, as Joseph Roach observes, "intensified networks of production and consumption" undeniably, if invisibly, drew on the nation's West Indian investments; coffeehouse readers of Steele's periodical "refreshed themselves with stimulating beverages extracted from the labor of West Indian slaves" in a physical space where "sales of slaves were conducted."⁶⁸ Steele owned enslaved peopled, numbered slaveholders among his friends and associates, and designed his published work for readers similarly immersed in a culture of captivity. Nearly contemporaneous with Steele's attempts to dispose of the Barbados estate was his initiation of *The Spectator* and his retelling of the Inkle and Yarico narrative. Frank Felsenstein suggests that "as a result of his inheritance," Steele's "attention would have first been drawn to" Richard Ligon's *A True and Exact History of the Island of Barbados,* the known source for "Inkle and Yarico."⁶⁹ The relevance of Ligon's description of Barbados extends beyond "Inkle and Yarico," however; the details it provides about the island, England's relationship with the colony, and the treatment of both the enslaved and the indentured also shape *The Conscious Lovers.*

The length of time Steele spent writing this play, its circulation in manuscript, and its popular cultural presence before it even actually appeared on the stage, make clear how Steele carefully—almost obsessively—planned the minute elements of the text. His attention to the details of class, geography, and economy were central to his efforts to present merchants as a new "Species of Gentry."[70] Crucially, the exemplary merchant in this text, Mr. Sealand, is intimately engaged in a trade dependent on the labor of enslaved Africans. The world in which Sealand's wealth is created is one in which, in John O'Brien's words, the slave trade is absolutely central "to the normal operations of the commercial system."[71] Steele composed the play during a decade in which the state's direct engagement in the trade in enslaved Africans (with the *asiento*) increased, as did the possibilities for the captivity of British subjects (through imprisonment, transportation, or indenture). Steele's desire to rehabilitate the perception of members of the merchant class and demonstrate their emotional capacity and refined sensibilities is a desire to valorize those (like himself) attempting to build wealth with the labor of enslaved people. Yet the merchant Sealand does not weep for those toiling on his West Indian plantations. Despite its sentiment, its calculated emotional effect upon the audience, and its comic resolution, *The Conscious Lovers* at base is a play structurally dependent on enslavement, captivity, and oppression.

Bristol, Captivity, and *The Conscious Lovers*

The culminating moment of *The Conscious Lovers* occurs in act V. The well-known and persistently popular sentimental comedy focuses on the apparently orphaned Indiana and her relationship with Bevil Jr., engaged to Lucinda, who is the daughter of the "great *India* Merchant" Mr. Sealand (I.i.49). Bevil, having rescued Indiana from the threat of debtors' prison, financially supports her and her Aunt Isabella in London. Although in love with Indiana, Bevil feels compelled by filial duty to agree to marry Sealand's daughter Lucinda at his father Sir John Bevil's request. In act V, Mr. Sealand, believing Indiana to be Bevil's mistress, appears at her lodgings to learn more about her. He wants to assess the nature of her relationship with Bevil and determine whether to allow the marriage between Bevil and Lucinda to proceed. In the course of Mr. Sealand and Indiana's conversation, the increasingly distraught Indiana thinks she will have to face a life without Bevil. Ripping off her dead mother's bracelet she exclaims, "O, could I be any other Thing than what I am—I'll tear away all Traces of my former Self, my little Ornaments, the Remains of my first State, the Hints of what I ought to have been" (V.iii.156–59).

Mr. Sealand recognizes the bracelet as one he had given his late wife and realizes Indiana is his long-lost daughter. The benevolent Sealand, whose

"Passions are too strong for Utterance," then bestows his tears and his fortune upon her (V.iii.181–82).[72] With a gesture that financially rewards virtue and explicitly joins commerce with sentiment, the merchant Sealand is fashioned as a modern and desirable breed of man. He fully occupies the place he claimed for himself as part of "a Species of Gentry": "[W]e Merchants," he tells Sir John, "are a Species of Gentry, that have grown into the World this last Century, and are as honourable, and almost as useful, as you landed Folks" (IV.ii.50–53).[73] The "last century" to which he refers coincides exactly with the growing dominance of Britain in the trade in enslaved Africans, an endeavor with which Sealand is specifically associated. Sealand rejoices that "our Sorrows past o'erpaid by such a Meeting" (V.iii.199), a reunion providing the "Joy too exquisite for Laughter," the marker of sentimental comedy Steele describes in the preface to the play (299).

Yet moments before the reunion with her newly discovered father, Indiana provides details about her life that complicate interpretations of Steele's play purely within the generic confines of sentimental comedy.[74] The description of both the past Indiana experienced and the future she anticipates without Bevil have often been read as metaphorical descriptions of distress aligned with the overwrought, often hyperbolic language consistent with the genre. Indiana's language holds much greater meaning when situated within a culture of captivity, however. Indiana does not speak abstractly or metaphorically about the dangers she, unprotected, would confront in a treacherous world; rather, she speaks quite specifically about the material realities of an indebted woman with no financial support who potentially faces confinement, victimization, and captivity in the form of indentured servitude, debtors' prison, or transportation to the colonies. Further, Sealand's repeatedly specified origins in Bristol, England's top slaving port in 1722, make the British Atlantic trade in enslaved Africans a foundational element of the play. Slavery is the financial structure upon which this new "Species of Gentry" depends (the very word "species" marking the ways in which humans are increasingly categorized). The text's potent details draw on recognizable cultural codes of the Atlantic trade in England and undeniably situate *The Conscious Lovers* within a culture of captivity. When the play excludes representations of Black interiority or enslaved characters, it displaces the experience of objectification, captivity, and dehumanization onto the younger white female characters. It filters the structural mechanisms of captivity through the narrated experience of Indiana, making her subjugation (and ultimate "liberation") fodder for the audience's sentimental reaction. Steele lacks the capacity to represent the experience of, say, a Yarico on stage. He can, however, parse elements of her captive experience through Indiana. Steele displaces violence upon the invisible yet absolutely present enslaved, translating it into symbolic violence (that could easily tip into actual violence) upon the body of the unprotected Indiana. The white female figure becomes an aesthetic accessory to the text, engendering a sentimental response from the audience and bearing (and, in fact, baring) the experiences of captivity.

Indiana characterizes her life as one defined by captivity at every moment, lamenting her inauspicious beginnings as "An Infant Captive!" (V.iii.139), a narrative Bevil amplifies in his description to his servant Tom. As a child in Bristol, Indiana begins a journey to Barbados after her father sends for his wife and "little Family" to "follow him to the Indies" now that his fortunes are restored. (As the aspirational investment of Martin Madan, Steele, and others demonstrates, the West Indies held a strong appeal to those seeking financial gain, even if that gain could only be realized through the labor of the enslaved.) Indiana's mother, "impatient" to join her husband, "would not wait the leisure of a Convoy, but took the first occasion of a single Ship." As a result she "lost her Liberty, and Life" (I.ii.171–75). Describing her aborted journey from Bristol to the West Indies, Indiana recounts her own abduction by a French privateer. The term privateer can refer dually to the actual ship (an armed vessel holding a government commission that authorizes the capture of merchant shipping belonging to an enemy nation) or to the commander of such a ship. Steele uses the term in both senses. Again, Steele seems to draw on personal knowledge here. The brother of Steele's first wife, Major Robert Ford, left Barbados in 1705 and later died on a French privateer, a detail that may have informed the narrative of Indiana and Isabella. French privateers commonly intercepted ships en route to or from Barbados. George Aitken describes how, when England and France were at war in the late seventeenth and early eighteenth century, "vessels from the West Indies were often captured by the French."[75] A 1709 petition signed by Steele and ten other Barbados plantation owners sought greater protection for transatlantic voyages to Barbados because of their particular vulnerability to privateers. Details of Indiana's narrative emerge from material practice, not imaginative hyperbole.

After her abduction and her mother's death, Indiana ends up in a foreign land, dependent on the kindness of the privateer, a man from Toulon who adopts her.[76] However, after that captain, "her Benefactor," was later "kill'd at Sea" (I.ii.189–90), his brother "found (among his other Riches) this blooming Virgin, at his Mercy" (I.ii.192–93). Indiana is suddenly subject to the sexual demands of the avaricious brother who threatens to imprison her for debt ("demanding her to account for all her Maintenance, from her Childhood") unless she capitulates to his advances (I.ii.199). Bevil sees Indiana's guardian "draging [sic] her by Violence to Prison" (I.ii.200–201), a pattern in a life narrative marked by aggression and imminent peril. The financial accounting and the reference to the threat of debtors' prison would have been transparent to any eighteenth-century reader or viewer. Debtors were among the largest component in the eighteenth-century prison population. By one estimate, nearly ten thousand people a year were imprisoned for debt, a "crime" that affected anyone of any class (including, of course, Richard Steele).[77] The volatility of the financial marketplace meant fortunes were easily won and lost. Certainly, the memory of the recent stock collapse of the South Sea Company was very fresh in viewers' minds. Indiana's potential imprisonment materializes the subjectivity and powerlessness of her existence; that her potential imprisonment hinges on debt extends its relevance.

The bereft Indiana's salvation comes only when Bevil, the "most Charming of Mankind . . . set me free" (V.iii.140–41). Although Bevil ostensibly liberates Indiana by rescuing her from the privateer's brother, he in fact moves her to another, distinctly different, state of captivity. Bevil pays for her lodgings (which Sealand estimates to amount to £1,000 a year), creating a liminal, suspect space in which she resides. Further, Myrtle's repetition of the possessive pronoun "your"—"your *Indian* princess, for your soft Moments of Dalliance, your Convenient, your Ready *Indiana*" (IV.i.149–51)—reinscribes Bevil's ownership-like control over Indiana and insinuates her sexual availability (an availability Isabella worries about, reminding Indiana "don't see [Bevil] in a Bed-chamber" [II.ii.112–13]).[78]

Indiana internalizes her subjected state when describing the future she envisages for herself if forced to live without Bevil's financial support: "What have I to do, but sigh, and weep, to rave, run wild, a Lunatic in Chains, or hid in Darkness, mutter in distracted Starts, and broken Accents, my strange, strange Story! [. . .] All my Comfort must be to expostulate in Madness, to relieve with Frenzy my Despair, and shrieking to demand of Fate: why—why was I born to such Variety of Sorrows?" (V.iii.126–33). Indiana describes herself as "a Lunatic in Chains." Although the language is suggestive of confinement in an institution like Bethlehem Hospital or "Bedlam,"[79] within the context of the play the language more powerfully evokes the very present and immediate use of chains on humans in captivity: convicts, the indentured, and the enslaved. Indiana anticipates the geographic displacement associated with her captivity as signaled by the characterization of hers as a "strange, strange story"; it is strange because it is "unaccountable" but it is also strange because, when told, it will "belong to another country" or be told in a "place different from her own." Faced with debt and absolutely no means of support, a woman in Indiana's position, if placed in debtors' prison, might be transported to the colonies as a convict or might choose to essentially sell herself into indentured servitude merely to survive. Without Bevil's support Indiana will face an ambiguous future, one that might reasonably include any of the states of captivity referenced in the play.

The only comfort Indiana anticipates lies in what she lacks at present: the opportunity to speak freely. In predicting her state of woe, she imagines she will have the "comfort . . . to expostulate," to complain of her grievances. Only in her irredeemably altered state, displaced from the confines of English culture, can she speak truthfully of her situation, freed from patriarchal silencing. Indiana's preoccupation with speech and her freedom to narrate her plight has great resonance with Yarico's situation. Yarico similarly lacks not only power to speak freely but also mastery of English. Inkle and Yarico "had learn'd a language of their own, in which the voyager communicated to his mistress."[80] The one-sided direction of the conversation—Inkle speaks to Yarico—embodies their asymmetrical power relationship. Indiana and Bevil's interactions mirror Inkle and Yarico's idiosyncratic and largely silent communications. Indiana can only interpret Bevil, not speak to him directly or at least not speak freely. She laments and predictably realizes "The Goodness and Gentleness of his Demeanour made me misinterpret all" (V.iii.108). Even when they converse, the power of what he does not say is telling. Indiana relies on what "his Eyes have only made me think" (V.iii.106).

Steele amplifies Indiana's silence with a two-stanza song "design'd" to be sung to her as "Entertainment" arranged by Bevil at the beginning of act II. While ostensibly a gesture of flattery and diversion the song, as planned, would have rather reinscribed Indiana's passive, silent state. "[F]or want of a Performer" the song appeared instead in the published Preface to the play where Steele described it as "the Distress of a Love-sick Maid."[81] Tellingly, the imagined emotional state of the "Love-sick Maid" replicates the oppression and displacement Indiana experiences before the support of Bevil, a condition to which she anticipates she will return. That Steele designed this song as the "Entertainment" Bevil planned for Indiana reiterates her fully naturalized state of submission and captivity. The condition of the "Love-sick Maid" also shares qualities with the plight of enslaved or captive people:

> From Place to Place forlorn I go,
>   With downcast Eyes a silent Shade;
> Forbidden to declare my Woe;
>   To speak, till spoken to, afraid.
> My inward Pangs, my secret Grief,
>   My soft consenting Looks betray:
> He Loves, but gives me no Relief:
>   Why speaks not he who may?[82]

Displaced and silenced, the maid is "forbidden to declare [her] woe." Although the description does not specify gender or race (an absence heightened by the song's isolated presence in the play's preface), the phrase "Place to Place" conjures the displacement inherent in the colonial space and the forced movement—enslavement, transportation, indentured servitude, or a kidnapped Indiana—central to Steele's text and his culture's economy. (It is the dark manifestation of Indiana's status as a "Rambling Captive" [IV.i.149]). In a captive state, the speaker wanders with "downcast Eyes" and does not "speak till spoken to." Speech—or "woe"—is "forbidden"; grief must remain "secret." Silent "looks" appear "consenting," but that voicelessness merely replicates the inevitable lack of consent accorded women, especially in a captive state. The interiority conveyed in the song ("My inward Pangs") anticipates the forced silencing Indiana fears; she remains unable to share or display her considerable emotions. Like the final climatic scene, the song initially seems simply to align with the overwrought emotions that characterize this new genre—sentimental comedy.[83] However, it also clearly reiterates the material condition of those subjugated within a culture of captivity—they exist as perpetually displaced, silent shades. "Shade" summons associations of both the spectral (the unseen, invisible presence of enslaved people) and the darkness. Indiana's restoration to a life of financial security comes only after her protracted confinement and threatened abuse, and the song implicitly reiterates the kinds of financial trade and traffic essential to her father Mr. Sealand.

Steele discussed his vision for the character of Mr. Sealand in the Saturday, January 9, 1720, issue (No. 3) of his short-lived periodical *The Theatre*. He clearly stated his investment in the elevation of merchants to what he terms a *"third gentry."* Individuals who deal with goods rather than various forms of paper credit deserve a nation's gratitude and recognition for the important role they play. As Steele writes in the June 7, 1709, issue of the *Tatler* (No. 25), the citizen merchant makes "all men he deals with . . . the better." Steele describes Sealand as "Gentleman" "formerly what is call'd a Man of Pleasure about the Town; and having, when young, lavish'd a small Estate, retir'd to *India,* where by Marriage, and falling into the Knowledge of Trade, he laid the Foundation of the great Fortune, of which he is now Master."[84] That depiction is as dense and coded as the description of Inkle. It places Sealand's dissipation or rakish behavior as a "Man of Pleasure" in the past. Having lost one estate, Sealand uses his "knowledge" of trade to build another outside of his domestic home. In some ways, this sequence (minus the relocation to the colonial space) might be seen to mirror the trajectory of Richard Steele, another "Man of Pleasure" about the Town, who "by Marriage" certainly gained the means to lay the foundation for a fortune, even if that fortune remained largely unrealized.

In *The Conscious Lovers*, Steele refined his treatment of Sealand beyond the description in *The Theatre*, accelerating the specific use of place names to heighten Sealand's undeniable connection with the slave trade. Identifying Mr. Sealand as "an Eminent Merchant of *Bristol*" early in act I unequivocally marks the transatlantic slave trade as the economic foundation for the actions within the play (I.ii.164). By the time *The Conscious Lovers* debuted in 1722, Bristol, as Madge Dresser details, was "the nation's number one slaving port, eclipsing London as well as its newer rival Liverpool."[85] Fifty-two percent of all slave-trading voyages had originated in Bristol the previous year.[86] During this period Bristol "broke London's dominance" on the slave trade and for "a score of years it was the leading English slave port," notes James Rawley, "and for the century as a whole it stood second only to Liverpool in volume of slave ventures."[87] Thus to a 1722 audience, Bristol would immediately and absolutely code Sealand's economic gain as linked, in some form, to commerce dependent on enslaved people and their labor. Although Sealand is not specifically identified as someone engaged directly in the slave trade, "many eminent Bristol merchants who did not specialize in slaving nevertheless made investments in slaving voyages"; "slave-trading played" a wide role "in the city's economic life."[88] Further, just as Steele never specifically names Inkle as a slaver—describing him only as one seeking "to improve his Fortune by Trade and Merchandize"—he also doesn't have to name Sealand as someone engaged in the trade of the enslaved; the connections were that powerful. A mark of The Conscious Lovers' association with Bristol might also be found in the fact that the play was chosen for opening night of the Bristol Old Vic on May 30, 1766.[89]

Bristol and its merchant class had deep and well-known financial investments in the West Indies with particularly extensive investments in Barbados, the location of Steele's own plantation; in fact the Barbados settlement of "Speightstown was known as 'Little Bristol' because the preponderance of Bristol ships trading there" was so great.[90] Kenneth Morgan marvels at "the sheer extent to which Bristol was connected with the West Indies in the eighteenth century."[91] Additionally, immediately prior to the production of The Conscious Lovers, the published efforts of Bristol merchants to more fully control the price of enslaved people in Barbados appeared regularly in newspapers of the period. "A Letter from a Merchant in Bristol, Touching the Trade to Africa, as It Relates to the Out-ports of Great Britain" details how the African Company's "Pretences for an Exclusive Trade, have very much allarm'd the City of Bristol." "[I]f this Trade is to be lock'd up," asks the author, "what must become of the Out-ports of Great Britain, who have little or no Trade left, but that to the Plantation, which increases or diminishes in Proportion to the number of Negroes imported there, which produce the Commodities with which our Ships are usually loaded, and enables the Planters to live well, and purchase great Quantities of our British Commodities."[92]

In addition to its association with the trade in enslaved Africans, Bristol also served as a "major exit point" for white transportees including indentured servants and, subsequently, convicts. A "number of prominent Bristol merchants gained lucrative contracts shipping" British subjects to the West Indies.[93] Of the 50,000 convicts sent from Britain between 1718 and 1775, 10,000 were sent from Bristol. The categories of individuals who might be classed as "convicts" were actually quite complicated. Street children were kidnapped to provide labor (and might be considered "convicts" because they were probably deemed vagrants); similarly, political prisoners, especially the Irish and Monmouthshire rebels, might be considered another category. Once "the convict trade was officially established in 1718 as an important secondary punishment for certain criminal offences," it helped satisfy the "constant demand for cheap white labour" in the British colonies where, as Morgan notes, "convicts sold for about a third of the price" of enslaved Africans.[94] The transportation of white laborers, another kind of domestic captivity, would also certainly be part of the consciousness of a 1722 theater audience. Bristol dominated England's role in the sugar industry, which depended on the labor of enslaved people for the planting, harvesting, and refining of sugar cane. Bristol merchants often filled "both functions" of merchant and planter and the "overlap among personnel in the sugar and slave trades at Bristol" was pervasive.[95] (Indeed Sealand's name, delineating the two spheres of his economic activity—sea and land—implicitly reiterates that dual involvement.)

Mr. Sealand's financial history as detailed by Bevil in the first act of the play is the centerpiece of all discussions of him. Sealand, in Bevil's words, was "a Younger Brother of an Ancient Family and, originally an Eminent Merchant of *Bristol;* who, upon repeated Misfortunes, was reduced to go privately to the *Indies.* In this Retreat Providence again grew favorable to his Industry, and, in six Years time, restored him to his former Fortunes" (I.ii.164–69). "The mark of a successful Barbados planter," notes Richard Dunn, "was his ability to escape from the island and retire grandly to England."[96] Sealand's history richly codes this situation. His characterization as an "Eminent Merchant of Bristol" might suggest his membership in Bristol's Society of Merchant Venturers.[97] Membership in the Merchant Venturers signaled a man's economic and social power in Bristol. The Merchant Venturers comprised the dominant group of leading Bristol merchants who, in addition to contributing to the civic improvement of Bristol, worked assiduously to preserve its economic interests in the West Indies, lobbying Parliament and individual MPs. Peter Mathias notes that within the society's petitions "the slave trade emerges as the most important single issue, with efforts to preserve the conditions of existence of the trade in general and the position of the port of Bristol in particular."[98] Indeed, in the period immediately prior to *The Conscious Lovers,* the Bristol's Society of Merchant Venturers renewed its efforts to minimize the Royal African Company's role in the transatlantic slave trade.

Before he emerges as a man of wealth, however, Sealand was forced "to go privately to the *Indies*," a phrase with ambiguous meaning. It can, of course, simply suggest the need to leave secretly, due to debt or scandal. "Privately" might also connote the mercenary nature of his venture, a move to preserve only his own private—rather than public or civic—interests, or suggest perhaps sailing without the protection of the British Navy. "Providence" grammatically controls the action of the sentence: "Providence again *grew* favorable . . . and . . . *restored* him to his Fortunes." While Sealand's "Industry" is noted, just as Sealand is the object of Providence's bounty, so too the real industry is of course displaced upon those actually laboring on his plantation. That passive construction renders him object rather than subject, and continues in his own self-narration where he details how "Misfortunes drove me to the *Indies*." (Like Steele himself, Sealand does not assume responsibility for his own failures.) Although an owner within the oppressive system, Sealand fashions himself as the one largely buffeted by economic forces beyond his control, as another individual trapped in the culture of captivity. Yet, for a 1722 audience member, there would be no doubt that Sealand's wealth derives from the labor of enslaved people. Just as Steele offers no judgment of Inkle—nor of course of someone like Codrington—so too Sealand's role remains unremarked upon.

Locating Sealand in Barbados, the site of Steele's own plantation, further complicates Steele's characterization of the "*third* gentry." Accounts of Barbados plantations from the period detail the notoriously harsh conditions for both enslaved Africans and white indentured servants. In *A True and Exact History of the Island of Barbados,* Richard Ligon characterizes both groups strictly as "commodities": "The Commodities these Ships bring to this Island, are *Servants* and *Slaves*, both men and women."[99] Ligon's detailed account of the island suggests that because "the slaves and their posterity" represent a greater long-term financial investment, "being subject to their Masters for ever," they are "kept and preserv'd with greater care than the servants" whose owners hold "but for five years, according to the law of the land."[100] Ligon asserts that "the servants have the worser lives, for they are put to very hard labour, ill lodging, and their dyet very sleight." Hilary Beckles describes Barbados as the "worst poor man country" in the British Atlantic.[101] For the poor, the marginalized, or those deemed "criminal," transportation by choice or by force was a regular occurrence throughout the century. Indeed there was a persistent slippage between slavery and servitude in the British imagination where, as Roxann Wheeler notes, there was a "tendency to see British labor through the lens of slavery."[102] Thus the specter of transportation hangs over the play, implicitly a possible fate for Indiana (or perhaps some audience member?) and, more troublingly, an established mechanism for obtaining unfree labor and removing "undesirable" people from British soil.

The play also foregrounds the better treatment domestic servants receive in England as opposed to the treatment of those in the colonies or during an indistinct past. Steele carefully delineates between the treatment Sir John and Bevil's servants receive and the current norm, presenting the two men as enlightened and benevolent employers. Sir John's servant Humphrey notes that he has passed forty years in service "without much . . . Labour" (I.i.8), attending Sir John who claims to regard him "more like a humble Friend than a Servant" (I.i.19–20). Similarly, Tom notes that his "Master" Bevil "scorns to strike his Servants" (I.i.138), situating corporal punishment of servants as something existing only in the past; Tom goes on to assert "my Master is my Friend" (I.i.239–40).[103] This treatment is consistent with the construction of British masculinity among the elite, a group, Steele suggests, possessing a demonstrated capacity for sentiment and exercising a benevolent form of mastery. Yet, this characteristic of benevolent mastery does not extend beyond British servants on domestic soil, nor is it applied to Mr. Sealand. That absence, in light of Steele's familiarity with Ligon and the treatment of enslaved people in Barbados, might suggest that Bevil's benign mastery could translate from a domestic to a colonial setting, but the play does not mix those categories. The text, as if by design, elides any discussion of the treatment of enslaved people despite their indisputable (absent) presence as the source of the financial underpinnings of the text.

Ligon, Women, and *The Conscious Lovers*

The Conscious Lovers' connection with Richard Ligon's *History of Barbados* becomes explicit in its treatment of the text's marriageable women. The circumscribed role for a woman, and her institutionalized lack of control over her own sexuality, defines conversations about Mr. Sealand's other daughter Lucinda, who experiences another kind of domestic confinement with the prospect of a forced marriage to either Bevil or the foolish aristocrat

Cimberton. Despite Indiana's imperiled state that is the centerpiece of the play's dramatic action, in many ways Lucinda is actually the female character most tightly confined by the expectations of gender for a woman of her class. Her servant Phillis complains that neither Myrtle or Bevil will "Attempt to set her at Liberty" and she recognizes Lucinda's state of captivity (IV.iii.23–25), perhaps because of her own status as a female domestic servant, a group always at risk for various kinds of violence.[104] Phillis, who marries Bevil's servant Tom by play's end, remains vulnerable to the unwanted attentions of the rakish Myrtle (even though he claims he "cannot live" without Lucinda [IV.iii.71]). The stage direction explicitly details their exchange. Myrtle "*Catches and kisses* [Phillis], *and gives her Money*" (365). This casual assault conforms to Steele's "comic" subplot, yet it displaces sexuality and potential violence onto the lower classes, and reveals the accepted indifference to the sexual vulnerability of female servants. However, Phillis's response bears note: "O Fie! my Kisses are not my own; you have committed Violence; but I'll carry 'em to the right Owner. (Tom *kisses her*)" (IV.iii.64–65). The "Violence" referenced—anticipating perhaps the kinds of "amorous violence" to which women in domestic service were routinely subject, as Eliza Haywood reminds us—refers to something very real.[105] Phillis does not possess or "own" her body, and her rapid movement from Myrtle to Tom reinforces that condition. Phillis and Tom's physical, broadly comic relationship stands in stark contrast to the dramatic saga of Indiana and Bevil. Nevertheless, this scene's placement immediately before act V, where Indiana reunites with a father who promptly gives her to Bevil, anticipates, in a different register, the adjacent powerlessness of Indiana and Lucinda whose body, kisses, and wealth are also not their own.

Lucinda's mother similarly seeks to exert complete control over the circulation of her daughter's body and financial resources. Mrs. Sealand wants Lucinda to marry Cimberton to satisfy her own interest in finding "a Means, to keep the Blood as pure, and as regularly descended as may be" (III.215–16). Steele's manuscript memorandum on *The Conscious Lovers* describes Mrs. Sealand as "rejoicing in her own high Blood, Dispising her husbands Pedigree, and Effecting to Marry her Daughter to a Relation of her Own, to take of [off] the Stain of the lowe Birth of her husbands Side."[106] Her position as the wife of a man financially benefitting from the slave trade perhaps has intensified her preexisting sensitivity to the "blood" of her progeny. Sealand actually shares this preoccupation with breeding, although it is differently directed. In his first exchange with Sir John, Seal-and describes the two men as members of "projecting Races" (IV.ii.64). They are men who anticipate the future and seek to fashion a new breed of men to meet it, and Sealand specifically thinks in terms of "Races."

The same language of breeding appears throughout Ligon's *A True and Exact History of the Island of Barbados*. Although he was impoverished, Ligon, using the first-person inclusive pronoun, narratively allies himself with plantation owners when he details their desire for strong genetics: "We breed both Negroes, Horses, and Cattle" in an effort to "supply the moderate decayes which we finde in all those."[107] A shortage of any such "stock" threatens the estate. Lucinda's proposed fiancé Cimberton similarly seeks to breed in order to avoid any "decay" in his stock. He admits "I Marry to have an Heir to my Estate" (III.308) but he claims he does not want "to beget a Colony, or a Plantation" (III.309). The explicit sites for breeding—colonial plantation and domestic estate—places them on a continuum and structurally figures their inhabitants, whether English subject or enslaved African, as analogous. Cimberton's domestic estate adopts the model of a colonial plantation, a model that raises further questions about his behavior within the family unit. Cimberton notes the need for a kind of personal economy and self-restraint, recognizing he "must depend upon my own Reflection, and Philosophy, not to overstock my Family" (III.320–22). Children, like livestock, constitute another commodity, another resource to be domesticated or husbanded. Nevertheless, Cimberton admits that "pregnant undoubtedly she will be yearly. I fear, I shan't, for many Years, have Discretion enough to give her one fallow Season" (III.290–92). Like land to be tilled, Lucinda will rarely lie uncultivated.

Mrs. Sealand and Cimberton's ensuing discussion of Lucinda's desirability, like her own commentary upon their conversation, echoes Ligon's description of the process of purchasing the enslaved Africans. Just as planters "choose them [enslaved Africans] as they do Horses in a Market," so too Lucinda believes she has been "survey'd like a Steed at Sale" (III.294), "barter'd for, like the Beasts of the Field . . . but for encrease of Fortune" (III.183–86).[108] Bevil, although speaking hypothetically, not of Indiana directly, notes that the "great Expense" he has paid to support her is less than that "Men lay out upon an unnecessary Stable of Horses" (II.iii.134–35). Myrtle anticipates that Cimberton "will examine the Limbs of his Mistress with the Caution of a Jockey," treating her as "if she were a meer breeding Animal" (II.i.46–48). Indeed, Cimberton admits he considers her "but as one that is to be pregnant" (III.288).

Plantation owners' emphasis on the breeding capacity among enslaved Africans, notes Ligon, means that "the strongest, youthfullest, and most beautiful, yield the greatest prices."[109] Ligon offers sustained descriptions of "the shapes of these people," paying particular attention to the "ordinarily very large breasts . . . [of] The Young Maides."[110] Consequently, Ligon notes, when "Planters buy them out of the Ship . . . they find them stark naked, and therefore cannot be deceived in any outward infirmity."[111] Lucinda feels she too has been "expos'd, and offer'd," subject to scrutiny of her physical characteristics (III.174). Finding Lucinda "very well limb'd" (III.295–96), Cimberton atomizes her with a particular focus on her breeding characteristics: the "Pant of her Bosom" (III.268), "Her forward Chest" (III.270), and "her Arms—her Neck" (III.277). He even praises the "Elasticity in her Veins and Arteries!" (III.281). Lucinda herself compartmentalizes her experience, asserting that while one may "have this Body of mine," without her affection, it "is nothing" (III.154–55). Cimberton's assertion of privilege and the perpetuation of his patrilineal line mimics the common approach of plantation owners to the sexuality of enslaved women. Their "reproductive potential," notes Marisa Fuentes, "placed their bodies in a position to reproduce the future of slavery and the white wealth this created."[112] Of course Lucinda's life of white, European privilege is at a far remove from the enslaved women of color Fuentes describes. The text does not directly represent Black domestic captivity in a colonial site. Rather, Lucinda becomes a kind of narrative surrogate for that experience. Nevertheless Cimberton, linking reproductive capacity and economics, situates her in a subjected and sexualized position (one that uncomfortably echoes Inkle's financial gain with Yarico's pregnancy). The play's language elides racial difference. Lucinda cannot be literally sold into slavery like Yarico, nevertheless structurally the two situations align: Cimberton's desire for financial gain through breeding, the elimination of Lucinda's agency, and her legal invisibility once a married woman. Although the exchange between Cimberton and Lucinda is often regarded as just another "comic subplot" of the play, it reiterates the text's larger message of exploitation. Much like the "comic subplot" of Southerne's Oroonoko in which the Welldon sisters seek husbands, this narrative thread amplifies and reinforces the text's representation of human commodification, exploitation, and exchange.

Lucinda and Indiana, both betrothed at the end of the play, enter into confining institutional relationships that legally eliminate their personhood. While the two women are obviously never subject to anything comparable to racially based enslavement, they manifest what Moira Ferguson observes as the striking "analogies between female subalternity and the state of colonial slavery."[113] (The same culturally pervasive dynamic discussed in chapter 1.) Indiana's excessive self-abnegation—"All the rest of my life is but waiting till he comes. I live only when I'm with him"—remains completely consistent with the constructed ideology of female passivity, dependence, and restraint. The language associated with marriage similarly reiterates its perpetual condition and pointedly echoes the language of servitude: "If he takes me for ever, my purpose of Life is only to please him," asserts Indiana (II.ii.75–76). When he embraces her at the end of act V, pronouncing her his "ever-destin'd . . . acknowledg'd Wife," she identifies him as "my Lord! My Master!" (V.iii.224–25), the last words Indiana utters in the play—words allied with the power relationships to which enslaved people are subject. With Steele's text, these words are to be understood as not just normative, but positive.

At the beginning of the play, Sir John discusses with his servant Humphrey the behavior of his son Bevil. Acknowledging the "Freedom" with which he has lived "in some part of my Life" (with impunity and "without Reproach"), Sir John wants his son to also live with "Liberty" (I.i.28–30). Thus he "indulged him in living after his own manner," knowing it "wou'd be . . . little injurious to my Son" (I.i.30–31). He casts this gesture as a means to "judge of [Bevil's] Inclination" (I.i.32). The "liberty" and "freedom" to which Sir John refers have nothing to do with a release from bondage or independence from a state power. Rather, the terms here refer purely to the condition of being able to act without hindrance, of having the power to do as one likes. It bespeaks privilege predicated on class, gender, and, most obviously, race. Freedom, tellingly, can also connote acting with a certain frankness or familiarity, often in conversation. The language of "freedom" and "liberty" points to a tradition of libertine behavior as historically represented on stage and practiced by men of Sir John's class and predisposition. Although that behavior is located in the past it is not marked as outmoded. Sir John presents this bald assertion of power and privilege as innocuous; a means of determining one's authentic "inclinations," even within in a play that ostensibly asserts the supremacy of morality, virtue, and sentiment. The displacement of the libertine behavior onto Bevil's servant Tom does not trouble the text's putative morality. Tom rakishly pursues Lucinda's maid Phillis, but because Phillis's virtue has limited social value (aside from a pragmatic desire that she avoid pregnancy), even Tom can pursue "freedom" relatively "without reproach."

Sir John essentially endorses his son Bevil's "freedom" because, as he asks, "what can be concluded from a Behaviour under Restraint and Fear?" (I.i.33–34). While "restraint" can mean a sense of self-control or self-restraint, in this context it most certainly encompasses those meanings of restraint associated with confinement, deprivation, or restriction (as the grammatical formation "under restraint" connotes). "Restraint" can mean not just the act of limiting someone's behavior—such as a father might do a son—but the very physical mechanism or device by which one is restrained, like the chains to which Indiana alludes in act V. Fear, like restraint, governs the actions of Indiana, who, as a lovesick maid, remains "afraid" "to speak, till spoken to."[114] The restraint and subsequent fear reside primarily in anticipated financial consequences of inappropriate behavior, a common condition for almost any disempowered person.

Although Sir John's comment stems from concerns that Bevil, bound by duty, cannot speak truthfully to him as his father, that question, only thirty lines into the play, captures a dynamic that shapes essentially all the relationships Steele presents. Restraint and fear, obscured by the generic force of sentimental comedy, fundamentally determine the actions and decisions of all but the most empowered within this text. The differences between slavery, marriage, and indentured servitude are of course vast. Yet, especially for women, they exist on a continuum in which male "freedom" or "liberty" generates power that can be strategically used. Sealand ultimately obscures that real delineation of power, however, when he suggests to Sir John that Bevil has become "enslav'd" by Indiana, noting that "Very wise Men have been so enslav'd" (IV.ii.82). This (common) metaphor for romantic love advances the idea that (at least until marriage) power lies with the woman. It marks not only how casually metaphors of enslavement were deployed, but how easily the language inheres in a text that normalizes asymmetrical power relationships, sentimentalizes captivity, and displaces the central economic engine of the text, that is, institutionalized enslavement. Like all the tears and emoting attached to the financially empowered men, the metaphor also obscures the real power dynamic the play advances. *The Conscious Lovers*, ostensibly a text of sentiment, draws upon the largely invisible world of enslavement, brutality, and oppression to create one of the most popular plays of the eighteenth century.

The next chapter explores an author who performs a similar sleight of hand within a tremendously popular genre. Penelope Aubin uses tales of Barbary captivity to simultaneously obscure and highlight the dangers confronted by women daily within a domestic culture of captivity.

· CHAPTER 4 ·

Barbary Captivity

Penelope Aubin and The Noble Slaves

The previous chapter showed how Richard Steele used the generic weight of sentimental comedy to obscure the darker forces of enslavement, confinement, and control that shape human interactions within *The Conscious Lovers* and, arguably, much of eighteenth-century England as a whole. Steele presents a world of subjugation with the language of sentiment. The apparent generosity of characters like Sealand and Bevil serves to mask the dehumanization inherent in the financial model and imperial gains the play celebrates. That *The Conscious Lovers* was among the century's most successful plays affirms the cultural work the text performed, and bespeaks a desire to segregate the "benevolent" uses of West Indian wealth from the violence and oppression fundamental to it. The elaborate display of sentiment, directed to imagined domestic rather than actual colonial suffering, further avoids the anguish of enslavement and the experience of the kidnapped African subject.

Like Steele, Penelope Aubin enjoyed commercial success as an author, although in a distinctly different genre. And, like Steele, Aubin was writing in a decade in which British social norms and attitudes toward unfree labor were profoundly shaped by the centrality of the slave trade as an economic driver, the increasing use of transportation as a punishment for those deemed "criminal," and the state's commitment to colonial expansion. Certainly, as discussed below, Aubin explicitly draws on these elements within her fiction. Her characters' wealth, global movement, and domestic operations repeatedly depend upon the labor of or profit from enslaved people. However, Aubin focuses even more closely on another kind of captivity that also resulted from increased global trade and mobility—Barbary captivity or the confinement of abducted Europeans by North African corsairs. Within a period between October 1, 1721 and July 23, 1723, Aubin published three successive novels that foreground Barbary captivity. Aubin tapped into a persistent anxiety about, and, frankly, fascination with, the capture and enslavement of English subjects, particularly women. This experience of captivity figures centrally in her fiction as she, like many of her contemporaries, dramatically details the captivity of European subjects held in North Africa for an eager reading public.

Yet Barbary captivity itself is not Aubin's real focus, however marketable it proved to be. Rather, Aubin strategically uses fictional narratives of Barbary captivity as a vehicle to advance her more immediate concern: women's persistent confinement within a restrictive European patriarchal order. Aubin makes a sustained and ultimately subversive critique of the domestic captivity of women under a system of legal, economic, and sexual oppression, a condition familiar to her female readers. The culturally accepted patriarchal assumptions about power, force, and privilege that structurally fuel the global colonial enterprise and the transatlantic slave trade have domestic manifestations that foundationally shape the experience of European women. When held in Barbary captivity eighteenth-century European women experienced a "loss of freedom of action" within a "climate of coercive violence," qualities that equally defined their "non-captive" existence.[1] Legally denied personhood, women already lack in a domestic setting those things apparently stripped from them in a condition of captivity abroad. For Aubin's fictional female subjects, being held in Barbary captivity reproduces foundational elements of their condition of domestic disempowerment; that context (for both Aubin's reader and her fictional subjects) newly reveals to them the constraints in which they live when "free." Aubin, with her savvy knowledge of business, empire, and popular culture, keenly understood the potential risks to women in a world that afforded them little authorized power, less financial autonomy, and essentially no legal status.

In truth, comparatively few women would actually be held in Barbary captivity.[2] But every eighteenth-century woman lived within a restrictive gender hierarchy (and many, as the previous chapters suggest, observed the horrific effects of enslavement). Aubin's narratives may suggest pockets of autonomy within or provide avenues for escape from Barbary captivity;

they also demonstrate how no such options exist within domestic captivity. More importantly, within Aubin's fiction, the loss of freedom, the coercive violence, and the lack of agency women suffer explicitly and repeatedly come at the hands of *European*, not Barbary, captors (often the same men implicated in the transatlantic slave trade). It is not the Barbary corsair or the Muslim sultan who threatens women. Rather, it is the husband, the father, or the lover; it is the social customs limiting marriage between disparate classes; it is the restrictive construction of gender that silences women and affirms male privilege; it is the nonconsensual sexual encounters and condoned libertinism; and it is the inheritance laws that limit women's right to property. Women confront male aggression, passion, and violence in their own homes. Domestic relationships, not Barbary captivity, are the most onerous and dangerous form of confinement Aubin's characters endure. Consequently, the women in Aubin's fictional world, like many women in England, rarely escape a culture of captivity.

This narrative strategy—using Barbary captivity to advance the real object of her critique—appears throughout Aubin's 1720s fiction, but her 1722 novel *The Noble Slaves*, popular, widely read, and reprinted six times in the century, provides perhaps the most vivid example.[3] In *The Noble Slaves*, women are abducted, pursued, drugged, trepanned, imprisoned, seduced, coerced, captured, sold, traded, silenced, raped, exploited, and chained. Almost without exception, these actions are either performed or precipitated by European men. Her fictional women are, like those in Behn's *The Emperor of the Moon*, doubly subject—restrained when held by Barbary masters and, when liberated, captive again in the strictures of a patriarchal-imperial culture. Certainly, as Aubin recounts and this chapter details, men held in Barbary captivity confront their own unique challenges. But in Aubin's representations, generally male privilege translates as readily across cultures as women's persistent state of captivity. This chapter first explores Barbary captivity, Aubin's unusual knowledge of it, and the compelling reasons for its appearance in her narratives. The chapter then closely examines how *The Noble Slaves*, through a complex series of interpolated narratives, powerfully represents the persistent challenges to women's autonomy, safety, and personal freedom.

"The General Subject of Discourse"

Just months before Penelope Aubin (1697–1738) published *The Life and Amorous Adventures of Lucinda* (1721), her first novel touching directly on Barbary captivity, five London newspapers the week of March 26, 1720, featured a letter from the "Administrator for the Redemption of the Captives at Algiers" to the "Commander" of the Trinitarian Order "for the same Purpose at Cartagena."[4] The widely published missive recounts the harrowing story of "The Lady Bourk." The daughter of "the Marquis de Varennes, Lieut. General in the French King's Army" and the wife of Sir Toby Bourk, "an Irish Gentleman, formerly Envoy Extraordinary of the King of Spain to the late King of Sweden,"[5] Lady Bourk, traveling by ship from her native France to Spain with her two children and retinue, was "driven by a Storm upon the Coast of Barbary."

"Barbary" comprised three provinces on the north coast of Africa—Algiers, Tunisia, and Tripoli—each governed by a pasha or bey and all part of the Ottoman Empire.[6] For a 1720 reader, however, the term served as a familiar if inaccurate shorthand for essentially the whole of North Africa, including Morocco. The Barbary States become what Nabil Matar describes as "a defining region" within the British imagination.[7] Amplified by the etymological slippage with "barbarous" or "barbaric," the very word "Barbary" summoned distinct and powerful associations with pirates, peril, and, particularly, captivity.[8] The highly organized, state-funded raids or abductions by Barbary pirates or corsairs provided a sponsoring entity (governor, official, local leader) with a reliable funding stream. Whether stripping wrecked ships, accosting travelers in transit, or raiding Mediterranean settlements, the corsairs operated not as random, renegade actors but often as part of a concerted state effort. The goods obtained from a ship and its passengers, coupled with the revenue generated by ransoms, protection money, or the acquisition of what Matar terms "human commodities," provided lucrative resources for the sponsoring countries.[9]

Shipwrecked upon Barbary's treacherous coast, Lady Bourk and her eight-year-old son who threw "himself into his mother's arms" were immediately killed "by the Moors of Cuco." "A Spanish woman who waited on her" and "three other Domestics" met the same fate and "[a]ll the Ship's crew were either drowned or made Slaves." Among the newly enslaved were Lady Bourk's nine-year-old daughter, a priest described as "her relation," and two other servants who were "Stript . . . of all they had," which "yielded some thousands of Crowns." Captors commonly took the clothes and belongings (what the letter terms "Booty") of their conquests to further increase their potential profit.

Once stripped and bound, the captured would typically be paraded before the port population of their captors for public viewing. Residents, "along with the officials who had financed the privateers," would come out to inspect the captives, before they were led to one of the local leaders who was often also "the chief share-holder in all privateering ventures."[10] Those not chosen to be enslaved by the highest-ranking persons moved to "the bagnios, the public bathhouses, which were used as holding pens for captives and slaves."[11] The survivors of the Bourk party were delivered "stark naked" to a "Priest of Barbary" to await sale, transport, or ransoming.

At this point, however, the young Miss Bourk, "who hath more Wit and Good Sense, then is allowed to Persons of so Tender an Age," acts independently and secures the group's freedom. Fluent "both in French and Spanish," the young girl "wrote with her own Hand an Account of the Misfortune which had befallen them."[12] She composes the document "at a time when there were Fathers of our Order [Trinitarians] for the Redemption in the Country." Such "Redemptive Orders" played an important part in the freeing of captives. Redemptive practices differed widely by country in part because of a fundamental ambiguity about who bore responsibility for generating the necessary ransoms. Captives often made direct appeals to family members or churches, but a large number of those held were poor men serving on ships, men of unremarkable status with no one able or willing to pay for their release. England was notoriously stingy in its redemption practices (in fact, Charles II famously diverted funds allocated for ransoming captives for his own use).[13] In the face of inconsistent state commitment to pay ransoms for captives, two religious orders—the Mercedarians and the Trinitarians—had, since the thirteen century, dedicated themselves to securing the "redemption" of Barbary captives from Catholic countries.[14] These two religious orders organized fundraising among citizens, pursued the release or "redemption" of the captives, and generally focused on administrative details of ransoming. They also, of course, addressed the captives' spiritual redemption when necessary.

Reading the young Miss Bourk's letter (which is never shared with the London audience),[15] a member of the order recognized her as a daughter of privilege. Her bilingual literacy immediately alerted the European "Re-deemers" to her considerable worth. However, clothed in only "a sack, like the Moors upon the Mountains," the "distinction" of Lady Bourk's daugh-ter remained invisible to her captors, enabling her redeemer to secure her ransom "for little more than eight hundred Pieces of Eight, which in any other Place would have cost above ten thousand." The author of the let-ter attributes this low ransom price to the inability of the "brutish" Moors "to know any Distinction of Persons." Miss Bourk's captors and redeemers operate within different cultural economies, making her value legible only within a Eurocentric context. However, the young Miss Bourk's capacity to construct an "Account of the Misfortune" "with her own Hand" elevates her beyond the four people with whom she is traveling (including the priest) and essentially ensures her salvation. Her narrative transforms her from a "stark naked" body to a written text. After this extraordinary experience, the young girl returns to Europe and, perhaps, a more routine continua-tion of her life story. The newspaper account concludes: "N.B. Miss Bourk is since arrived in Marseilles, with Monsieur Dussuant, Envoy of France; when she is set out for Spain, to go to her Relations." She returns to a family structure and social network, presumably for reintegration into a more conventional path for a young girl of her rank.[16]

The published letter recounting the events, like the ordeal of Miss Bourk itself, sounds fantastic, even novelistic. A plucky young girl shorn of familial protection, imperiled by external forces, uses her literacy and rhetorical skills to write a compelling narrative that secures her release.[17] The account of events, with excessive language describing her confinement, reads as incredible, a fictional construction rather than an experience based in a historical reality. Yet, as Daniel Vitkus notes, "piracy, slavery, and forced labour were business-as-usual in the Mediterranean and Atlantic mari-time world."[18] While Miss Bourk's redeemer may have been embellishing his published letter for a London audience eager for graphic details, the experience recounted—Barbary captivity—remained a persistent and not unfounded concern for those traveling by sea. Daniel Defoe saw the fear as widespread. "[A] Sailor . . . in a Merchant Ship," writes Defoe, can't help but feel "some secret Tremor," "horror," or "a little panick fear upon his Spir-its" that "sometime or other it may be his lot" to be carried to "the Coast of *Algier,* or *Tunis,*" and "sold for a Slave."[19] Further, incursions of Barbary corsairs both into Mediterranean settlements and onto English soil, with stories of captives taken from England, Wales, or Ireland, seemed cause for alarm. "Not an Inhabitant on the Coast of *Spain* or *Italy*, no not from *Gibraltar* to the City of *Venice*," continues Defoe, escapes the "constant apprehensions of being surpriz'd in their Beds" and taken captive.[20] For British and Irish subjects, "the fear of Barbary was very real," asserts Linda Colley, initiating what she terms a "captivity panic"[21] or what Matar describes as "social anxiety about captivity"[22]—an anxiety a writer like Aubin exploited to great effect.[23]

The number of European captives in North Africa bears out the causes for concern. Robert Davis posits that between 1530 and 1780 "there were almost certainly a million and quite possibly as many as a million and a quarter white, European Christians enslaved by the Muslims of the Barbary Coast."[24] Even these numbers, suggests Matar, underreport the actual incidence of European enslavement.[25] (Matar also reminds us that North Africans in turn were also captured and enslaved, a largely underreported practice.) Included in these calculations are the estimated 20,000 Britons enslaved by Barbary corsairs between 1660 and the 1730s. During that same period the number of captives redeemed by the British government likely represents "only a portion of the total number of English captives held."[26] Miss Bourk's narrative points to the random, often indiscriminate nature of Barbary captivity. Statistically, more men than women were seized simply because men comprised the bulk of maritime travelers and laborers; the overwhelming majority of women taken into Barbary captivity were taken in land raids. Yet ships bearing the wealthy or influential remained high-value targets and female captives were quite desirable, if rarer.[27] Part of the cultural anxiety lay in the fact that Barbary captivity could randomly affect almost anyone traveling by sea—the wealthy and well-connected were not immune. Just as the number of captives is incalculable, so too the actual duration of an individual's captivity remains largely unrecoverable, as Colley notes. Illustrating Britons' vulnerability to shipwreck, piracy, or capture, the Bourk narrative presented a 1720s reader with a vivid description of the dangers of sea travel and potential encounters with Barbary corsairs.

If London readers wanted to read tales of capture, they also desired narratives of release. Less than two years after Bourk's experience, 280 unnamed male British subjects returned to London having been redeemed by King George I. *Applebee's Original Weekly* of Tuesday, December 9, 1721, details how the hundreds of "English Captives march'd in their Moorish

Habits . . . thro' a great Part of this City to the Cathedral of St. Paul's."[28] In an ironic inversion of the parade before Barbary officials that would have marked the men's initial step into captivity, the "English Captives" now process before British officials and a London throng eager to celebrate their liberty. After listening to the subsequently published sermon by William Berriman (1688–1750) rejoicing in their return from the "various Miseries of such a Captive State,"[29] the "Captives" went to St. James's Palace "to return Thanks to his Majesty, for interposing on their Behalf." The movement of the "English Captives" through London attracted so "vast" a "Multitude of People that crowded to see them" that "they were forc'd to divide themselves into several Companies, and to take different Ways thither."[30] Unlike Miss Bourk, these "English Captives" are as nameless and indistinct as the "multitude" that watches them. In their apparent liberation, they also illustrate the complicated situations to which many return—a situation invoked by the very term "English Captive," which anticipates the oxymoronic "freed slaves" subsequently used by Mary Barber (as discussed in chapter 1). When returned to domestic soil, the "English Captives" confront a rigid English social structure, few opportunities for employment, and a world without a social safety net; they are captive to the limitations of the culture in which they live, the culture to which they are returned.

The fascination that drove Londoners into the streets to see the returning captives also shaped their reading habits. As the *St. James's Post* of December 11–13, 1720 notes, the "Redemption of the Slaves" from Morocco has "occasion'd that Kingdom to be the general Subject of Discourse." Like many of her contemporaries, the market-savvy Aubin recognized that anything that became "the general Subject of Discourse" could be used to increase the appeal of her novels within that same, relatively compressed window of time.[31] Tales of fictional characters held in Barbary captivity appeared regularly in fiction of the period. Defoe's *Robinson Crusoe* (1719), Eliza Haywood's *Idalia; or, The Unfortunate Mistress* (1723), and *Philadore and Plancentia* (1727) all contain details about treatment at the hands of Barbary captives. *A Select Collection of Novels in Four Volumes* (1720) includes three novels, each of which draws specifically and explicitly on the fascination with North Africa. William Rufus Chetwood's novel *The Voyages and Adventures of Captain Robert Boyle* (1726) recounts the Barbary captivity of Robert Boyle, "son of the owner of a merchant ship that traded to the West Indies"; the novel tells of the captivity of a man whose business is the captivity of others. The text also includes a particularly harrowing embedded narrative of an English woman similarly held who, like Boyle, is centrally implicated in the trade in enslaved Africans.[32]

Like Chetwood, Haywood, and Defoe, Aubin knew the value of Barbary captivity in marketing her novel, and she specifically highlights *The Noble Slaves'* connection to Barbary captivity with her mention at the end of the novel of the "return [of] . . . a great number of Christian Slaves,"[33] referencing the 280 English captives redeemed in December 1721. The public attention ("The whole City rang of this Strange Story" [178]) offered a specific, relevant, and saleable dimension to her fictional narratives. And, without a doubt, Aubin's primary motivation was to sell books. "If this Trifle sells," wrote Aubin in the preface to her first novel *The Strange Adventures of the Count de Vinevil and His Family* (1721), "I conclude it takes, and you may be sure to hear from me again; so you may be innocently diverted, and I employ'd to my Satisfaction."[34] Aubin's commercial focus persisted. In the preface to *The Life of Charlotta Du Pont* (1723), Aubin claims to fulfill her promise "to continue writing if you dealt favourably with me. My booksellers say, my Novels sell tolerably well."[35] With her fifth novel, she pointed to her ability "to entertain the Publick, and not with ill success; which has encouraged me to proceed."[36] Tellingly, she consistently positions her fictional texts as if in competition with the accounts of current events, insisting that her novels "might agreeably entertain you at the time when our News-Papers furnish nothing of moment" (*Charlotta Du Pont*, v). Fiction, claims Aubin, can improve on journalism and provide more engaging information.

Although Aubin clearly perceived a market advantage in focusing on North African captivity, she also possessed unique insights into the perils of maritime travel as well as the horrors of the slave trade, two factors that also shape the focus of her fiction. Her merchant husband, Abraham Aubin, one of twelve children, had two seafaring brothers who between them experienced piracy, shipwrecks, hurricanes, slave rebellions, and global maritime travel. Elements of Aubin's fiction often dismissed as utterly fantastic actually emerge from the experiences of men she knew personally. As Aubin remarks in the preface to *The Adventures of Count Vinevil*, "I know no reason why this [text] should thought a Fiction."[37] In command of naval ships and merchant vessels, her brother-in-law David Aubin witnessed and participated in commercial activities advancing British imperial interests in the West Indies specifically and the British Atlantic generally. His own personal financial interests rested in the "Sugar Islands." After his naval career, David Aubin later lived in Barbados and, as Debbie Welham—who has deeply researched the Aubin family—notes, "received patents for irrigation and sugar refining there," squarely implicating him in the economic infrastructure of a slave-based economy.[38]

David Aubin's maritime career was also fodder for Aubin's fiction. In a June 1720 letter to Aubin's husband, David Aubin vividly detailed his experience of being captured by pirates in the West Indies. Recounting the two-hour fight against the fifty men who boarded his ship, David Aubin describes how "the Enemy Came in Furiously with their lances and Cutlasses, and fell a Cutting me and my Poeple [sic] in a Most Barbarous Manner."[39] "Stripped and Beaten most unmersifully," Aubin and his men "kild 13 of the Privateers Or, Rather the Pirats Men, and Wounded about 18 or 20 More of which several are since Dead." Such details appear almost seamlessly in Aubin's *Life of Charlotta Du Pont, an English Lady, Taken from Her Own Memoirs,* and they clearly color descriptions in *The Noble Slaves* as well.

Another of Aubin's brothers-in-law, Phillip Aubin, served initially on ships in the Royal Navy and then exclusively on slaving ships. As Welham details, he served aboard the *Ormond* "operating between the Bight of Benin and Antigua" as well as other slaving ships operating in the Gulf of Guinea, and he ultimately captained the *Crocodile,* "a ship involved in several known slaving journeys, to and from Jamaica."[40] His survival of a hurricane-caused shipwreck off the coast of West Africa appears in David Aubin's letter: "I am informed the Brother Phill has bin Cast away on the Coast of Guiny," writes David, "& is since gon Mate of a French Ship to Petiguaves on Hispaynola [Petit-Goâve, on the coast of what is now Haiti]." Welham posits that Aubin's brother-in-law may also be the "Phillip Aubin" who served on the *Ferrers,* a ship that experienced a particularly violent rebellion of the enslaved people on board.

The involvement of both of her brothers-in-law in slaving voyages likely gave Aubin a more than rudimentary understanding of trade in the British Atlantic; she may, in fact, have understood the implications with some detail. The frequency with which enslaved Africans appear in her fiction certainly suggests she had naturalized slavery within her cultural and fictional landscape. Some critics, such as Eve Tavor Bannet, assert that frequent representations of enslaved Africans in *The Noble Slaves* mark Aubin's "clear argument for abolition."[41] While I agree that, as Bannet notes, Aubin knew "people of all nations were being enslaved," Aubin remains largely uncritical of the enslavement of Africans or indigenous peoples in her books. She focuses on individual instances of enslavement rather than offering broadly based opinions, provides limited narrative detail about non-European characters, and generally withholds commentary on the larger economic or institutional structures perpetuating institutionalized enslavement. Despite the pivotal role of people of color in her texts, her narratives erase their humanity.

Beyond information gleaned from her brothers-in-law, Aubin possessed firsthand knowledge of the financial stakes of shipping activities in the Caribbean and was a businesswoman in her own right. For example, in 1702 she advised Thomas Fairfax, fifth Baron Fairfax of Cameron, and Richard Savage, fourth Earl Rivers, in a salvaging expedition to the Caribbean.[42] Further, Aubin's husband, a captain in the French army, was frequently absent prior to his 1712 retirement from the military. As a result, Aubin assumed responsibility for parts of his business, playing an active role within the larger web of financial and familial relationships. (Frederick Burwick and Manushag Powell call her a "she-merchant.")[43] While Aubin, like Judith Madan with her similarly absent husband, might have keenly felt the difference between authority and responsibility, burdened with the latter but gaining precious little of the former, she seems to have acted independently with some ease.

Within the business community, Aubin also developed a reputation for her unique store of information. In 1709 she testified before the Board of Trade about the feasibility of a project to repatriate British pirates living in Madagascar. The board's interest in the pirates was purely financial: the pirates, also known as "Madagascar men," were allegedly holding large amounts of money of which the state sought a percentage. Asked to "organize a petition of wives and dependents of the pirates at Madagascar" to help persuade the men to return to England, Aubin presented as someone tapped into a network of mercantile contacts (authorized and otherwise).[44] Ultimately she refused the invitation to organize and also advised against the repatriation scheme.

The recognized global insights Aubin derived from her brothers-in-law, coupled with her own knowledge and sensitivity to the marketability of Barbary captivity, intensified her focus on the perils and experiences of European women in North Africa. Aubin's focus on Barbary captivity provides her with a point of market differentiation in the competitive 1720s book trade in a number of ways. First, she capitalized on her readers' familiarity with the language of captivity—spiritual captivity. The state of Barbary captivity materially reiterated the metaphorical condition of all Christians as understood in popular discourse. The sermon William Berriman preached and then published celebrating the liberation of the 280 Christian slaves in December 1721 makes explicit the slippage between spiritual and physical captivity. As he writes, "Such then, as we have seen, being the grievous Hardships which attend Captivity; it is not to be wonder'd, that the wretched Corruption of our Nature, should in Scripture be so often represented under this Similitude, and they, in whom it prevails, should be reckon'd *Slaves* to *Sin,* and *Captives* of the *Devil.*"[45] People hearing about the state of the spiritual captives every Sunday, or reading sermons reiterating their condition, came to a fictional text like Aubin's with a predisposition to both understand and accept the ostensibly moralistic narrative she offers. Like Lady Bourk's ordeal, those elements that seem outlandish or fantastic to a contemporary reader would be, to some degree, normalized for a 1722 reader who saw the world through the frame of—and had the ready vocabulary for—spiritual captivity.

Aubin also distinguished her fiction in another way. Despite the sexuality, sensuality, and titillation Aubin includes in her descriptions of women's experiences in North Africa, the popular, unnuanced misunderstanding of Islamic culture offered a rigid (and false) binary between the virtuous, Christian captives and the immoral, "brutish" Muslim captors by whom they are victimized. That tension, widespread in the "general . . . Discourse," advanced the allegedly moralistic aim of Aubin's fiction. The rich history and cultural practice of the Ottoman Empire was flattened by such simplistic or reductive representations more easily presented in the popular press and consumed by readers. This preexisting binary structure enabled Aubin both to disguise her rather more complicated messages about women's domestic captivity, and to obscure her fiction's more subversive and sensationalistic qualities. Aubin's desire to problematize the responsibility for women's captivity—ultimately placing it in the hands and homes of European men, not Barbary captors—can be subsumed or accommodated by the more simplistic albeit more sensational depictions of captivity in North Africa. Her fiction's titillating appeal comes from its newness and the unfamiliarity of its locales.

The same technique applies to the apparently pious tone in Aubin's fiction. Aubin strategically used moralistic language to increase her marketshare, a practice has been recognized by scholars like Chris Mounsey,

Sarah Prescott, and Adam Beach.[46] This moralistic pose, frequently read as completely authentic by early critics, served to distinguish her writing from contemporaries like Eliza Haywood, perceived as a more scandalous writer. The preface to Aubin's posthumous collected works, A Collection of Entertaining Histories and Novels (1739), advances this image of Aubin as a purely pious novelist, claiming on the title page that her novels "promote the author of Virtue and Honor." Similarly, Samuel Richardson's preface to that collection praises the "Purity of Style and Manners" of Aubin's novels.[47] He ensures that "nothing may be contained in them that has the least tendency to pollute or corrupt the inexperienced Minds, for whose Diversion they are intended."[48] The belief that Aubin writes primarily "pious polemic" for "inexperienced minds" stems from a fundamental misapprehension about her textual focus and an underestimation of her abilities as a writer.

Aubin's persistent reputation as a moralizing author erodes further within The Noble Slaves. Divided into eighteen largely independent chapters, the carefully structured text does not demand a linear reading. Rather, each chapter presents a relatively self-contained narrative concerning either a dominant or subordinate character. While the travails of the four main characters continue throughout the entire novel, each chapter still provides a complete story within each embedded narrative. The novel's structure would enable first-generation readers to read selectively or in a nonlinear, episodic fashion as their time and interest allowed. Aubin's message about domestic captivity and the threats to women appear in every chapter, making it a persistent through line to the narrative. The structure also established a pattern of meaning, a strategic repetition, leaving a more powerful impression on the reader than simply the elaborated story of one or two characters would have. The peril, anxiety, and captivity affecting essentially all female characters are woven through all eighteen chapters. By contrast, Aubin's extensive moralizing is not. Most chapters include some language praising the providential nature of God and the importance of virtue, but those sporadic sentiments come from the mouths of characters, not Aubin herself, and then usually only at times of extreme peril. Moralistic commentary from her narrative authorial persona appears infrequently and with limited scope. Aubin also withholds the "moral" of the story until the very last pages of the text and even then it is expressed only in equivocal language. The isolated placement of that ambivalent statement, discussed below, raises questions about its authenticity. As Mounsey observes, "All her claims to piety are couched in ambiguity."[49] He rightly suggests Aubin's paratextual materials have "an ironic edge, which served to fool the gullible into believing the plots were moral"; those "gullible" might include the first-generation reader, or those policing the reading habits of the same.[50] To consider Aubin primarily as a moralistic novelist flattens the complexity of her narrative, reducing it to a vehicle for conformist ideology and a simplistic worldview. Instead, Aubin writes with wit, insight, and a great deal more sophistication than she has previously been given credit for. As the following discussion of *The Noble Slaves* argues, Aubin destabilizes the assumptions about gender, power, and confinement in a highly nuanced and subversive way.

The Noble Slaves: Mark(et)ing Captivity

The very title of Aubin's structurally sophisticated novel signals the centrality of captivity to her narrative. Its oxymoron, with echoes of *Oroonoko's* subtitle "The Royal Slave" or the journalistic descriptor "English captives" for those men redeemed from Barbary captivity the month before the novel's publication, marks the complexity and ambiguity of her fictive world, one filled with liminal spaces, shifting status, and unfamiliar locations. The title page provides a detailed plot summary, one that appears nearly verbatim in advertisements for the novel in London newspapers the last weeks of March 1722, alerting readers to the narrative on which they are about to embark:[51]

> Two LORDS and two LADIES, who were shipwreck'd and cast upon a desolate Island near the *East-Indies,* in the Year 1710. The Manner of their living there: The surprizing Discoveries they Made, and strange Deliverance thence. How in their return to *Europe* they were taken by two *Algerine* Pirates near the Straits of *Gibraltar.* Of the Slavery they endured in *Barbary;* and of their meeting there with several Persons of Quality, who were likewise Slaves. Of their escaping thence, and safe Arrival in their respective Countries, *Venice, Spain,* and *France,* in the Year 1718. With many extraordinary Accidents that befell some of them afterwards.
>
> Being a History full of most remarkable Events.

The description flags numerous marketable elements of the text: the Crusoe-esque "desolate island";[52] the focus on "Lords and Ladies" and

"Persons of Quality"; the appearance of "*Algerine* Pirates." Aubin promises a narrative "full of most remarkable Events." The language of personal trials, near escapes, happy coincidences, and exotic locales also summons the characteristics of romance, certainly an influence on Aubin.

The advertisement's geographic and chronological details (many typographically highlighted with italics) move the description from being merely marketable to being topical. All place names distinctly mark the period's dependence on maritime commerce, enslavement, and imperial expansion. The dangers presented by the "Straits of *Gibraltar*"—the strategic and contested point of entry to the Mediterranean so crucial to commercial interests—were well known and long-standing. France and Spain, like their active economic competitor England, similarly depended upon the labor of the enslaved in their colonial efforts. The "*East-Indies*," an area of increasingly concentrated British activity since the charter of the East India Company in 1600, represented a site of emergent British imperial expansion and colonial enslavement with 15 percent of British imports coming from India by 1720. Venice, controlled by the Ottoman Empire after 1718, serves as a reminder of the impermanence of colonial power, and, of course, the raids by Barbary corsairs and "*Algerine* Pirates."

But if Aubin grounds her title page with specificity and detail, her dedication gestures toward her need to obscure the more subversive aspects of her text when she asks her dedicatee, Lady Colerain, to "skreen" her "from the ill-natured Croud of Criticks" (vi). Although asking protection from critics was a stock rhetorical move in dedications of the period, Aubin's use of the term "skreen" invokes the recent investigation of the 1720 South Sea Company scandal (a company itself rooted in the slave trade), which earned Prime Minister Robert Walpole the sobriquet "The Screen."[53] The South Sea Company was itself a corporation whose business was supplying enslaved people to the Spanish West Indies (although that reason also became obscured when the company assumed the national debt). With this gesture Aubin signals the multiple layers, or the screen, within her own narrative—the story about Barbary captivity screening another, more urgent story about women's domestic captivity. Both stories have as their unspoken landscape the global trade in enslaved Africans. Aubin similarly "screens" her personal aims, claiming her "ambitious Desire" is only to secure "the Happiness" of her "Friend" Colerain. However, with this, her third novel, Aubin clearly harbors ambitions well beyond personal friendship.

The "screening" continues with the first line of the preface: "In our Nation, where the Subjects are born free, where Liberty and Property is so preserv'd to us by Laws, that no Prince can enslave us, the Notion of Slavery is a perfect Stranger" (ix). Because England's "excellent Constitution will always keep us rich and free," Aubin continues, "it must be our own Faults if we are enslav'd, or impoverish'd" (x). Aubin highlights the fundamental ambiguity of British "liberty," distinguishing England as a nation "where the subjects are born free" and "the Notion of Slavery is a perfect Stranger." While institutionalized enslavement of Britons may be a "stranger" to England, certainly the "notion" or concept of slavery is quite familiar given England's significant financial investment in the institution of slavery and the slave trade. By 1722, an increasing portion of the British economy was driven by resources, services, or goods either directly connected to participation in the slave trade or derived from the labor of enslaved people. Aubin's personal connections to individuals intimately engaged in the transportation of the enslaved also makes her claim that England is a "Stranger" to slavery disingenuous.

Further, liberty is a deeply contingent concept that varies according to status and depends upon race, gender, and property ownership.[54] Liberty is not freedom or equality; rather it is primarily the protection of property, as Aubin begins to suggest with her leveling of the two terms. While England may "preserve" property "by Laws" (laws that of course classify enslaved humans as property), those same laws also determine that women do not have access to that most basic form of liberty. Indeed, as discussed in chapter 1, women themselves constitute a form of property within marriage.[55] The significance of this legal disappearance of a married woman lies not simply in her transition to property, but also in the other subordinate legal categories with which that disappearance aligns her. "Blackstone assumes that all propertyless members of a community necessarily exist 'under the immediate dominion of others,'" explains Teresa Michals, quoting Blackstone.[56] Consequently, wives, children, servants, and enslaved people unquestionably fall under the dominion of the male property owner. "The inferior hath no kind of property in the company, care, or assistance of the superior, as the superior is held to have in those of the inferior," writes Blackstone.[57] Thus, the father, the husband, and the master have "liberty," but, as Aubin well knows, it is a form of liberty to which women have no access. That context complicates Aubin's concluding comment that "it must be our own Faults if we are enslav'd, or impoverish'd." The inclusive first-person pronoun "our," while perhaps pointing to British subjects, certainly does not extend to women.

Aubin not only destabilizes the concept of "liberty" in her preface, she also describes her novel's purpose with a fundamental ambiguity. Characterizing "Books of Devotion" as "tedious, and out of Fashion," Aubin states that "Novels and Stories will be welcome" (xii). With "[t]he charming Masquerades being at an end," opera "almost" tiring "our Ears . . . with *Italian* Harmony," and "extravagant Gaming" having "empty'd" our "Pockets . . . of Money," young women, particularly, will "be glad of new Books to amuse" them because "time" hangs "heavy on our Hands" (xii). Aubin's book serves as an antidote to "a time when we have so much occasion for something new, to make us forget our own Misfortunes" (1–2), a tellingly inclusive first-person pronoun. The presumptive female reader exists in a condition of limitation characterized by tedium, "Misfortunes," and too much time on her hands (especially having exhausted the diversions of masquerade, opera, and gambling). Restrictive social expectations and rigid construction of gender compel women to seek other forms of amusement. Aubin claims to "imprint noble Principles in the ductile Souls of our Youth, and setting great Examples before their Eyes, excite them to imitate them" (xi). Ostensibly, the "great examples" of imitative behavior Aubin provides are those of unwavering Christian devotion at moments of extreme peril. The Christian belief in the captivity of the sinner and the nonbeliever and their redemption or deliverance from that state of captivity—the rhetoric explicitly used in the 1722 sermon celebrating the release of the Barbary captives—underpins much of the discourse around Barbary captivity. But in fact what quite likely "excites" most readers are Aubin's descriptions of desire, sensuality, and seduction, not "pious" Christian behavior. The language of piety and Christian devotion are overwhelmed by far more sensationalized material in the narratives of the primary characters and the individuals they encounter.

The "noble Slaves" of the title are two European couples: the Spaniards Don Lopez and Teresa and the French subjects, Count de Hautville and Emilia. Over a period of seven years, these two couples—who marry relatively early in the narrative—initially shipwrecked individually on a remote island, join forces and secure passage home. However, when they reach the Straits of Gibraltar on their return to Europe,[58] they are captured by a

Barbary corsair and subjected to a variety of trials over seven years until, ultimately, the two couples all reunite in France. Through a series of interpolated narratives, the novel also presents the stories of four additional European couples, each held in North Africa.

As depicted by Aubin, vulnerability to Barbary captivity often results from the aggression, duplicity, or misdirected passions of European men who imperil themselves and the women with whom they associate. Once captured, the experiences of male and female captives differ sharply. Men have the capacity to use their wealth, skills, or sexuality to improve or alleviate their position, if only temporarily. By contrast, women, having been endangered, threatened, or abused by a European man, often discover in Barbary captivity their previously unrealized capacity for independent action and enjoy freedoms unthinkable within the restrictive culture from which they came. Cross-dressing, unmonitored female intimacy, economic self-sufficiency, geographic mobility, and demonstrations of physical strength become part of some captive women's new lives. Many of these activities result from harsh necessity—bodily vigor wards off unwanted sexual assault; economic self-sufficiency stems from the need to eat; geographic mobility enables escape. Nevertheless the text suggests a fuller range of possibilities for women, even if these freedoms and newfound capabilities are short-lived. Like the young Miss Bourk, these women, when "freed," actually return to a much more proscribed and more dangerous existence.

"A French West-India Captain": The Codes of Captivity

From its first line, The Noble Slaves points simultaneously to an increasingly visible world of the enslavement of kidnapped Africans initiated and controlled by the British, and a familiar world of domestic captivity that legally, economically, and socially restricts women. By situating her novel within a broader and geographically specific landscape of enslavement, Aubin reminds readers that the forces of white, European patriarchy that drive the colonial domination responsible for the enslavement of kidnapped Africans also construct a world of domestic captivity for women. These forms of captivity are mutually reinforcing, if, of course, dramatically different in scale. And, in Aubin's fiction, the two represent much more onerous forms of captivity than those imposed by the Barbary corsairs. Every structuring device of The Noble Slaves explicitly locates the text within a world of colonial enslavement. The first sentence of the novel reads: "A French *West-India* Captain just return'd from the Coast of *Barbary,* having brought thence some Ladies and Gentlemen, who had been Captives in those Parts, the History of whose Adventures there are most surprizing, I thought it well worth presenting to the Publick." This captain provides the catalyst for the narrative by returning to Europe the "Ladies and Gentleman" "whose Adventures" are "most suprizing" and "well worth presenting to the Publick"—that is, he returns the "noble slaves" (1). Yet the unnamed captain appears only in these first words; then he completely disappears from the novel. And, he could easily be shorn from an awkward opening sentence that refuses to parse grammatically and demands the reader's additional attention to its individual components.

Immediately recognizable for a 1722 reader, a "French *West-India* Captain," like Aubin's brothers-in-law, would most commonly be engaged in transporting the commodities associated with the slave-based economy of the British Atlantic. However, rather than carry enslaved Africans from the west coast of Africa to the West Indies, this captain returns "noble slaves" from the "coast of Barbary" to Europe, creating a different kind of triangle trade. (He also facilitates or transports the literary commodity of Aubin's novel.) The West Indies and Barbary visually stand as the two recognized sites of enslavement. Both depend on a (differently realized) slave-based economy, a dependence that connects the global forms of enslavement and captivity that operate as the novel's economic drivers.[59] This first sentence underscores Aubin's desire to construct a narrative world—one that mirrors the material world—in which enslavement and captivity come in myriad and mutually reinforcing forms.[60]

The geography and sociopolitical power of the title's four "noble slaves" also situates each of them within a country whose economy depends upon enslaved and unfree labor. In this fictional world, as Edward Kozaczka notes, "slavery is endlessly possible."[61] Aubin reveals the structural alliance between imperial and commercial power and the racist and sexist assumptions underpinning both. The threat of oppression resides not purely externally—in the complex networks of empire—but also internally within the domestic structures that ultimately prove as, if not more, imperiling for women. The text's numerous interpolated narratives—which themselves confine the reader—vividly reiterate the persistent dangers to which women of all ages, classes, and national origins are always already subject.

The structural repetition of the tales of captivity acts as a narrative drumbeat sounding the persistence of the captive state of women. Aubin presents literally a world—a global situation—of dangerous possibilities for women. The hierarchical culture that affirms male dominance in any country also naturalizes the oppression, subjection, and dehumanization of women and the enslaved.

The novel's four main characters live in countries whose national economic structures depend upon unfree labor. Teresa's father flees Spain for New Spain or Mexico to establish his fortune as a colonial venturer. There, he owns multiple plantations and generates extensive wealth derived from the labor of the enslaved people; in fact Teresa herself initially relies on the enslaved Domingo who shares her boat when it goes adrift at the beginning of her narrative.[62] In the sixteenth century, New Spain had more enslaved Africans than any other colony in the Western Hemisphere. During a three-hundred-year period, more than 200,000 Africans were brought to New Spain where they labored in silver mines, on sugar plantations, in textile factories, and in households. In New Spain, "African slaves were both a form of wealth," writes Michael Guasco, "and a necessity for the maintenance of that wealth through the production of goods."[63] Published less than a decade after the *asiento* granting England monopoly slave-trading rights in the Spanish South Seas, an area of slave trading previously controlled by the Spanish, *The Noble Slaves* draws on readers' awareness of the Spanish involvement and investment in the trade in enslaved people. It also points to England's profound investment and deep penetration into the slave trade, something considered highly desirable—indeed essential—to England's economic growth. At this point in the century, the Spanish would, in fact, be purchasing enslaved people from the English. Don Lopez, the man who pursues and marries Teresa, is similarly implicated in this exploitative colonial enterprise as the son of the governor of New Spain.

Engagement with the economy of enslavement also marks the French subjects Emilia and Count de Hautville, the man who becomes her husband. France's involvement with colonial sites of oppression facilitates the kidnapping of Emilia by the captain of a ship destined for Quebec. The French initially planned to use enslaved Africans as a labor source in that colony, although an insufficiently deep harbor and incompatible labor needs diminished the number of enslaved people actually transported. More importantly, however, when the count begins his journey to find Emilia after her abduction, he invests all his money in the East India Company. The East India Company not only structurally depended on a slave-based economy in its colonization of India, but also purchased and internally transported enslaved Africans (primarily from the east coast of Africa), using Madagascar as the hub for that activity.[64] Aubin's knowledge of this particular aspect of the East India Company would have been quite keen in light of her January 1709 testimony about the "Madagascar Men."

The four main characters who become the "noble slaves" of the novel's title all depend upon the wealth generated by enslaved people, a key narrative detail. The text's landscape of permanently enslaved, unnamed, and largely unspecified non-European people of color sits uncomfortably adjacent to the minutely described temporary captivity of the "noble slaves" and the other Europeans they encounter while held in North Africa. Although the text includes enslaved Africans, indigenous people, and other racialized characters, it does not give voice (or ultimately even much consideration) to those figures. Instead it centralizes the situation of privileged European white women (albeit abducted and held captive), which differs profoundly from the experience of an enslaved African subject to the racialized and inheritable category of enslavement. Although the text documents the naturalization of enslavement and oppression foundational to both states of confinement, Aubin does little to represent Black subjectivity.

The Captivity of Women

Women's lack of financial independence dooms many female characters in The Noble Slaves to forms of captivity; they lack the "liberty" or property to which Aubin refers in the preface. The narrative of Emilia, one of the title's "noble slaves," encapsulates the challenges confronted by European women of any country in early eighteenth-century patriarchal society. Lovely, nobly descended, and virtuous, Emilia lacks a sufficient fortune to be acceptable to the father of her suitor Count de Hautville. Upon the death of her own father Emilia learns that "the Estate was entail'd, and could not descend to a Daughter" (12). She becomes immediately dispossessed, forced to live with her unmarried aunt. Appearing to be a generous and moral soul, the aunt instead proves to be "a sordid, malicious old Maid" (12). She conspires with the count's father to pay a ship captain three hundred crowns to kidnap Emilia and take her to French Quebec. The aunt's competitive jealousy drives her vindictive actions, which temporarily ally her with the male power structure. In a scene reminiscent of the kidnapping of Oroonoko, the captain, who is already friendly with the family, invites Emilia and her aunt to a "Treat" and "Entertainment" aboard the ship (13). There, the count's father and the aunt give Emilia "Wine with an Infusion of Opium" and, once the aunt disembarks, the ship sails to Quebec (13). The novel's first display of sexual violence comes at the hands of this ship captain, who attempts to make Emilia his mistress and provides an early example of the rapacious sexuality that characterizes European, not North African, men.

The pattern of violence affects secondary characters as well. Eleanora, the Venetian daughter of a wealthy merchant by his second wife, suffers a similar threat of sexual violence at the hands of a European. As she details to the count and Don Lopez in chapter 6, at thirteen, she falls in love with her mother's kinsman, Andrea Zantonio, and the two plan to wed secretly, since "the Custom and Laws of that State will not permit ['the eldest son of a *Venetian* Senator'] to marry out of a noble Family" (62). However, on the journey to the secret wedding ceremony at her father's country seat, she is kidnapped by Alphonso, the much older "rich Captain of a Ship, who had cast his Eyes upon me in my Infancy, and was one of the first that entertain'd me with the Discourses of Love" (62). The abduction is swift and violent. Eleanora is "bound and gagg'd," as she and her enslaved companion, "poor Black Attabala," are rowed out to the captain's ship and sail away (63).

Physically confined aboard ship, Eleanora is forcibly transported from her home to an unknown location. Eleanora reacts to the abduction as if it is an arranged marriage. "I saw myself in the hands of a Man whom I hated," recounts Eleanora, "and no way left to escape" (64). That statement accurately records the situation for both a physically abducted woman and a married woman in an age without divorce. Justifying his physical aggression as a "bold deed . . . to manifest my Love," the captain rhetorically turns his act of violence into an appropriate gesture of devotion (64). Conflating demonstrations of power with demonstrations of love, he naturalizes the threat of gendered violence that always lies beneath the surface (or, that in this case, has come to the surface). He instructs Eleanora to "fear nothing more, you are now in the hands of a Man that adores you, and it is your own fault if you are not happy" (64). That relationship is completely asymmetrical—his excessive emotion fills every part of their interactions.

That statement, essentially blaming Eleanora if she is "not happy," echoes Aubin's claim in the preface that any in England who are "enslav'd, or impoverish'd" similarly have only themselves to blame.

Aware that any sexual interaction with Eleanora will be nonconsensual, Alphonso plans to marry her that night so that he "will not be a Ravisher, but having secured your Person and your Hounour, take what will be then my Due" (65). He relies on the legal impossibility of rape within marriage; as Matthew Hale details, women cannot "retract" the consent implicit in the marriage vows.[65] Alphonso would have legal, physical, and, essentially, social control over Eleanora. He also points explicitly to the permanent condition of marriage: "whilst I possess you, you shall be mine, and only Death can free you from me" (65). The situation drains her words of any power; with Alphonso as her only interlocuter, her language has no meaning. "Rage on . . . fond Girl," he taunts (65). Neither speech or silence can help her. He also has the ability to invest her silence with unintended meaning. He reminds her that "Silence . . . does give Consent" (66), making her refusal to "speak those Words, or answer" during the wedding ceremony a hollow gesture (66).

Eleanora's freedom from Alphonso comes, ironically, when she is captured by Barbary pirates and taken to the governor in Algiers who, over eight years, "love[d] me passionately, and . . . deny'd me nothing" (67). In a pattern distinctly at odds with the consumer model of male sexuality frequently represented in contemporaneous prose fiction, the governor "gave [Eleanora] the Preference" and throughout her captivity "loved [her] with the same Ardour as at first" (68). Her inability to produce an heir ultimately cools his passion, but she still controls key aspects of her own life (her home, her activities, and her companions), and has more autonomy than most other women in the novel. This (relative) autonomy also gives her the capacity to help Don Lopez and the count escape after they are purchased by the governor; seeing the men in chains, she declares "I will free you" (56). Initially, her own confinement by the governor made her loath to share her personal history; she admits, "whilst I was a Slave I was not willing to be known" (61). But now she takes "Pleasure to entertain" them with her story. Her narrative of abduction, sexual violence, and captivity becomes a diversion, a form of entertainment (just like Aubin's novel). If Aubin is offering examples for her readers to imitate, Eleanora is an instructive one. Her pragmatism is rewarded. After living with an Algerian governor for nearly a decade, she is reunited with Zantonio, now a hermit living in North Africa who escaped the sexual advances of the governor of Tunis. When they are reunited, Zantonio embraces Eleanora "with as much Joy as if she had been a Virgin," his "Passion being sincere as ever" (149).

The enslaved man Attabala "whom [Eleanora] fancy'd" (58) helps "deliver" Eleanora, Don Lopez, and Count de Hautville from their Barbary captivity. Attabala, "a young *Black* . . . purchased when a Child" by Eleanora's father, is a significant element in Eleanora's narrative. Also abducted by the captain in Eleanora's initial kidnapping in Europe and then, subsequently, captured by the governor, Attabala occupies a liminal position in Barbary captivity, he is essentially doubly captive. Although captive herself, Eleanora persuades the governor to first "purchase" and then free "Attabala at [her] request" (57); she also convinces him to give Attabala "a little House and Garden, which he used in the Summer to repair to for his Pleasure, to fish on the Sea-coast, and take the Evening Air on the Water with his Pleasure-boat" (58). He appears to have some independence, to possess domesticity, and to remain someone in whom Eleanora "could confide" (58). Despite this apparent intimacy between the two, and his freedom from Barbary captivity, Attabala cannot shed his role as Eleanora's slave. In fact, the text never terms him anything other than "Slave," and Eleanora retains her role as "his dear Mistress." He regularly brings "little Presents of Fish and Fruits, as grateful Acknowledgements of the Favour [his 'freedom'] she had done him" (58), a "freedom" that is not fully realized. Attabala is the vehicle for the Europeans' escape, bringing them horses and allowing them to stay at his house until they all flee together. Despite the humanity, Christianity, and emotion Aubin accords to Attabala, ultimately, he remains only a narrative accessory. When he "escapes" with the Europeans, he leaves an independent domestic space to go into an unknown and largely unchronicled fate. When he returns to Venice with Eleanora, "poor *Attabala*," as he is called, "was much caress'd for his faithful Service to his Lady" (178), but his status as free or enslaved is unclear; he is not mentioned again.

Following the chapter containing Eleanora's story, Charlot shares her narrative of captivity with Emilia and Teresa. Like Eleanora, Charlot experiences imprisonment at the hands of a European when she is abducted by a professed lover. Charlot's "Father's Ambition was so great" that he "refused to give [her] to" several "good Tradesmen and Merchants"; rather he hopes to secure an alliance with the nobleman Victor Amando, Count Frejus (154), who actually has no intention of marrying someone of Charlot's rank. The phrasing—"give her to"—marks her utter lack of participation in the decision. This paternal ambition leaves Charlot vulnerable to the sexual advances of Victor Amando, to whom her father permits "all the Liberty imaginable" (155). As in *The Conscious Lovers*, here too "liberty" points to a kind of personal freedom to which women do not have access without consequence. The actions of Victor Amando embody Aubin's critique of male libertinism, which she characterizes, in part, as a lack of personal restraint accepted in men. Just as Sir John encouraged his son Bevil to live with "liberty," so too Charlot's father encourages Victor Amando to take "liberty" with his daughter.[66]

Amando's liberty leads to Charlot's captivity. Victor Amando abducts and rapes Charlot, leaving her in the hands of her (duplicitous) maid Phillis and two servants "who watched me as a Prisoner" (156). "[S]o well watched," she is held physically captive, a state compounded by her admission that "I loved the Villain that had undone me" (156). He holds her as a prisoner for five years, a period during which she bears him three children and "never appear'd abroad, but with a Masque" (157). Amando suffers no consequences for his abduction, sexual violation, and imprisonment of Charlot. His father took "little notice of his keeping a Mistress" (157), his term for the captive Charlot.

Ironically, in the novel's preface Aubin points to precisely this kind of sexual behavior as a distinguishing element of the "Turks" whose Monarch "thinks it no Crime to keep as many Women for his Use, as his lustful Appetite excites him to like" (x). To characterize such behavior as normative for aristocratic European men demonstrates that captivity rests on gender as much as (if not more than) national identity or religion. While Barbary men may hold women captive for set periods of time, European men, with their assertions of gender privilege, can hold women into perpetuity. A woman sold into or ransomed from Barbary captivity certainly circulates as an item of value, yet that exchange does not establish an ongoing relationship between the two men; it is fundamentally transactional.[67] By contrast, women married within a patriarchal-imperial European structure strengthen the connection between the two men advancing their own social, economic, or political interests.

When Amando marries another women, he does not free Charlot. Rather he "sold [her] to an *Arabian* Captain, or Chief of a Tribe" (159), echoing the plot of the contemporaneous memoir *The Unfortunate Marriage* by the Marchioness de Frene (1722). That popular first-person narrative tells of how the marchioness is taken aboard a ship for what is ostensibly an evening's entertainment with her husband and maid in attendance. (The same device used in *Oroonoko* or with Aubin's character Emilia.) The two women are given the "fatal Draught" that "so disturb'd" their "Reason" that they "prattled, and suffer'd our Tongues to run at random for some time, scarcely knowing what we either did or said, we fell into a sound Sleep, which continued for Twenty-four Hours. My Husband . . . made use of this Opportunity to finish" his design.[68] The marchioness awoke to realize she "was now" the captain's "Slave" (73). In a pattern consistent with Aubin, the marchioness's Barbary "husband" proves more devoted than her European one.[69] Similarly, Charlot, once sold by Amando, finds the treatment by her Arabian owner Abenbucer much gentler than her experience at the hands of Amando. Amando kidnaps, rapes, and sells her. By contrast, "the brave *Arab* used me kindly, lov'd and prefer'd me before all his Women" (159). Like Eleanora, Charlot finds strategic opportunities within her captivity and within her narrative to preserve the opportunity to tell her own story.

Conversely, unlike Charlot and Eleanora, Maria, the novel's ostensible exemplar of female virtue in extremity, does not tell her own tale of kidnapping, self-mutilation, and confinement. Her experience, shared early in the novel's fourth chapter, is the first interpolated narrative in the text. Her Persian husband Tanganor recounts it to the newly shipwrecked "noble slaves." Tanganor and Maria's relationship began with an economic transaction: Tanganor bought Maria, "a *Spanish* Girl, a virgin of but 13 Years of Age" for 100 crowns (25–26). His explicitly sexual plans change when the thirteen-year-old's "Fear and Grief" "cool'd" his "Blood" (28). Although her youth defers his immediate sexual violation of her, it does not eliminate his desire. Maria averts the threat of sexual assault by offering to marry Tanganor if he converts to Christianity, thus alleviating her "Shame" (28). Initially the agreement appears to invert their power dynamic. Mimicking the supplicant role of a suitor, Tanganor treats her "as if [he] had been her Slave," obscuring his actual ownership of her person (29). However, before Tanganor can marry her, she attracts the attention of the emperor, initiating a toxic competition between the two men. The emperor's desire to dominate her, and by extension Tanganor, is evident in his determination to show "what a *Persian* Monarch can bestow on her he loves" (32).

This encounter is typical for this text in the aggression it attributes to the emperor. Aubin writes that he "stifled" Maria with kisses, a verb of particular violence (32). Stifling means either to kill someone, or to deprive them of consciousness by covering their mouth or nose; it is essentially suffocating someone. The range of contemporaneous meanings ("to destroy, crush, suppress") amplifies the inherent violence of the emperor's gestures and also his desire to silence Maria, another meaning of stifle.[70] Repeating the words Alphonso uses with Eleanora aboard ship, the emperor asserts that "Force must I find procure me now what your Consent shall afterwards secure me of" (33). As an already enslaved woman, Maria doubly lacks the capacity to consent. Rather than witness her own "Shame" or "more inflame Mankind" with her beauty, Maria tears out her own eyeballs and throws them at the emperor (33).[71] Like Oroonoko, Maria practices self-harm and mutilation as a gesture of (fleeting) revenge against her enslaver. (Ironically, before her own act of violence, the emperor declares that Maria's "Vertue charms me more than your Eyes" [32–33].) The emperor interprets this gesture as a demonstration of Maria's love for Tanganor, not a marker of her shame, and pronounces her future husband "happy," wishing he had been "so fortunate to be beloved like you" (33). Although the emperor returns her to Tanganor, who has "black'd" his "Face and Hands, and changed" his "Dress for that of a Slave" (30) in order to enter the palace unobserved (a reminder of the invisibility of the enslaved Africans), he does so with reluctance: "Blind as you are, you charm me" (33). Certainly the emperor's attempted sexual violation precipitates this extreme act. But he does not physically mutilate her. Maria's disfigurement and blindness result from her own stringent application of a European gendered morality that explicitly endorses self-harm.

When Tanganor shares Maria's experience with the Europeans in chapter 4, she, now twenty-eight, has lived with him for fifteen years, bearing him three children. Remaining "much in her Chamber . . . because of her being blind," Maria is as imprisoned by her lack of sight as her self-imposed closeting (34). Wearing a black ribbon "that cover'd her Eyelids," her beauty "could not be altogether eclipsed" (37). In fact, Emilia remarks, "The want of Sight adds to your Charms, and causes us to love and admire you," aligning her disability—or rather inability to be seduced by visually appealing things—with her virtue (38). Certainly Maria's blindness echoes the visual iconography of the virgin Saint Lucy who, in versions of her narrative told after the fifteen century, is represented with her eyes covered after she gouged them out to put off a persistent suitor.[72] Alternately, Aubin could also be undercutting the power of Maria's narrative. The image of her as a woman with her eyes covered by a black ribbon in 1722 invokes a prostitute in a mask in the pit of a London playhouse or a woman disguised at the kind of masquerade to which Aubin refers in the preface. The absence of Maria's eyes may signify her virtue, but, within the visual markers of 1720s London, the associations with the mask itself complicates an unambiguous interpretation of the image within the novel. It also reminds us that Maria is never actually harmed by the threatening sexual advances of the Barbary captor; rather she is a victim of self-harm and an overly solicitous adherence to Christian principle. Maria's narrative appears very early in the novel and constitutes the first fully drawn moment of female captivity and threatened sexual violation; the extreme reaction of Maria, determined not to "see her Shame," sets a high bar for the rest of the women in the protection of their own virtue.

Maria's story has a greater effect on Don Lopez and the count than on Emilia and Teresa. In fact, after hearing Maria's narrative, Don Lopez immediately wants to marry Teresa, only thirteen, and he aggressively polices her chastity. Like all the women in this novel, Teresa is extremely young, twelve when first adrift at sea (only three years older than the "young Miss Bourk"). Some critics suggest that the unusually young age of Aubin's heroines indicates her target audience—as though she were writing young adult literature for the eighteenth century.[73] I would suggest rather that Aubin marks how profoundly and quickly young women are acculturated—groomed if you will—for a life of subservient domestic captivity. Their youth is all the more relevant in an era when the age of consent for a girl was ten. The tender age of her fictional female subjects serves both as warning and reality. Don Lopez fell in love with the twelve-year-old Teresa "from the Moment he first saw her" (19). Even at twelve Teresa possesses such "stature and beauty" that "she was admired by all Men, and envied by all the Women"; she "inspired Love with every Glance" (2). After her disappearance when her pleasure boat goes adrift, Don Lopez pursues her, a gesture that initially appears one of devotion and commitment (as well, of course, as an essential plot device); however, it also marks how wealth, power, and unencumbered mobility enable men to pursue the objects of their passions.

This compulsion to pursue Teresa anticipates Don Lopez's aggressive focus upon her virtue and intensified desire to marry her after hearing about Maria's experience. His "proposal" to the thirteen-year-old embodies the kinds of coercive pressure indicative of the novel's European men.

Conflating "Heaven's Will" with his own, Don Lopez provides no opportunity for Teresa to refuse him (38). Although using words rather than physical violence, he knows that consent can be gotten through force, persuasion, or persistence (or some combination of the three): "I know that you are not insensible or ignorant of my Passion for you, nay I even hope that you love me; do not longer, charming Maid, defer to make me happy. . . . Tho you are very young, yet you are of Years to marry. Fate has decreed you mine, keep me no longer languishing; . . . yield to Heaven's Will" (38). Her emotions are immaterial; he "hope[s]" she loves him but, like the succession of male characters in the novel, doesn't really concern himself with her feelings. Her reply conflates the language of marriage and enslavement: "Tho with much confusion I consent to make you Master of *Teresa's* Heart and Hand, do as you please" (39).[74] The text omits meaningful or romantic verbal exchanges between Teresa and Don Lopez, or between any European lovers in the novel.

After they marry, Don Lopez amplifies the alarming nature of Maria's story when the two couples are captured by the Turkish captains and taken to Algiers. He and the count both torment their teenaged wives with vivid descriptions of the horrors that could befall them, subjecting them to a kind of emotional pornography: Don Lopez warns Teresa (although "big with Child") that she will be "ravished from me by some powerful Infidel, who will . . . force you to his curst Embraces" (42). "[R]avished from me" reveals his concern is as much for the loss of the property his wife represents as for her falling prey to sexual violence. Consistent with his prior excessive demonstrations of possessiveness, Don Lopez vows "my Arms shall grasp [you] even in Death" (43). The men extract the women's promise to "die rather than live a Vassal to a vile *Mahommetan's* unlawful lust" (42). The language tellingly conflates an anti-Islamic sentiment, "vile Mahommetan," with the language of European class oppression, "live a Vassal" (42). This overwrought language explicitly urges the women to self-harm rather than submit.

Don Lopez's language contrasts sharply with the tone and demeanor of the women's North African captors. The governor of Algiers, Teresa and Emilia's first captor, "one of the most beautiful and accomplish'd Men of his Nation" (45), treats the women with "civility" (41). His physical beauty matches his gentle and seductive demeanor. Courting Teresa "with all the Eloquence Love can inspire" (46), he is "generous and compassionate" (47).

He provides the women with wine and food, and he allows them to keep their personal belongings. A subsequent captor, the "very amorous and gallant" Muley Arab, creates a similarly inviting environment. He speaks to Teresa in Spanish, saying "the most tender and passionate things to her that Love could dictate" (107). He offers "the most delicious things that please the Taste," "Wine, Sherberts, Sweet-meats, Cold-meats" (105). Perhaps most importantly, while attracted to the women's beauty, he claims it is their "Wisdom [that] charm'd him" (108). When Teresa explains their situation to him, "the Prince listned [sic] as if he had heard some *Syren* sing, and grew more mad in Love" (108).[75] This kind of treatment—attentive listening, kind words, respectful physical distance—contrasts sharply with the women's experience with European men within Aubin's fiction.

These generally positive descriptions of Barbary captors, consistent with others in the novel, create a fundamental ambivalence within the text. Adam Beach, drawing on Orlando Patterson, reminds us that the master never performs any act of "generosity" authentically.[76] Rather, such gestures comprise a larger strategy to overpower the captive subject. Similarly, Madeline Zilfi warns scholars of "blind spots" in accepting a "sanitized" "popular image" of slave practices in Barbary.[77] Scholars such as Colley and Matar, who offer insightful descriptions of the state of captivity, might be seen as succumbing to a narrative that reads captivity in North Africa as a system with a kind of "benevolent paternalism" and a potential route for some "to status and security."[78] Such examples certainly exist. Zilfi concedes that Barbary captivity, like Ottoman slavery, is "scarcely comparable in intent or practice" to slavery in North America or the Caribbean.[79] However, the imbalance of power, the foundation of violence, and, most of all, the use of coercion infects all of forms of enslavement. Aubin's ambivalent characterization of Barbary captors aligns with the romanticized image Zilfi cites, but frankly, Aubin seems less concerned about accurately representing Barbary captivity than she does about foregrounding the dangerous, if naturalized, gendered violence practiced by European men. Emilia and Teresa's experience of Barbary captivity highlights the failings of European men who, unlike their Barbary counterparts, don't listen, don't offer, and don't act with civility.

Indeed, for Teresa the most horrific moments of violence and sexual assault occur at the hands of a European man after she has returned to a life of apparent normalcy. Having survived seven years in a "continued Scene of Misfortunes" after initially going adrift on the open sea as a twelve-year-old, Teresa encounters the greatest threat to her safety and well-being in Spain from her husband's own cousin Don Fernando de Medina. Proximity provides opportunity. Seeing the now-nineteen-year-old Teresa, Fernando "gazed away his Liberty" (193) and "burn'd to possess her" (196). His language reveals the twisted inversion by which the psychological desire ("love") overtakes a man, costs him his "liberty"—"captivates" him—prompting acts that result in the physical confinement or captivity of a woman. Such a rhetorical gesture—a stock feature in sonnets, for example—obscures the man's unwavering physical, legal, and economic dominance. Fernando knows Teresa's "Virtue render'd all means but Force impracticable" (194). He is undeterred by either the prospect of cuckolding his own cousin or resorting to sexual violence after he has "resolved to possess" her (194). Fernando secures a house in a remote location where he constructs "a Chamber strong as a Prison" to hold Teresa and he arranges for two "old Hags" to care for her after her abduction (194).

The physical extremity Teresa experiences at the hands of the four European men hired to kidnap her exceeds anything she encountered over the previous seven years. She is "bound Hand and Foot," gagged, forced "into a Horse-litter," and transported "twenty Miles" (196). At the house where Fernando will hold her captive, she is "laid . . . bound upon the Bed" in the "horrid Room where the old Hags attended to watch her" (196). The scene (which anticipates the capture and confinement of Samuel Richardson's Clarissa Harlowe) contrasts sharply with the physical comforts offered during captivities she previously endured. Teresa's verbal pleas "would have melted the Hearts of *Barbarians*" (196). Aubin slyly conflates the meaning of Barbarian as one from Barbary with barbarian as an uncivilized person speaking a different language. Teresa's words could soften the most obdurate, but have no effect on a European captor. Aubin sharply contrasts this episode with moments when Teresa had successfully redirected the passions of her North African captors. For example, the governor of Algiers, after her verbal defense, promises to "never use base Force" and vows to "leave [her] to Repose, and not presume to urge [her] farther" (47). Her words to an Algerian captor have power; her words to a European man remain impotent. Similarly, unlike the gentle "eloquence" of the governor, Fernando verbally abuses Teresa with "threats" and then sexually assaults her, "rudely kissing and embracing her" (197). The contrast could not be starker.

To create a diversion to facilitate her escape, Teresa enforces the "civilities" offered by her Barbary captors and urges Fernando to take a gentler approach: "if I must be yours, shew that you love me" (197). Taking up her challenge, Fernando pours her wine, which she promptly throws in his face. Yet she cannot escape. Falling down the stairs, Teresa suffers a compound fracture to her right leg "short of the Instep. . . . the Shin-bone was shiver'd, so that it had cut thro the Skin and Sinews, and appear'd" (198). Fernando carries the immobilized Teresa to the bed with the intention of continuing his assault upon her now-wounded body, but "the sight" of her injury "dash'd his amorous Fires" (198). Fernando summons a village surgeon for treatment, and successfully uses the myth of female irrationality to drain her words of meaning. Because Fernando claims Teresa is "his Wife, who was a lunatic, and had broke loose, and endeavour'd to escape" (198), the doctor ignores what she says. He "drest her, not regarding her Complaints" (198). Fernando renders Teresa as silent as if he had put his hand over her mouth.

Ironically, words spoken while delirious save her, another mark of the cultural silencing of women. When the surgeon returns the next day to check on Teresa, he finds her "light-headed, with a strong Fever which had seized her" (199). In her febrile state, she talks of "Don *Lopez, Emilia,* her Child, and of being stole" (199). The last phrase underscores how fully she has internalized her own objectification. She perceives herself as "stole," a verb most commonly used in connection with moveable property, not people. She has been taken like any other of Don Lopez's possessions. Yet the surgeon still does not act upon this information until, some days later, he "heard" of "great Inquiry being made after *Teresa*" from a male authority, and alerts Don Lopez (199). Her words do not spur action; only the wider consensus of the community (the "great Inquiry") moves him. Even when rescued, Teresa's silencing persists. After shooting Fernando through the head, her husband Don Lopez "hush[es] her" and refuses to exact justice on her behalf (200). Rather than pursue "a Trial, or private Injury, from *Fernando*'s family," he "absconded" to France to live with Emilia and the count (200). The primary motivation for Don Lopez to even consider seeking justice lies not in Teresa's kidnapping but in the "great . . . Injury" he himself sustained (200). Teresa's violent experience sits within a broader landscape of coercion the novel details. Although Teresa recovers, she is "lame, and never expects to do otherwise whilst she lives" (200–201). Like Maria, she bears the mark of male aggression and predatory sexual violence. Unlike

Miss Bourk who can literally write her own deliverance, Teresa, despite her eloquence, cannot narrate her liberation. She can only display the physical mark of the violence of European men after her so-called "freedom" from Barbary captivity.

The Barbary Captivity of Men

If, as this chapter asserts, European men prove to be culpable in the confinement of women, what happens to these male European captors when they themselves are held captive? Aubin represents the male experience in Barbary captivity as starkly different: affirming the gendered divide that characterizes the world in which they live and reminding readers that men of privilege often manage to retain that privilege across diverse contexts. Within Aubin's text, men's captivity generally enables them either to preserve elements of their privileged European status (including libertine sexual practices) or to improve their status through specialized skills or knowledge that increase their value to their captor.[80]

After Don Lopez and the count's capture by the Algerian governor, the men, although chained to the floor, receive a mattress and quilts, food and wine. Their Turkish captors recognize the financial and cultural power that resides with the two men "by the vast Treasure they found in the Ship, and their Habit" (44); knowing they are "Persons of Quality" they reward the men with preferential treatment and the opportunity to secure ransom.[81] The benefits of the men's status extend to the advantage they gain in personal interactions, and the capacity to use their charms and sexuality to secure their escape. Eleonora, the previously discussed Venetian woman enslaved by a governor, offers to free the men on the promise of an appropriate expression of "gratitude" from Don Lopez who "was too well skill'd in the fair Sex, not to perfectly understand this Lady's meaning" (56). Although he is "not altogether insensible of Eleonora's Charms," he also realizes "no other means but this was left to free them" (56–57). Even in captivity, men of privilege retain the opportunity to replicate libertine behavior. Aubin, in a rare moment of authorial interjection, reflects on Don Lopez's actions and distinguishes between men's emotional and sexual capacity: "he was a Man, and tho he was intirely devoted to Teresa, yet as Man he could oblige a hundred more: Life is sweet, and I hope my Reader will not condemn him for what his own Sex must applaud in justification of themselves: for what brave, handsome young Gentleman would refuse a beautiful Lady, who loved him, a Favour?" (56–57). Scholars have read Aubin's fiction as bearing an antilibertine strain (certainly borne out by other moments in this novel). Initially this episode seems to validate, if not endorse, Don Lopez's actions in a way that might complicate such an antilibertine reading.[82] Don Lopez's preternatural sexual capacity epitomizes libertine excess ("his own Sex must applaud"), here justified when channeled to a heroic end. Yet, Aubin's hyperbole (his ability to "oblige a hundred more"), subtle understatement (he's doing Eleonora a "Favour" in gratifying her desires), and gendered reading of the situation ("my Reader" versus "his own Sex") suggest she is actually satirizing the situation and the libertine impulse. His patently ridiculous statements to Eleonora ("a Dungeon with such a Companion would be pleasant"; "Your Charms would even render Confinement supportable") feed her words she knows to a false (she "suffer'd her self to be deceived"). The statement "Life is sweet" within the middle of a novel representing diverse forms of captivity begs the question "for whom?" In this small but significant moment, Aubin signals the degree to which privileged European men retain their "liberty" (and libertinism) even in these moments of captivity, which, of course, their female counterparts cannot.

If Don Antonio willingly provides a sexual "Favour" to Eleanora in a situation in which he retains some control, the Frenchman Clementine, when captured, has a different experience. Clementine tells his story, which appears in chapter 9, to the four central characters, interweaving it with the experience of his wife Clarinda. Clementine's narrative highlights the range of captive states to which men of more limited economic means could be subject, unlike men of privilege. Equally important, his experience marks European men's ability to impose restrictions upon women even while the men themselves are held captive. As the third son, Clementine, although from a wealthy family, must pursue a vocation since he is barred from inheritance in a country with primogeniture. "Destined to the Church," he is "ordain'd a Secular Priest at twenty" (81). However, his "Inclinations do not suit the Habits" he wears (82) and, taken ill, he retires to his family's summer home where he sees the fifteen-year-old Benedictine nun Clarinda. "[R]esolved to possess" Clarinda, Clementine steals jewels from the reliquary, hires a boat, and removes Clarinda from the convent (82). At this moment Clementine likens himself to "[t]he sad Prisoner who has lived long confined in a dark loathsome Vault"; no one "feels . . . a greater Joy at

the sight of Day and Liberty than I did then" (84). Shorn of religious or so-
cietal checks on his behavior, that "Liberty" for Clementine manifests itself
in "enjoy[ing] the Maid I so much languished for" and only then marrying her, doubly breaking his vows (84). (The utter absence of Clarinda in
that statement raises the question of consent.) Male liberty entails the unchecked "possession" of a woman's body. Clementine plans to sail to England with Clarinda.

In this novel, the European men, in a state of displacement, do not have
ready access to the status their property accords them in their native country. Like the men in Behn's *The Rover* (1677), Aubin's male subjects exist in a
kind of exile and seek to reconstitute their authority in a contingent fashion,
often through acting on libertine sexual impulses. In *The Noble Slaves*, they
demonstrate that liberty directly through their imposition upon the female
body, which they repeatedly claim as property. This pattern of behavior,
and the attendant language of "liberty" persistently associated with it, complicates the assertion in the preface that an English constitution facilitates
liberty and property (both always already limited to men). The most common form of liberty Aubin illustrates within the text is the sexual liberty of
men. Whether held in Barbary captivity or free in Europe, male liberty
and authority derive primarily from the confinement and subjugation of
women. When Clementine sails to England, he imagines there he "should
be free in all respects," "where I should rather be applauded than condemn'd
for what I had done" (85). That language from Clementine bears note. He
repeats the word—"applaud"—figuring his self-conceptualization as a libertine, despite his newly married state. Further, what Clementine "had done"
for which he anticipates "applause" includes theft, abduction, seduction,
and abrogation of vows. That statement from Clementine advances Aubin's
sustained critique of English society generally, and her indictment of libertine behavior specifically. If, as Clementine imagines, England is a "place
where I should live free from all Constraint," it is not a place conducive to
the safety of women. Clementine conflates liberty and freedom, making
his move to England about his own personal freedom, not a political state.

En route to England, the now-married lovers are captured by Barbary
corsairs. They pose as siblings and are bought by Admela, "a Merchant's
Widow" (85). Although Clementine admits he had not "been bred to work,"
he can "write, cast Accompt, play upon several sorts of Musick" (86), all
gentleman's skills. However, his owner Admela quickly lets him know she

"liked his Person" and "gave [him] to understand what she expected" and she compels him into a state of sexual slavery (86). As Don Lopez must satisfy the "beautiful" Eleonora, Clementine is forced "to oblige the lustful Hag" who "was old, and very disagreeable" (86). In an inversion of the libertine structure, Clementine becomes the object rather than the initiator of sexual liberty. Yet even within an exploitative relationship, he retains vestiges of male privilege and improves his personal and financial power. He is "treated as the Master of all, [and] . . . was deny'd nothing" (86). That mastery extends to his wife (posing as his sister) who also labors for Admela. During the period he serves Admela, Clementine also "often" "stole to Clarinda's Room" to take "the privilege of a Husband to enjoy my vertuous Wife" (87). Clementine has gone from celibate priest to de facto adulterer.

When his marriage and sexual relationship with Clarinda is exposed, Admela has Clarinda kidnapped, prompting Clementine to "resolve to shun Admela's lustful Arms and Bed" (89) until he learns what has become of his wife. When Admela (who he describes as his "Devil-mistress") threatens to have Clarinda killed, Clementine capitulates to continuing their sexual activity. Clementine must continue to appease Admela and "caress [her] in an extraordinary manner" over the next two years (88). Her sexual demands take their toll and Clementine describes symptoms comparable to victims of domestic abuse. Clementine lives "in perpetual Torment, and Anxiety of Mind . . . I was no longer the same Man" (89). The situation does not change until Admela's death when her family has him "turn'd out to be used as a Slave, with a clog chain'd to my Leg" (90). This subsequent enslavement and hard labor come only after Clementine has led what one scholar describes as a "polygamous life in Barbary according to Islamic marital laws" akin to what a British reader might compare with libertine behavior.[83] Khalid Bekkaoui suggests that Aubin's representation "creates intense moral confusions" and a "complex configuration of gender and nationhood . . . disoriented by moral inconsistencies."[84] While the reader might be "disoriented," Aubin most certainly is not. She quite strategically represents such so-called "inconsistencies" to illustrate male inconstancy, patriarchal privilege, and an undeniable double standard. The rigid morality imposed upon women repeatedly, and predictably, proves irrelevant for men.

However, Clarinda's treatment highlights the continuity between the state of Barbary captivity and the state of domestic captivity although, as with every other European woman in the novel, her worst treatment comes at the hands of European, not North African, men. Prior to her elopement with Clementine, Clarinda is confined in a convent. For financial reasons, her family places her (the youngest of six children, three daughters) in a nunnery rather than seek a husband for her. Her secret marriage to Clementine perpetuates her confinement. When owned by the widow Admela, Clarinda lives in a state of captivity, laboring for Admela and subject to Clementine's secret conjugal sexual demands. After their relationship is discovered, Clarinda is (again) abducted, imprisoned, and "chain'd by the leg" for two years (89). During this period, Clarinda receives unwanted sexual advances from her jailor, the Irishman Macdonald, who offers freedom in exchange for "the Enjoyment of Your Person" (90). On her promise of sexual favors, he secures her escape. When he demands his compensation, she stabs him with his own bayonet, leaving him for dead. The response to this stabbing from the priest from whom she seeks aid crystallizes Aubin's ironic deployment of her allegedly "pious" discourse. "[C]ould you find no way to touch his Soul?" the priest asks. "Why did you not rather call earnestly to God to deliver you?" (96). The priest's reaction seems patently absurd, urging utter passivity and faith in divine intervention at a moment of great peril; it is part parody, part antipatriarchal or anti-Catholic sentiment from Aubin. Although liberated from successive states of physical confinement, Clarinda finds the most restrictive situation exists within the dominant patriarchal culture of her own country. The inflexible application of morality repeatedly proves disastrous for the women in Aubin's text, as the end of the novel suggests.

Aubin's Final Words

The novel ends with an image as irregular as its very awkwardly phrased first sentence. In reflecting on the previous eighteen chapters, Aubin compares her fictional women "who will pull out their Eyes, break their Legs, starve, and chuse to die, to preserve their Virtues" to "The Nuns of *Glastenbury* [sic], who parted with their Noses and Lips to preserve their Chastity" (202). She pronounces the nuns the last women "the *English* Nation can boast of" so devoted to their virtue. Ostensibly, Aubin praises the self-mutilating women, willing to inflict self-harm, self-violence, or self-violation, before submitting to a loss of virtue. Self-mutilation, or what one scholar terms "sacrificial mutilation," performed by medieval nuns to avoid rape certainly did occur.[85] The most famous Anglo-Saxon example was Ebba the Younger (d. 870) of Coldingham who cut off her nose and lips under the threat of impending sexual violation. A new translation of William Camden's *Britannia,* also published in 1722, describes the "famous House of Nuns, whose Chastity is recorded in ancient Writing, for their cutting off (together with Ebba their Prioress) their Noses and Lips; chusing to secure their Virginity from the Danes, rather than preserve their Beauty."[86] The story gains new currency in 1722.

Yet, Aubin incorrectly places these virtuous women in Glastonbury, the fabled site of the mythical King Arthur and the knights of the round table, rather than correctly locating them in Coldingham. The year 1722 also saw the publication of *The History and Antiquities of Glastonbury,* a massive tome with a comprehensive history of that legendary place. Perhaps Aubin simply misattributed the location. Perhaps Aubin confused the two places or the two books. (Aubin was famously creative in her geography.) Or perhaps Aubin is slyly suggesting that in her own age women of such determined chastity are as mythical as the figures in the Arthurian legend. *The History of Glastonbury* points to "many incredible Stories that have been reported" about King Arthur, likening his history to something "little better than a Romance."[87] The emphatic classification of these extreme actions as components of *"English"* women (italics Aubin's) seems part praise, part myth (202). Aubin's subsequent lines cast doubt on the entire practice of self-sacrificing virtue, suggesting "the fair Sex" of "this Age" would do "well" just to "stand the Trial of soft Persuasions; a little Force will generally do to gain the proudest Maid" (202). The sentence simultaneously laments the lax morality of women susceptible to "soft Persuasions" while acknowledging the seemingly inevitable sexual violence from men, whose "Force will generally do to gain the proudest Maid" (202).

However, this specific allusion to self-mutilation invokes another fictional precursor, making the image a kind of palimpsest. For the savvy reader, references to self-severed noses and lips would also immediately summon the final actions of Oroonoko, who "cut a piece of Flesh from his own Throat, and threw it at" his captors.[88] Thomas Southerne's *Oroonoko* (1696) had just been performed at the Theatre Royal in Drury Lane in January and February of 1722, the two successive months leading up to the publication of *The Noble Slaves.* The play was reprinted with "Elsiver Letter" at least twice that year as recently as March. Behn's *Oroonoko* also appeared in a new edition in August 1722, and the November 6, 1722, *St. James Evening Post* contained advertisements for both Behn's novel and *The Nobles Slaves*.[89] In the final lines of her novel Aubin reiterates the point she made in the first: the inextricable connection she perceives between the domestic captivity of women and the enslavement of kidnapped Africans, both driven by the white, patriarchal, imperial impulse. The next chapter looks at the ways in which these same impulses affect other British subjects such as indentured servants, trepanned wives, or kidnapped children who find themselves under the power of brutal American masters in the North American colonies.

CHAPTER 5

"Indentured Slaves"

Eliza Haywood, Edward Kimber, and
British Captivity in Colonial America

As discussed in the previous chapter, Penelope Aubin uses Barbary captivity as a vehicle for her potent, ultimately subversive representation of women's domestic captivity. She suggests the real danger for women lies at home, in familiar, not foreign, spaces. The perceived external threat casts into sharp relief structural gender inequities and threats of confinement women confront within British culture. Her fictional male subjects in captivity, by and large, retain the privileges accorded their class and gender in their native country; displaced, they find strategies for reasserting that dominance until they return home. This chapter also explores texts that document the captive experiences of displaced British male subjects as well as experiences of confinement on English soil. Two books are the focus of this chapter: Eliza Haywood's *Memoirs of an Unfortunate Young Nobleman* and Edward Kimber's *The History of the Life and Adventures of Mr. Anderson*. They depict the enslavement of male British subjects within colonial America and consider the effects of that captivity on the national construction of idealized, imperial masculinity.

Based on historical events, both texts detail the childhood abduction of young boys in England, their transportation to the colonies, and then their sale and subsequent captivity until adulthood. Eliza Haywood's *Memoirs of an Unfortunate Young Nobleman* (1743) recounts the actual experience of James Annesley, the Irish heir to the Barony of Altham to whom Haywood was distantly related.[1] James was kidnapped as a child by his uncle (who wanted to claim the title himself) and sent to the American colonies as an "indentured slave."[2] Definitively attributed to Haywood by her bibliographer Patrick Spedding, *Memoirs* was Haywood's fourth most popular novel, due in part to the widespread fascination with Annesley, his ordeal, and the well-publicized trial for his title upon his return.[3] A decade later Edward Kimber's *The History of the Life and Adventures of Mr. Anderson* (1754) tells of the childhood kidnapping and enslavement in the colonies of the young Tom Anderson, drawing on an allegedly true story Kimber learned during his two-year foray in the American colonies. Like the real figure of James Annesley, the fictional Tom Anderson's abduction interrupts an anticipated life of privilege and security in England.

Both narratives hinge on indentured servitude; that is, the voluntary or involuntary sale of an individual and the labor they provide for a specified period of time in a colonial site. As discussed below, the practice of indentured servitude, like the risk of kidnapping or abduction, disproportionally affected the poor, the young, or the unskilled. However, the narratives by Haywood and Kimber present something quite different: young boys—destined for inheritance and lives in the gentry or aristocracy—being kidnapped on English soil and relegated to a life as an "indentured slave" in an American colony. The texts situate the British male subject in a colonial location of captivity that is shorn of opportunities for the kind of compensatory libertinism or hopes of ransom found, for example, in Aubin's texts on Barbary corsairs. The narratives of unprotected and unformed young boys give voice to anxieties about the potential erosion of male British identity while simultaneously assuaging that anxiety by illustrating the degree to which that identity remains inviolate or "innate" even in a corrosive climate where ignorant, bullying Americans are the young boys' captors. The ability to retain—indeed cultivate, with the assistance of captive female subjects—the ennobling elements (rationality, benevolence, sensibility) central to the idealized construction of British masculinity distinguishes these young boys (who become men within the narrative). This colonial captivity of males who would, in England, lead lives of privilege and power, does not derail the men's progress toward ascendance into that condition. Actually, within these texts, the captivity serves to consolidate the dominant construction of British masculinity.

This construction of the male British subject contrasts sharply with the less reflective, less cerebral, and physically violent American planters who hold them captive. These plantation owners, geographically and ideologically separated from England, embody a purely acquisitive, debased version of masculinity that ultimately represents an illegitimate (yet largely insurmountable) power. By extension, in a kind of negative relief, the colonial American owner also serves to implicitly valorize (and in a sense legitimate) the British colonial agents in the West Indies with whom they are explicitly (and unfavorably) compared. The enslavement of a British youth under the control of an American plantation owner narratively obscures the much more horrific British actions against enslaved Africans in a West Indian colonial site. The very qualities that distinguish these abducted and subjected youths—intellect, benevolence, sympathy—are projected upon the absent British (not present American) planter class, existing at spatial and cultural distance. Further, while these texts reveal the abhorrent conditions for "indentured slaves," they simultaneously reinforce the classist and racist ideologies that foundationally underpin the British colonial efforts.[4] Like Behn and Aubin, Haywood and Kimber—despite an awareness of the horrors of slavery—do not condemn enslavement as a global practice underpinning now-institutionalized economic practices. The male subjects' stint in captivity, rather than resulting in an abhorrence of unfree labor, serves ultimately to reinforce the superiority of the British as "natural" and legitimate masters and the need for hierarchical structures. Indeed, that the young men's captivity occurs within a landscape literally populated by enslaved Africans, themselves kidnapped, abducted, and transported in a far more inhumane fashion, goes largely unremarked. The atrocity acted upon the enslaved Africans in the American colonies, while condemned in both pieces, really operates to illustrate the inhumanity of the colonial American planter and his discredited form of masculinity rather than to document barbarous treatment of all humans within institutionalized slavery, including those controlled by the British.

Finally, the texts' delineation of gender extends this construction of British superiority into a domestic realm. In both narratives, the young boys, desirous of education, turn specifically to women to supply them with the cultural touchstones of their native country. These women also exist in a state of domestic captivity either as fellow "indentured slaves" or as victims of the legal and economic confinement of women within a patriarchal system. Yet, despite their own subjugation, these women assume responsibility for preserving male British identity in the face of colonial captivity. Even as the women remain unable to effect any change in their own status, replicating in microcosm the conditions for women in England, they become essential actors in these kidnapped men's acculturation to the dominant British culture to which they will eventually return.

This chapter first looks at the practice of voluntary and involuntary indentured servitude in the early eighteenth century. During this period, nearly 200,000 English, Irish, and Scottish subjects entered into the contractual agreement for a set term of service (with varying degrees of understanding and consent). The prevalence of indentured servitude, especially during the late seventeenth and early eighteenth century, made it a familiar story to be sure; but it also suggests the degree to which many British subjects—lacking opportunities, resources, or a meaningful future—allowed themselves to become what William Moraley (1698–1762), documenting his own colonial experience of indenture, termed "bought servants," willingly trading one kind of confinement for another, hoping for an improved result. The main focus of the chapter is Haywood's and Kimber's texts, which illustrate that not all servitude was voluntary. Haywood, capitalizing on the intense public scrutiny of Annesley, used details of his narrative to fashion her own extremely popular text. The Annesley trial may have informed Kimber's novel somewhat as well, although he claims it emerged instead from the history of a man he met during his travels in America.[5] Like Memoirs, The History of Mr. Anderson presents multiple states of captivity affecting individuals from multiple points of society. These texts not only demonstrate the British capacity for mastery with restraint (in contrast to the unbridled cruelty of American captors), but also extend the sites of captivity representing confined states in both domestic and colonial locations. Even as these texts provide examples of the kinds of domestic captivity to which individuals might be subject in both locations, they both ultimately figure England as a potential site of liberation for men (even as their texts prove it to be otherwise); at the same time they highlight, and essentially elide, the forms of domestic captivity to which the most vulnerable members of eighteenth-century culture could still be subject.

"Bought Servants," Unfree Labor, and "Voluntary Slaves"

A contract for indenture is a deceptively simple document. Blank spaces wait to be filled with the name, age, and destination of the signatory. The initial phrase of the document, "be it remember'd," implicitly speaks to an oral culture where memory serves in place of written words. One does "by Indenture ... agree to serve." Although the document guarantees the person entering the indenture specified items such as "necessary Cloathes, Meat, Drink, Washing, and Lodging," the amount and quality of these items remain unquantified. One receives "as other Servants in such cases are usually provided for, and allowed." That phrase, "usually provided for," is an imprecise and ultimately relative measure. The language speaks of service, apparently in exchange for "necessary" things. Certainly for many, particularly those in dire straits, that simple subsistence exceeded their current situation. Many of these contracts vividly document their signatory's lack of access to these details. A simple mark—an "X," a circle, or perhaps a well-practiced letter—reveals the world of literacy unavailable to them. Thus, reading a stack of indenture agreements invites, or perhaps demands, an imaginative reconstruction of the circumstances involved. When sixteen-year-old William Holt made his mark, X, on October 21, 1736, obliging himself to six years in Jamaica, did his mother "being present" as the document notes suggest moral support or coercion? Eighteen-year-old Mary Alexander's confident signature might proclaim her literacy, or perhaps simply a studied ability to sign with more than a single letter or random symbol. For many, entering a term of indentured servitude represented either a desperate effort at survival or an opportunity for a new beginning.

William Moraley presented himself as in a bleak situation when recounting his experience in *The Infortunate: The Voyage and Adventures of William Moraley, an Indentured Servant*.[6] Originally published in Newcastle in 1743, the same year at Haywood's *Memoirs*, the text provides insights into the condition of indentured servants in colonial American. Moraley's urban experience of indenture in Philadelphia differs significantly from the plantation-based captivity Haywood's and Kimber's texts record. However, his decision to become what he terms a "voluntary slave" offers an example of the factors motivating many entering into this condition.[7] His father suffering losses in the collapse of South Sea Company stock, Moraley was pulled from an apprenticeship as a law clerk to a less promising one as a watchmaker. However, upon his father's death and mother's remarriage, he loses his last means of support and decides to "sell myself for a Term of Years into the American plantations."[8]

He recounts seeing the "printed Advertisements fix'd against the walls" of the Royal Exchange offering bound passage to the colonies—the opportunity to self-commodify. "[O]ppress'd by Dame Fortune," Moraley does not care where he goes; "All Places are alike to me." He seeks only "some view of Bettering my Condition of Life, though I might have expected a better Fate than to be forc'd to leave my Native Country."[9] His situation— a lack of opportunity in his "Native Country"—makes a departure inevitable. Held captive by the inability to imagine "bettering his condition" at home, he must place himself in a different state of confinement—as he puts it, "sell myself"—to improve his plight. He clearly understands the fundamental contradiction of his situation as a member of a group of "Voluntary Slaves." They, he writes, "are the least to be pitied."[10] The instance the individual has the greatest power over himself—the moment of entering into a contract—is the point that power completely disappears (at least for the term of the indenture). As Moll Flanders's mother notes, "such as were brought overs by Masters of Ships to be sold as servants, such as we call them, . . . are more properly call'd *Slaves*."[11] While Moraley also connects the situation of the servant and the slave—seeing them both as sources of unfree labor—he draws clear distinctions in their condition during his own experiences in Philadelphia. Repeatedly citing the "severity of the Laws" that discriminate against enslaved Africans in terms of punishment, Moraley also reminds his reader of the inheritable state of enslavement: "all their Posterity are Slaves without Redemption."[12] His attention to and commentary on the condition of the enslaved differs sharply from that of Haywood and Kimber.

But not all transportation of white laborers from Britain to the colonies was voluntary.[13] Affecting a vulnerable segment of the population was the act of "spiriting" away individuals to be sold in the colonies, a practice originating in the seventeenth century with the escalating needs for labor. As early as 1649, William Bullock details in *Virginia Impartially Examined* how the colonial need for labor resulted in the practice of what essentially amounted to kidnapping. "The usuall way of getting servants," writes Bullock, "hath been by a sort of men nick-named *Spirits*, who take up all the idle, lazie, simple people they can intice, such as have professed idlenesse, and will rather beg then work; who are perswaded by these *Spirits*, they shall goe into a place where food shall drop into their mouthes: and being thus deluded, they take courage, and are transported."[14] The stories about "spirits" specifically targeting children, coaxing them onto ships to sell them in the colonies, also circulated widely and continued into the eighteenth century, fueling interest in texts like Haywood's and Kimber's. "The theme of the abducted servant and of the cheating agent who had deceived him into crossing the Atlantic became part of a well-rehearsed narrative."[15] Children's lack of status increased their vulnerability. Describing the kidnapping of children in eighteenth-century Ireland, James Kelly notes that because of their young age, abducted children "possessed no agency"; thus, he asserts, "a closer equation can legitimately be made between their lives and that of a slave, since they were exchanged in a commercial transaction that was conducted without their approval."[16] Additionally, the children's lack of agency, the inability to offer consent, and the use of their bodies in an commercial exchange structurally aligns them with women similarly accorded only limited powers.

Vulnerable adults also succumbed to kidnapping in the early eighteenth century. In her autobiography *Some Account of the Early Part of the Life of Elizabeth Ashbridge* (1774), the author (1713–55) describes her experience in 1732 of being "kidnapped," "lured onto a ship and held prisoner for three weeks."[17] Although she was rescued from that initial experience by the water-bailiff, she embarked on another ship for which she signed an indenture. After being "sold" in New York, she endured a series of hardships ranging from wearing inadequate clothing ("I was not allowed decent clothes; I was obliged . . . to go barefoot in the snow"), performing "the meanest drudgery," and suffering sexual abuse at the hands of her master.[18] She also described how, after displeasing her master by telling other women of this sexual abuse, her master "sent for the town's whipper to correct me."[19] As John Donoghue asserts, in colonial America "the prevalence of servitude, in tandem with the growth of slavery, made unfreedom of varying degrees the common dominator of colonial work until the American Revolution."[20] The line between indenture and enslavement was often blurred, a "fine distinction that an unsuspicious public was not disposed to make."[21] Ashbridge's detailing of her "cruel servitude" not only highlights the utter lack of agency accorded to an indentured servant, but also another way in which individuals could profit from their fellow English subjects.[22]

As discussed, individuals were also transported to the colonies as a result of increasingly draconian punishments for any crimes against property.[23] The transportation of convicts proved another opportunity to provide labor to the colonies from a captivity originating in a domestic location (with the explicit desire to remove the individual from that space).

Moll Flanders's mother, reflecting on colonial Virginia, observes that "the greatest part of the Inhabitants of that Colony came thither in very indifferent Circumstances from *England.*" Many, as she details, are those "Such as are Transported from Newgate and the other Prisons, after having been found guilty of Felony and other Crimes punishable, with Death."[24] When Moll is later transported to Virginia she describes herself as existing "in the despicable quality of transported convicts destined to be sold for slaves, I for five years."[25] Such fictional representations often advance the idea that transportation, like indentured servitude, could result in rehabilitation or a positive outcome. In the *London Magazine,* Kimber recounts the use of "Convicts that are transported here," observing that they "sometimes prove very worthy Creatures." Echoing the words of Moll Flanders's mother, Kimber notes that "several of the best Planters, or their Ancestors, have in the two Colonies, been originally of the Convict-Class." However, these words of (tacit) praise do not stop Kimber from regarding transported convicts, like "Volunteer Servants," as "a Commodity."[26] The landscape into which Haywood and Kimber place their fictional subjects, two young boys who consider themselves "indentured slaves," abounds with multiple forms of unfree labor.

Eliza Haywood's *Memoirs of an Unfortunate Young Nobleman*

The advertisement for *Memoirs of an Unfortunate Young Nobleman* alerts readers that this "story founded on Truth" represents the dangers of captivity that potentially exist for all but the most protected—even "an unfortunate young nobleman" can be subject to thirteen years of "Slavery." Eliza Haywood (ca. 1693–1756), known primarily as an author of amatory fiction, women's periodicals, and, later, more developed prose fiction, recognized the cultural fascination with Annesley, whose story had all the elements of an engaging narrative: parental rejection, questions of paternity, change of fortune, alienation of affections, allegations of adultery. It was, as Patrick Spedding notes, a "life story . . . every bit as romantic as any that Haywood invented."[27] James Annesley (1715–60), the son of Arthur Annesley, fourth Baron Altham, was initially acknowledged as the legitimate heir to the barony. However, his parents' estrangement, coupled with his father's financial need to sell some leases on which James would be a claimant, created a breach that cast doubts on his legitimacy. Following the death of his father, the title went to his father's younger brother Richard Annesley. To solidify his claim on the title, Richard had James secretly kidnapped and sold as an indentured laborer.[28]

Long thought dead, the first notice of Annesley appeared in the February 12, 1741 *Daily Post* when he returned to England on the *Falmouth* following his rescue by Vice Admiral Edward Vernon (1684–1757), who discovered and identified him in Jamaica.[29] The brief newspaper account reports that "at eight years old just upon the death of his father [he was] sold as a slave into Pennsylvania for seven years, before the expiration where of he attempted to make his escape, but was retaken, & by a law of the country oblig'd for his elopement to serve seven years more; & that a little before the end of this second slavery" again escaped and found passage to Jamaica.[30] After Annesley's arrival in England, he promptly initiated court proceedings to claim his title. The trial began on November 11, 1743, although its progress was slowed by Annesley's involvement in a hunting accident in which he killed a man. While Annesley ultimately received a favorable decision recognizing his claim, the ongoing process of appeals and strategic delaying tactics by his uncle kept him from ever actually realizing his inheritance.

From his return to England in 1742 until after the conclusion of the trial in 1745, Annesley was the focus of more than sixty publications. These titles targeted diverse segments of the reading public with varying degrees of sophistication and disparate price points. Publications ranged from the expensive detailed transcripts of the legal proceedings to satiric poems, ballads, and chapbooks priced at sixpence. Almost without fail, regardless of the intended audience, the narratives foreground Annesley's enslavement. *The Trial in Ejectment* (1744) details how Annesley was "sent into *America*, and there sold for a *common Slave* . . . and continued about 13 Years in Slavery."[31] The poem *The Richardiad* (1744), satirizing his nefarious uncle, poetically recounts Annesley's "painful life": "he wastes in slavish chains / While in his spoils th' exulting tyrant reigns."[32] Elizabeth Boyd's poem *Altamira's Ghost* (1744) describes his physical punishments, the "cruel Stripes, / Whose Marks he daily wore" as he exists "as Slave."[33] Like most of these publications, Boyd highlights the disparity between Annesley's class as the heir to a title and his captive status, calling him a *"noble Slave"* in the prefatory letter.

Publications targeted to a less sophisticated audience, perhaps a group existing in a state of greater economic insecurity, provide more sensationalized depictions of both the treachery of Annesley's uncle and Annesley's thirteen years of "slavery." For example, *The Cruel Uncle; or, The Wronged Nephew* (1744), a chapbook, advertises itself as "an Account of the hardships, and 13 year Slavery at Virginia, of that Unfortunate young Nobleman *James Annsly* [sic] who was sent abroad by his Uncle." It reminds readers how "some Relations, will so base behave, / To gain the wealth, will make the Heir a Slave."[34] Like Boyd's poem, the text charts the great distance between heir and slave, and ominously details how quickly that distance is lost. The chapbook's woodcuts emphasize both the transatlantic and the transactional nature of Annesley's kidnapping. The second woodcut titled with the heading "*The* Captain *selling the boy to the Planter*" shows a planter adorned with wig, sword, and cravat being persuaded to buy a small, young boy whose clothes are noticeably in rags. The planter, reluctant to purchase the child because "he was two [sic] small," offers a "hogshead of Tobacco."[35] The hogshead of tobacco (about 1,000 pounds in weight)—so valuable in colonial American as to essentially serve as currency—represents the product of the intense labor to which Annesley, once sold, will be subject. "So to this Planter there this Child he sold / This is enough to make ones blood run cold." When the ballad assumes the child's point of view, he narrates his own period of enslavement: "i Labour'd hard according to strength / Thus thirteen Years with Labour and great Pain, / in Cruel Slavery i did remain."[36] (The lower-case "i" for the first-person pronoun, though a sign of the diminished quality of this low-status publication, visually highlights the boy's own diminished status.) This chapbook, like contemporaneous publications, sensationalized the snatching of a young boy from English soil, a narrative personalized with the fame of Annesley and his plight.

Always a savvy marketer, Haywood correctly anticipated the cultural fascination with Annesley, publishing her first volume nine months before the start of his trial. Haywood capitalized on the topicality and interest in the Annesley affair, an interest that was persistent and widespread. In fact, when Tobias Smollett included the Annesley affair in a section of *Peregrine Pickle* (1751),[37] he felt the story was so well known that he did not need to provide details or a context for the narrative. Haywood's publication of the first volume of her account before the start of the trial fueled Spedding's speculation that she had privileged knowledge based on a family connection. Haywood tapped into the relevance of Annesley's plight and the immediacy of the story. Although Haywood altered the names in the texts, "it seems that few contemporary readers would have needed a key."[38] Significantly, Haywood appeared to add "very little" to the narrative. Just as Aubin notes that her novels, despite their fantastic elements, are texts founded in "truth," so too Haywood asserts that veracity in her preface to Volume 2. "[I]f Time permits this Book to live to After-ages, the Reader will look upon it as fictitious." But, she avers the accuracy of the portrait of Count Richard, "a Monster . . . without the least mixture of *Humanity.*"[39] Haywood tapped into the persistent anxiety tinged with fascination about the fundamental issues of national identity raised by Annesley's captivity. Haywood's two volumes follow the entire journey of Annesley, including his escape and eventual return to England when he then initiated legal proceedings against his uncle Richard to reclaim his inheritance. That approach proved successful. As Spedding details, Haywood's *Memoirs of an Unfortunate Young Nobleman,* by any metric, was among the ten most popular texts Haywood published; in terms of the frequency with which it was published, *Memoirs* was her single most popular work.[40] *Memoirs of an Unfortunate Young Nobleman* was "Haywood's fastest selling work by far," with five complete editions printed in London in 1743 and an abridgement published in the *Gentleman's Magazine.*[41]

Haywood uses the scope of the narrative to focus initially on James Annesley's domestic captivity in England. His condition reveals the utter absence of resources for an unprotected child, and the hardships of service in the colonies for those children spirited or coerced away. Young James's particular situation stems largely from his father's hedonism and profligacy. His father's excessive spending creates its own form of captivity: tremendous debt from which he cannot extricate himself. Although he was "Master of a good Sum of ready Money," he "squander'd all . . . [and] became so extremely destitute that he wanted even the common Necessaries of Life."[42] His father's brother Richard, who subsequently arranges James's kidnapping, urges James's father to "raise Money by giving Leases in reversion of a very great Estate, which must infallibly devolve on him at the Demise of the present Possessor who was extremely ancient" (41–42). Yet, the young James represents "an Impediment to the Execution. . . . No body being willing to purchase Leases which they knew would not stand good without Consent of the Heir" (42). For immediate economic gain, his father and uncle put Annesley in "a private place"—as a laborer in a school—and spread a report "that he was dead" (42). This decision initiates a form of domestic captivity on British soil long before James's kidnapping, abduction, and enslavement in the colonies.

In this "private" isolated location, James's constrained conditions become worse when his father stops paying for his board. He experiences an emotional and physical withholding. James begins to feel "the Want of those Things his young Apprehension made him know he stood in need of—all that could cherish or delight him was denied" (43). Annesley lacks things that define a familial relationship or offer the foundational preparation for a young man destined to a position in the ruling class. Wearing "tatter'd" clothing long outgrown, he lacks a basic sartorial marker of his position.[43] No "Recreations" of mind or body are permitted. He does not receive any "Tenderness" or "soft Indulgence," only beatings, reprimand, and reproach. While his physical labor—"drawing Water, cleaning Knives," and other "servile Offices"—is not particularly taxing, it prohibits him from receiving the "Exercises of Learning" enjoyed by "others of his Age." Over the course of two years he serves as "a Sweeper of that School he should have studied in." Even at this young age, he realizes (and hungers for) the education he considers essentially his birthright. Occupying a space with an inverted hierarchy, Annesley is displaced socially, as he serves as "the Drudge of those he ought to have commanded" (43). The meaning of the word "drudge" extends beyond one employed in particularly servile work; at the time it also meant simply "a slave."[44] And his awareness of that inequity further distinguishes him. As he is "grown more sensible" he increasingly realizes his treatment constitutes "ill usage."

His complaints of this "ill usage" have no purchase. Rather he is told "if he did not like his way of Life he might go and seek a better" (43). That statement tellingly lacks any specific speaker conveying the message; it is uttered by a collective and unnamed "they." That anonymity underscores the pervasive indifference to his plight—or the plight of any unprotected child in that particular cultural moment. There is no "better" for him to seek. Frustrated with his situation and determined to find his father, James runs away. Homeless, hungry, and confused in the metropolis, the ten-year-old boy "knew not how to ask Relief" (44). "[E]xposed half naked to the inclement Air,—no Lodging but the open Street,—his Food cold Scraps . . . a Companion for Vagabonds,—unknowing, uninstructed in every thing that raises the human Species above Brutes," James lives as a beggar (46). He possesses neither the education appropriate to his class nor the hardscrabble experience necessary for the world in which he finds himself. His existence as one uninstructed and unknowing dehumanizes him; he possesses nothing. By locating the delineation between human and brute in knowledge and education Haywood speaks to the precarious nature of Annesley's situation, and also points to the need for women to be educated. The only way anyone—male, female, free, enslaved—can distinguish their humanity is through knowledge and education. Further, Annesley's narrative of homelessness and indigence exemplifies a much broader problem of unknown numbers of children and adults who live the same way, the unnamed domestic captivity so many seek to escape.

Living on the streets and beaten by a number of boys who taunt him with "Dog, Scoundrel, Blackguard, and such like foul Names," James proclaims his identity as the son of a lord (47). Haywood asserts a physical difference in James (much as Behn did with Oroonoko): "a certain Nobleness in his Air," coupled with "the fine Proportion of his Limbs, with the loveliest Hair in the World," evidence Annesley's distinguished birth (51). His declaration attracts the attention of an "inquisitive" woman who runs an inn (49). Hearing his tale after taking him in, she recognizes the descriptions of his father and his "wicked Uncle" Richard, whom she promptly contacts (53). Her realization of his identity marks the power of informal, oral networks of communication.

Knowing the threat James presents to his own inheritance of his brother's holdings, his uncle Richard constructs a plan of "sending him into *America* to be disposed of as a Slave, whence there was little Probability he would ever return." He contrived "the Means to make him what none who are happy enough to be baptized into the Christian Faith either ought or legally can be" (53–54). The uncle secures his passage with "the Master of a Ship bound for *Pensilvania* [*sic*]" and instructed the captain "to make what Advantage he could of him, by disposing him in the Plantations to who bid most" (55). Before the ship leaves, the baron dies but "the young Chevalier, now real Baron, was kept too close a Prisoner to hear anything of this Change in his Family" (56).

On board, James, who "passionately long'd to be Master of those Accomplishments he had seen in others" (53), believes this sea passage will take him "to an Academy for Education" (58) to compensate for the years of tutelage he's already missed. James can't understand his ill-treatment while at sea. He objects to the conditions he experiences, finding his food, "Salt

Beef and Peas," of quality and "in such a Manner, as but in the short Time
he was a Vagrant in Streets, he had never even seen" (58). But more troubling to him is his shipmates' disregard for him; he "could not imagine the
Reason for their not paying him the Respect due to his Birth" (58). His
focus on "birth," and the attendant associations of blood, lineage, and rights
accorded, speak rather uncritically to the classism that governs human interactions, a classism the text ultimately endorses. He has internalized his
own birth status, creating cognitive dissonance with his current situation.

James learns "that instead of being made an accomplished Nobleman,"
the status to which he is born, "he was going into the worst kind of Servitude" (58). The phrase "worst kind of Servitude" acts as an odd intensifier.
Servitude marks the condition of "being the property of another person."
The Oxford English Dictionary variously defines the word as "the condition being a slave" (1.a.) or "a condition resembling slavery" (1.d.).[45] The
added intensifier "the worst kind" may stem from the difference in condition any kind of servitude would mark for one born a nobleman; it may
signal James's intuitive understanding of the perils of indentured servitude;
or it might flag James's recognition that, given his youth and completely
unprotected state, he has no control over the duration of his term of services or the conditions in which he labors—making it "the worst kind of
servitude." His immediate response is self-harm, repeating the pattern
of Oroonoko. Haywood echoes many elements of Behn's characterization.
Like Oroonoko, James is endowed with a natural superiority and possesses
"a Heart that knew no Guile," a quality that contributes to the capture of
both individuals (60). Fearing the young boy will throw himself overboard,
"and by that means deprive him of the Advantage he might make of him,"
the captain puts James in the hold, the interior section of the ship below
deck, under "a Watch set over him till he became more reconciled to his
Destiny" (59). When James "refused all Sustenance," the captain attempts
unsuccessfully to have him force fed. This pattern, from being placed in
the hold to resisting with a hunger strike, similarly echoes (albeit in greatly
reduced form) Oroonoko's. Only the captain's financial interest "in his Life,
and the Recovery of his good Looks" compels him to moderate his behavior (61). Just as in The Conscious Lovers, where sentiment screens the
economic drivers within the play, so too here self-interest is obscured by
apparently benevolent behavior.

To sustain Annesley for the duration of the journey, the captain brings
him to his own cabin, feeds him, and "began to sooth him with the kindest

Words he could make use of" (59-60). Deceptive language has a palliative effect on the young boy's state of mind. This section of the text not only replicates—at the level of language—the experience Behn describes with *Oroonoko*, but also structurally repeats the strategies used by Haywood's predatory male characters attempting to seduce or violate a vulnerable young woman. Throughout her oeuvre, Haywood reminds her female readers of the dangers of "too easily giving Credit to what we hear," as she writes in *The British Recluse* (1722).[46] The captain's soothing and "kindest" words similarly should be ignored—but are not. When the captain claims ignorance "that his Men had dealt so ungently with" James, he promises to "do his utmost to place him where he should be well used" (60). The language obscures the reality of the situation. He is selling James, not "placing" him; that sale situates the child in a system of unfree labor founded on discipline and abuse—no one is "well used."

James's greatest concern for the future remains his lost opportunity for education: "*But I shall have no Learning and shall be a Slave*" (60). Dismissing his concerns, the captain exploits the common slippage of descriptors for unfree labor in the colonies. "*[Y]ou will have Opportunities enough to learn any thing—nor is there any thing so terrible in the Name of Slave as you imagine—'tis only another Name for an Apprentice*" (60). The imprecise language, while part of the captain's rhetorical manipulation, marks the instability of the three dominant terms for unfree labor in the colonies—apprentice, indentured servant, and slave. In the Delaware and Pennsylvania systems of unfree labor, as Sharon Salinger notes, "servants and slaves were members of interchangeable labor forces."[47] James's statement returns to his earlier understanding of the connection between ignorance and enslavement. Not only does his status as a "slave" deny him education; a lack of education itself constitutes a perpetual form of captivity. The two conditions are mutually reinforcing. Although ostensibly focused on Annesley's condition, Haywood's description invokes the longstanding arguments that denying women access to appropriate education ensures their condition of domestic captivity. Contemporaneous with *Memoirs,* Haywood published *The Female Spectator* (1744-46), which identifies female education, reflection, and understanding as imperative for women and focuses on providing them with (vicarious) opportunities to learn about their world. The relevance to women readers of James's concern about education increases when, as discussed below, a female indentured servant educates Annesley and, as a result, moves him closer to reclaiming his birthright.

Annesley's Colonial Captivity

Once in the colonies, the captain's promise to "place" James favorably disappears in the face of financial gain; he seeks instead "to dispose of his Property to the best Advantage he could for himself." In a commercial transaction that underscores James's dehumanization, the captain sells him to "a rich Planter" in Newcastle County, Delaware, named Drumon, "who immediately entered him among the Number of his Slaves" (61). After sleeping "but one Night in the House of Bondage," at daybreak James was "sent to work in the Field with his Fellow-Slaves" (62). The work initially assigned to James—cutting timber to make pipe staves,[48] lies so beyond the strength and skill of "our noble Slave" "that he had many Stripes for his Awkwardness before he had any Meat" (62). He quickly bears the physical marks of his subjection.

James's dehumanization is institutionalized by the labor structure: "he was as absolutely as an Ox or an Ass, or any other Property he had made purchase of" (62). Like those beasts of burden, James is an expendable, exploitable commodity. The "cruel monster" Drumon seemed "to do every thing in his Power to degenerate them [laborers] from the human Species, and render them on a Level with the mute Creation" (62–63). Previously in the narrative, Haywood observes that James lacked "every thing that raises the human Species above Brutes" because of his early oppressors' strategic withholding of knowledge and material objects commensurate with his birth (46). Now, Drumon actively imposes physical and emotional brutality to intentionally "degenerate" James and the enslaved from the "human Species" and put them on the same level as "the mute Creation" (63). The repetition of the term "Species" within this context is significant. For Drumon, like his plantation-owning contemporaries, all unfree laborers—the enslaved, the indentured, or those like James in a liminal condition—constitute nothing more than essentially a "species" of labor. Their degradation complete, these laborers possess no humanity; they serve only as bodies marked, like James, by the "many Stripes" of Drumon's deliberate punishment.

The colonies' legal structure reinforces the purely economic attitude toward indentured servants. A planter like Drumon can manipulate the system in order to extend a laborer's term of service. The "barbarous Policy" of such Planters is to intensify the conditions, "to use their Slaves ill," particularly "when the Time for which they are bound is near expir'd" to prompt them to attempt escape (65). Should they run away, "by the Laws of that Country," if they are "retaken, as they commonly are, they are mulcted for that Disobedience, and oblig'd to pay by a longer Servitude all the Expenses and Damages the Master pretends he has sustained by their Elopement, so that by this means some of them serve double the Years they are contracted for" (65). The term "mulcted" specifically refers to exacting a financial penalty or punishing someone with a fine. For individuals in this condition of confinement, the only "currency" available to them is their own bodies, their dispossessed labor, over which they no longer have control.[49]

Of course other kinds of punishment exist. While James is on the plantation, another "slave," Jacob, escapes, taking "a Bag of Money" and "several small Pieces of Plate" (74). When he is captured twenty-seven miles away from Drumon's plantation, he is "script down to the Waste," receives "twenty Lashes from each of his Fellow-slaves," and is then "re-sold to a Planter in *Philadelphia*" (76). "By the Laws of that Country," he could also have been "branded on the Forehead" (76).[50] However, branding would both mar Jacob's physical appearance and mark him as someone unreliable or potentially troublesome, making him less appealing—and therefore less valuable—to a prospective buyer. "Thus," writes Haywood, "can the most cruel Tempers shew Mercy when they find it in their Interest to do so" (76–77). Just as the ship captain lessens the harsh treatment of James to preserve his value, so too Drumon withholds severe punishment not out of benevolence, but rather from pure financial self-interest.

The captivity James endures under Drumon is characterized as a specifically *American* form of servitude. The figure of the colonial planter in America, brutal and brutalizing, charts an important and persistent characterization of a distinctly colonial American masculinity. Drumon "took Delight in heightening the Calamities" of those under his control (63). "Nor Age, nor Sex, nor the Accidents which occasioned their being in his power" (63) move "him to the least Compassion" (64). Indeed, notes Haywood, "on the contrary, those received the worst Treatment from him that were intitled to the best" (64). No one under his command can "do anything to please him" (62). Sadistic, "he seemed to take a savage Pleasure in adding to the Misery of their Condition by continual ill Usage" (62–63). This perverse behavior stands completely at odds with the constructed ideal of the rational, benevolent landowner associated with the British ruling class.

Clearly, as the state of the poor in England and the enslaved in the British West Indies documents, this construction constituted a complete fantasy but one with cultural freight within this narrative.

Further, Haywood describes "the Hardships of an *American* Slavery" as "infinitely more terrible than that of a *Turkish* one" (63). The "Turkish" slavery refers to "Barbary captivity," a situation Haywood writes about in *Idalia* (1722) and *Philadore and Placentia* (1727). As discussed in detail in the previous chapter, between 1660 and the 1730s, thousands of Britons were taken captive and enslaved by Barbary corsairs. Just as the ranks of indentured servants were usually filled with individuals with limited options or means, so too Barbary captives most often were sailors, perhaps originally pressed into service, or other disfranchised members of British society. Like indentured servants, they commonly constituted a part of the population—the laboring poor—most vulnerable to financial instability. Within popular discourse, Turkish captivity was typically (although as some scholars remark, erroneously) viewed as less oppressive than other forms of enslavement not only because of the different nature of the labor entailed but also because, as Linda Colley notes, that captivity was, for some, "a potential gateway to opportunity and a fresh start for those who were disadvantaged in some way in their home society."[51] (Ironically, indentured servitude was also thought by many to provide a "fresh start.") The comparison of American and Turkish slavery ultimately privileges Turkish captivity as a less onerous, and in some senses, less alien form of confinement. The American planters—not the North African masters—emerge as the less familiar, more "foreign" captors. The Americans' viciousness, self-interest, and relentless use of violence, in Haywood's depiction, run completely counter to the rational behavior ascribed to a British elite.

Haywood also specifically compares James's condition in America with "the manner in which the Slaves or Servants to the *West-India* Planters in general live" (63). Haywood provides details about diet, clothing, and labor on the American plantation that reveal the abject conditions for "slaves," but does not distinguish between indentured servants and enslaved Africans in the "American" setting.[52] All held captive are categorized as "slaves." However, notably she retains the distinction between slaves and servants in a West Indian colonial site controlled by individuals identified as "British." Indeed, she suggests that "some Masters" in the West Indies "appear more human than *Drumon,* and soften in some measure the Severity of these poor

Creatures Fate by gentle Words" (63). While the adjective "some" may serve to qualify this sweeping generalization, the description runs completely counter to the well-documented horrific conditions in West Indian plantations. Further, that the power of language—the alleged "gentle words"—would mitigate any aspect of the treatment of the enslaved or other unfree labor seems risible. The persistent characterization of the West Indian colonies as avowedly British accounts for this perspective. Earlier descriptions of the West Indian plantocracy, as detailed in previous chapters, dwell on its avarice and atavistic and utterly inhumane treatment of the enslaved. Thus Haywood's relative praise of this group of plantation slaveholders sits in quite strategic opposition to the American planter, advancing her idealized presentation of a British elite and the construction of masculinity with which it is associated. The text extols those few who "know how to make a right Use of Power" in a world where most men "imagine they cannot be *Rulers* without being *Tyrants,* and this it is that gives Asperity to Subserviency" (77). In this formulation, the "subserviency" of enslavement, when enforced by an appropriately modulated "Ruler" does not produce "Asperity"; that severity or harshness is produced only by the base actions of a "Tyrant" like Drumon (77). Neither Haywood or anyone implicated within this institutionalized power structure questions the validity of the structure itself, only the individual manifestations of it.

Drumon has a range of individuals subject to his power. The specter of abduction and enslavement extends beyond unprotected children like James to other vulnerable members of society, including cast-off wives like the "Wife of a Person of some Consideration in *England*" who labors with James. This unnamed "female Slave of near sixty Years of Age" possessed an "Air and Aspect" that "denoted her to have been a Person little accustomed to the servile Offices she was now employed in" (64). The never-identified woman's "mean habit" cannot obscure her previously elevated station. Her "Bloom being past," as she tells James, her husband had her "trepanned" on board a vessel bound for Pennsylvania "where she fell to the Lot of the pitiless *Drumon*" (64).[53] Although never named, perhaps to remind readers her tale is not unique, the woman's situation receives detailed treatment. Haywood strategically provides the compelling story of an aging woman discarded by her husband, essentially moving from one form of legal captivity in marriage to another in indentured servitude. The narrative illustrates in the plainest possible terms the degree to which women, in England or in colonial sites, are particularly susceptible to commodification; their value, dependent on their strength, age, or physical appearance, always diminishes with the passage of time.

While Drumon initially designates this unnamed female for domestic work as a seamstress, "finding her Eyes were too much impaired by the Tears she shed at the unnatural Barbarity she had met with," he relegates her to increasingly demeaning forms of labor (64). In an ironic inversion of good housewifery, she is tasked with preparing and delivering the "wretched Sustenance allowed for the Slaves" to eat in the field (64). But "this was a Toil the Delicacy of her Constitution could not sustain" (64). The term "delicacy" marks a vestige of her previous life as a person of consequence in England, before being sold off by her husband; such delicacy, like her literacy and level of education, operates as a positive attribute in her prior life of gentility. In her state of colonial captivity, however, gentility is a liability. Seeking freedom, she attempts to send a letter to some friends in England "in hope of being redeemed, by the Money being returned to *Drumon* that he paid for her" (65). That gesture, like the term "redeemed," structurally aligns her with a Barbary captive seeking redemption in the form of a paid ransom from a domestic agent. When Drumon discovers her letter, "he made her be chastised with the most cruel Stripes by way of Example to the others"; the marks of his vindictiveness upon her body replace her written words upon a page (65). He affirms his commitment "to part with none of his Slaves" (65).

Drumon tries to reduce her to an object lesson, an "example to others," but she takes on the role of active tutor with James who "scarce could have been" more "dear to the old Slave . . . had he been her own Son" (67). Although her literacy proves disastrous for her, she uses it to improve James's condition. The "afflicted Woman" recognizes that James's primary lament, beyond his captive state, is "being deprived of an education suitable to his birth"—a birth clearly more elevated than Drumon's (66). She becomes "his kind Instructress" (67) during his captivity by drawing on her accumulated knowledge: "She had been a very great Reader, was well acquainted with History and the World; and tho' a Stranger to the dead Languages knew very well the Subjects on which the ancient Historians, Poets and Philosophers had wrote, by having been conversant with the best Translations of them" (66). Her education, which in many ways resembles that of the aspirational merchant class (having read the classics in translation rather than the original text, for example), marks her own relatively elevated position in England and allows her to offer James a subversive, covert form of education. Like Behn entertaining Oroonoko, the "afflicted woman" helps the "noble slave" become "acquainted with several remarkable Occurrences of the *Greek* and *Roman* Empires, as well as the Revolutions of a later Date and nearer Home" (66). Although she doesn't have any books with her, she draws on her own recollection of past learning, calling "every thing she could to her Remembrance" (66). Indeed, she creates a kind of textbook for James, writing "down on Paper" what she remembers and giving it "to him when she brought his Food" (66).

Secreting the scraps on which his ad hoc tutor has written those stories she can call to mind, "whenever he was a Moment out of sight he would pull out these little Pieces of Paper and read them till he got them by Heart" (67). Like his female tutor, James must depend on his memory alone to sustain his learning. (And he must do so outside the surveillance of the plantation system.) But, "[i]n this Employment being often catch'd he endured many Stripes for neglecting his Work, yet did not the Smart deter him; and never any Boy suffer'd more Correction for his little Propensity to Learning" (67). Just as the female indentured servant's preparation and delivery of unpalatable food ironically subverts idealized domestic female behavior, so too James topples the image of the reluctant schoolboy beaten for inattention; he, rather, is beaten for his studiousness. These small instances become microcosms of the unnatural conditions in which James and his unnamed female teacher live.

This process of education for Annesley not only helps construct a British identity, but also inserts him into a history he recognizes as his own. When "he found an Action great or noble done by some of his own Ancestors, his young Heart was ready to burst, between a generous Ambition and the Impossibility there was that he should ever be able to imitate them" (66–67). Although a captive, James is able to construct a past, if not yet imagine a future; even denied his birthright, he can still access elements of his lineage through the oral and written texts the "old" female "Slave" provides (67), a combination of tutorial and autodidacticism. Further, the older female slave provides him with a distinct history into which he can imagine himself, restoring a continuity with England. Despite her own alienated condition of captivity, her role as educator and avowedly British supporter further undermines the moral or cultural authority of Drumon

and those implicated in the distinctly colonial American, irredeemably barbarous planter class. As James grows older, with the foundation from the
female servant, he develops a more nuanced understanding of the world
and his position within it. "[A]s his Capacity enlarg'd with the Increase of
his Years, his Ideas of Men and Things still grew more clear and distinct"
(68). He questions men's "Motives," reflects on "the Vices of Mankind,"
and expresses contempt for "Avarice and Ingratitude" (68). His "judicious
Remarks" align him with idealized principles of rationality, benevolence,
and self-control. His "Contemplations" into the nature of things reveal his
superiority of mind, despite being "crush'd by such a Series of Cruelties
and Misfortunes!" (67). He explores first principles, sounding practically
Lockean on his assessment of property, enslavement, and the articulation
of wealth.[54] While he thinks deeply about his own enslavement, his mus-
ings do not provide any insight into the institutionalized systems of slavery
on which the American and West Indian colonies both depend.

James's learning—and eventual suitability to assume his title when he
returns to England—depends on the tutelage provided by an unnamed
British female subject. Yet, Haywood problematizes the value of women's
education in both a domestic culture in which they can be trepanned at will
and in a colonial setting where that comprehension can exacerbate the pain
of captivity. On the one hand, the unnamed servant's education crucially
advances James's liberation; she assumes the dangerous role of tutor "for
the Advantage of the noble slave." His eventual return to England would be
meaningless if he lacked the intellectual development to function in the class
to which he was born, a development she facilitates. However, her depth of
knowledge does absolutely nothing to ease her own suffering. Female education is foundational to the construction and continuity of idealized British masculinity, but only within limiting parameters and when affirming a
woman's subordinate position. James's liberation is advanced by his studies;
the unnamed female slave's captivity is only intensified by hers.[55] The inef-
fectiveness of her education except when in support of James's ascendance
is reiterated by the fragmented nature of her narrative. She simply disappears from the text. She tutors James for "four Years of the seven he was
bound to serve" (68), then dies. Without her his state of captivity becomes
unbearable: "He now felt all his Woes with double Weight, having none to
advise him how to bear them. His Slavery became . . . insupportable" (69).
She provided the emotional succor and the intellectual rigor essential to his
development, but that function complete, she has no place in the text.

The woman's instruction also helps James remain largely inoculated against his debased surroundings. "[H]is pure and florid Blood flow'd thro" his veins "untainted either with the inclement Air, coarse Food, or hard Labour" and his "Mind. . . . imbibing nothing of the Principles of those he was among, nor the least Tincture of their Manners" (67). This discussion of "blood," especially within the text's preoccupation with lineage, inheritance, and legitimacy, is doubly directed. While the text uniformly refers to James, his older female tutor, and the other laborers under Drumon's control as "slaves," that meaning here—while accurately describing them as unfree labor—completely elides the unmentioned landscape of the abducted Africans for whom enslavement is an inherited condition. James, presented with an opportunity to escape, contemplates the value of liberty if it requires a "base Action," something he disdains "even more than a mean Servitude" (75). He rationalizes the conditions of his own captivity: "as he was the Property of *Drumon,* and his Service purchased by him for a certain Time, it seem'd not strictly Just he should deprive him of himself without any Assurance of having it in his Power to return him as much Money as the residue of his Time with him might be worth" (75). This revelation essentially displays James's own self-commodification, willingly categorizing himself as "the Property of *Drumon.*" He attempts to calculate the monetary value "the residue of his Time" might be worth. His ability to see humans (even himself) as property, a "sentiment" "truly worthy of a Nobleman" in Haywood's words, doesn't really distinguish him from the baser attitude of Drumon with his classist and racialized notions of superiority. James does not lament the deplorable conditions in which he lives; they are "the least galling Portions of his Slavery" (78). His objection, rather, is philosophical; the "Reflections" upon the "unwarrantable and unnatural Act" that resulted in his enslavement are "infinitely severer than all his Body could endure" (78). Yet, he does not extrapolate from the history of his own condition—the "unnatural Act" that led to his captivity—to the condition of the enslaved Africans around him.

Ultimately James does run away, only to be captured and held for five weeks in a prison until he is recovered by Drumon, who "claim'd him as his Property" (86).[56] The justices "mulcted him for two Years, so that he had now four Years to remain a Slave" (87). The "revengeful Drumon" exacts a more violent punishment: he "set him Tasks utterly impossible to be perform'd, gave him Stripes without Mercy for his enforced Disobedience, and Food in such scanty Portions, that it might be said only was sufficient to keep him from perishing" (87). While Drumon is presented as a particularly heinous master, he is by no means unique. He subsequently sells James, who finds "the Person whose Property he was now become, being as cruel and inexorable a Disposition as *Drumon*" (88). Haywood paints American colonial captivity as unbearably bleak although she gives no sustained attention to the enslaved Africans who actually comprise the majority of the unfree with whom James labors. Haywood's representation, like Behn's description of Oroonoko, privileges James as a "noble slave," a phrase that appears repeatedly in the book. His education at the hands of a captive British woman distinguishes him from the unreflective American landowners and masters (and the legal system they construct and endorse) and aligns him with a British ruling class from which (and by which) he was kidnapped and to which, by the end of the volumes, he strives to return. That alignment, however, is significant. Like *Oroonoko*, the text never really interrogates the institutionalized asymmetries of power. In the hands of the rational and the benevolent, enslavement—either of the dispossessed British or kidnapped Africans—is presented as a viable system of unfree labor necessary to England's colonial efforts.

Edward Kimber and *The History of Mr. Anderson*

The construction of British masculinity, as contrasted with that of the colonial American planter and advanced through the efforts of an educating female, also shapes Edward Kimber's *The History of the Life and Adventures of Mr. Anderson*. Like Haywood, Kimber depicts a colonial landscape replete with unfree laborers and, with one exception, he similarly erases the narratives and the humanity of the enslaved Africans. He focuses instead on the experience of Tom Anderson an "indentured slave," who, like Haywood's Annesley, benefits from the instruction of captive women. Kimber's narrative never loses its focus on the ways captivity in colonial America proves a crucible forging Anderson's identity. However, he does expand his scope to include detailed descriptions of domestic captivity in England and a harrowing first-person account of the captivity of Fanny, Tom's eventual bride, that proves central to the narrative.

Kimber (1719–69) spent two years traveling in colonial America, chronicling his experience in a series of eight pieces published between August 1745 and December 1746 in the *London Magazine*, a periodical edited by his father Isaac (1692–1755).[57] Kimber's "Observations in Several Voyages and Travels in America" (or "Itinerant Observations" as a modern editor titled them) provided detailed descriptions of the culture, behavior, and social mores he encountered in the North American colonies.[58] A dispatch from July 1746 includes an abbreviated, and differently concluded, version of the story on which Kimber based *Mr. Anderson*.[59] An American planter tells Kimber his own story—of how he, as a six-year-old boy, had been separated from his father in Lincoln's Inn Fields sixty years earlier. Spotted by "Capt. —— Master of ——," he was abducted and "carry'd . . . in the Stage Coach to Bristol," a city associated with both the slave trade and the extensive transportation of convicts and indentured servants to the North American colonies. As in *Mr. Anderson,* the unnamed captain sells the young boy to a planter "for 14 years, for 12 Guineas."[60] The very currency used in the transaction, the gold guinea—its name a metonym for the West African region from which the precious metal came—reiterates the institutionalized investment in a British Atlantic economy based on slavery and other forms of captivity. The similarity between *Mr. Anderson* and Kimber's "Observations" in the *London Magazine* largely ends with the sale of the young boy, however. The person Kimber claims to have met was sold to "A Man of Great Humanity," a planter who "lik'd the youth more and more," "marry'd him to an only Daughter," and left "him at his Decease his whole Substance."[61] This aspirational narrative, designed for a metropolitan audience, satisfies the desire to see colonial America as a site of opportunity. While the basic premise of the kidnapping of a young boy remains, Kimber's novel differs starkly in the expanded retelling.

Beginning as abruptly as the abduction it recounts, *Mr. Anderson* focuses on the kidnapping of the young boy Tommy who, left momentarily unattended in Lincoln's Inn Fields by his merchant father, is taken by Bristol ship captain Williamson who promptly sets sail for Maryland. Kimber specifically identifies Captain Williamson as someone actively involved in transporting both enslaved Africans from "the coast of Guinea" and indentured servants and convicts from Bristol.[62] Williamson's engagement with the slaving "profession" has a deleterious effect on him, creating a "roughness and brutality" "mingled" with his "abominable vice" of pedophilia (49). Williamson is struck by Tommy's "enchanting countenance"; with "tresses curling in his neck," skin "fair as alabaster," and "little plump lips and cheeks" Tommy resembles Cupid (50). During the voyage to

Maryland, however, the young boy, subjected to Williamson's "most shocking and most unnatural lust" as well as his tyrannical behavior, loses "his colour and complexion" (50) and his physical condition rapidly deteriorates. Thinking Tommy near death because of his weakened state, Williamson, "actuated by avarice" (51), sells him for £10 sterling to the "eminent" Maryland planter Barlow who explicitly buys Tommy to serve as "a very ornamental attendant" for his daughter Fanny who is the same age (52). This first act of human commodification anticipates the subsequent treatment of Tommy and introduces him to a world peopled with the indentured and the enslaved.

From Workhouse to Indentured Servitude

Other indentured servants on Barlow's plantation offer detailed accounts of personal histories that illustrate the various forms of domestic captivity to which individuals can be subject in both England and the colonies. The oppressive toil of the workhouse, the crushing weight of debt, or the pain of an exploitative apprenticeship prompt British subjects to seek opportunities elsewhere, even if those opportunities entail confinement or captivity. The situations that motivate—or force—people into indentured servitude evidence the confinement in which people exist in colonial and domestic sites. The histories of Molly Beetle and her husband Mr. Ferguson, both owned by Barlow, reiterate the concentric circles of human captivity.

The life story of Barlow's cook Molly Beetle demonstrates the kinds of social confinement to which poor, unprotected children are subject, a confinement literalized by the increasingly restrictive physical spaces into which she is placed. (Notably, Molly does not tell her own tale; rather her husband Ferguson offers it "in fewer words" than he does his own, underscoring the way gender can exacerbate confinement.) Hers is a familiar narrative: "born in distress—nursed in poverty—educated in slavery—and all without any crime of her own; but merely from the misfortunes of her parents" (64). This text, like Haywood's, affirms the importance of birth families. Her father "was a tradesman at *Bristol*," but, insolvent, dies in debtors' prison. "[R]elations that could well have provided for her, had they either christianity or humanity," do not (63). Just as Thomas Clarkson (1760–1846) would later draw upon the negative associations of Bristol in his abolition writings, casting Bristolians as a people largely inured to and unreflective upon human suffering, so too Kimber repeatedly uses Bristol as a marker for a society damaged by its trade in human commodities, as a place defined by hypocrisy, callousness, and ill-will. Molly's relatives' indifference to her situation repeats that of the individuals in London who ignore the abduction of Tommy because they would not "busy their heads to do a humane or charitable action" (48). Abandoned by her Bristol relations, Molly is left "to the care of their parish" and sent to the workhouse (63).

Bristol was the site of the first workhouse in England. Bristol merchant and slaveholder John Cary (1649–1719) initiated the establishment of the Bristol Corporation of the Poor in 1696 and the organization established the original workhouse in 1698. As Cary detailed in *An Account of the Proceedings of the Corporation of Bristol in Execution of the Act of Parliament for Better Employing and Maintaining the Poor of that City* (1700), he envisaged the Bristol workhouse as a model that could be (and in fact was) replicated across England. The workhouse, seen as an alternative to "out-relief" or direct charity from a parish, was designed to harness the efforts of the homeless, indigent, and unprovided to realize some economic gain on the part of the state. The prevailing attitude was, as Roy Porter notes, that "to accept relief should mean loss of liberty."[63] The commissioners viewed the unemployed poor as what Anthony Brundage terms "a potential national resource."[64] While presented as an opportunity to provide education and activity to poor youth, the workhouse—as the name indicates—actually was designed to extract forced labor from its inmates.

Molly's experience aligns with Cary's description of the New Workhouse, Bristol's first, which held one hundred girls. In his account, Cary explains that the high number of "young Girls that were on the Poor's Books, and of such whose Parents took no due Care of them" led the commission to establish the initial workhouse specifically for young girls.[65] Cary and his committee clearly regarded these young women—who were expected to work spinning thread "Ten hours and a half every Day" in summer and "an hour less in the Winter"—as a potential source of economic revenue that would make the workhouse self-sustaining.[66] Yet, he casts those parents and family members "who formerly kept" the young girls as the mercenary parties, now causing a "great deal of trouble."[67] "Having lost the sweetness of their Pay" in the form of out-relief, parents and families "did all they could to set both those children and others against us."[68] While Cary does not specify the means of enforcement that guaranteed the conflict "was soon over," he does detail the instruments of compliance displayed for the young girls—"A Bridewel [sic], stocks, and Whipping-Post, always in their sights" provide them with appropriate motivation.[69]

The model of the Bristol workhouse expanded as workhouse management was farmed out to private contractors; chief among them was Matthew Marryott (1670–1731/2), who operated dozens of workhouses across England. His descriptions of his individual workhouses dwelled upon details of their "Confinement and Labour."[70] The institutional discipline includes a spartan diet, long work hours, and containment within the regulated space. As Marryott notes, "None are suffered to walk into the Town without leave," and all are "confined within the Precincts of the House, and are not to go out of it without Leave of the Master."[71] The titles assigned to the agents of control—master, overseer—replicate those in the colonial plantation system; the terms emerge conterminously.[72] Indeed, the inmates of the domestic poorhouse were explicitly compared to people enslaved in colonial sites. Matthew Hale expressed his hope that workhouses would "produce the orderliness among the London poor that he had observed in a Barbados slave plantation."[73] The privatization of workhouses invited corruption, and Molly believes her parish workhouse "would produce happiness and frugal plenty to the miserable, if the guttling of officers and committeemen, the embezzlement of collectors, and the extortion of the keepers, did not make misery more wretched" (64). While she repeats the common criticism that money collected for the poor was diverted into banquets for committeemen, her almost Swiftian language also marks how the poor themselves are, in a sense, "guttled" or consumed by the parish forces.

Following her stint in the workhouse, Molly is "bound out as an apprentice, to household drudgery"—that is, into domestic service (64). (Again the word "drudge" is doubly directed.) As children aged out of the workhouse, they would be placed in an apprenticeship, another responsibility of the parish. However, parish officers tasked with binding children out often "remained indifferent to the nature of the master or the suitability of the trade selected," as George Rudé notes.[74] The workhouse and the accompanying apprenticeship system, performed under the guise of charity and generosity, operate as vehicles of oppression and control. The woman to whom Molly is bound possesses a particularly Bristolian disposition; Kimber pointedly describes her as "a devotee in the same city" (65) who "daily humbled herself at church, and returned from thence to ill-use and plague her family" (64).[75] Molly's world of work resembles that described in Mary Collier's *The Woman's Labour*, discussed in chapter 1, which explicitly compares the life of an itinerant domestic servant to a kind of enslavement.[76] Molly finds her work as an apprenticed household maid "so hard and rigorous, that she could bear it no longer" and signs herself over to indenture "to be relieved from it" (64), although she was "of a disposition that merited a better fate, than to have been indented to such a master" as Barlow (54). That indentured service in the colonies seems an improvement on an apprenticeship in England illustrates the harshness of such a domestic state of confinement.

Like Molly, her husband, the Scotsman Mr. Ferguson, initially came to Maryland as an indentured servant seeking refuge from his conditions in London, only to be sold to Mr. Barlow. Orphaned as a boy, he was adopted by his wealthy, elderly uncle for whom he is designated as heir upon his decease; however, when that uncle marries a much younger woman "of more policy than honesty," Ferguson's status and inheritance are compromised (61). Upon his uncle's death, the woman, a "rapacious widow," sues Ferguson for a debt of £200 based on a bond she finds in her late husband's desk (62). Structurally the episode replicates in miniature the situation of Indiana in Steele's *The Conscious Lovers*, when her late guardian's brother demands repayment of her maintenance, compelling her to debtors' prison.[77] The note, as Ferguson explains, was designed to make him "diligent" and "respectful" to his uncle, not actually to obligate him financially (62). Yet the very existence of the bond subtly suggests that "respect" even within a familial relationship somehow must be purchased. Although Ferguson has trained at the University of Glasgow as a doctor, without funds and the "usual assistance" of his uncle, and now burdened with a £200 debt, he must flee to London to avoid debtors' prison. His stark change in fortunes would be familiar to an eighteenth-century reader. Ferguson goes from being a "successful practioner" to "subsisting" by "the meanest applications." Further, without what Ferguson terms "a respectable appearance" a man cannot prosper and his "sordid appearance exposed" him "to all the distresses and miseries of want and poverty" (62).

Just as Moraley describes his walk to the Royal Exchange in *The Infortunate*, so too Ferguson, on one of his "hungry melancholy walks," sees the bill inviting "servants of any profession" to a "passage, upon indenting themselves to the captain or agent for five years" (62). A physician, he "was soon engaged as a very necessary man" although he cannot escape the confinement of indenture. Arriving in Maryland, he "by way of bargain and sale, fell into Mr. *Barlow*'s hands" under whom he initially "endured all the miseries of subjection" (63). Once Barlow recognizes Ferguson's ability to cure "diseases that had for some time infected his *Negroes*, he began to use [him] in a milder sort" (63). Barlow moderates his pattern of behavior only out of financial interest, not sentiment, sympathy, or respect. When Ferguson's "obligation expired," Barlow gives him a "small plantation" where he is able to use his "industry" to raise tobacco and to practice his "professions of physic and surgery" (63). With the end of Molly's indenture the two marry and their narratives present a dimly optimistic vision of the possibility for socioeconomic improvement under the terms of indenture, more akin to those Kimber included in the *London Magazine*. Significantly, these secondary narratives sharply contrast with the dominant focus on Tom Anderson.[78]

A Place of Colonial Confinement

Molly and Ferguson arrive as adults, voluntarily indentured (to the degree the term "voluntary" can be used), consenting to enter into a specified contractual agreement. Tommy, by contrast, lacks any agency. When Barlow brings Tommy home to his wife, he declares him "my slave for life, and a good bargain he'll be" (55), and refers to him as "his purchase" (52). The linked terms of human subordination—"my slave"—and economic advantage—"good bargain"—define Barlow's character as revealed through his relationship with Tommy (55). Tommy's initial experience on the plantation is marked by confinement and terror. Traumatized after his prolonged exposure to Williamson, Tommy remembers "the old discipline of the whip" and reacts with immediate acts of submission when Barlow even threatens to abuse him; Tommy falls "upon his knees . . . with his little hands uplifted, beg[ing] pardon" (54). Despite his suppliant demeanor, he initially escapes corporal punishment only by his seclusion in increasingly confined spaces—he runs to the kitchen (in an outbuilding) and then, within that, he is "clap'd . . . into a cupboard" to hide (56). He remains a "little prisoner" (56). Throughout Tommy's childhood, Barlow treats him with "unreasonable severity and antipathy" moderated only by the remonstrations of his wife (56).

Like Annesley, Tommy finds some respite in his relationship with the women on the plantation, especially Mrs. Barlow and, later, her daughter Fanny. Although "a woman of sense and humanity, of many extraordinary endowments" (53) and "of the best descent in *Maryland*" (57), Mrs. Barlow lives in a state of "wedded inhumanity" (54). The text withholds details of how a woman of such refinement came to marry someone as coarse as Barlow; perhaps the prevalence of financially motivated marriages makes an explanation unnecessary. That narrative omission also increases her similarities to the indentured servants. Contractually bound within the marriage, Mrs. Barlow too must complete a term of service. She routinely suffers Barlow's verbal harassment and threats of violence and he treats her "with a moroseness very near bordering upon ill usage and brutality" (54). Hers is a geographically isolated and emotionally abusive condition of domestic confinement. Despite her own unhappy state, she attempts to ameliorate, to the degree possible, the condition in which all those on the plantation live (53). Because of her, for example, Molly Beedle "weathered her term with much less oppression than servants ever feel in this colony" (64).

Mrs. Barlow takes a particular interest in Tommy, vowing (much to her husband's displeasure) not only to bestow "the tenderness of a mother" upon him, but also to educate him alongside her daughter Fanny (55). She teaches him in two ways. First, because of her husband's commitment to maintaining a strict social distinction between his "slave" Tommy and his daughter Fanny, she teaches "the little cunning folks how they should behave to each other" when Mr. Barlow is present. Quick studies, they readily learn this form of social performance, obeying "her lessons so well, that when the husband appeared, miss shewed a haughty distance, and *Tom* a lowly reverence and respect" (57). As he matures, Tommy's devotion to Fanny intensifies, manifesting the submission to her that he previously feigned.

Second, Mrs. Barlow herself "had been well educated" and shares her knowledge with Tommy and Fanny. Instructing him "by stealth," Mrs. Barlow teaches him and Fanny how "to read, very prettily" (57). Originally, "prettily" and "pretty" meant cunning or crafty, extending and affirming the covert nature of their instruction. The two young people "amuse themselves" with Mrs. Barlow's "pretty female collection of the politest authors," a collection both aesthetically pleasing and also clever (57). But Fanny and Tommy quickly "exhausted her stock" (58) and "thirsted for more" (57). Their education continues when Mrs. Barlow contracts Mr. Gordon, a

Scottish clergyman, to teach Fanny, and secretly Tom, "to write and cast accompts" (58). With his "tolerable library . . . much enlarged . . . by orders from *England*," Mr. Gordon can offer the two a more complete education (58). Tommy establishes an invisible, but essential, economy of knowledge as "one by one" he peruses Gordon's "whole riches" (58). This "stock" of books and knowledge is the only commodity Tommy cares about—not people, livestock, or agricultural goods. The lessons Barlow believes *he* can "teach" Tommy—asserting "I shall make a man of him, I fancy, . . . but I think I should give him a little learning too"—remain unrealized and, for Tommy, undesirable (68). Rather, he pursues an education that enables him to recognize the limitations of the colonial American system under which he labors. While he is "sensible" he lives "in the condition of a slave," because he never "voluntarily made" himself Barlow's "property, by contract or indenture"—because he never gave his consent—he questions how he remains in this subordinate state (60). His questioning never extends to the enslaved Africans, shorn of consent, laboring beside him. He explicitly points to the "excellent" English constitution "that protects every individual in his freedom," but which has no purchase in the colonies (60). Like Aubin, Kimber pushes against the limitations of the English constitution. While Tommy cannot yet anticipate his ultimately triumphal return to England, his response to this education signals this foundational embrace of the English system so central to the construction of the masculinity of the ruling classes.

Mrs. Barlow, Mr. Gordon, and Mr. Ferguson who teaches Tommy "sciences," educate him in a style appropriate to his birthright (58). Over a four-year period, he becomes "proficient in *Latin* and *French*, in all the useful branches of *mathematics*, spoke and wrote correctly and elegantly" (59). He learns to play the flute and the violin; he also gains "the principles of religion and morality, which took so deep root, as no after misfortune" could ever tempt him to violate (59). Now known as "Tom" (no longer tagged by the diminutive Tommy), he embodies the values of the British gentleman he was born to be (and will become by the end of the novel). This process of education and accomplishment, coupled with "[t]he kindness of his behavior to the servants, his humanity and consideration of the *Negroes*, and their families, gained him all their loves" (69). Tom accrues an "importance" on the plantation and beyond, providing him with an alternative, more desirable power than that held by Barlow. The text affirms that Tom makes a "better" master and embodies a more desirable form of masculinity than Barlow in part because of the difference in the two men's level of education (67).

When Barlow exiles Tom as an overseer to a remote plantation, "a place of confinement" forty miles away to separate him from Fanny, Tom refashions himself as a kind of pastoral figure entering retirement (84). Taking his flute and a "quire of paper, some pens and some ink" and a "pocket *Horace*" (86) he "would retire to the shadiest and most private retreats of the woods to vent his love and grief . . . and the groves around, echoed to softest, saddest melody" (81).[79] Yet Tom must function as an overseer of the enslaved, not a gentleman in retirement. Tasked with increasing the profitability of this remote plantation, Tom understands that his own battered body will serve as the compensation for any financial shortfalls: Barlow promises that "every deficiency shall be had out of your hide with a good cow-skin" (80). He plans to make Tom's body a kind of account book. However, through his "sweet treatment" of the enslaved Africans, Tom makes the plantation more productive "than was ever seen . . . before"; the unremarked physical labor of the enslaved remains the unspecified currency. Tom "gained their good-will, and shewed that kindness and clemency to those miserable creatures will make them more serviceable than cruelty and brutality" (81). He transforms objects of commodification—enslaved humans—into objects of his benevolence, creating a financially profitable moral economy. Yet Tom's benevolence, though born of sensibility, does not lead him to liberate the enslaved Africans, only to increase the productivity of the so-called "miserable creatures" (81). Indeed, moments in the text reveal Tom's uncritical acceptance of the racialized system of enslavement, which remains completely uninterrogated by him (no matter how intensively he philosophizes about his own situation). Early in the text, Barlow demurs at Tom's offer to pull off his boots, observing "thy hands were made for somewhat better" (68). Tom tacitly endorses this opinion when, "overjoyed" he "soon found a proper person to do this office"—that is, an enslaved African (68).

While Tom's education provides him with the moral and emotional qualities the text frames as ideal for mastery, Mr. Barlow remains in utter ignorance. Barlow "had little notion of the necessity of knowledge himself, as he could but just write his name mechanically," like many of those signing indenture agreements in England (58). He is not alone in his ignorance. Colonel Carter, the wealthiest planter in Virginia, is completely "unlettered" (67); his son Young Carter possesses a "mind" "all low and mean" (73). Barlow's lack of education accelerates his need for physical malice; together his violence and illiteracy mark him as lacking moral authority over those he controls. For example, when Barlow overhears Fanny and Tom's declaration of love he responds with brute force. He beats Tom "'till weariness obliged him to give truce to his fury" (75). The beating is so savage that Mr. Gordon finds it likely "if he recovered" that Tom would "be a cripple all the days of his life" (78).[80] Barlow declares, "I'd rather be hang'd, by G-d, than see my daughter debauched by a scoundrel . . . that I have purchased with my money" (76). It is less Tom's status than the fact he was "purchased" by Barlow that rankles; he both transgresses a line demarcating their social difference and deprives Barlow of the full return on his original investment. Barlow's uncontrolled language, like his unbridled anger, a recurrent manifestation of what the text designates as his specifically "America[n]" form of masculinity, actually feminizes him (92). His inability to control his emotions, his limited education, and even the way his verbal outbursts appear on the printed page—passages filled with em-dashes and exclamation points—align him with the culturally constructed image of feminine behavior. The text discredits American forms of mastery, which always stand in stark contrast to Tom Anderson and other British masters at a geographic remove, whether in England or the West Indies.

Domestic Captivity of Colonial Women

Embedded within the narrative of Tom Anderson's captivity are representations of the domestic captivity of colonial women, captivities initiated by Barlow and his fellow plantation owners. As in Aubin's The Noble Slaves, here the threats of captivity and domestic confinement are local, familiar, and, perhaps most importantly, familial. The oppressive patriarchal forces that enable the enslavement, indenture, or oppression of unprotected individuals operate in microcosm on Mr. Barlow's daughter Fanny. Barlow plans to fully use the legal power he has over Fanny as her father to compel her to marry Young Carter, vowing to "do as he pleased with his own daughter and his own slave" (79), conflating the two terms. Seeking to augment his holdings and create a strategic financial alliance, Barlow plans to essentially sell Fanny to Carter's son as readily as Captain Williamson originally sold young Tommy to him. He will "barter" Fanny "for sordid expectations of worldly riches" (74). Both transactions, rooted in human commodification, replace familial or affectionate bonds with economic self-interest. Fanny is regarded by Barlow less as a woman (let alone as a daughter) than as a commodified body who figures within a brokered alliance. (Indeed, he repeatedly calls her "Frank," his diminutive for her name Francis.) Fanny's ordeal begins with verbal abuse and spectacles of violence and escalates to imprisonment and attempted rape as Barlow and Colonel Carter try to exact her compliance. Barlow's language toward and about Fanny transgresses all social and familial norms: he calls her a "hell-fir'd, little b—h" (76), exclaiming "D—m her, let her die—it's good enough for her—a disobedient b—h!" (77). He later calls her a "d—'d, dissembling, disobedient little b—h," and a "cunning w—e" (167). He dismisses any need for emotion within the marital union. "Marry first, and he'll put love into her afterwards" (70); "[H]e'll cure her I warrant him" (72). His words are as extreme as his attitude.

The verbal abuse escalates to threats of physical violence when Colonel Carter and Barlow lure Fanny to the colonel's distant plantation. They plan to force her to submit to Young Carter's "assiduities, solicitations and presents," and prevent her leaving "till the marriage was perform'd" (151). Young Carter, imitating the behavior of those who privilege power over emotion, abandons thoughts of earning Fanny's love and instead "began to lust after her possession" (88). The Carter plantation operates with extreme savagery and spectacular violence akin to that found in Behn's *Oroonoko*. Upon waking the first morning after her arrival, Fanny witnesses the younger Carter brutalizing an enslaved African in front of the window where she is eating breakfast: "The first scene that presented itself, a piece of gallantry to me I suppose, was a negroe ty'd up in a tree before the window, and the redoubted *Carter*, the younger, belabouring his sides with the *Cowskin*, whilst his father stood by, encouraging him to lay the strokes on home, tho' the poor creature's blood follow'd every one that was struck. This was a discipline I never in my life had seen before, for tho' my father perhaps us'd his slaves with little less cruelty, you know his executions of that sort were never perform'd near our house, or in our hearing" (157). Young Carter's demonstration of physical power, observed and condoned (indeed, encouraged) by his father marks their generational barbarity. The perversion of "gallantry" strikes the distance between British and American sensibilities; the ironic designation of "Carter, the younger" as "redoubted" points to his—and his father's—lack of moral authority. The vivid description draws on details about plantation life in the mid-Atlantic region Kimber gleaned during his travels. In "Observations," for example, he documents the use of the "Cowskin" as an instrument of punishment.[81] Both texts indicate the inescapable presence of human suffering within the plantation environment. Fanny views and hears a kind of discipline she "never in my life had seen before." But as Adam Beach observes, "the master's violence is always present and is constitutive of slavery itself."[82] The proximity of such arbitrary punishment to the domestic space is represented as uniquely "American." If, as discussed in chapter 3, the true "gentleman" or man of taste seeks to compartmentalize or decouple his identities as a slaveholder and as a gentleman, the colonial plantation owner in America does not achieve—or even strive for—that geographical or psychological separation.[83] Indeed, the demonstration of discipline is central to Young Carter's identity and to the plantation as a built environment. Fanny notes that her father's punishments, though "little less cruel," occur beyond her sight or hearing. When Fanny responds to this incident with utter and understandable revulsion, Carter's niece Betsey laughs at her, treating "the matter as a joke" (157).

This episode of the Carters' public inhumanity serves as an implicit warning to Fanny. By demonstrating the inescapable cruelty that controls the plantation, Young Carter signals the foundational exertion of power that would extend to his treatment of a wife. While he might never publicly violate Fanny's body as he does an unnamed enslaved Black man, his behavior toward her would be driven by the same impulses. Fanny recognizes that Carter would be "an unfeeling, unpitying husband": "this very morning you gave me a specimen of such brutality, that I shudder when I think what my fate would be" (160). Despite a life of exposure to her own father's relentless cruelty to the enslaved workers on his plantation, she is shocked by "such acts of unfeeling, obdurate inhumanity" (158). The inhumanity of the Carter plantation continues when father and son enjoy "laughing and joking at their late exploit, numbering up the poor fellow's groans and piercing cries, with a kind of triumph" (157). The audible suffering of others becomes yet another item to be quantified, "numbered up." Young Carter's further attempts to court Fanny, offered in halting, incomplete sentences, include boasting of the quantity of enslaved Africans on the plantation and detailing ways he will use them: "if you'll say the word—your coach shall be drawn by *Negroes* instead of horses" (159). This abhorrent offer threatens to literalize the dehumanization endemic to the entire colonial plantation culture. Kimber also explicitly points to Young Carter's sexual abuse of enslaved women. Lamenting Fanny's impending marriage, Tom finds specific "horror and distraction" in the fact that Fanny would be "in the possession of a wretch, who shall embrace [her beauties] . . . in common with the . . . slaves he is master of" (73).

The other warning Fanny receives about the dangers of the Carters is from an enslaved man Squanto, previously owned by her father.[84] Unlike any other character in the novel, Fanny recognizes the humanity of enslaved people and "ever consider'd the poor wretches as part of my own species and not upon the level of the brute creation" (157). She is "really glad to see *Squanto*" and her identification with him is profound as she "plac[es] him in the light of a fellow sufferer, from the same barbarous and inhuman people" (164). No one else held captive in this novel links their captivity with that of enslaved Africans; however, Fanny immediately embraces Squanto as a "fellow sufferer," explicitly connecting her status as a captive white female with his as an enslaved African. Squanto shares Fanny's recognition of the gravity of his situation and her own, pronouncing "here is de Hell" (164). Despite her affinity for him, her promises of freeing him, and their shared attempt at escape, the profound difference in their condition is revealed in their respective fates. Caught by the Carters and Barlow, Squanto is killed by "a series of punishments . . . that would terrify the hardest heart to conceive" (167) while Fanny is "Lock'd. . . . into a room" and observes that "to confine" her thus was actually "exercising mercy" relative to the fate of Squanto (an unusual turn of phrase that affirms the Carters' power even as it demonstrates their moral unfitness).[85] Her story foregrounds the experience of the enslaved yet ultimately subsumes it, replacing it or confining it within her own narrative of domestic captivity. It is not erased from the reader's mind or the narrative's consciousness (as the experience of enslaved people are from so many of these narratives) but it functions more to inject urgency into Fanny's narrative than to deeply engage Squanto's trauma or the grim end he suffers.

The situation of forced confinement, or what Fanny terms "durance" in "my prison," is a prelude to the use of sexual violence as a means of compliance. Entering Fanny's bedroom "in his night-gown," Young Carter fastens the door "on the inside," and drags her to "the middle of the floor, with disheveled hair and torn attire, and would have proceed to liberties that are shocking . . . even in idea" (173). Male sexual liberty, the freedom to act with impunity, always threatens the subjugation of others, and Carter's plan to sexually violate Fanny is interrupted only by a slave rebellion initiated by the "natives of Guinea" on the Carter plantation (170). The episode repeats a pattern in Kimber's text. While the least empowered individuals in the text can—wittingly or unintentionally—facilitate the liberation of more privileged white characters like Tom and Fanny, they cannot author their own freedom.

The first-person description of Fanny's kidnapping and confinement at the Carter plantation is the most extreme, detailed, and sustained narrative of domestic captivity told or experienced by a white female character in the text. While structurally, her narrative makes up three of the last four chapters in the novel, temporally it occurs prior to the "many years of [Tom's] absence" (150); the story is a reflection told in memory.[86] This departure from the style of the rest of the novel makes the piece the most disturbing in the text (intensified by its first-person voice); the structure also makes it an episodic, self-contained tale (appropriate to Kimber's journalistic background) that becomes a kind of set-piece of captivity the concludes the entire novel. While a brief final chapter provides narrative closure for all the other characters, Fanny's ordeal really serves as the conclusion to the work. Her captivity, with echoes of Clarissa Harlowe's experience, demands a similarly emotional response but has an expanded scope. The condensed, three-chapter retelling of her captive experience, which also embeds the story of Squanto, acts as a surrogate for the other untold stories of confinement, exploitation, and abuse brought upon the enslaved Africans the narrative omits or erases.

The material world of the colonial space is one relentlessly marked by human commodification, indifference to suffering, cruelty, aberrant sexuality, and unapologetic self-interest. For Tommy, while enslaved, the only respite lies in his belief that faith, virtue, justice, and sensibility exist—either in a spiritual world or, as finally realized, in England where he is ultimately restored to his elevated position and enjoys a surplus of financial resources: £20,000 from his parents, £700 p.a., and Fanny's £8,000.[87] He also receives a surplus of emotional resources; he receives not only the love of Fanny, but also now the love of "two mothers," Mrs. Barlow and his birth mother (179). Every individual Tom values emotionally (or who, in turn, shares his worldview) returns to England. Those British subjects who transgress the text's idealized construction of British masculinity—such as Captain Williamson who originally abducted and abused Tommy—ultimately end up dead or utterly marginalized. Despite his ostensibly ennobling characteristics that distinguish his British masculinity, Tom has simultaneously naturalized the world of human commodification in which he has circulated for more than twenty-five years as both master and slave. When finally reunited with Fanny, he considers her "recompense" "for all my pains and suffering" (149). The human form itself continues to operate as a meaningful currency. Like Sealand, Tom conflates emotional and financial rewards. In turn, Tom has the means to financially reward those who assisted Fanny. This text envisages a world in which patriarchal-imperial power, when properly channeled, can have positive effects for those subordinated by it or profiting from it. Unlike the irrational, irascible, and completely unreliable American colonial planter, men like Tom advance a specifically British vision of "good" mastery. Indeed, Tom's return at the end of the novel to the Yorkshire estate his birth parents purchased replicates the desired move of the West Indian planter who inoculates himself from the world of oppression and subjugation by returning to England. He affects the compartmentalization Simon Gikandi marks as essential, a compartmentalization underscored by the strategic placement of Fanny's narrative at the end of the novel. Tom distances himself from his own captivity, certainly, but his "success" as an overseer in a plantation environment ultimately makes him complicit in a larger system of oppression.

The text offers multiple narratives of captivity and oppression associated with the colonial space: personal stories of servants who sell themselves into indentured servitude, the details of Fanny's captivity, and consequences of an unsuccessful rebellion of enslaved Africans. Just as Aubin's sequence of embedded narratives in *The Noble Slaves* reiterates the repetition of domestic captivity, so too *Adventures of Mr. Anderson* reiterates the inescapable condition within the colonial plantation system Anderson depicts. The cumulative effect of these narratives and the consequences of the specifically American colonial space creates a hierarchy of cultural and geographic spaces in the British Atlantic.

Together these mid-century texts by Haywood and Kimber document how fully the role of the elite British male as appropriate "master" had been naturalized by mid-century. Those participating in West Indian plantation culture, although never individually shown, emerge as an idealized—if absent—model of rational, enlightened, and benevolent domination, particularly in contrast to the emotional, arbitrary, and brutal impulses of their colonial American counterparts. Yet both texts remove the male figure, and for Tom Anderson his dependents, from the colonial site and return them to England. That gesture essentially elides—indeed erases—the forms of captivity the men witnessed (and to which they were subject) in colonial America as well as the continuing conditions of domestic captivity of other British subjects that still remained.

Domesticating Captivity

This book asks what happens when we use captivity as a lens for reading popular texts of multiple genres from the Restoration and early eighteenth century. Captivity shaped creative expression, concepts of self, and human interactions, laying bare the discrepancy between the "liberty" so central to British identity and its limited meaning in the actual lives of many British subjects—the unprotected child, the impressed sailor, the indigent laborer, or the indentured servant. Domestic captivity presses forcefully upon women, whose narratives reveal the consequences of the legal, financial, and social constraints imposed daily upon them. Foundational to these confining, oppressive situations, and their literary representations, is England's deep investment (financially and psychologically) in global slavery, to which domestic captivity is inextricably linked. While many texts occlude the voices of enslaved people or erase their experiences, subsuming those important, often fragmented stories within another's tale, they still bear the undeniable marks of England's institutionalized, state-sponsored commitment to the exploitation of kidnapped Africans. Although the most visible forms of enslavement existed at a geographic remove from the British Isles, it infused domestic culture—as the texts in this study reveal. When the metaphor of language is situated within material culture, it unveils the presence of domestic captivity, the intricate web of dominance and subordination, and the normalized, accepted world of violence and human commodification.

And that world can be summoned, vividly, with just a single word. The casual aside or pointed comment provides a window into forms of subjection and the naturalization of domestic captivity always lurking at the edges of a text. *Pride and Prejudice* (1813) contains the casual mention of "flogging" in chapter 12 when Kitty and Lydia return to Longbourn and report the "information" from the militia stationed in the town of Meryton: "Much had been done, and much had been said in the regiment since the preceding Wednesday; several of the officers had dined lately with their uncle, a private had been flogged, and it had actually been hinted that Colonel Forster was going to be married."[1] The inattentive reader can easily miss the reference to flogging in that line, situated as it is between dining and a prospective marriage. Indeed, that is Austen's point. As Tim Fulford observes, Lydia and Kitty's description "shows military life to be a routine . . . in which brutal punishment seems just another amusing and ordinary event in the social round . . . as an unremarkable detail."[2] By inserting flogging into Lydia's news of the day, Austen brings the markers of captivity into the physical space of the Bennet's domestic dwelling and into the narrative space of the domestic novel.

Such an episode evinces the complete naturalization of the culture of captivity—a naturalization Austen resists. Here Austen knowingly gives a glimpse of a world that includes the corporal punishment of privates—but of course invokes other kinds of flogging, specifically the cruelty upon the enslaved. A devoted reader of Thomas Clarkson and his *History of the Abolition of the Slave Trade* (1808), Austen certainly knew of the treatment of enslaved people.[3] Similarly, while heavily debated by the time Austen began writing *Pride and Prejudice*, the flogging of soldiers in the army and navy was a common and widely known practice. In fact, in his *Letters on Slavery* (1788), William Dickson uses the army's practice of flogging as a baseline for discussing the treatment of the enslaved in Barbados—the two represent analogous acts. The punishment of an enslaved person was legally limited to forty lashes from a "cow-skin," an "instrument of correction" made of leather "hard platted and knotted, like that of a horse-whip but thicker" with "some degree of elasticity." Dickson characterizes the punishment of an enslaved African with this whip as "more severe, perhaps, though less tedious, than two hundred from the cat-o-nine tails used in the army."[4] That "tedious" act of two hundred lashes is the event to which Lydia and Kitty refer.[5]

By inserting flogging into a novel defined by gentility, civility, and propriety, Austen points to a world in which those qualities coexist with confinement, brutality, and enslavement. She gestures toward what Bharat Tandon terms "the invisible world" that shapes her fictive one and in doing so she summons a culture of captivity.[6] With two beloved brothers serving in the West Indies, an aunt Jane Leigh-Perrot who owned a plantation in Barbados and had a Black servant in England, and a sister-in-law Fanny who was raised in Jamaica, Austen also had an intimate understanding of West Indian colonial life and its reverberations in England.[7] While her nuanced prose makes hers, perhaps, a most oblique reference, the mention of flogging epitomizes the ways captivity, domestic confinement, and forms of control persist. Her novel does not—cannot—accommodate the graphic descriptions of violence that we see, for example, in *Oroonoko* or *The Adventures of Mr. Anderson*. But it does not need to. The formative cultural work performed by texts like the ones discussed in this book naturalizes the landscape of domestic captivity and the role of the British subject within it.

. but women also de-naturalize it

PROLOGUE

1. Historian Linda Colley uses the phrase "culture of captivity" to characterize a period in the eighteenth century during which cultural anxiety about individual citizens' potential captivity in other countries existed simultaneously with widespread patriotic pride in British commercial and colonial success built upon the captivity of others. Linda Colley, *Captives: Britain, Empire, and the World, 1600–1850* (New York: Anchor Books, 2002), 78. Colley, in the passage quoted, is looking at the ways in which the situation for Barbary captives held in North Africa resonates with the laboring poor and their particular vulnerability. That astute observation, as I am suggesting, actually extends well beyond the situation for Barbary captives and resonates to a broader sweep of the population than perhaps even Colley herself accounts for. Her study as a whole examines captivity, primarily of white Britons, in the Mediterranean, North America, and India; she does not look at the captivity of indentured servants in the Caribbean nor at the enslavement of Africans. While I use her term quite differently, and her study pursues very different avenues of investigation, her book deeply informs my thinking.

2. Felicity Nussbaum, *Limits of the Human: Fictions of Anomaly, Race, and Gender in the Long Eighteenth Century* (Cambridge: Cambridge University Press, 2003), 156. Nussbaum identifies this pattern as prevalent "before abolitionist discourse coheres" (143), which is the period under exploration in my project.

3. Richard Pinder, *The Captive (That Hath Long Been in Captivity) Visited with the Day-Spring from on High* (London, 1660), 5.

4. Peter Linebaugh, *The London Hanged: Crime and Civil Society in the Eighteenth Century* (Cambridge: Cambridge University Press, 1992). The same

year, the colonial legislature also passed "An Act for the good Govern-ing of Servants, and Ordering the Rights between Masters and Servants," which similarly capitalized on the degree to which indentured servants functioned as property to be "sold and disposed of" (26), often conflated the status of "servant" and "slave," and categorized the time a servant was bound to service as a currency comparable to sugar or specie. See *Acts of Assembly, Passed in the Island of Barbadoes from 1648, to 1718* (London, 1721), 22–29.

5. Elizabeth A. Bohls, *Slavery and the Politics of Place: The Colonial Caribbean, 1770–1833* (Cambridge: Cambridge University Press, 2014), 3, 7.

6. Arthur H. Williamson, "An Empire to End Empire: The Dynamic of Early Modern British Expansion," *Huntington Library Quarterly* 68, no. 1/2 (2005): 245.

7. K. G. Davies, *The Royal African Company* (1957; rpt. New York: Octagon Books, 1975), 39.

8. Robin Law, "The First Scottish Guinea Company, 1634–9," *Scottish Histor-ical Review* 76, no. 202, pt. 2 (1997): 185–202.

9. Davies describes how "all gold obtained in West Africa was delivered to the Mint" (*Royal African Company*, 181), which coined 548,327 guineas between 1673 and 1713 (39).

10. Holly Brewer, "Slavery, Sovereignty, and 'Inheritable Blood': Reconsider-ing John Locke and the Origins of American Slavery," *American Historical Review* 122, no. 4 (2017): 1049.

11. *The Several Declarations of the Company of Royal Adventurers of England . . .* (London, 1667), 8.

12. The company expanded its activities beyond slave trading in 1731, and then dissolved in 1752.

13. *Certain Consideration Relating to the Royal African Company of England . . .* (London, 1680), 5.

14. For a discussion of the significance of the South Sea Company in the his-tory of the Atlantic trade and in the construction of the public imagination see Abigail L. Swingen, *Competing Visions of Empire: Labor, Slavery, and the Origins of the British Atlantic Empire* (New Haven: Yale University Press, 2015); John O'Brien, *Literature Incorporated: The Cultural Unconscious of the Business Corporation, 1650–1850* (Chicago: University of Chicago Press, 2016); and Sean Moore, "Exorcising the Ghosts of Racial Capital-ism from the South Sea Bubble: Pent-up Racist Liquidity and the Recent Four-Year Stock Surge," *Eighteenth-Century Studies* 54, no. 1 (2020): 1–13.

15. Davies, *Royal African Company*; William A. Pettigrew, *Freedom's Debt: The Royal African Company and the Politics of the Atlantic Slave Trade, 1672–1752* (Chapel Hill: University of North Carolina Press, 2013).

16. Linebaugh, *The London Hanged*, 45. Other enslaved persons were branded with RAC upon their chests. This practice continued with other companies trading in enslaved Africans. For example, the South Sea Company, which, after the *asiento* had trading rights to supply the Spanish with enslaved Africans, branded each enslaved person with the letter A (for "*asiento,*" O'Malley posits) when they stopped in Jamaica en route to the Spanish territory. See Gregory E. O'Malley, *Final Passages: The Intercolonial Slave Trade of British America, 1619–1807* (Chapel Hill: University of North Carolina Press for the Omohundro Institute of Early American History and Culture, 2014), 219.

17. The work of Catherine Hall and the Centre for the Study of the Legacies of British Slavery (https://www.ucl.ac.uk/lbs/) builds on two previous projects that trace the impact of slaveholding on the formation of Britain: the Legacies of British Slave-ownership project and the Structure and Significance of British Caribbean Slave-ownership 1763–1833. The work reveals slaveholding and individuals' involvement with that practice to have been much more widespread in its presence and influence than originally thought. The focus of the center, and the accompanying database mapping both the location in Britain of slaveholders and, to a more limited degree, the Caribbean location of estates and plantations, targets a period later than the focus of my study, in part because it draws heavily on the 1834 compensation records awarding £20 million to former slaveholders. The records reveal the pattern of slaveholding, the geographic and demographic diversity of that group, and the tremendous influence of the wealth they generated. The approach foundational to the database, and its accompanying volume (Catherine Hall, Nicholas Draper, Keith McClelland, Katie Donington, and Rachel Lang, *Legacies of British Slave-ownership: Colonial Slavery and the Formation of Victorian Britain* [Cambridge: Cambridge University Press, 2014]), asks questions and suggests connections that have resonance for an earlier period as well. Consequently, this work, and much of the scholarship that has responded to or benefited from its findings, has informed my thinking.

18. Holly Brewer, "The Fashion for Slavery" (Paper presented at the Restoration and the British Empire Symposium, University of Maryland, April 29, 2016).

19. Peter Fryer, *Staying Power: The History of Black People in Britain* (London: Pluto Press, 1984), 2.

20. Catherine Molineux, *Faces of Perfect Ebony: Encountering Atlantic Slavery in Imperial Britain* (Cambridge, Mass.: Harvard University Press, 2012), 23.

21. Ibid., 58. In chapter 1 of her book, Molineux describes how such portraits sought to imbue "permanence, derived from an artistic legacy, into a domestic relationship that runaway advertisements suggest was much more tenuous" (59). She discusses the vernacular iconographies of racial slavery. As she and others have noted, many of these images contain a young enslaved African male with a silver collar around his neck. The use of a collar, albeit brass not silver, also appears in advertisements seeking enslaved individuals fleeing their slaveholder. "Runaway the 30th of January, a Negro Man of a Tawny Complexion . . . walks with his Chin in his Bosom, having a piece of one of his Ears cut of[f], with a Brass Collar about his Neck." *London Gazette,* March 7, 1689.

22. In addition to Molineux, Patricia A. Matthew's "Look Before You Leap," *Lapham's Quarterly,* November 4, 2019, like the exhibition and accompanying booklet *Figures of Empires: Slavery and Portraiture in Eighteenth-Century Atlantic Britain* (New Haven: Yale Center for British Art, 2014), draws attention to the ways white portrait subjects appeared with Black servants, often identified as enslaved.

23. *The Character of a Town Miss* (London, 1675), 7.

24. Gretchen Gerzina, *Black London: Life before Emancipation* (New Brunswick, N.J.: Rutgers University Press, 1995), 2.

25. Madge Dresser and Andrew Hann, eds., *Slavery and the British Country House* (Swindon, UK: English Heritage, 2013), 14. This rich collection of essays shares the revisionary focus of Hall et al., *Legacies of British Slave-ownership.* See too Kathleen Chater, *Untold Histories: Black People in England and Wales during the Period of the British Slave Trade, c. 1660–1807* (Manchester: Manchester University Press, 2009).

26. Until the Mansfield decision in *Somerset v. Stewart* in 1772, in which Lord Mansfield ruled that English common law did not support slavery, an enslaved individual brought from a colonial site to England was still considered enslaved.

27. *London Gazette,* July 6, 1684.

28. *London Gazette,* October 1, 1685.

29. *London Gazette,* October 13, 1692. Branding had long been a punishment; those pleading the clergy were to be branded upon their thumb as a mark of their previous conviction. Toward the end of the seventeenth century,

as John Beattie details, there was a movement to make the branding more visible and a 1699 act changed the "usual mark" from the thumb to "'the most visible part of the left cheek nearest the nose'" (*Crime and the Courts in England, 1660–1800* [Princeton, N.J.: Princeton University Press, 1986], 490). This change was later repealed since the "visible stigmatization" of the individual made it difficult for them to subsequently secure legitimate employment.

30. *London Gazette,* August 4, 1692.
31. *London Gazette,* July 6, 1684.
32. *London Gazette,* October 22, 1694.
33. *London Gazette,* December 6, 1688.
34. *London Gazette,* August 18, 1711.
35. *Evening Post,* December 24, 1730.
36. The most detailed discussion of transportation can be found in Beattie, *Crime and the Courts in England.* See also M. J. Daunton, *Progress and Poverty: An Economic and Social History of Britain 1700–1850* (Oxford: Oxford University Press, 1995); James J. Willis, "Transportation versus Imprisonment in Eighteenth- and Nineteenth-Century Britain: Penal Power, Liberty, and the State," *Law & Society Review* 39, no. 1 (2005): 171–210; Kenneth Morgan, "English and American Attitudes towards Convict Transportation 1718–1775," *History* 72, no. 236 (1987): 416–31; and Linebaugh, *The London Hanged,* among others.
37. Quoted in Beattie, *Crime and the Courts in England,* 473. As Beattie also details, transportation was increasingly viewed as a way to rid communities of individuals viewed as undesirable. Quoting Acts of the Privy Council, Beattie notes that magistrates were authorized to transport "'vagabonds, idle and disorderly persons, [and] sturdy rogues and beggars' to be 'disposed of in the usual way of servants for the space of seven years'" (478).
38. Linebaugh, *The London Hanged,* 17.
39. Swingen, *Competing Visions of Empire,* 14. See also Carl Wennerlind, *Casualties of Credit: The English Financial Revolution, 1620–1720* (Cambridge, Mass.: Harvard University Press, 2011).
40. Jonathan Swift, *A Beautiful Young Nymph Going to Bed* (London, 1734).
41. George Boulukos, "Review Essay: Social Liberty and Social Death: Conceiving of Slavery beyond the Black Atlantic," in *Invoking Slavery in the Eighteenth-Century British Imagination,* ed. Srividhya Swaminathan and Adam R. Beach (Farnham, UK: Ashgate, 2013), 177. Beach and Swaminathan's excellent collection expands the understanding of the concept

of "slavery," and the multiple ways the term and concept were deployed throughout the long eighteenth century.

42. The *London News* of June 3, 1721, details the range of punishments from transportation, standing in the pillory, being "burnt in the Hand or order'd Whipt." Three men were also executed "for returning after Transportation before their Time." *The Gentleman's Journal, and Tradesman's Companion,* June 3, 1721, 2. The men's return suggested how the imaginative and perhaps geographic distance between England and the colonies had narrowed.

43. *Daily Post,* March 24, 1725.

44. *Daily Post Boy,* April 18, 1732.

45. *London Gazette,* April 20, 1702.

46. *Daily Post Boy,* March 13, 1733. Although beyond the scope of this study, the effect of the colonial presence and the slave trade on natural history and the collection of specimens is well documented. See, for example, Kathleen S. Murphy's discussion of the role of slaving ship surgeons in the collection of specimens in "Collecting Slave Traders: James Petiver, Natural History, and the British Slave Trade," *William and Mary Quarterly* 70, no. 4 (2013): 637–70.

47. Richard Steele, *The Spectator,* No. 69, in *The Spectator,* vol. 1, ed. Donald Bond (Oxford: Clarendon Press, 1965).

48. Emma Rothschild, *The Inner Life of Empires: An Eighteenth-Century History* (Princeton, N.J.: Princeton University Press, 2011), 2.

49. *Reasons Humbly Offer'd, Why a Duty Should Not Be Laid on Sugars* (London, 1698).

50. Molineux, *Faces of Perfect Ebony,* 13. Kathleen Wilson, *A Sense of the People: Politics, Culture, and Imperialism in England, 1715–1785* (Cambridge: Cambridge University Press, 1995), 56. Bridget Orr, *Empire on the English Stage, 1660–1714* (Cambridge: Cambridge University Press, 2001). Elizabeth Maddock Dillon, *New World Drama: The Performative Commons in the Atlantic World, 1649–1849* (Durham, N.C.: Duke University Press, 2014).

51. John A. Richardson, *Slavery and Augustan Literature: Swift, Pope, Gay* (London: Routledge, 2004), 21, 15. Simon Gikandi, *Slavery and the Culture of Taste* (Princeton, N.J.: Princeton University Press, 2011), 113.

52. *The Assiento; or, Contract for Allowing to the Subjects of Great Britain the Liberty of Importing Negroes into Spanish America* (London, 1712).

53. Wennerlind, *Casualties of Credit,* 199.

54. Herman Moll, *A View of the Coasts, Countries and Islands within the Limits of the South-Sea Company* (London, 1711). The map contained in the volume, "A New & Exact Map of the Coast, Countries and Islands within the

Limits of the South-Sea Company," while illustrating primarily southern North America and all of South America, also includes the west coast of Africa.

55. Raymond Williams, *Marxism and Literature* (New York: Oxford University Press, 1977), 128–35.

56. Felicity Nussbaum, "Between 'Oriental' and 'Blacks So Called,' 1688–1788," in *The Postcolonial Enlightenment: Eighteenth-Century Colonialism and Postcolonial Theory,* ed. Daniel Carey and Lynn Festa (Oxford: Oxford University Press, 2009), 139.

57. Paula R. Backscheider details how Defoe engaged in the practice of selling people in 1688. *Daniel Defoe: His Life* (Baltimore: Johns Hopkins University Press, 1989), 487. For a discussion of slavery in *Robinson Crusoe,* see Daniel Carey, "Reading Contrapuntally: *Robinson Crusoe,* Slavery, and Postcolonial Theory," in *The Postcolonial Enlightenment: Eighteenth-Century Colonialism and Postcolonial Theory,* ed. Daniel Carey and Lynn Festa (Oxford: Oxford University Press, 2009), 105–36.

58. The narrator in *Oroonoko* reads with a similar lens when she imagines that the untranslated words and gestures of the indigenous people directed toward her and her brother to be signs of their admiration. When the indigenous people come "swarming out, all wondering, and crying out Tepeeme: taking their hair up in their hands, and spreading it . . . as if they would say (as indeed it signified), Numberless wonders, or not to be recounted. . . . [W]e thought they would never have done admiring us." The interpretation of their actions as admiration is quickly followed by a gesture of dominance as Behn's brother "kisses" the "very young wife" of the Indian peeie. Like Crusoe, the brother's assumption about dominance colors all personal interactions.

59. Lynn Festa, *Fiction without Humanity: Person, Animal, Thing in Early Enlightenment Literature and Culture* (Philadelphia: University of Pennsylvania Press, 2019), 220.

60. See slavevoyages.org/voyage/database.

61. *A Modest Proposal* (Dublin, 1729) also reiterates the confinement and starvation of the Irish under British colonial oppression as it intricately connects that treatment to colonization in the West Indies, both the exploitation of enslaved labor and the need for the impoverished to "sell themselves to the Barbadoes." From the initial Letter "I" that visually mimics the seal of the Royal African Company to the discussion of the "constant breeders" and the profit to be made from them, the text represents the state of captivity common to both locations.

62. Nancy Armstrong, "Captivity and Cultural Capital in the English Novel," *Novel: A Forum on Fiction* 31, no. 3 (1998): 360. Armstrong's sophisticated argument extends the assertions of *The Imaginary Puritan* and suggests how the narrative of colonial captivity advanced the construction of British national identity, and continued—in modified form—well into the nineteenth century.

63. For a discussion of the function of Sally Godfrey, see Charlotte Sussman, "'I Wonder Whether Poor Miss Sally Godfrey Be Living or Dead': The Married Woman and the Rise of the Novel," *Diacritics* 20, no. 1 (1990): 86–102.

64. Not only do we know that Richardson printed some of Aubin's texts, so, too, as William Warner demonstrated, he clearly appropriated many of the elements of her fiction and reinserted it in his own, more "morally focused" texts. William B. Warner, "The Elevation of the Novel in England: Hegemony and Literary History," *ELH* 59, no. 3 (1992): 557–96.

1. CULTURES OF CAPTIVITY

1. Martin Madan served as a soldier for twenty-nine years, leading troops at Dettingen (1743) and Fontenoy (1745), both central battles in the War of Austrian Succession (1740–48). In the Prince of Wales's household he was first an equerry (1736–49) and then a groom of the bedchamber (1749–51). He served as an MP from Wooton Bassett between 1747 and 1754. *The History of Parliament: The House of Commons, 1715–1754,* ed. Romney Sedgwich (London: Her Majesty's Stationery Office, 1970).

2. Falconer Madan, *The Madan Family and the Maddens in Ireland and England: A Historical Account* (Oxford: Oxford University Press, 1933), 270. There has been limited treatment of Judith Cowper Madan and her poetry. Most notably, Valerie Rumbold discusses her in *Women's Place in Pope's World* (Cambridge: Cambridge University Press, 1989) and "The Poetic Career of Judith Cowper: An Exemplary Failure?" in *Pope, Swift, and Women Writers,* ed. Donald C. Mell (Newark: University of Delaware Press, 1996), 48–66. Claudia Thomas discusses Madan's *Abelard and Eloisa* in *Alexander Pope and His Eighteenth-Century Women Readers* (Carbondale: Southern Illinois University Press, 1994). See, too, Laura Alexander, "Rewriting Pope's *Eloisa to Abelard*: Judith Cowper's *Abelard to Eloisa* and Early Gothic Sensibility," *English Studies: A Journal of English Language and Literature* 97, no. 5/6 (2016): 608–17.

3. MSS. Eng. lett. c. 284, f. 121, July 12, 1731; MSS. Eng. lett. c. 285, f. 21, February 19, 1739/40; MSS. Eng. lett. c. 284, f. 131, Martin Madan to Judith, September 16, 1731; MSS. Eng. lett. c. 284, f. 202, July 12, 1734. All

Madan family letters and papers quoted in this chapter are in the Bodleian Library, Oxford.

4. Toby L. Ditz's classic essay "Shipwrecked; or, Masculinity Imperiled: Mercantile Representations of Failure and the Gendered Self in Eighteenth-Century Philadelphia," *Journal of American History* 81, no. 1 (1994): 51–80, provides an example of similar articulation of failure and frustration by eighteenth-century Philadelphia merchants.

5. MSS. Eng. lett. c. 284, f. 129, August 15, 1731.

6. Simon Gikandi, *Slavery and the Culture of Taste* (Princeton, N.J.: Princeton University Press, 2001), 150.

7. Numerous examples of well-known and persistent contradictions characterize the founding of the North American colonies. Later in the eighteenth century, Samuel Johnson famously asked in the pamphlet "Taxation No Tyranny" "How is it that we hear the loudest yelps for liberty among the drivers of Negroes?" Susan Amussen reminds us, "John Locke argued that slavery was 'directly opposite to the generous temper and courage of our Nation,' but he invested in the Royal African Company." Susan Dwyer Amussen, *Caribbean Exchanges: Slavery and the Transformation of English Society 1640–1700* (Chapel Hill: University of North Carolina Press, 2007), 219. Multiple instances of such inconsistencies appear throughout the period under discussion.

8. Another dimension of Martin's capacity to subjugate includes the culture of the British military, the institution in which he spent most of his adult professional life, characterized by accepted, often arbitrary violence. The flogging of soldiers in the army and navy was a common practice, although one heavily debated by the end of the eighteenth century. The knowledge of such treatment, justified as necessary for a disciplined serviceman, was widespread.

9. Eliza Haywood, *The History of Miss Betsy Thoughtless,* ed. Christine Blouch (Peterbough, Canada: Broadview Press, 1998).

10. MSS. Eng. lett. c. 285, f. 32, undated letter.

11. MSS. Eng. lett. c. 285, f. 58.

12. MSS. Eng. lett. c. 285, f. 48, October 1, 1741.

13. MSS. Eng. lett. c. 285, f. 289, undated letter.

14. MSS. Eng. lett. c. 285, f. 145, September 15, 1744.

15. MSS. Eng. lett. c. 284, f. 128 October 21, 1731.

16. MSS. Eng. lett. c. 285, f. 49, October 8, 1741. Early in their marriage he neglects to leave her money before he departs.

17. MSS. Eng. lett. c. 285, f. 55, March 31, 1742.

18. MSS. Eng. lett. c. 285, f. 151, September 25, 1744.

19. MSS. Eng. lett. c. 285, f. 62, April 25, 1742.

20. MS Eng. Misc., d. 637, f. 6.

21. MSS. Eng. lett. c. 285, f. 145, September 15, 1744.

22. MSS. Eng. lett. c. 285, f. 72. undated letter.

23. MSS. Eng. lett. c. 285, f. 80, October 31, 1742.

24. MSS. Eng. lett. c. 285, f. 209, c. 1740–42.

25. MSS. Eng. lett. c. 284, f. 107, June 7, 1729.

26. MSS. Eng. lett. c. 284, f. 130, February 12, 1731/2.

27. MSS. Eng. lett. c. 284, f. 107, June 7, 1729.

28. MSS. Eng. lett. c. 285, f. 198, July 21, 1748.

29. MSS. Eng. lett. c. 284, f. 245, undated letter.

30. MSS. Eng. lett. c. 285, f. 71, Friday, August 27, 1742.

31. MSS. Eng. lett. c. 284, f. 245, undated letter from 1736.

32. MSS. Eng. lett. c. 285, August 18, 1743.

33. MSS. Eng. lett. c. 285, f. 144, f. 151, September 15, 1744.

34. MSS. Eng. lett. c. 285, f. 80, September 18, 1742. At other moments Martin seeks to "buy 10 negroes a year," MSS. Eng. lett. c. 284, f. 142, August 13, 1732.

35. MSS. Eng. lett. c. 285, f. 131, August 18, 1743.

36. MSS. Eng. lett. c. 285, f. 131, August 18, 1743.

37. MSS. Eng. lett. c. 285, f. 131, August 18, 1743.

38. MSS. Eng. lett. c. 284.

39. The eight volumes of *Letters Writ by a Turkish Spy, Who Lived Five and Forty Years, Undiscover'd, at Paris* by Giovanni Paolo Marana, was published in French in 1684 and then in English in 1687. Significant discussions of this text appear in Ros Ballaster, *Fabulous Orients: Fictions of the East in England, 1662–1785* (Oxford: Oxford University Press, 2005), 145–62; and Srinivas Aravamudan, "Fiction/Translations/Transnation: The Secret History of the Eighteenth-Century Novel," in *A Companion to the Eighteenth-Century English Novel and Culture*, ed. Paula R. Backscheider and Catherine Ingrassia (London: Blackwell, 2005), 75–96.

40. While "Bashaw" is an earlier form of the Turkish title pasha, it can also figuratively suggest a haughty or imperious man. Judith's epistle seems quite earnest, despite the persistent patterns of tension within the marriage.

41. MSS. Eng. lett. c. 284, f. 129, August 15, 1731.

42. *Cowper Family Miscellany* kept by Ashley Cowper, BL Add MS. 28101, d. 144 r.

43. Ibid.

44. Ibid.

45. MSS. Eng. lett. c. 284, f. 189, February 20, 1734.

46. MSS. Eng. lett. c. 284 f. 123, July 21, 1731.

47. That quotation appeared in verses enclosed in an October 18, 1722, letter in which Pope praised her writings as "very good, & very entertaining." *The Correspondence of Alexander Pope*, ed. George Sherburn, 5 vols. (Oxford: Clarendon Press, 1956), 2:139.

48. The poem appeared in William Pattison, *The Poetical Works of Mr. William Pattison* (London, 1728), 67–77. It is quoted here from a modern reprinting in *British Women Poets of the Long Eighteenth Century: An Anthology*, ed. Paula R. Backscheider and Catherine E. Ingrassia (Baltimore: Johns Hopkins University Press, 2009), 280–85, line 1.

49. Patrick Delany's letter to Mrs. Charlotte Clayton, February 2, 1731, which appears in Mary Granville, Mrs. Delany, *Autobiography and Correspondence*, ed. Augusta Hall (Cambridge: Cambridge University Press, 2011), 1. 321, describes Barber, known the "Citizen's Housewife Poet," as "excellently educated, perfectly well-disposed and utterly unprovided for."

50. Mary Barber, "On Seeing an Officer's Widow Distracted, Who Had Been Driven to Despair, by a Long and Fruitless Solicitation for the Arrears of Her Pension," in *Poems on Several Occasions* (London, 1736), 242, 30.

51. Mary Barber, "The Widow Gordon's Petition: To the Right Hon. The Lady Carteret," ll. 12, 22 in *British Women Poets of the Long Eighteenth Century*, ed. Backscheider and Ingrassia, 473.

52. "Verses Said to Be Written by Mrs. Mary Barber. To a Friend Desiring an Account of Her Health in Verse," *Gentleman's Magazine* 7 (March 1737): 179, ll. 21–22, 27–28. Although this poem ostensibly recounts Barber's experience and confinement as a result of illness, Adam Budd persuasively suggests it might also draw upon her brief experience of imprisonment in 1734 following her arrest for transporting Jonathan Swift's *Epistle to a Lady* to England. Budd, "'Merit in Distress': The Troubled Success of Mary Barber," *Review of English Studies* 53, no. 210 (2002): 204–27.

53. Mary Barber, "On Seeing the Captives, Lately Redeem'd from Barbary by His Majesty," in *Poems on Several Occasions* (London, 1734), 271–74. Discussions of this poem appear in Catherine Ingrassia, "Contesting 'Home' in Eighteenth-Century Women's Verse," in *Home and Nation in British Literature from the English to the French Revolutions*, ed. A. D. Cousins (Cambridge: Cambridge University Press, 2015), 154–68; Suvir Kaul, *Poems of Nation, Anthems of Empire: English Verse in the Long Eighteenth Century* (Charlottesville: University of Virginia Press, 2001), chap. 1; and Linda

Colley, *Captives: Britain, Empire, and the World, 1600–1850* (New York: Anchor Books, 2002), 101, where she characterizes it as "one of [Barber's] dreadful poems." Moira Ferguson also discusses Barber's poem in *Subject to Others: British Women Writers and Colonial Slavery, 1670–1834* (New York: Routledge, 1992), 16–18, in the context of Barbary captivity, and she reads it as both Barber's unironic celebration of King George and Sir Charles Wager, the merchant assisting in the ransoming of the captives, and as a precursor to "expressions of gratitude half a century later toward prominent abolitionists and emancipationists" (17). My reading differs from Colley's and Ferguson's.

54. *Daily Journal*, November 12, 1734.

55. As Peter Linebaugh details in chapter 1 of *The London Hanged: Crime and Civil Society in the Eighteenth Century* (Cambridge: Cambridge University Press, 1992), the London poor of the eighteenth century regularly witnessed evidence of slavery and domestic captivity (although he doesn't use that term) throughout the eighteenth century.

56. Ironically, Barber does the opposite of many popular, circulating accounts of Barbary captivity, which, as Robert C. Davis notes, "attempt to distract the reader from the fact of unfree labour and suffering within English society." *Christian Slaves, Muslim Masters: White Slavery in the Mediterranean, the Barbary Coast, and Italy, 1500–1800* (Houndmills, UK: Palgrave Macmillan, 2003), 35.

57. A similar contradiction can be seen as well in the naturalization of a dual culture of confinement and freedom embodied on the title page of the *asiento*, which grants "the Subjects of Great Britain the Liberty of Importing Negroes," or what William Pettigrew calls "the liberty to trade in the enslaved." William Pettigrew, *Freedom's Debt: The Royal African Company and the Politics of the Atlantic Slave Trade, 1672–1752* (Chapel Hill, NC: University of North Carolina Press, 2013), 150. For a discussion of *Rule Britannia*, see Nicolas Hudson, "Britons Never Will Be Slaves: National Myth, Conservatism, and the Beginnings of British Antislavery," *Eighteenth-Century Studies* 34, no. 4 (2001): 559–76; Kaul, *Poems of Nation, Anthems of Empire*, chap. 1

58. See Nancy Armstrong and Leonard Tennenhouse, *The Imaginary Puritan: Literature, Intellectual Labor, and the Origins of Personal Life* (Berkeley: University of California Press, 1992).

59. Daniel J. Vitkus, "English Captivity Narratives," in *Colonial and Postcolonial Incarceration*, ed. Graeme Harper (London: Continuum, 2001), 29; Elizabeth Foyster, "The 'New World of Children' Reconsidered: Child

Abduction in Late Eighteenth- and Early Nineteenth-Century England," *Journal of British Studies* 52, no. 3 (2013), 672–73; Robert Darby, "Captivity and Captivation: Gulliver in Brobdingnag," *Eighteenth-Century Life* 27, no. 3 (2003): 124–39; Denver Brunsman, *The Evil Necessity: British Naval Impressment in the Eighteenth-Century Atlantic World* (Charlottesville: University of Virginia Press, 2013), 6.

60. Stephen Duck, "On Poverty," in *Poems on Several Subjects . . .* (London, 1730), 26–27, ll. 12–13, 16–18.

61. John Wareing, *Indentured Migration and the Servant Trade from London to America, 1618–1718: 'There Is Great Want of Servants'* (Oxford; Oxford University Press, 2016), 3.

62. Mary Collier, known as the "washerwoman poet," published *The Woman's Labour: An Epistle to Mr. Stephen Duck; in Answer to His Late Poem, Called The Thresher's Labour* (London, 1739), 7, l. 41. She subsequently published *Poems on Several Occasions* (London, 1762).

63. Roxanne Wheeler, "Slavey, or the New Drudge," in *Invoking Slavery in the Eighteenth-Century British Imagination*, ed. Srividhya Swaminathan and Adam R. Beach (Farnham, UK: Ashgate, 2013), 153, 154.

64. Sarah Fyge Egerton, "The Emulation," in *British Women Poets of the Long Eighteenth Century*, ed. Backscheider and Ingrassia, 593, ll. 2–3, 15.

65. Lady Mary Chudleigh, "Solitude," in *Poems on Several Occasions* (London, 1703), 87.

66. Elizabeth Thomas, "On Sir J— S— saying in a sarcastick Manner, My Books would make me Mad," in *British Women Poets of the Long Eighteenth Century*, ed. Backscheider and Ingrassia, 847, l. 2. Thomas echoes the words of Chudleigh, with whom she corresponded and whom she greatly admired. In the preface to her 1703 volume of poems, Chudleigh writes that women are "inslav'd to Custom."

67. Judith Drake, *An Essay in Defence of the Female Sex* (London, 1721).

68. Barber, "The Conclusion of a Letter to the Rev. Mr. C—," in *Poems on Several Occasions*, l. 12.

69. Eliza Haywood, *The Distressed Orphan; or, Love in a Madhouse* (London, 1726). Speaking of the fortune that makes her the target of her uncle's (who is her guardian) avaricious plan, Annilia states, "The Love of Liberty is natural to all, and I should have more Reason to regret, than be pleased with the large Fortune left me by my Father, if it must subject me to eternal Slavery" (30). Annilia's description of the other inmates' experience within the madhouse details "the Fetters on their Legs fast bolted into the Floor," the "poor Pitance of Food," and the regular beatings ("they

saluted them with Stripes in a manner so cruel, as if they delighted in inflicting Pain," 38).

70. *Mist's Weekly Journal,* May 21, 1726.
71. William Blackstone, *Commentaries on the Laws of England,* 4 vols. (Oxford, 1765–69), 1:430.
72. George Savile, *The Lady's New-Year's Gift; or, Advice to a Daughter,* 7th ed. (London, 1701), 21–22. This discussion of the status of women in marriage draws on my headnote to "Poems on Marriage" in *British Women Poets of the Long Eighteenth Century,* ed. Backscheider and Ingrassia, 610–13.
73. See Sybil Wolfram, "Divorce in England, 1700–1857," *Oxford Journal of Legal Studies* 5, no. 2 (1985): 155–86; Lawrence Stone, *The Road to Divorce: England, 1530–1987* (Oxford: Oxford University Press, 1990).
74. Mary Chudleigh, "To the Ladies," in *British Women Poets of the Long Eighteenth Century,* ed. Backscheider and Ingrassia, 615, ll. 3–4.
75. Matthew Hale, *The History of the Pleas of the Crown* (London, 1736).
76. Elizabeth Foyster, *Marital Violence: An English Family History, 1660–1857* (Cambridge: Cambridge University Press, 2005), 9.
77. Ferguson, *Subject to Others,* 19. Ferguson explores this commonality in significant detail; however, her focus, considering how antislavery protest contributed to a feminist expression, differs from my own concerns here.
78. Mary Astell, *Reflections on Marriage,* 3rd ed. (London, 1706), 23.
79. Richard Allestree, *The Ladies Calling in Two Parts* (Oxford, 1720), 181, 244.
80. Egerton, "The Emulation," l. 15.
81. Anne Finch, "The Unequal Fetters," in *British Women Poets of the Long Eighteenth Century,* ed. Backscheider and Ingrassia, 616, ll. 18, 20.
82. Laetitia Pilkington, "A Song," in *Memoirs,* 3 vols. (London, 1747–54), 1:149.
83. Elizabeth Thomas, "The Monkey Dance," in *Poems on Several Occasions* (London, 1726), 264.
84. Lady Mary Wortley Montagu, "Epistle from Mrs. Yonge to Her Husband," in *British Women Poets of the Long Eighteenth Century,* ed. Backscheider and Ingrassia, 278, ll. 22–23.
85. *The History of Miss Betsy Thoughtless,* 501.
86. Mary Astell, *Political Writings,* ed. Patricia Springborg (Cambridge: Cambridge University Press, 1996), 9. Astell of course anticipates Mary Wollstonecraft's similar pronouncement: "I call women slaves" in *A Vindication of the Rights of Woman* (London, 1792), chap. 12, "On National Education," 18.
87. Blackstone, *Commentaries,* 4:433.

88. Stephen Pincus, *1688: The First Modern Revolution* (New Haven: Yale University Press, 2009), 12.

89. Elizabeth Thomas, "On Sir J— S— saying in a sarcastick Manner, My Books would make me Mad. An Ode," in *British Women Poets of the Long Eighteenth Century,* ed. Backscheider and Ingrassia, 847–50, ll. 85–86.

90. Bruce McLeod, *The Geography of Empire in English Literature, 1580–1745* (Cambridge: Cambridge University Press, 1999), 1.

2. CAPTIVATING FARCE

1. Scholars also situate Behn's work within Mediterranean histories of slavery. For example, Adam Beach suggests that Behn was interested in "depicting Old World forms of human bondage," which must be taken into account "to form a more complete understanding of Behn's views on slavery." Adam R. Beach, "Global Slavery, Old World Bondage, and Aphra Behn's *Abdelazer,*" *Eighteenth Century: Theory and Interpretation* 53, no. 4 (2012): 413.

2. *London Gazette,* December 29, 1678. Other newspaper accounts record similarly graphic details: "By a Vessel arrived from Surinam, the States have Letters from the Governor of the 16 of October in which he gives them an account that the Indians continue to do the Planters much harm, ruining their Plantations, burning their Mills, killing their Negro's [*sic*] and Servants, & c., and that without a speedy and considerable assistance from hence, it would be impossible for him to preserve that Colony." "We here thence that the Indians, fell upon some of the Dutch there, and killed an Ensign fleying of his Skin, and put it on a stake, burning the body. Upon which the Dutch assaulted them and killed their cheif [*sic*]" (West-Indies, Surinam, *Monthly Recorder,* April 1, 1682). Aphra Behn, *Oroonoko; or, The Royal Slave,* in *The Works of Aphra Behn,* vol. 3, ed. Janet Todd (Columbus: Ohio State University Press, 1995), 84. Subsequent citations will be to this edition and appear parenthetically in the text.

3. *London Gazette,* September 19–22, 1687.

4. Charles Dibdin concludes his entry on Behn in *The Complete History of the English Stage,* 5 vols. (London, 1800) with his only mention of *The Emperor of the Moon* by writing "With *The Emperor of the Moon,* performed also in 1687, we shall take leave of Mrs. BEHN for the present, which was nothing more than a farce borrowed from an Italian opera that had been translated into French. It was whimsical, and had some success" (4:203).

5. K. G. Davies, *The Royal African Company* (1957; rpt., London: Octagon Books, 1975), 16–17.

6. William A. Pettigrew, *Freedom's Debt: The Royal African Company and the Politics of the Atlantic Slave Trade, 1672–1752* (Chapel Hill: University of North Carolina Press, 2013), 23.

7. That number was determined by a search of the *Transatlantic Slave Voyages Database*, slavevoyages.org/voyage/database.

8. Davies, *Royal African Company*, 41.

9. Gary A. Puckrein, *Little England: Plantation Society and Anglo-Barbadian Politics, 1627–1700* (New York: New York University Press, 1984), 61.

10. Catherine Hall, Afterword to *Imagining Transatlantic Slavery*, ed. Cora Kaplan and John Oldfield (Basingstoke, UK: Palgrave Macmillan, 2009), 197.

11. Pettigrew, *Freedom's Debt*, 11.

12. As has been well-rehearsed by other scholars, Oroonoko's own involvement with enslavement—whether the enslaved people he presents to Imoinda as his first gift to her or those vanquished opponents he sells—is neither racialized nor based purely on a desire for profit.

13. Paula Backscheider, "From *The Emperor of the Moon* to the Sultan's Prison," *Studies in Eighteenth-Century Culture* 43 (2014): 16.

14. Jane Jones, "New Light on the Background and Early Life of Aphra Behn," *Notes & Queries* 37, no. 3 (1990): 293.

15. Puckrein, *Little England*, 75.

16. Ibid.

17. Michael Craton, "Reluctant Creole: The Planter's World in the British West Indies," in *Strangers within the Realm: Cultural Margins of the First British Empire*, ed. Bernard Bailyn and Philip D. Morgan (Chapel Hill: University of North Carolina Press, 2012), 329, 335. "West Indian plantations," Craton continues, "were a machine for creating wealth and aiding upward mobility."

18. Sarah Barber, "Power in the English Caribbean: The Proprietorship of Lord Willoughby of Parham," in *Constructing Early Modern Empires: Proprietary Adventures in the Atlantic World, 1500–1700*, ed. L. H. Roper and B. Van Ruymbeke (Boston: Brill, 2007), 197. Willoughby's fascinating and somewhat peripatetic personal history included his time in Barbados from 1650 to 1652, an interlude to England (1652–63) before the Restoration (a period when he was jailed for royalist activities), that, after the Restoration, resulted in the return of his British estates and a formalized expansion of his power in the West Indies. He was named royal governor of the islands and also retained his claim to Surinam. For a popular history of Willoughby, see Matthew Parker, *Willoughbyland: England's Lost Colony* (New York: St. Martin's Press, 2015). See too Michael A.

LaCombe, "Willoughby, Francis, fifth Baron Willoughby of Parham (bap. 1614, d. 1666)," in *DNB*, https://doi.org/10.1093/ref:odnb/29597.

19. Sarah Barber details how "[h]e offered every settler in Surinam fifty acres freehold, plus a further acreage, depending on gender, age, and status. . . . Single people, without the means to transport themselves, would be carried at Willoughby's expense, to become his personal servants and tenants." "Power in the English Caribbean," 197.

20. Ibid. As was typical, Surinam also welcomed any kind of religious practice. Henry Adis praises "the freedom of our Liberties in the service of our god, according to what was promised by your Lordship" (Henry Adis, *A Letter Sent from Syrranam* . . . [London, 1664], 3). In his reply, Willoughby reiterates his commitment to "the free liberty and enjoyment of your Consciences in the Worship of God" (7).

21. Adis, *Letter,* 5, 3, 6.

22. Barber, "Power in the English Caribbean," 199.

23. Ibid., 198.

24. William Byam, *The Most Execrable Attempts of John Allin, Committed on the Person of His Excellency Francis Lord Willoughby* (London, 1665), 3, 8. Janet Todd, Shannon Miller, and others suggest that *Oroonoko* generally and the representation of Willoughby specifically were informed by contemporaneous accounts. See Shannon Miller, "Executing the Body Politic: Inscribing State Violence onto Aphra Behn's *Oroonoko,*" in *Violence, Politics, and Gender in Early Modern England,* ed. Joseph P. Ward (New York: Palgrave Macmillan, 2008), 173–206.

25. Byam, *Most Execrable Attempts of John Allin,* 3.

26. Aphra Behn, *The City-Heiress,* ed. Rachel Adcock, in *The Cambridge Edition of the Works of Aphra Behn,* vol. 4, *Plays 1685–1696,* gen. ed. Claire Bowditch, Mel Evans, Elaine Hobby, and Gillian Wright (Cambridge: Cambridge University Press, 2021), 34.

27. Adis, *Letter,* 7.

28. Janet Todd, *The Secret Life of Aphra Behn* (New Brunswick, N.J.: Rutgers University Press, 1996), 52.

29. Although, as Shannon Miller notes in "Executing the Body Politic," Behn could also look around her in England for evidence of physical brutality exacted upon the resistant political figure (beginning of course with Charles I).

30. Susan Dwyer Amussen, *Caribbean Exchanges: Slavery and the Transformation of English Society 1640–1702* (Chapel Hill: University of North Carolina Press, 2007), 174.

31. Marisa J. Fuentes, *Dispossessed Lives: Enslaved Women, Violence, and the Archive* (Philadelphia: University of Pennsylvania Press, 2016), 38.

32. Moira Ferguson, *Subject to Others: British Women Writers and Colonial Slavery, 1670–1834* (New York: Routledge, 1992), 320. The word "obliged" appears in *Oroonoko* more than two dozen times and, almost without exception, it is used to convey requests or demands placed on Behn's persona, Imoinda, or Oroonoko after his enslavement.

33. Alan Marshall, "'Memoiralls for Mrs. Affora': Aphra Behn and the Restoration Intelligence World," *Women's Writing* 22, no. 1 (2015): 17.

34. Janet Todd and Francis McKee, "The Shee Spy," *Times Literary Supplement*, September 10, 1993, 5. Todd and McKee additionally detail how Behn's letters written during this period express "her increasing frustration with the perceived niggardliness of her employers, who let her spend her own money on her work and even pawn her rings to keep herself" (4).

35. Marshall, "'Memorialls for Mrs. Affora,'" 28.

36. Of course, enslaved people were also increasingly visible in the English country estates. See Madge Dresser and Andrew Hann, eds., *Slavery in the English Country House* (Swindon, UK: English Heritage, 2013).

37. Amussen, *Caribbean Exchanges*, 221. "Black slaves were valuable property; what they stole by running away was themselves" (223).

38. Gretchen Gerzina, *Black London: Life before Emancipation* (New Brunswick, N.J.: Rutgers University Press, 1995), 53. Gerzina goes on to note that such youths, when they hit puberty, were often sold back into plantation slavery.

39. For a discussion of portraits of this type, see Catherine Molineux, *Faces of Perfect Ebony: Encountering Atlantic Slavery in Imperial Britain* (Cambridge, Mass.: Harvard University Press, 2012). Any number of portraits from the period represent this relationship, e.g., Pierre Mignard, *Louise de Kéroualle, Duchess of Portsmouth* (1682); Peter Lely, *Elizabeth Murray, Countess of Dysart, with Black Servant* (1650); and John Closterman, *Charles Seymour, 6th Duke of Somerset, with a Black Page* (ca. 1690).

40. Quoted in Folarin Shyllon, *Black People in Britain, 1555–1833* (New York: Oxford University Press, 1977), 77.

41. *Public Advertiser,* January 19, 1762.

42. Quoted in Peter Fryer, *Staying Power: The History of Black People in Britain* (London: Pluto Press, 1984), 23.

43. *London Gazette,* September 19–22, 1687.

44. Fuentes (*Dispossessed Lives*) also explores in detail the meaning of what she terms "runaway advertisements" of enslaved people.

45. Aphra Behn, *The Adventure of the Black Lady,* in *The Works of Aphra Behn,* vol. 3, ed. Todd, 319.

46. Janet Todd, introduction to *The Works of Aphra Behn,* vol. 1, ed. Todd, xviii. "Aphra Behn and the Restoration Theatre," in *The Cambridge Companion to Aphra Behn,* ed. Derek Hughes and Janet Todd (Cambridge: Cambridge University Press, 2004), 30.

47. Aphra Behn, *Sir Patient Fancy,* in *The Works of Aphra Behn,* vol. 6, ed. Todd, 6.

48. Montague Summers, *The Works of Aphra Behn,* 6 vols. (London: W. Heinemann; Stratford-on Avon: A. H. Bullen, 1915), 1:lvii.

49. *The Works of Aphra Behn,* vol. 6, ed. Todd, 159, l. 1.

50. As Behn laments in the Epilogue to *The Emperor of the Moon,* "Not one is left will write for thin third day." Behn, *The Emperor of the Moon,* ed. Elaine Hobby and Alan James Hogarth, in *The Cambridge Edition of the Works of Aphra Behn,* 4:529, l. 16. Subsequent citations will be to this edition and appear parenthetically in the text cited by page and line number.

51. Behn, Epilogue, *The Second Part of The Rover,* in *The Works of Aphra Behn,* vol. 6, ed. Todd, 297, ll. 6–7.

52. Quoted in Todd, introduction to *The Works of Aphra Behn,* vol. 1, xvii.

53. Quoted in Todd, *Secret Life,* 324–25.

54. *The Young King* is a text with a protracted composition history still being investigated. Mel Evans's recent stylometric study suggests that Behn either wrote or significantly revised *The Young King* in the 1670s. As my discussion suggests, given Behn's foregrounding of "America" as an influence on the piece, the actual date of composition is less relevant than its content (Mel Evans, "Style and Chronology: A Stylometric Investigation of Aphra Behn's Dramatic Style and the Dating of *The Young King,*" *Language and Literature* 27, no. 2 [2018]: 103–32). For a discussion of source material for the text, see Judy Hayden, "Representations of 'Times of Trouble': Aphra Behn's *The Young King; or, The Mistake* and Calderon's *Life Is a Dream,*" in *Aphra Behn: Identity, Alterity, Ambiguity,* ed. Guyonne Leduc, Bernard Dhuicq, and Mary Ann O'Donnell (Paris: Harmattan, 2000), 49–58.

55. Behn, *The Young King,* in *The Works of Aphra Behn,* vol. 7, ed. Todd, 83. Subsequent citations will be to this edition and appear parenthetically in the text cited by page and line number.

56. Anita Pacheco states, "Behn's decision to write a tragicomedy about restoration, embracing the most popular genre and theme of the early 1660s, helps to date *The Young King* to the beginning of her career, as does the play's feudal setting" ("'Where Lies this Power Divine?': The

Representation of Kingship in Aphra Behn's Early Tragicomedies," *Journal for Eighteenth-Century Studies* 38, no. 3 [2015]: 318). She suggests that Orsames's tyrannical attitude simply "replicates the only relationship of which he has any knowledge: that between divine power and human submission to that power" (318). She also notes that Act II indicates that "by this early stage of her career, Behn had already embraced the free-thinking attitudes that are now recognized as an integral aspect of her work" (319). Orsames possesses a "rapacious libido" that is "entirely unsocialized" (319) and "his passion remains inseparable from a tyrannical determination to exercise absolute power of the lives of his subjects" (320). Although Pacheco does not connect the text to Behn's experience in Surinam, it does not seem unreasonable to consider that such a characterization may reflect what Behn might have heard about Willoughby or seen in other colonial leaders. Other discussions of *The Young King* can be found in Derek Hughes, "Rape on the Restoration Stage," *The Eighteenth-Century: Theory and Interpretation* 46, no. 3 (2005): 227–32. In *The Complete History of the English Stage*, Dibdin writes, "*The Young King*, performed in 1683, is a tragi-comedy, and as incongruous as any thing that ever bore that designation. Mrs. BEHN's dedication of this play is in natural and glowing language" (4:202).

57. For some readers, the reference to a "castle or prison on the sea" might summon the imagine of the "slave castles" or forts build by the English (and others) as essentially human warehouses for kidnapped Africans prior to their transportation and experience of the Middle Passage.

58. His notion that "low submissive souls" should regard him with "fear" and "awe, as thou hast of the Gods," anticipates the language of power Behn uses to describe Oroonoko while he is still in Africa.

59. Richard Ligon, *A True and Exact History of the Island of Barbados*, ed. Karen Ordahl Kupperman (Indianapolis: Hackett Publishing, 2000), 97.

60. Ibid., 93.

61. Ramesh Mallipeddi, *Spectacular Suffering: Witnessing Slavery in the Eighteenth-Century British Atlantic* (Charlottesville: University of Virginia Press, 2016), 22.

62. *The Several Declarations of the Company of Royal Adventurers of England Trading into Africa . . .* (London, 1667), 8.

63. *The Oxford History of the British Empire*, vol. 1, *The Origins of Empire: The British Overseas Enterprise to the Close of the Seventeenth Century*, ed. Nicholas Canny (New York: Oxford University Press, 1998). See also in this volume, George Braddick, "The English Government, War,

Trade, and Settlement, 1625–88," 286–309. Braddick writes, "[T]here is a strong case for arguing that by the 1670s, England was a nascent empire" (299).

64. George Warren, *An Impartial Description of Surinam upon the Continent of Guiana in America with a History of Several Strange Beasts, Birds, Fishes, Serpents, Insects and Customs of That Colony, etc. / Worthy the Perusal of All, from Experience of George Warren* (London, 1667), 14. Oroonoko, in attempting to rally the fellow enslaved, urges them to refuse "to perish by the hand of the tyrant's whip" (116, l. 157), referencing the regular brutality.

65. Todd, *Secret Life*, 150. Todd comments that "probably Surinam had an effect" on the play, as this chapter demonstrates, 64.

66. Ibid., 336. In *The Younger Brother*, the last name is spelled "Marteen"; in *Oroonoko*, it is spelled "Martin." When quoting directly, I spell as it appears in the text; otherwise, I use the traditional spelling of the family name—Marten.

67. Parker, *Willoughbyland*, 179.

68. Todd, *Secret Life*, 52.

69. Andrew J. O'Shaughnessy, "Codrington, Christopher (1639/40–1698)," in *DNB*. See also *Strangers within the Realm: Cultural Margins of the First British Empire*, ed. Bernard Bailyn and Philip D. Morgan (Chapel Hill: University of North Carolina Press for the Omohundro Institute of Early American History and Culture, 1991).

70. Todd, *Secret Life*, 39.

71. Aphra Behn, *The Younger Brother*, ed. Margarete Rubik, in *The Cambridge Edition of the Works of Aphra Behn*, 4:746–47. Subsequent citations will be to this edition and appear parenthetically in the text.

72. Todd, *Secret Life*, 336.

73. Ibid., 337.

74. Ibid., 336.

75. Sarah Barber, *A Revolutionary Rogue: Henry Marten and the English Republic* (Stroud, UK: Sutton, 2000), 194. Chapter 6 has information about Henry's brother George Marten who owned enslaved people, had an estate in Barbados on the east coast in the parish of St. John, and became "an establishment name among settlers" (131). See also Robert Sanford, *Surinam Justice . . .* (London, 1662).

76. Michael J. Jarvis, *In the Eye of All Trade: Bermuda, Bermudians, and the Maritime Atlantic World, 1680–1783* (Chapel Hill: University of North Carolina Press, 2010), 322.

77. Mallipeddi, *Spectacular Suffering*, 41. He uses this phrase to describe Oroonoko's body but, in the world of thoughtless and leveling commodification, the same forces apply to the animal.

78. Richard Altick observes, "Of all these importations, the one that most excited Restoration London was 'the strange Beast called the Rynnoceros.' Evelyn, like most of the learned, identified the breed with the fabled unicorn, although the reality somewhat belied the myth, for 'it more ressembled a huge enormous Swine, than any other Beast amongst us.' Arriving aboard an East Indiaman in August 1684, the 'Rhinincerous' (the spelling presented insuperable difficulties to contemporary pens) was valued at £2000—an impressive indication of its worth as a commercial showpiece. The Rhinenceras was immediately put up for sale and was 'bought for £2320 by Mr. Langley one of those that bought Mr. Sadlers well at Islington & in a day or two will be seen in Bartholomew faire.' But Mr. Langley was unable to raise the money and lost his £500 deposit; whereupon the owners took back their Rhinoceros and put it up for resale, 'but noe person bid a farthing soe lyes upon their hands.' By the end of September the Rhynonceros was at the Belle Sauvage inn at the foot of Ludgate Hill.... The Rhynoceros continued to attract crowds until its premature death two years later (September 1686); 'the serverall proprietors haveing Ensured £1200 on her life the Ensurers are catched for much money.'" Richard D. Altick, *The Shows of London* (Cambridge, Mass.: Belknap Press of Harvard University Press, 1978), 37.

79. Ibid.

80. Davies estimates that between 1672 and 1711, the RAC sold more than 90,000 enslaved Africans by auction in the West Indies (*Royal African Company*, 299).

81. "[N]ewspapers show that at Lloyds, Garraways and other London coffee houses, casks of wine, bales of silk, ships' cargoes, and even the ships themselves were auctioned by 'an inch of candle.'" (E. Carleton Williams, "The Aldermaston Candle Auction," *Berkshire Archaeological Journal* 51 [1948–49]: 35–40). This type of auction is where the expression "you could hear a pin drop" emerges. Such auctions were "very popular" in the second half of the seventeenth century, something Williams ascribes to "the reckless spirit of the age" (35).

82. PRO T 70/57, f. 50. Royal African Company to Barbados Agents, London, November 11, 1690. Quoted in David W. Galenson, *Traders, Planters, and Slaves: Market Behavior in Early English America* (Cambridge: Cambridge University Press, 1986), 82.

83. George Frederick Zook, *The Company of Royal Adventurers Trading into Africa* (Lancaster, Pa.: Press of the New Era Printing Company, 1919; reprinted from *Journal of Negro History* 4, no. 2 [April 1919]), 209.

84. Trevor Burnard and Kenneth Morgan, "The Dynamics of the Slave Market and Slave Purchasing Patterns in Jamaica, 1655–1788," *William and Mary Quarterly* 58, no. 1 (2001): 224.

85. Candle auctions were actually legalized two years after the appearance of *The Younger Brother* in part to facilitate the sale of goods imported from the East Indies. The coffeehouse Lloyd's in Lombard Street, established in 1691, became the center of these sales. See Warren R. Dawson, "The London Coffee Houses and the Beginnings of Lloyd's," *Journal of the British Archaeological Association* 40 (1935): 104–34.

86. Behn also represents the troubling objectification of female characters. The ironically named Lady Youthly refers to her niece as "My inventory"; Marteen's sister Olivia likens her arranged marriage to "Prostitution in the lewdest manner" (756, l. 43). Prince Frederick atomizes women, focusing on Mirtilla's "Dimpl'd Mouth, her Neck, her Hand, her Hair" (764, l. 221). Yet Behn reserves her sharpest critique for the sale of a privileged white male.

87. Katherine Mannheimer, "Celestial Bodies: Gender and the Spectacle of Readerly Rapture in Aphra Behn's *Emperor of the Moon*," *Restoration* 35, no. 1 (2001): 40.

88. Al Coppola, "Retraining the Virtuoso's Gaze: Behn's *Emperor of the Moon*, the Royal Society, and the Spectacles of Science and Politics," *Eighteenth-Century Studies* 41, no. 4 (2008): 481–506; Judy A Hayden, "Harlequin Science: Aphra Behn's *Emperor of the Moon* and the Plurality of Worlds," *English: The Journal of the English Association* 64, no. 246 (2015): 167–82; Paula R. Backscheider, "From *The Emperor of the Moon* to the Sultan's Prison," *Studies in Eighteenth-Century Culture* 43 (2014): 1–26.

89. Derek Hughes, *The Theater of Aphra Behn* (Cambridge: Cambridge University Press, 1979), 171. See also Judith Milhous, "The Multimedia Spectacular on the Restoration Stage," in *British Theatre and the Other Arts, 1600–1800*, ed. Shirley Strum Kenny (Washington, D.C.: Folger Books, 1984), 41–66. Milhous, who calls *The Emperor of the Moon* a "machine farce," details how the play was written "to capitalize on the staging capabilities of Dorset Garden without incurring the sort of expense an opera entailed" (45).

90. He was a member of the Committee of the Honourable East India Company (1683–91), and his father-in-law Josiah Child wrote *Discourse about*

Trade (1690, reprinted as *A New Discourse on Trade* in 1693), which included his *Proposals for the Relief and Employment of the Poor* that advocated sending people to the colonial plantations as indentured servants.

91. Behn, *The Emperor of the Moon*, in *The Works of Aphra Behn*, vol. 7, ed. Todd, 431n17.

92. Paula R. Backscheider, *Spectacular Politics: Theatrical Power and Mass Culture in Early Modern England* (Baltimore: Johns Hopkins University Press, 1993), 104.

93. Aphra Behn, *The Luckey-Chance*, ed. Kate Aughterson and Claire Bowditch, in *The Cambridge Edition of the Works of Aphra Behn*, 4:226–27, ll. 30–31.

94. See Mallipeddi, *Spectacular Suffering*; and Laura Brown, *Ends of Empire: Women and Ideology in Early Eighteenth-Century English Literature* (Ithaca, N.Y.: Cornell University Press, 1993).

95. Fuentes, *Dispossessed Lives*, 38.

96. Ligon, *True and Exact History of the Island of Barbados*, 102.

97. Coppola, "Retraining the Virtuoso's Gaze," 482.

98. Consistent with that, in their introduction to the Cambridge edition of *The Emperor of the Moon* Hobby and Hogarth observe that the language of the text has slippage between Naples and London, creating a "melded Naples-London," offering moments when the "London audience are firmly on home ground" (4.376). That observation accords with Behn's warning about the use of spectacle in both colonial and domestic locations.

99. This concern, of course, is not unique to *The Emperor of the Moon*, or to Behn. For example, in *The Widdow Ranter* (1690), upon arriving in Virginia, Friendly observes that "This Country wants nothing but to be People'd with a well-born Race to make it one of the best Collonies in the World." (*The Widdow Ranter*, ed. Anita Pacheco, in *The Cambridge Edition of the Works of Aphra Behn*, 4:582, ll. 115–16).

100. *The Works of Aphra Behn*, ed. Todd, 7:438n123.

101. Baliardo's hierarchical notions about breeding extend to his servants as well; although his servant Scaramouch wants to be "rewarded" with the young women's lady's maid Mopsophil, the Doctor has already "promis'd her to a Farmer for his Son" (442, l. 161), a slight elevation in status. With that gesture, Baliardo simultaneously objectifies her and enforces strict class distinctions. (Indeed, Mopsophil herself asks "was I made a Property?" [480, l. 61].)

102. This language also echoes Richard Allestree's declaration that his conduct book, when appropriately used, will "penetrate the Heart of the Reader,"

another subtle process of social indoctrination. Richard Allestree, *The Gentleman's Calling* (London, 1664), dedication.

103. The play's spectacular finale serves a similar ideological purpose as an "important vehicle for mediating representations of alien cultures in public pageants and major theatrical forms" (Mallipeddi, *Spectacular Suffering*, 25). See also chapter 2 of Backscheider, *Spectacular Politics*.

104. John Patrick Montaño, "The Quest for Consensus: The Lord Mayor's Day Shows in the 1670s," in *Culture and Society in the Stuart Restoration*, ed. Gerald MacLean (Cambridge: Cambridge University Press, 1995), 51.

105. Ibid., 32.

106. And, as Barthelemy notes, the published narrative descriptions of these pageants "reflects the seriousness with which these projects were undertaken by both the poet-playwrights and the sponsoring guilds" (*Black Face, Maligned Race: The Representation of Blacks in English Drama, from Shakespeare to Southerne* [Baton Rouge: Louisiana State University Press, 1987], 45).

107. "Jordan, Thomas (ca. 1614–1685), actor, poet, and playwright," in *Oxford Dictionary of National Biography* (Oxford: Oxford University Press, 2004). See also Backscheider, *Spectacular Politics*, 38–40.

108. Barthelemy, *Black Face, Maligned Race*, 47.

109. Diana Henderson, "Theatre and Controversy, 1572–1603," in *The Cambridge History of British Theatre*, vol. 1, *Origins to 1660*, ed. Jane Milling and Peter Thomson (Cambridge: Cambridge University Press, 2004), 256.

110. Thomas Jordan, *London Triumphant* (London, 1672), 4. It is significant that these descriptions clearly distinguish between the use of Africans and of Europeans in blackface; whites "performing" as Black retain a privileged presence. For example, in this same pageant, the text specifies that "an Imperial person alone, in Royal habit," will have "his Face black, and likewise his Neck and Arms" and on his head "short curl'd black wool-like-Hair" (3–4). This "Indian *Emperour*" also has the first speech.

111. Thomas Jordan, *The Triumphs of London* (London, 1678), 3. The subsequent description of the young boy points to elements of cultural appropriation stemming from colonial dominance; he "is habited in an Indian Robe of divers Colours, a wreath of various-colour'd Feathers" on his head (3).

112. Thomas Jordan, *The Triumphs of London* (London 1675), 13.

113. I appreciate Paula Backscheider's assistance on considering the participation of free Africans in both the Lord Mayor's pageants and Behn's play.

114. Janet Todd describes this "final spectacular scene" as something requiring "ten blacked actors." The visual and descriptive similarity between this display and contemporaneous Lord Mayor's pageants in which Africans appear is striking. Felicity Nussbaum details how Ira Aldridge, known as "the African Roscius," was the first Black actor to appear on the English stage in a speaking part (*The Limits of the Human: Fictions of Anomaly, Race, and Gender in the Long Eighteenth Century* [Cambridge: Cambridge University Press, 2003], 214), but no one has yet fully explored the use of free Africans as extras or "walkers" in Restoration productions.

115. Backscheider, "From the *Emperor of the Moon* to the Sultan's Gate," 5.

116. The *DNB* details how, as part of a group of violent "young rakes," Albemarle was involved in the death of a beadle "during a brawl in a brothel"—an incident for which he had to seek a pardon in 1671. Robin Clifton, "Monck, Christopher, second duke of Albemarle (1653–1688), army officer and colonial governor," in *Oxford Dictionary of National Biography* (Oxford: Oxford University Press, 2018).

117. Ibid. For a discussion of Albemarle's journey to Jamaica, see Abigail L. Swingen, *Competing Visions of Empire: Labor, Slavery, and the Origins of the British Atlantic Empire* (New Haven: Yale University Press, 2015), 135–38.

118. As Richard Frohock observes, "Behn occupies a position somewhat analogous to that of the hero she describes: the poet seems to act out of honorable motives—reverence for the noble person celebrated—but in fact harbors unacknowledged material ambitions." Richard Frohock, *Heroes of Empires: The British Imperial Protagonist in America, 1596–1764* (Newark: University of Delaware Press, 2004), 57.

119. Ibid., 68.

120. Behn, *To the Most Illustrious Prince Christopher, Duke of Albemarle, on His Voyage to His Government of Jamaica a Pindarick* (London, 1687), 2, ll. 11–12. Subsequent citations appear parenthetically in the text by page and line number.

121. Edward Ward, *A Trip to Jamaica: With a True Character of the People and Island* (London, 1698), 16.

122. All long ago eradicated—only Maroons remained. So Behn was either misinformed or making a conscious choice to use this language.

123. "They never speak to any Subject, Sir, when they appear in Royalty, but by Interpreters" (523, ll. 147–48).

124. The performance notes list at least five other instances in the first decade of the eighteenth century when the performance is designated as for "the Entertainment" of "several Foreigners" (December 31, 1703, February 7,

1704), often "Foreign Ministers" (December 20, 1704). It also lists an April 19, 1703, performance for the entertainment of His Excellency Hodgha Bawhoon, envoy to Her Majesty from the great king of Persia. http://www.eighteenthcenturydrama.amdigital.co.uk/LondonStage/Database.

125. *London Evening Post,* November 13, 1729.

126. "On Tuesday Night their Royal Highnesses the Prince and Princess Royal, and the Princess Carolina, were at the Theatre Royal Lincolns'-Inn-Fields, to See the Farces of The Emperor of the Moon, Flora, and the Sorcerer." *British Journal,* October 3, 1730.

3. DOMESTICATING CAPTIVITY: RICHARD STEELE'S *THE CONSCIOUS LOVERS*

1. John O'Brien, *Literature Incorporated: The Cultural Unconscious of the Business Corporation, 1650–1850* (Chicago: University of Chicago Press, 2016), 83. As is well known, that arrangement led to the wild inflation and then total collapse of the South Sea Company stock in 1720 in an event known as the South Sea Bubble.

2. See Simon Gikandi, *Slavery and the Culture of Taste* (Princeton, N.J.: Princeton University Press, 2011), particularly chapter 3.

3. *English Trader, Indian Maid: Representing Gender, Race, and Slavery in the New World: An Inkle and Yarico Reader,* ed. Frank Felsenstein (Baltimore: Johns Hopkins University Press, 1999). As is well known, in *Spectator* No. 11, Steele describes how he was "amusing myself with *Ligon's* account of *Barbadoes*" where "in his fifty fifth page, the History of *Inkle* and *Yarico*" appears (86). As Felsenstein notes, Steele could have been citing "either the first (1657) or the second (1673) edition of Ligon, since Yarico's story appears on the same page (55) in both" (86n8). Unremarked-upon is a similar narrative Steele shares in his short-lived periodical *The Lover.*

4. Nicole Horejsi, "'A Counterpart to the Ephesian Matron': Steele's 'Inkle and Yarico' and a Feminist Critique of the Classics," *Eighteenth-Century Studies* 39, no. 2 (2006): 201–16.

5. Peter Craft, "'The Doves Are Censured While the Crows Are Spared': Steele's 1711 Inkle and Yarico Adaptation," *Journal of Commonwealth and Postcolonial Studies* 1, no. 2 (2013): 3.

6. Quoted in Felsenstein, *English Trader, Indian Maid,* 88. As Anthony Pollock details, "Steele offers no cognitive judgment, either about Inkle's economic imperatives (linked explicitly to Freeport's) or about his exploitative sexuality; rather, Mr. Spectator's sentimental impotence emblematizes the

ethical position of the privatized reader framed by Addison and Steele's essays." "Neutering Addison and Steele: Aesthetic Failure and the Spectatorial Public Sphere," *ELH* 74, no. 3 (2007): 725.

7. John Loftis, *Steele at Drury Lane* (Berkeley: University of California Press, 1952), 184. Part 4, chapter 1 discusses the composition of the text at length. See also Shirley Strum Kenny, "Richard Steele and the 'Pattern of Genteel Comedy,'" *Modern Philology* 70, no. 1 (1972): 30; as well as her introduction to *The Conscious Lovers* in *The Plays of Richard Steele* (Oxford: Clarendon Press, 1971), 275. Nathalie Wolfram, "'I Am My Master's Servant for Hire': Contract and Identity in Richard Steele's *The Conscious Lovers*," *Eighteenth Century: Theory and Interpretation* 53, no. 4 (2012): 456, 458. The same argument, I would assert, could also suggest the degree to which Steele's involvement in the Barbados plantation also generated some "ideological threshing."

8. Peter Hynes, "Richard Steele and the Genealogy of Sentimental Drama: A Reading of *The Conscious Lovers*," *Papers on Language and Literature* 40, no. 2 (2004): 145.

9. *The Correspondence of Richard Steele*, ed. Rae Blanchard (Oxford: Clarendon Press, 1941), 332. All subsequent references to correspondence will be to this edition and cited by letter number and date.

10. Letter No. 562, July 16, 1717. The delays in production stemmed in part from Steele's conflict with the Duke of Newcastle, who, serving as Lord Chamberlain, revoked Steele's royal theatrical license on January 23, 1720.

11. And the play was seen by many theater-goers: between 1723 and 1773, *The Conscious Lovers* had 316 performances on the London stage. Additionally, as Jason Shaffer details, the play was performed to specific political ends in the West Indies and the American colonies between 1771 and 1776. *Performing Patriotism: National Identity in the Colonial and Revolutionary American Theatre* (Philadelphia: University of Pennsylvania Press, 2007), 126-31.

12. Richard Steele, *The Theatre*, No. 3, January 9, 1720, ed. John Loftis (Oxford: Oxford University Press, 1962), 12.

13. Nicole Horejsi, "(Re)Valuing the 'Foreign Trinket': Sentimentalizing the Language of Economics in Steele's *Conscious Lovers*," *Restoration and Eighteenth-Century Theatre Research* 18, no. 2 (2003): 16, 12.

14. Jennifer Donahue, "Bringing the Other into View: Confronting the West Indian Creole in *The Conscious Lovers* and *The West Indian*," *Restoration and Eighteenth-Century Theatre Research* 26, no. 1/2 (2011): 41-56.

15. O'Brien, *Literature Incorporated*, 103.

16. Emma Rothschild, *The Inner Lives of Empires: An Eighteenth-Century History* (Princeton, N.J.: Princeton University Press, 2011), 9. The "invocation of colonial servitude in the Western plantations" that Bridget Orr identifies as present on the Restoration stage continues, indeed intensifies, in *The Conscious Lovers. Empire on the English Stage, 1660–1714* (Cambridge: Cambridge University Press, 2001), 227.

17. Calhoun Winton, *Sir Richard Steele, M.P.: The Later Career* (Baltimore: Johns Hopkins University Press, 1970), 221.

18. *Correspondence of Richard Steele*, ed. Blanchard, 202n3. Moira Ferguson describes Steele's first wife as a "Caribbean heiress" (*Subject to Others: British Women Writers and Colonial Slavery, 1670–1834* [New York: Routledge, 1992]).

19. PRO document C6 /352/ 2, quoted in John Owen and Arthur L. Cooke, "Addison vs. Steele, 1708," *PMLA* 68, no. 1 (1953): 314.

20. Calhoun Winton, "Steele, Sir Richard (bap. 1672, d. 1729)," in *Oxford Dictionary of National Biography* (Oxford: Oxford University Press, 2004). Winton's previous characterization of Stretch's legacy in his biography of Steele, *Captain Steele*, is more modest: "she left her husband in a comfortable financial situation" (*Captain Steele: The Early Career of Richard Steele* [Baltimore: Johns Hopkins University Press, 1964], 86).

21. Rae Blanchard, "Richard Steele's West Indian Plantation," *Modern Philology* 39, no. 3 (1942): 282.

22. George A. Aitken, *The Life of Richard Steele in Two Volumes* (1889; rpt. New York: Greenwood Press, 1968), 1:64.

23. Winton, "Steele, Richard."

24. Letter No. 221, August 30, 1707. Like Madan, Steele obscures his financial situation in romantic verbiage.

25. Felsenstein, *English Trader, Indian Maid*, 88.

26. Letter No. 418, March 1713/14. Steele's attitude anticipates Martin Madan's approach in correspondence with his wife Judith where he too acknowledges a lack of financial resources for which he offers emotional currency instead.

27. Letter No. 226, September 3, 1707.

28. Ibid.

29. Ibid.

30. Blanchard, "Richard Steele's West Indian Plantation," 282.

31. PRO, Cal. State Papers, C.O. 5, 210, 7, quoted in Willard Connely, *Sir Richard Steele* (Port Washington, N.Y.: Kennikat Press, 1967), 102. The full document, written January 6, 1707, is summarized in *Calendar of State*

Papers Colonial, America and West Indies, vol. 23, *1706–1708,* ed. Cecil Headlam (London: His Majesty's Stationery Office, 1916), 344–66, http://www.british-history.ac.uk/cal-state-papers/colonial/america-west -indies/vol23/pp344-366. The third Earl of Sunderland was appointed secretary of state in December 1706 and was dismissed June 1710.

32. Thomas Tickell, *Oxford. A Poem. Inscrib'd to the Right Honourable the Lord Lonsdale* (London, 1707), 6.

33. Gikandi, *Slavery and the Culture of Taste,* 120.

34. Ibid., 150.

35. Addison's brother Gulston owned an estate in India.

36. Item 1256, *Calendar of State Papers Colonial, America and West Indies,* ed. Headlam, 23:628–32, http://www.british-history.ac.uk/cal-state-papers /colonial/america-west-indies/vol23/pp628-632. The full document is C.O. 319, 1, 116–17.

37. James Alsop, "Richard Steele and Barbados: Further Evidence," *Eighteenth-Century Life* 6, no. 1 (1981): 21. Alsop explains that the men were referring to "the bitter, drawn-out controversy which surrounded Mitford Crowe's governorship of the island" (21). He notes that in August 1709, around the same time as the petition, "seventy-six gentlemen with interests in Barba-dos" petitioned the House of Commons on "the necessity for the establish-ment of a joint-stock company for the African trade with Barbados" (22).

38. Connely, *Sir Richard Steele,* 127.

39. Item 1256, *Calendar of State Papers Colonial, America and West Indies,* ed. Headlam, 23:628–32.

40. "America and West Indies: January 1709," Item 321, 193–214, *Calendar of State Papers Colonial, America and West Indies,* vol. 24, *1708–1709,* ed. Cecil Headlam (London: His Majesty's Stationery Office, 1922), 193–214, http://www.british-history.ac.uk/cal-state-papers/colonial/america-west -indies/vol24/pp193-214. Full document available C.O. 28, 12, No. 7.

41. Alsop, "Richard Steele and Barbados," 22. The August 1709 document, which is not signed by Steele, is titled "A Letter from the most Consid-erable Proprietors of the Island of *Barbadoes,* to the Several Persons in *Great Britain* interested in the said Island, requesting their Application to the Honourable the House of Commons, for Establishing the African Trade by a Joint-Stock." It complains that since the "Trade to Africa" had been "laid open" in 1697, eroding the monopoly rights of the Royal Af-rican Company, the price of enslaved Africans had "arisen gradually to such a height, that as there is no purchasing of them now on the Coast of Guinea, for less than about 8 or 10 l. per Head at least; so these have

been sold again in Barbadoes, from 25l to about 40 l. per Head; . . . Nor have the Plantations been, of late Years, supply'd with sufficient Number of Negroes, even at any rate."

42. During that same period in 1709, Steele also successfully requested an advance of his pension as gentleman waiter. In August 1709, he borrowed £1,000 from George Doddington.

43. Letter No. 239, October 8, 1707.

44. Letter No. 243, October 16, 1707. Speculation about the identity of Codrington is in *Correspondence of Richard Steele,* ed. Blanchard, 211n1.

45. Letter No. 251, December 8, 1707.

46. Letter No. 309, October 14, 1708.

47. Letter No. 290, September 9, 1708. For a discussion of the relationship between the two men, see James H. Averill, "The Death of Stephen Clay and Richard Steele's *Spectators* of August 1711," *Review of English Studies* 28, no. 111 (1977): 305–10.

48. Connely, *Sir Richard Steele,* 134.

49. Perhaps Steele's preoccupation with time also echoes his internalization, if from a distance, of the degree to which the sugar plantation resembled an industrial operation. As Trevor Burnard and John Garrigus assert, the integrated sugar plantation shared fundamental elements with an industrial operation including the use of hundreds of laborers, an industrial-style production process, and, most relevant here, a careful attention to time. Trevor Burnard and John Garrigus, *The Plantation Machine: Atlantic Capitalism in French Saint-Dominique and British Jamaica* (Philadelphia: University of Pennsylvania Press, 2016), 2.

50. Letter 269, June 4, 1708. Owen and Cooke ("Addison vs. Steele") describe Tryon as a "shrewd and rather shady agent." But J. D. Alsop suggests that, despite Steele's claim that Tryon was "incorrectly withholding funds due from the sale of the property," he was in fact an honest broker. "New Light on Richard Steele," *British Library Journal* 25, no. 1 (1999): 26.

51. Ibid. Blanchard is uncertain whether "Mrs. Tryon" is the spouse of William Tyron or his brother Rowland Tryon. Both men were signers of the petition on behalf of Barbados owners and both were "on the same side as Steele in the controversies over the governorships of Mitford Crowe at Barbados" and other political issues related to the colony (Alsop, "New Light on Richard Steele," 27). Rowland Tryon, according to Alsop, was a London merchant and "agent for Barbados merchants" who, as mentioned above, was "formally appointed" trustee for the sale of the estate in early 1708. "In this capacity," notes Alsop, "Tryon acted primarily on behalf of

the tenant and purchaser, George Walker" (26). All the existing scholar-ship on Steele and his associates strongly suggests Rowland Tryon was the Tryon in question.

52. Letter No. 272, June 7, 1708.

53. Letter No. 339, January 31, 1708/9.

54. Letter No. 341, March 2, 1708/9.

55. Letter No. 345, April 19, 1709.

56. Letter No. 295, September 21, 1708.

57. Blanchard notes that "particulars are lacking" in relation to Steele and his financial problems, but proposes he had been in a sponging-house on Vere Street in August 1710 (*Correspondence of Richard Steele*, ed. Blanchard, 265n1). Blanchard also suggests that on May 2, Steele was previously arrested for debt (although it is not clear whether he was imprisoned) (254n1).

58. Winton, *Captain Steele*, 95.

59. Letter No. 324, November 16, 1708.

60. Letter No. 349, May 5, 1709.

61. Winton, *Captain Steele*, 94.

62. Winton, "Steele, Richard."

63. Steele's proposal, published in 1718, was titled *An Account of the Fish-Pool: Consisting of a Description of the Vessel So Call'd, Lately Invented and Built for the Importation of Fish Alive, and in Good Health, from Parts However Distant* (London, 1718).

64. Blanchard, "Richard Steele's West Indian Plantation," 284. Blanchard de-tails the four successive deeds to the property, the trustees involved, and the final disposition of the estate.

65. Letter No. 272, June 7, 1708.

66. Letter No. 410, September 27, 1712.

67. Felsenstein, *English Trader, Indian Maid*, 88.

68. Joseph Roach, *Cities of the Dead: Circum-Atlantic Performance* (New York: Columbia University Press, 1996), 75. As Brian Cowan notes, during this period "coffee shifted from being a specialty product . . . to a colonial plantation crop, harvested primarily by slave labor," grown primarily in the West Indies. Brian Cowan, *The Social Life of Coffee: The Emergence of the British Coffeehouse* (New Haven: Yale University Press, 2005), 76. See also S. D. Smith, "Sugar's Poor Relations: Coffee Planting in the British West Indies, 1720–1833," *Slavery and Abolition* 19, no. 3 (1998): 68–89.

69. Felsenstein, *English Trader, Indian Maid*, 14.

70. Richard Steele, *The Conscious Lovers*, in *The Plays of Richard Steele*, ed. Shirley Strum Kenny (Oxford: Clarendon Press, 1971), IV.ii, l. 51. Subsequent references will be to this edition and cited parenthetically in the text by act, scene, and line number. In the preface, Steele maintains that "a Play is to be Seen" (in no small part, because it advanced his own financial interest), and that "the greatest Effect of a Play in reading is to excite the Reader to go see it," 299.

71. O'Brien, *Literature Incorporated*, 87.

72. Steele also records his own moments of sentimental reaction; in a letter to two of his daughters he writes "I Love you all so tenderly that my Tears are ready to flow when I tell you that I am, Dearest Creatures, Y^r most Affectionate Father and Most Humble Servant" (Letter No. 621, February 11, 1721/22).

73. Lisa A. Freeman explores "good breeding" in *The Conscious Lovers*, describing how Steele works to demonstrate "how 'good breeding' could support the audience's material interest in breeding well." *Character's Theatre: Genre and Identity on the Eighteenth-Century English Stage* (Philadelphia: University of Pennsylvania Press, 2002), 213. My essay, while taking a different approach with its effort to situate Sealand within the transatlantic trade in enslaved Africans (and its attendant concerns with "breeding"), seeks to complement her fine discussion.

74. While Nicole Horejsi suggests the play is concerned with the characters' sources of wealth, her focus is more on the role of enslaved Africans, Indiana's perceived racial difference, and Steele's ideological message rather than the subjects discussed here. "(Re)Valuing the 'Foreign Trinket,'" 13.

75. Aitken, *The Life of Richard Steele in Two Volumes*, 1:132.

76. Ibid., 1:132n4. For additional information about privateers see, among others, Jon Latimer, *Buccaneers of the Caribbean: How Piracy Forged an Empire* (Cambridge, Mass.: Harvard University Press, 2009) or Kenneth Morgan, "Bristol and the Atlantic Trade in the Eighteenth Century," *English Historical Review* 107, no. 424 (1992), which specifically discusses "the impact of war on shipping" during the War of Spanish Succession, a period chronologically consistent with the privateer moment to which Indiana and Isabella refer (630).

77. Stephen Ware offers this number in connection with the latter half of the eighteenth century. "A Twentieth-Century Debate about Imprisonment for Debt," *American Journal of Legal History* 54, no. 3 (2014): 352. See also

Paul Haagen, "Imprisonment for Debt in England and Wales" (PhD diss., Princeton University, 1986).

78. The French did not begin transporting convicts until 1853, so Indiana's association with transportation as either convict or indentured servant is exclusive to her time in England.

79. Although Bethlehem Hospital or Bedlam did use manacles to restrain some patients (and does, of course, represent another form of captivity), that practice declined as the century progressed. For a history of the hospital see Jonathan Andrews et al., *The History of Bethlehem* (London: Routledge, 1997). Pages 214–17 specifically discuss the history of restraints. See also Patricia Allderidge, "Bedlam: Fact or Fantasy?" in *The Anatomy of Madness: Essays in History of Psychiatry*, vol. 2, *Institutions and Society*, ed. W. F. Bynum, Roy Porter, and Michael Shepherd (London: Tavistock Publications, 1985), 17–33. Allderidge acknowledges that some inmates were chained but interrogates some of the common assumptions about Bedlam.

80. Felsenstein, *English Trader, Indian Maid*, 88.

81. The complete poem was first printed in *The Theatre*, No. 18, March 1, 1720, as detailed by Loftis in *Steele at Drury Lane*, 26n1.

82. *The Occasional Verse of Richard Steele*, ed. Rae Blanchard (Oxford: Clarendon Press, 1942), 26.

83. In her introduction to the text, Kenney notes that "[a] multitude of pathetic heroines . . . sighed and wept through intolerable situations in the comedies . . . following the greatest stage popularity of *The Conscious Lovers*" (287).

84. *The Theatre*, No. 3, January 9, 1720, ed. John Loftis (Oxford: Clarendon Press, 1962), 12. Steele continues, extoling "the great, and rich Families of Merchants, and eminent Trades, who . . . are so far from being below the Gentry, . . . and deserve the Imitation of the modern Nobility. . . . He is a Man that does Business with the Candour of a Gentleman, and performs his Engagements with the Exactness of a Citizen" (12).

85. Madge Dresser, *Slavery Obscured: The Social History of the Slave Trade in Bristol* (2001; rpt. Bristol: Redcliffe Press, 2007), 8. Dresser notes how Bristol "played a crucial role in the trade's early development" and "helped to establish an effective trading and political infrastructure to support the trade," illustrating "the wider impact African merchants made on the city's development" (28). For a detailed discussion of the history of the slave trade in Bristol, one which informs Dresser's discussion, see David Richardson, *Bristol, Africa, and the Eighteenth-Century Slave Trade*

to America, 4 vols. (Bristol: Bristol Record Society, 1986–96) and his *The Bristol Slave Traders: A Collective Portrait* (Bristol: Bristol Historical Association, 1985). See also David Harris Sacks, *The Widening Gate: Bristol and the Atlantic Economy, 1450–1700* (Berkeley: University of California Press, 1991).

86. William Pettigrew, *Freedom's Debt: The Royal African Company and the Politics of the Atlantic Slave Trade, 1672–1752* (Chapel Hill: University of North Carolina Press, 2013), 224, appendix 1.

87. James A. Rawley with Stephen D. Behrendt, *The Transatlantic Slave Trade: A History*, rev. ed. (Lincoln: University of Nebraska Press, 2005), 164; see also chapter 8 for a sustained discussion of Bristol. Rawley delineates Bristol's "pre-eminence in the English slave trade," which he attributes, in part, to the ability of Bristol merchants to exchange "commodities in a broad trading area" (148), producing "exports and transport for the African business" (149). Sugar was, of course, the primary import good of Bristol, and the city's role in the sugar trade (and the refinement of sugar) is well documented. Kenneth Morgan notes that by 1750, Bristol had twenty sugar refineries in operation "a larger number than at any other British out port" (*Bristol and the Atlantic Economy in the Eighteenth Century* [Cambridge: Cambridge University Press, 1993], 185); he goes on to describe the sugar trade as "the greatest success story in Bristol's eighteenth-century Atlantic trade" (221). Rawley also details how the Bristol Society of Merchants was active in fighting the monopoly of the Royal African Company (and blocking efforts to restore the company's privileges) and gained equal representation with London and Liverpool on the parliamentary committee managing the Company of Merchants Trading to Africa (Rawley, *Transatlantic Slave Trade*, 151). For a full discussion of the changes in the Royal African Company's monopoly of the slave trade see William Pettigrew, "Free to Enslave: Politics and the Escalation of Britain's Transatlantic Slave Trade, 1688–1714," *William and Mary Quarterly* 64, no. 1 (2007): 3–38.

88. Dresser, *Slavery Obscured*, 28–29.

89. See David Roberts, "First Night in Bristol: Reflections on a 250th Anniversary," *New Theatre Quarterly* 32, no. 3 (2016): 203–9. The powerful associations of Bristol with the slave trade persisted well through the eighteenth century. Not only did Thomas Clarkson use Bristol as his example for the dangerous effects of the slave trade in *Essay on the Impolicy of the African Slave Trade* (1788), so too Jane Austen explicitly draws on the city's powerful and longstanding association with the slave trade in

Emma (1815). See Catherine Ingrassia, *"Emma,* Slavery, and Cultures of Captivity," *Persuasions* 38 (2017): 95–106.

90. Dresser, *Slavery Obscured,* 14.

91. Kenneth Morgan, "Bristol West India Merchants in the Eighteenth Century," *Transactions of the Royal Historical Society* 3 (December 1993): 185–208. See also Morgan, "Bristol and the Atlantic Trade in the Eighteenth Century"; and his book *Bristol and the Atlantic Economy in the Eighteenth Century.* For a discussion of representations of "Indies" merchants during the Restoration, see Orr, *Empire on the English Stage,* 225–38.

92. "A Letter from a Merchant in Bristol, Touching on the Trade to Africa, as It Relates to the Out-ports of Great Britain" (London, 1711), quoted in Pettigrew, *Freedom's Debt,* 102n31.

93. I appreciate Madge Dresser's assistance in refining those categories. For discussions about the transportation of convict labor, and its relationship with the enslavement of Africans, see, too, Peter Wilson Coldham, *Emigrants in Chains: A Social History of Forced Emigration to the Americas of Felons, Destitute Children, Political and Religious Non-Conformists, Vagabonds, Beggars, and other Undesirables, 1607–1776* (Baltimore: Genealogical Publishing Co., 1994), 173–76; A. Roger Ekirch, "Bound for America: A Profile of British Convicts Transported to the Colonies, 1718–1775," *William and Mary Quarterly* 42, no. 2 (1985): 184–200; David Eltis, "Labour and Coercion in the English Atlantic World from the Seventeenth Century to the Early Twentieth Century," in *Slavery & Abolition* 14, no. 1 (1993): 207–26; and his "Slavery and Freedom in the Early Modern World," in *Terms of Labor: Slavery, Serfdom, and Free Labor,* ed. Stanley L. Engerman (Stanford, Calif.: Stanford University Press, 1999), 25–49. Between the middle of the seventeenth and beginning of the eighteenth century, plantation owners also transitioned from using white indentured servants to enslaved Africans. That shift in unfree labor, commonly seen as contributing to the accelerated growth of a slave-based plantation economy, has been extensively discussed by scholars of the British Atlantic. See, for example, James Thornton, *Africa and Africans in the Making of the Atlantic World, 1400–1800* (Cambridge: Cambridge University Press, 1998). For a further discussion of the transformation of these patterns, see Hilary Beckles, *White Servitude and Black Slavery in Barbados, 1627–1715* (Knoxville: University of Kentucky Press, 1989).

94. Morgan, "Bristol and the Atlantic Trade," 637. J. S. Cockburn details how records of the first government contracts immediately following the Transportation Act show that a few convict ships had served as slave

ships, suggesting the slippage between the two categories. ("Punishment and Brutalization in the English Enlightenment," *Law and History Review* 12, no. 1 [1994]: 155–79). See also Rae Blanchard, "Richard Steele's Maryland Story," *American Quarterly* 10, no. 1 (1958): 79.

95. Morgan, *Bristol and the Atlantic Economy*, 203.

96. Richard Dunn, *Sugar and Slaves: The Rise of the Planter Class in the English West Indies, 1624–1713* (Chapel Hill: University of North Carolina Press, 1972), 116. In "Bristol West India Merchants," Morgan traces the various paths Bristol merchants used to build and consolidate their wealth, including investing in ownership of plantations in the West Indies to supplement (and complement) their shipping or mercantile interests in ways that might illuminate the context for considering Sealand's narrative.

97. John Latimer, *History of the Society of Merchant Venturers* . . . (Bristol: J. W. Arrowsmith, 1903).

98. Peter Mathias, review of *Politics and the Port of Bristol in the Eighteenth Century* (1963), by W. E. Minchinton, *Economic History Review* 20, no. 2 (1967): 400. Morgan also discusses the Merchant Venturers. The Society of Merchant Venturers contributed to the public debate in the 1690s resulting in Parliament's passage of the African Trade Act in 1698, which "opened the slave trade to all English citizens for a period of thirteen years on payment of a 10 percent duty on imports and exports" (Pettigrew, "Free to Enslave," 5). Pettigrew also notes that when the act expired in 1712, opening up the trade, the number of annual voyages in service of the slave trade rose from 37 in 1686 to 120 in 1730 (5).

99. Ligon, *True and Exact History of the Island of Barbados*, 89. Thomas Phillips, a late seventeenth-century trader, observes slaves "have a worst apprehension of Barbados than we [Europeans] have of hell." Thomas Phillips, *A Journal of a Voyage Made in the Hannibal of London, 1693, 1694*, in *Collection of Voyages and Travels*, ed. Awnsham Churchill and John Churchill (London, 1746), 6:219, quoted in Ramesh Mallipeddi, "'A Fixed Melancholy': Migration, Memory, and the Middle Passage," *Eighteenth Century: Theory and Interpretation* 55, no. 2/3 (2014): 239. For a discussion of Ligon in connection with *Inkle and Yarico* see Laura Martin, "'Servants Have the Worser Lives': The Poetics and Rhetorics of Servitude and Slavery in *Inkle and Yarico's* Barbados," in *Invoking Slavery in the Eighteenth-Century British Imagination*, ed. Srividhya Swaminathan and Adam R. Beach (Farnham, UK: Ashgate, 2013), 115–32.

100. Ligon, *True and Exact History of the Island of Barbados*, 93.

101. Beckles, *White Servitude and Black Slavery in Barbados*, 167.

102. Roxann Wheeler, "Slavey: or, The New Drudge," in *Invoking Slavery in the Eighteenth-Century British Imagination*, ed. Swaminathan and Beach, 166.

103. For a discussion of servants in *The Conscious Lovers*, see Wolfram, "'I Am My Master's Servant for Hire.'"

104. The sexual vulnerability of female domestic servants is well documented. See, for example, Bridget Hill, *Servants: English Domestics in the Eighteenth Century* (Oxford: Clarendon Press, 1996).

105. Eliza Haywood, *Fantomina*, in *Fantomina and Other Works*, ed. Margaret Case Croskery, Anna C. Patchias, and Alexander Pettit (Toronto: Broadview Literary Texts, 2004), 52. Haywood further represents the threats to female servant in *Anti-Pamela* (1741), which more extensively explores the challenges women confronted in domestic service.

106. Steele, *The Theatre*, 126–27.

107. Ligon, *True and Exact History of the Island of Barbados*, 188.

108. Ibid., 97.

109. Ibid.

110. Ibid., 103. In his examination of American slaveholding and its legacies, Clint Smith notes a similar practice. The narrative of James Roberts, a man enslaved in Louisiana in the late eighteenth century, details how a certain number of enslaved women "were kept constantly for breeding." *How the Word is Passed: A Reckoning with the History of Slavery Across America*, (New York: Little, Brown and Company, 2021), 69.

111. Ibid., 197.

112. Marisa Fuentes, *Dispossessed Lives: Enslaved Women, Violence, and the Archive* (Philadelphia: University of Pennsylvania Press, 2016), 93.

113. Ferguson, *Subject to Others*, 335n67.

114. Steele, *The Occasional Poems of Richard Steele*, 26.

4. BARBARY CAPTIVITY: PENELOPE AUBIN AND *THE NOBLE SLAVES*

1. Robert C. Davis, *Christian Slaves, Muslim Masters: White Slavery in the Mediterranean, the Barbary Coast, and Italy, 1500–1800* (Houndmills, UK: Palgrave Macmillan, 2003), xxvii.

2. Davis estimates that the proportion of Christian females enslaved in Barbary may have been as low as 5 percent "among the generality of European slaves there" (ibid., 36). He goes on to note (207n28) that "it must be remembered, however, that such estimates that are currently available represent only those women who were ransomed; whether the percentage was the same for those captured overall remains an open question, but it

is highly likely that many women, once absorbed into the harems of North Africa, converted to Islam and were never offered for ransom at all."

3. Eve Tavor Bannet also notes the text's popularity in the colonies. See chapter 2, *Transatlantic Stories and the History of Reading, 1720–1810: Migrant Fictions* (Cambridge: Cambridge University Press, 2011).

4. Between October 1721 and July 1723, Aubin published *The Amorous Adventures of Lucinda* (October 1721), *The Noble Slaves* (March 1722), and *The Life of Charlotta Du Pont* (July 1723). She published two additional novels during this same period, *The Adventures of Count Vinevil* (July 1721) and *Lucinda* (October 1721), which touch on but do not squarely focus on Barbary captivity. During this period, the newspaper advertisements in the London papers demonstrate the fascination with all things exotic and international. For example, the *St. James Evening Post* of November 6, 1722, has an advertisement for books printed for E. Bell at the Cross-Keys and Bible in Cornhill. It lists twenty-four books, three of them Aubin's (*The Noble Slaves, Count Vinovel* [sic], and *Life and Amorous Adventures of Lucinda*). The first item, in a font larger than all the rest, was "The Arabian Nights Entertainment; Consisting of One Thousand and One Stories; in 8 Vols."

5. This exact narrative appears in the *Weekly Journal or British Gazetteer*, Saturday, April 2, 1720; the *Post Boy*, March 27–29, 1720; the *Weekly Journal or Saturday's Post*, Saturday, April 2, 1720; the *Original Weekly Journal*, April 2, 1720; and the *St. James Evening Post*, March 29, 1720. The story, although not this precise narrative, appears in a much longer, slightly different format in 1736 as Philémon de La Motte's *Several Voyages to the Barbary* (London, 1736). This text contains a long narrative recounting in great detail the events surrounding the departure, shipwreck, and subsequent redemption (see especially pages 21–41). This version of the narrative names the woman as "De Bourk." The *DNB* does not include an entry for her husband under Bourk, De Bourk, or any other variant spelling.

6. Morocco, although also technically part of the Barbary, was not part of the Ottoman Empire but was, intermittently, a trading partner of England.

7. Nabil Matar, *Britain and Barbary, 1589–1689* (Gainesville: University Press of Florida, 2005), 3.

8. The term "barbarian" in its broadest sense refers to someone who is "foreign," which originally meant non-Hellenic, non-Roman, or non-Christian. While that broad sweep would encompass inhabitants of North African and what would become the Barbary States, it did not refer to

them exclusively or originally. The *OED's* last documented usage of the word "barbarian" in reference to a native of the Barbary States is 1709. The word has the additional connotation of one who is uncivilized or savage. "Barbarous" shares that non-Hellenic, non-Roman meaning, with a particular emphasis on differences in language, speech, and culture.

9. See *Piracy, Slavery, and Redemption: Barbary Captivity Narratives from Early Modern England,* selected and edited by Daniel J. Vitkus, introduced by Nabil Matar (New York: Columbia University Press, 2001), 17.

10. Matar, *Britain and Barbary,* 7.

11. Ibid.

12. The 1736 version of this narrative notes Miss Bourk wrote her letter upon "the Beginnings and Ends of some Books" carried by her steward (La Motte, *Several Voyages to the Barbary,* 26).

13. Linda Colley elaborates on England's "meanness" in terms of generating the fund to redeem Barbary captives in *Captives: Britain, Empire, and the World, 1600–1850* (New York: Anchor Books, 2002), 53ff. Moira Ferguson observes that "the historical contradiction between helping kidnapped Europeans and upholding colonial slavery remained." "Seventeenth-Century Women," in *Culture and Society in the Stuart Restoration: Literature, Drama, History,* ed. Gerald Maclean (Cambridge: Cambridge University Press, 1995), 225.

14. The Royal, Celestial, and Military Order of Our Lady of Mercy and the Redemption of the Captives, also known as the Mercedarians, is a Catholic mendicant order established in 1218. The Order of the Most Holy Trinity and of the Captives, often shortened to the Order of the Most Holy Trinity, or Trinitarians, is a Catholic religious order founded at the end of the twelfth century. For a fuller discussion of the Redemptive Orders and their interactions with different European countries and principalities, see Jarbel Rodriguez, *Captives and the Saviors in the Medieval Crown of Aragon* (Washington, D.C.: Catholic University of America Press, 2007); and Gillian Weiss, *Captivity and Corsairs: France and Slavery in the Early Modern Mediterranean* (Stanford, Calif.: Stanford University Press, 2011). Colley notes, "captives from Britain and Ireland . . . sometimes felt bereft" (since the Trinitarians and Mercedarians focused on redeeming Catholic captives) (54).

15. Perhaps tellingly, her letter is also withheld in the 1736 version of events. That text includes two versions of the incidents. In the first, the author claims to have been an eyewitness; I "myself being at Tunis when M. Du Sault [Bourk's steward] arrived there, very early in 1720. There I heard most of the Circumstances, partly from that ancient Gentleman's

own Mouth, as he related them to the French Consul, M. Bayle, and others" (La Motte, *Several Voyages to the Barbary*, 36). The other is an abbreviated version by "another French Writer, M. Laugier de Tassy," "then on the Spot" (35). No version of the narrative includes the letter from the young Miss Bourk. The 1735 version of "de Bourk's" ordeal, *Voyage to Algiers and Tunis, for the Redemption of the Captives*, details her time in captivity, the habits of the Moors (including food, living conditions, and rituals), and the protracted means of securing her release. However, the 1735 and 1736 versions differ markedly from the 1720 account in the cause of death of Lady de Bourk. The later, amplified versions recount how she and a large number of her traveling companions drown when their ship sinks in "a most furious Tempest" (37).

16. Notably, the 1735 version of the narrative underscores what is, perhaps implicit in the 1720 letter: Miss Bourk's possible fate if not ransomed. "The *Sheikh* was absolutely determined to retain M. *De Bourk*, designing her as a Wife for his Son, who was fourteen Years old, and not (he said) any way unworthy of her, even had she been the King of France's own Daughter, his Son being the Offspring of a King of Mountains and consequently not her inferior" (ibid., 31). For a modern edition of the 1735 version of Bourk's narrative with a contextualizing introduction, see Khalid Bekkaoui, *White Women Captives in North Africa: Narratives of Enslavement, 1735–1830* (New York: Palgrave Macmillan, 2011).

17. Nancy Armstrong and Leonard Tennenhouse argue that the captivity narratives coming from America provide one of the templates for the eighteenth-century novel, citing Richardson's *Pamela* as an immediate and obvious text dependent upon that model. They do not discuss narratives of Barbary captivity. *The Imaginary Pilgrim: Literature, Intellectual Labor, and the Origins of Personal Life* (Berkeley: University of California Press, 1992). See also Michelle Burham, *Captivity and Sentiment: Cultural Exchange in American Literature* (Hanover, N.H.: University Press of New England, 1997).

18. Daniel Vitkus, "The Circulation of Bodies: Slavery, Maritime Commerce, and English Captivity Narratives in the Early Modern Period," in *Colonial and Postcolonial Incarceration*, ed. Graeme Harper (London: Bloomsbury, 2001), 29.

19. Daniel Defoe, *A General History of Discoveries and Improvements in the Useful Arts* [. . .] (London, 1725), 148.

20. Ibid.

21. Colley, *Captives*, 63.

22. Matar, Introduction to *Piracy, Slavery, and Redemption*, ed. Vitkus, 5.

23. Chris Mounsey writes of the "conversion panic" that besets Aubin's characters. The anxiety about capture certainly lies, in part, in the "panic" about forced conversion to Islam, but it also resides in a more global apprehension about captivity. "Conversion Panic, Circumcision, and Sexual Anxiety: Penelope Aubin's Queer Writing," in *Queer People: Negotiations and Expressions of Homosexuality, 1700–1800*, ed. Chris Mounsey and Caroline Gonda (Lewisburg, Pa.: Bucknell University Press, 2007), 256.

24. Robert C. Davis, "Counting European Slaves on the Barbary Coast," *Past & Present* 172 (2001): 87–124. Alan G. Jamieson concurs, suggesting that "one million Christian captives" were "taken by the Barbary corsairs between 1500 and 1800." *Lords of the Sea: A History of the Barbary Corsairs* (London: Reaktion Books, 2012), 17.

25. In doing so, Matar asks scholars to also consider "European captivity of, and violence against, Muslims" (*Britain and Barbary*, 114).

26. See Colley, *Captives*, chap. 3. My description of the incidence of Barbary captivity is informed by Colley's detailed and effective description.

27. Moira Ferguson details the ransoming of female captives in chapter 1 of *Subject to Others: British Women Writers and Colonial Slavery, 1670–1834* (New York: Routledge, 1992).

28. "News," *Applebee's Original Weekly*, December 9, 1721.

29. William Berriman, *The Great Blessing of Redemption from Captivity. A Sermon Preached at the Cathedral Church of St. Paul, December 4, 1721. Before the Captives Redeem'd by the Late Treaty with the Emperor of Morocco* . . . (London, 1722), 9.

30. *London Journal* and *Applebee's Original Weekly* of December 9, 1721, include the exact same story, and *Applebee's* lists the names of all the redeemed captives.

31. Many writers told stories of Barbary captivity or included a reference to it. *A Select Collection of Novels in Four Volumes* (London, 1720) includes three novels, each of which draws specifically and explicitly on the fascination with North Africa in its presentation. For example, *The Happy Slave*, subverting the model of North Africa as a site of anxiety, instead asserts that, "*Barbary* it self is Barbarous only by Name": "Love is of all Countries" (3). Further, and not insignificantly, Bannet notes that Mary Rowlandson's captivity narrative was also reprinted in London in 1720 (*Transatlantic Stories*, 55).

32. Interestingly, Chetwood's narrative, like Aubin's, creates a world in which the threats from English men far exceed those from the Barbary captors.

For example, "Mrs. Villars," the orphaned daughter of a wealthy Bristol merchant, is abducted, threatened with gang rape, and verbally brutalized by an English sea captain previously in her father's employ. The associations with slaving and his likely role in it are abundant. After her abduction by a Barbary captain, however, even though he describes her as "a slave of mine, that I have lately taken," he restores the jewelry, books, and personal items taken by the English captain. "He treated her with Decency, allowing her every thing but Liberty; with the conveniency of a Study of Books, which the Captain had procur'd by his Piracy; and even left in her Closet, her Jewels and other things of Value, that he had taken out of the ship" (*Select Collection*, 88).

33. Penelope Aubin, *The Noble Slaves* (London, 1722), 201. Subsequent citations will be to this edition and appear parenthetically in the text. In referring to the redemption of captives, Aubin may also have been anticipating the release of captives in Madrid that was announced in the *Daily Post* of May 17, 1723, which reads: "Christian Slaves lately redeemed from their Captivity in Barbary by the Fathers of the Order of the Trinity, made their publick Entry into this City on the 29th past."

34. Penelope Aubin, *The Strange Adventures of the Count de Vinevil and His Family [. . .]* (London, 1721), 8.

35. Penelope Aubin, Preface, *The Life of Charlotta Du Pont, an English Lady, Taken from Her Own Memoirs* (London, 1723), vi.

36. Penelope Aubin, *The Life and Adventures of the Lady Lucy [. . .]* (London, 1726), ix.

37. Aubin, *Strange Adventures of Count Vinevil*, 6.

38. Debbie Welham, "Delight and Instruction: Women's Political Engagement in the Works of Penelope Aubin" (PhD diss., University of Winchester, 2009), 95.

39. The National Archives SP 78/168/6. David Aubin, a merchant, to his brother, June 3, 1720, Barbados. *Captain Singleton*, by Daniel Defoe, ed. Manushag N. Powell (Peterborough, UK: Broadview, 2019), Appendix B.2, 352.

40. Welham, "Delight and Instruction," 96.

41. Bannet, *Transatlantic Stories*, 58.

42. Joel H. Baer and Debbie Welham, "Aubin, Penelope (1697–1738), novelist and translator," in *Oxford Dictionary of National Biography* (Oxford: Oxford University Press, 2004).

43. Frederick Burwick and Manushag N. Powell, *British Pirates in Print and Performance* (New York: Palgrave, 2015), 106.

44. Welham, "Delight and Instruction," 111. For a further discussion of the Madagascar men, see Burwick and Powell, *British Pirates*, 106–7, and Joel Baer, "Penelope Aubin and the Pirates of Madagascar: Biographical Notes and Documents," in *Eighteenth-Century Women: Studies in Their Lives, Work, and Culture*, vol. 1, ed. Linda V. Troost (New York: AMS Press, 2001): 49–62. The appendix to Baer's article includes a transcription of the PRO document with Aubin's deposition regarding the "pirats of Madagascar" (58–59).

45. Berriman, *Great Blessing of Redemption*, 9.

46. Sarah Prescott, "Penelope Aubin and the Doctrine of Morality: A Reassessment of the Pious Woman Novelist," *Women's Writing* 1, no. 1 (1994): 102.

47. Many contemporary critics take Aubin's claims at face value. John Richetti early labeled her one of the "pious polemicists," and subsequent scholars echoed that position (see chapter 7 in *Popular Fiction before Richardson: Narrative Patterns 1700–1739* [Oxford: Clarendon Press, 1969]). William Warner sees her as offering "exemplary originals for her readers to copy" (*Licensing Entertainment: The Elevation of Novel Reading in Britain, 1684–1750* [Berkeley: University of California Press, 1998], 183–84). Jerry Beasley attributes to her a "genuine cultural anxiety over the weakening moral structures" ("Politics and Moral Idealism," in *Fetter'd or Free?: British Women Novelists, 1670–1851*, ed. Mary Anne Schofield and Cecilia Machesky [Athens: Ohio University Press, 1986], 218). Susan Staves describes how Aubin crafts her female characters "didactically as models for the reader's imitation" (*A Literary History of Women's Writing in Britain, 1660–1789* [Cambridge: Cambridge University Press, 2006], 194).

48. In "Politics and Moral Idealism" Beasley attributes the preface to *A Collection of Entertaining Histories* . . . to Samuel Richardson which, given Richardson's own preoccupations with the morality of prose fiction, may account for the skewed representation of Aubin as a purely pious novelist. Michael McKeon describes the preface as "attributed to" Richardson and similarly focuses on Richardson's praise of Aubin "against the negative example of contemporary female authors." Michael McKeon, *The Secret History of Domesticity: Public, Private, and the Division of Knowledge* (Baltimore: Johns Hopkins University Press, 2005), 642. The preface appears in *A Collection of Entertaining Histories and Novels*, 3 vols., by Penelope Aubin (London, 1739).

49. Chris Mounsey, "'. . . bring her naked from her Bed, that I may ravish her before the Dotard's face, and then send his Soul to Hell': Penelope Aubin,

Impious Pietist, Humourist, or Purveyor of Juvenile Fantasy?" *British Journal for Eighteenth-Century Studies* 26, no. 1 (2003): 58–59.

50. Ibid., 60.

51. Advertisements for *The Noble Slaves* appeared in the *Post Boy* for March 1720, 1722, and March 31–April 3, 1722.

52. The description also echoes the title page to Woodes Rogers, *A Cruising Voyage round the World* (London, 1718), which contains similar place names—South Seas, East Indies, Cape of Good Hope—and chronological markers.

53. For a discussion of this widely known nickname, see Edward Pearce, *The Great Man: Sir Robert Walpole* (London: Pimlico, 2008), 126–27.

54. Teresa Michals, "'The Sole and Despotic Dominion': Slaves, Wives, and Game in Blackstone's *Commentaries*," *Eighteenth-Century Studies* 27, no. 2 (1993/94): 198.

55. Susan Staves, *Married Women's Separate Property in England, 1660–1833* (Cambridge, Mass.: Harvard University Press, 1990).

56. William Blackstone, *Commentaries on the Laws of England*, 4 vols. (Oxford, 1765–69), 1:171; Michals, "'The Sole and Despotic Dominion,'" 200.

57. Blackstone, *Commentaries*, 3:143.

58. Colley notes that before the discovery of longitude (1714) any ship "sailing close to the dangerous North African coastline, especially in poor weather, was at risk of something there" (*Captives*, 67).

59. This novel has been noted for its rather fanciful sense of geography, a world in which Japan is close to Mexico. Certainly, Aubin had a keen knowledge of the reaches of the British Empire—between her engagement with her ship captain brother-in-law David Aubin, whose activities in the West Indies were known to her, and her own engagement with Madagascar, the West Indies, the Barbary Coast, and East and West Africa. This irregularity may stem from Aubin's fundamental misconception of the area or her strategic plan to retain the fictional dimensions of her novel. Ryan Holroyd, "Whatever Happened to Those Villains of the Indian Seas? The Happy Retirement of the Madagascar Pirates, 1698–1721," *International Journal of Maritime History* 29, no. 4 (2017): 752–70.

60. This initial statement may also highlight Bannet's observation that "Aubin argued that people of every nation should realize they must not make slaves of others precisely because people of every nation were being enslaved" (*Transatlantic Stories*, 59).

61. Edward J. Kozaczka, "Penelope Aubin and Narratives of Empire," *Eighteenth-Century Fiction* 25, no. 1 (2012): 200. Aubin's "treatments of

gender, mercantilism, and slavery constitute, to some extent, a critical position of empire in general and the growing British Empire in particular" (202).

62. "Slavery was already a well-established institution in Spain, Portugal, and their colonies by the late fifteenth century" (Vitkus, "The Circulation of Bodies," 27).

63. Michael Guasco, *Slaves and Englishmen: Human Bondage in the Early Modern Atlantic World* (Philadelphia: University of Pennsylvania Press, 2014), 230. See also Herman Lee Bennett, *Africans in Colonial Mexico* (Bloomington: Indiana University Press, 2005); Herbert Klein and Ben Vinson, *African Slavery in Latin America* (Cambridge; Cambridge University Press, 2009); Colin Palmer, *Human Cargoes: The British Slave Trade to Spanish America, 1700–1739* (Urbana: University of Illinois Press, 1981); Frank Proctor III, *Damned Notions of Liberty: Slavery, Culture, and Power in Colonial Mexico* (Albuquerque: University of New Mexico Press, 2010); Verene A. Shepherd, *Slavery without Sugar: Diversity in Caribbean Economy and Society since the 17th Century* (Gainesville: University Press of Florida, 2002); and Elena Schneider, "African Slavery and Spanish Empire: Imperial Imaginings and Bourbon Reform in Eighteenth-Century Cuba and Beyond," *Journal of Early American History* 5, no. 1 (2015): 27.

64. As Holroyd details, "the 1715 reinterpretation of the East India Act of 1698 . . . allowed the legal transportation of slaves directly from the Indian Ocean to British America" ("Whatever Happened to Those Villains of the Indian Seas?" 767).

65. See the discussion of Matthew Hale in chapter 1 of this book. Matthew Hale, *The History of the Pleas of the Crown*, 2 vols. (London, 1736). Marital rape was not illegal in the UK until 1991. Blackstone subsequently wrote of what amounted to the legal disappearance of women within marriage, which "served to legitimate the propertization of women through marriage. Wives were viewed as their husbands' chattel deprived of all civil identity" (Anne Dailey, "To Have and to Hold: The Marital Rape Exemption and the Fourteenth Amendment," *Harvard Law Review* 99, no. 6 [1986]: 1256).

66. Aubin's use of names here, and throughout, seems strategic and reiterates the compulsory nature of Amando's power. Not only does his first name mean "conqueror" in Latin, his surname is the Latin gerundive for "amo"—literally meaning he who must be loved.

67. This fundamental anthropological argument has been foundationally made in Gayle Rubin's "Traffic in Women: Notes on the 'Political

Economy' of Sex," in *Toward an Anthropology of Women*, ed. Rayna R. Reiter (New York: Monthly Review Press, 1975), 157–210.

68. Marchioness de Frene, *The Unfortunate Marriage* (London, 1722), 72–73.

69. Ibid., 74.

70. S.v. "stifle, v." *OED* online.

71. For a relevant discussion of rape on the Restoration stage, and similar acts of violence, see Jennifer Airey, *The Politics of Rape: Sexual Atrocity, Propaganda, and the Restoration Stage* (Newark: University of Delaware Press, 2012).

72. See the *Manual of Prayers and Other Christian Devotion* (London, 1720), 67.

73. Mounsey, "Penelope Aubin, Impious Pietist, Humourist, or Purveyor of Juvenile Fantasy?" 59.

74. Other moments of coercion exist within the text. After hearing Eleanora's story, for example, Antonio found "an opportunity of pressing the charming Anna to make him likewise happy." When the still-fifteen-year-old Anna's "Youth and Innocence made her hard to be persuaded to yield," he uses the enthusiasm of the assembled group to compel her compliance. (150).

75. Adam Beach is correct to assert the women's inability to grant free consent—the manipulative, inherently suspect nature of apparent generosity on the part of Moorish captors. However, we must consider its significance in the absence of similar moments of generosity from Europeans. Even those men perhaps best-positioned to model emulative behavior—Don Lopez and Count de Hautville—display limited empathy, gentleness, or subtlety in their actions. Their homosocial intimacy transcends their connection with either woman. "Aubin's *The Noble Slaves*, Montagu's *Spanish Lady*, and English Feminist Writing about Sexual Slavery in the Ottoman World," *Eighteenth-Century Fiction* 29, no. 4 (2017): 583–606.

76. Ibid., 591.

77. Madeline Zilfi, *Women and Slavery in the Late Ottoman Empire* (Cambridge: Cambridge University Press, 2010), 115.

78. Ibid.

79. Ibid., 151.

80. Mounsey, "Penelope Aubin, Impious Pietist, Humourist, or Purveyor of Juvenile Fantasy?" 60.

81. When "Spanish or Italian aristocrats . . . fell into Barbary corsair hands, [t]heir governments and friends rushed to get them ransomed as soon as possible, willingly paying heavy ransoms" (Jamieson, *Lords of the Sea*, 139).

82. Staves notes Aubin's "attacks on libertinism" (*A Literary History of Women's Writing*, 194). Paula Backscheider observes "embryonic expressions of longing for the utopian husband" in Aubin's novels ("The Rise of Gender as a Political Category," in *Revising Women: Eighteenth-Century Women's Fiction and Social Engagement*, ed. Paula R. Backscheider [Baltimore: Johns Hopkins University Press, 2000], 40).

83. Beach similarly cites a "larger confusion" and "contradictory impulses" in Aubin's text ("Aubin's *The Noble Slaves*," 602). As my discussion makes clear, I don't think Aubin is confused at all; rather she seeks to destabilize the assumptions and draw attention to male privilege in multiple forms.

84. Khalid Bekkaoui, "White Women and Moorish Fancy in Eighteenth-Century Literature," in *"The Arabian Nights" in Historical Context: Between East and West*, ed. Saree Makdisi and Felicity Nussbaum (Oxford: Oxford University Press, 2008), 163.

85. Jane Tibbets Schulenburg, "The Heroics of Virginity: Brides of Christ and Sacrificial Mutilation," in *Women in the Middle Ages and the Renaissance*, ed. Mary Beth Rose (Syracuse, N.Y.: Syracuse University Press, 1986), 48. See too Anne Clark Bartlett, *Male Authors, Female Readers: Representation and Subjectivity in Middle English Devotional Literature* (Ithaca, N.Y.: Cornell University Press, 1995).

86. *Britannia; or, A Chorographical Description of Great Britain and Ireland . . .*, 2 vols. (London, 1722), 2:1179. Saint Margaret of Hungary (d. 1270), as Patricia Skinner notes, not only threatened to cut off her lips to repel possible "pagan aggressors" but also, in a Maria-like move, "declared that she would rather cut off her nose and lips, and gouge out her eyes, than marry any of the three royal suitors proposed" ("Marking the Face, Curing the Soul? Reading the Disfigurement of Women in the Later Middle Ages," in *Medicine, Religion, and Gender in Medieval Culture*, ed. Naoë Kukita Yoshikawa [Suffolk, UK: Boydell & Brewer, 2015], 188). She goes on to note that for many of these medieval examples, "the threat of self-mutilation, rather than its actual practice, . . . was an effective deterrent" (189). My thanks to Sachi Shimomura for bringing this essay to my attention.

87. Charles Eyston, *The History and Antiquities of Glastonbury . . .* (Oxford, 1722), 145.

88. Aphra Behn, *Oroonoko*, in *The Works of Aphra Behn*, vol. 3, ed. Janet Todd (Columbus: Ohio State University Press, 1995), 116.

89. *London Journal*, August 25, 1722.

5. "INDENTURED SLAVES"

1. Patrick Spedding attributes Haywood's ability to publish *Memoirs of an Unfortunate Young Nobleman* nine months prior to the trial where Annesley sued his uncle for the title to "the intriguing possibility that she first heard of Annesley's story" through her family connections (*A Bibliography of Eliza Haywood* [London: Pickering and Chatto, 2004], 384). He also suggests that she may have been particularly intrigued by Annesley's tale because of the similarity between Annesley and the plight of her former associate Richard Savage (1697–1743), who famously claimed a similarly noble birthright.

2. Andrew Lanor, ed., *The Annesley Case* (Edinburgh: William Hodge Company, 1912), 6.

3. Spedding provides compelling evidence for the attribution of the first two volumes of this text to Haywood, most centrally the entry in the printed sale catalog of Frances Cogan's copyright, the catalog that also establishes her authorship of *Anti-Pamela* (*Bibliography of Eliza Haywood*, 388). However, the third volume, which has, as Spedding notes, "no stylistic continuity" with the first two volumes (388), was likely not written by Haywood. Indeed, it more closely resembles court transcripts from the case (382).

4. As Suvir Kaul observes, "considerably more than three-hundred thousand Irish and Scots poor were forced into indentured servitude in British America during the course of the eighteenth century." *Poems of Nation, Anthems of Empire: English Verse in the Long Eighteenth Century* (Charlottesville: University Press of Virginia, 2000), 3.

5. The trial received consistent coverage in the *London Magazine,* edited by Kimber's father Isaac, with stories appearing in volumes 13 (1743) and 14 (1744).

6. William Moraley, *The Infortunate: The Voyage and Adventures of William Moraley, an Indentured Servant,* ed. Susan E. Klepp and Bill G. Smith (University Park: Pennsylvania State University Press, 2005).

7. Ibid., 28.

8. Ibid., 14.

9. Ibid.

10. Ibid., 28.

11. In *Moll Flanders,* indentured servants coexist with all other unfree laborers during their term of service. Defoe paints a faintly optimistic picture about what happens upon the conclusion of their contract: "Among the rest, she often told me how the greatest part of the inhabitants of the colony came thither in very indifferent circumstances from *England.* 'When they

come here,' says she, 'we make no difference; the Planters buy them, and they work together in the Field till their time is out. When 'tis expired,' *said she*, 'they have encouragement given them to plant for themselves; for they have a certain number of acres of Land allotted them by the country, and they go to work to Clear and Cure the land, and then to Plant it with Tobacco and Corn for their own use; and as the Tradesmen and Merchants will trust them with Tools, and clothes, and other necessaries, upon the Credit of their Crop before it is grown, so they again Plant every year a little more than the Year before, and so buy whatever they want with the Crop that is before them.' 'Hence, child,' *says she*, 'many a Newgate-bird becomes a great Man, and we have,' *continued she*, 'several Justices of the Peace, Officers of the Trained Bands, and Magistrates of the Towns they live in, that have been burnt in the Hand.'" Daniel Defoe, *Moll Flanders*, ed. G. A. Starr (Oxford: Oxford University Press, 2011), 72.

12. Moraley, *The Infortunate*, 58.

13. And, obviously, the abduction and forced migration of the enslaved Africans was also not a voluntary passage.

14. William Bullock, *Virginia Impartially Examined* . . . (London, 1649), 14.

15. Elizabeth Foyster, "The 'New World of Children' Reconsidered: Child Abduction in Late Eighteenth- and Early Nineteenth-Century England," *Journal of British Studies* 52, no. 3 (2013): 672–73.

16. James Kelly, "'This Iniquitous Traffic': Kidnapping of Children for the American Colonies in Eighteenth-Century Ireland," *Journal of History of Childhood and Youth* 9, no. 2 (2016): 236.

17. Elizabeth Ashbridge, *Some Account of the Early Part of the Life of Elizabeth Ashbridge* (Philadelphia, 1773), 10.

18. Ibid., 11.

19. Ibid., 15.

20. John Donoghue, "Indentured Servitude in the Seventeenth-Century English Atlantic: A Brief Survey of the Literature," *History Compass* 11, no. 10 (2013): 893.

21. Matthew Mason, "Slavery, Servitude, and British Representations of Colonial North America," *Southern Quarterly* 43, no. 4 (2006), 116.

22. Ashbridge, *Some Account*, 16.

23. For a discussion of the changes in capital punishment and the strategic use of the same by the state, see such foundational studies as Douglas Hay et al., *Albion's Fatal Tree: Crime and Society in Eighteenth-Century England* (New York: Pantheon, 1976); or Peter Linebaugh, *The London Hanged: Crime and Civil Society in the Eighteenth Century* (Cambridge: Cambridge

University Press, 1992). The most popular play of the eighteenth century, John Gay's *The Beggar's Opera* (1728), depends on the cultural familiarity with the language of transportation, as well as the punishments for crimes against property.

24. Defoe, *Moll Flanders*, 31.

25. Ibid.

26. Edward Kimber, "Observations . . . ," *London Magazine*, July 1746, 326.

27. Spedding, *Bibliography of Eliza Haywood*, 382.

28. Haywood's two volumes follow the entire journey of James Annesley, which is beyond my interest here. Annesley successfully escaped to Jamaica, where, on June 11, 1740, he joined the HMS *Falmouth*, part of Vice Admiral Vernon's fleet. When the officers on board learned his identity, he was discharged when the *Falmouth* reached England. He then initiated legal proceedings to reclaim his inheritance. A hunting accident in which James killed a man, slowed the process but the case began on November 11, 1743. As Volume 3 of the *Memoirs* details, much of the testimony centered on the identity of James's mother. While Annesley received a favorable decision, the ongoing process of appeals and strategic delaying tactics by his uncle kept him from ever claiming his inheritance.

29. Vernon, who would ultimately become vice admiral of the British Navy, established his reputation in the Battle of Jenkins' Ear. In the January 3, 1745, issue of the *Female Spectator*, Haywood describes Vernon as "A Most brave and worthy Admiral." The *Female Spectator*, in *The Selected Works of Eliza Haywood: Part II*, vol. 2, ed. Alexander Pettit and Kathryn R. King (London: Pickering & Chatto, 2001), 377.

30. For a twentieth-century account of the trial, see Lanor, ed., *The Annesley Case*.

31. *The Trial in Ejectmen (at Large) between Campbell Craig, Lessee of James Annesley Esq. . . . and the Right Honourable Richard Earl of Anglesey* (London, 1744), 3.

32. *The Richardiad. A Satire* (London, 1744), 15, ll. 130–35. The footnote to those lines also details how Richard "the Usurper" "seiz'd his Person, and sent him as a Slave to Banishment" (15).

33. Elizabeth Boyd, *Altamira's Ghost; or, Justice Triumphant. A New Ballad. Occasion'd by a Certain Nobleman's Cruel Usage of His Nephew. Done Extempore* (London, 1744). *A Letter to a Nobleman* details how Annesley was "spirited away to *Delawar* River, where he was fairly sold to a Planter." "[H]e remained thirteen Years there, in the same low and abject Condition of a Servant, sold for a Term of Years which he was bound to fulfil . . . groaning

under the heavy Load of Slavery in *Virginia,* far from his Native Country."
A Letter to a Nobleman in the Country . . . (London, 1744), 28–29. The date
at the end of the letter is December 24, 1743.

34. *The Cruel UNCLE; or, The Wronged NEPHEW* . . . (Dublin, 1744), 2, ll.
15–16.

35. Ibid., 5.

36. *The Cruel UNCLE,* 6. A broadside ballad, *A Christmas Box,* recounts how
"Two ruffians put the youth on board" a ship going to America "With
hardships there to toil, /Among the woods, each tedious day, / Till thirteen years did roll." *A Christmas Box for a Certain Old Fox; or, A Sequel to
the Children in the Wood* (Dublin, 1744).

37. Lillian de la Torre demonstrates the "general accuracy of Smollett's account of Annesley" in "New Light on Smollett and the Annesley Case," *Review of English Studies* 22, no. 87 (1971): 274–81. In that article de la Torre
describes the *Memoirs* as "an unreliable novelization of the Annesley affair" (276). De la Torre's focus is on substantiating Annesley's accounts
following, not during, his time of captivity. See also her piece with Lewis
M. Knapp, "Smollett, MacKercher, and the Annesley Claimant," *English
Language Notes* 1 (1963): 28–33. Additional biographical information on
Annesley can be found at John Martin, "Annesley, James (1715–1760),
peerage claimant," in *Oxford Dictionary of National Biography* (Oxford:
Oxford University Press, 2004), https://doi.org/10.1093/ref:odnb/564;
and George Rousseau's "Introduction" to Tobias Smollett, *The Adven-
tures of Peregrine Pickle,* ed. John P. Zomchick and George S. Rousseau
(Athens: University of Georgia Press, 2014), xxvii–lxvii and footnotes
55–133; 797–98n55–153. This edition, like Spedding's *Bibliography of Eliza
Haywood,* also confirms Haywood's authorship of the text (see Rousseau,
"Introduction," 797n60).

38. Spedding, *Bibliography of Eliza Haywood,* 383.

39. Eliza Haywood, *Memoirs of an Unfortunate Young Nobleman, Part the Second* (London, 1743), 29.

40. Spedding, *Bibliography of Eliza Haywood,* appendix J, 775–76. Spedding
counts by three different metrics: ten most popular works excluding
translations and adaptations; most popular including translations and adaptations; and most popular in order of the frequency with which they
were republished.

41. Ibid., 389. Additionally, two Dublin abridgements and an Italian translation (1745) also appeared.

42. Eliza Haywood, *Memoirs of an Unfortunate Young Nobleman, Return'd from a Thirteen Years Slavery in America, Where He Had Been Sent by the Wicked Contrivances of His Cruel Uncle. A Story Founded on Truth, and Address'd Equally to the Head and Heart* (London, 1743), 41. All subsequent references are to this edition and will appear parenthetically in the text.

43. Just as Haywood here details how "his Fare was hard and allow'd him but in scanty Portions," so too *A Letter to a Nobleman* remarks that when James stayed at "The House of the Connaugh the Dancing Master," he could not bear his "usage": "he was debarred of his Liberty, and cut short of his Victuals" (20).

44. "One employed in a mean, servile, or distasteful work; a slave, a hack; a hard toiler" (s.v. "drudge, n.," *OED* online).

45. *OED* definitions commonly describe this as the state of utter servitude.

46. Eliza Haywood, *The British Recluse* (London, 1722), 1.

47. Sharon V. Salinger, *"To Serve Well and Faithfully": Labor and Indentured Servants in Pennsylvania, 1682–1800* (Cambridge: Cambridge University Press, 1987), 15.

48. Pipe staves, a "Commodity" that "is a considerable Branch of the Traffic of the County" (62), are the lengths of wood used to make barrels—the same hogsheads mentioned in the chapbook on Annesley.

49. Moraley also describes that practice. When a bought servant escapes and is captured, "the Servant is oblig'd to serve longer time" (*The Infortunate*, 61). Haywood's conversance with these legal nuances (also mentioned specifically by Kimber) suggests colonial policies were widely known in England.

50. In *Moll Flanders*, Moll's mother tells her that "she was one of the second sort of inhabitants herself . . . and 'here's the Mark of it, Child,' *says she*, turning up the Palm of her Hand, and showed me a very fine white Arm and Hand, but branded in the inside of the Hand, as in such cases it must be" (73).

51. See also the previous chapter's discussion of Madeline Zilfi's *Women and Slavery in the Late Ottoman Empire* (Cambridge: Cambridge University Press, 2010) as well as Linda Colley, *Captives: Britain, Empire, and the World, 1600–1850* (New York: Anchor Books, 2002), 119.

52. In the issue of the *Female Spectator* published almost contemporaneously with *Memoirs*, Haywood reveals some knowledge of the economic interests of the West Indies and casts the merchant/planters as essentially more heroic than those British subjects engaged in the navy: "more was

done against the Enemy [the Spanish] by those Ships which were equipt by the Trading Part of the nation than by the whole Royal Navy." The *Female Spectator* 2:309.

53. Given Haywood's preoccupation throughout with the dehumanization of Annesley it is interesting to note that the verb "trepan" can also be applied to an animal. When the female indentured servant describes herself as having fallen into "the lot" of Drumon, Haywood replicates the language Behn uses to describes the sale of enslaved people in Surinam. A more detailed discussion of this unnamed servant and the significance of the figure in Haywood's oeuvre can be found in Catherine Ingrassia, "Eliza Haywood's Captive Message," *Restoration* 44, no. 1 (2020): 67–86; for a discussion of captivity over the scope of Haywood's career, see Ingrassia, "Eliza Haywood and Captivity," in *A Spy on Eliza Haywood: Addresses to a Multifarious Writer*, ed. Aleksondra Hultquist and Chris Mounsey (New York: Routledge, 2022), 75–94.

54. For a discussion of Haywood and Locke, see Jonathan Kramnick, "Locke, Haywood, and Consent," *ELH* 72, no. 2 (2005): 453–79.

55. While Alexander Pope's *Epistle to a Lady* represents women of a very different class, his observation that "time and thought" are "foes to fair ones" remains relevant to the unnamed female slave. Although her labors preclude much "time," it does not prohibit thought.

56. James actually is assisted by a runaway wife and her lover who robbed her husband of "everything she could conveniently take" and planned to live in a foreign country (84). The couple is executed, a punishment James avoids when he proves he has had nothing to do with their plans.

57. Biographical information on Kimber can be found in Kevin J. Hayes's "Introduction," to *Itinerant Observations in America*, by Edward Kimber (Newark: University of Delaware Press, 1998); Jeffrey Herrle, "Kimber, Edward (1719–1769), journal editor and writer," in *Oxford Dictionary of National Biography* (Oxford: Oxford University Press, 2004); and Sidney A. Kimber, "The 'Relation of a Late Expedition to St. Augustine,' with Biographical and Bibliographical Notes on Isaac and Edward Kimber," *Papers of the Bibliographical Society of America* 28 (1934): 81–96.

58. See Edward Kimber, *Itinerant Observations in America*, ed. Kevin J. Hayes (Newark: University of Delaware Press, 1998).

59. "Itinerant Observations in America," *London Magazine*, July 1746, 326–27. During the years of James Annesley's trial and attendant publicity, the *London Magazine* published detailed accounts that might also have provided Kimber with more source material for his novel. For discussion

of Kimber's novel, see Alpen Razi, "Narratives of Amelioration: Mental Slavery and the New World Slave Society in the Eighteenth-Century Didactic Imagination" (PhD. diss., University of Toronto, 2016). Razi suggests that the novel is concerned with "the problem of *mental slavery*" (71), reading the text as "a kind of Protestant discourse, one that traffics in assumptions about the universal character of mental slavery, rather than a strictly colonial or racialist discourse" (72). See too the discussion of Kimber by George E. Boulukos, *The Grateful Slave: The Emergence of Race in Eighteenth-Century British and American Culture* (Cambridge: Cambridge University Press, 2008), 116–29.

60. Kimber, *Itinerant Observations in America*, 326.

61. Ibid. Both narratives include a scene in which the grown man confronts his original captor, the ship captain, facilitated by the former captive's participation as an actor, rather than a commodity, in the exchange of "bought labor." *Itinerant Observations* describes how "When a Ship with Convicts" comes in, the man, though previously sold himself as a youth, "went to purchase some Servants," demonstrating his unreflective integration into a system to which he had once been subject (327).

62. Kimber, *The Life and Adventures of Mr. Anderson*, ed. Matthew Mason and Nicholas Mason (Toronto: Broadview Literary Texts, 2009), 48–49. Subsequent citations will be to this edition and appear parenthetically in the text.

63. Roy Porter, *The Penguin Social History of Britain: English Society in the Eighteenth Century* (London: Penguin, 1980), 131.

64. Anthony Brundage, *The English Poor Laws, 1700–1930* (Basingstroke, UK: Palgrave Macmillan, 2002), 11.

65. John Cary, *An Account of the Proceedings of the Corporation of Bristol* (London, 1700), 6.

66. Ibid., 13.

67. Ibid.

68. Ibid.

69. Ibid.

70. Matthew Marryott, *An Account of Several Work-Houses for Employing and Maintaining the Poor* [. . .] (London, 1725), 34.

71. Ibid., 35, 100.

72. See the *OED* definition for "overseer" (*OED* online).

73. Linebaugh, *The London Hanged*, 68.

74. George Rudé, *Hanoverian London, 1714–1808* (Berkeley: University of California Press, 1971), 134.

75. By contrast, Molly's experience working exclusively for Mrs. Barlow creates a situation with "much less oppression than servants ever feel in this colony" (64).

76. Mary Collier, *The Woman's Labour: An Epistle to Mr. Stephen Duck; in Answer to His Late Poem, called The Thresher's Labour* (London, 1739).

77. As Peter Earle details, "the legal system was weighted on the side of the creditor" (115) and "the full rigor of the laws" worked against debtors. *The Making of the English Middle Class: Business, Society, and Family Life in London, 1660–1730* (Berkeley: University of California Press, 1989), 124. Consequently "there were normally several hundred London debtors languishing in prison at any one time" (124).

78. For details on how their narrative aligns with what Kimber saw in the Georgia colonies, see Eve Tavor Bannet, *Transatlantic Stories and the History of Reading, 1720–1810: Migrant Readings* (Cambridge: Cambridge University Press, 2011), 115–25.

79. The choice of Horace as the Roman author Tom takes with him is resonant. Horace's father too was once a slave who, when freed, ensured his son had an exemplary education in Rome.

80. This savage beating prompts Mr. Gordon, "who was independent of Mr. Barlow," to encourage Mrs. Barlow to "publish" the account of Williamson's original theft and sale of Tommy (78). Gordon also hopes to use the system of human commodification to try to liberate Tom, and plans to try "to purchase him of his master for the same sum he had given for him," betting that Barlow's "avaricious temper" will prompt him to unload a servant who may have limited physical skills (78).

81. Kimber, *Itinerant Observations*, 49.

82. Adam R. Beach, "Aubin's *The Noble Slaves*, Montagu's *Spanish Lady*, and English Feminist Writing about Sexual Slavery in the Ottoman World," *Eighteenth-Century Fiction* 29, no. 4 (2017): 601.

83. Simon Gikandi, *Slavery and the Culture of Taste* (Princeton, N.J.: Princeton University Press, 2011), 100.

84. The only access to Squanto's voice is through Fanny's narrative and his language is rendered in a racist dialect. He has nothing but words of praise for Tom and Fanny, to whom he proclaims "You lovee poor negroe, no beatee them—no whippee!" (161).

85. Fanny and Squanto are also accompanied by Fanny's maid Martha, another indentured servant who meets a similarly grim end: Barlow "us'd her with great severity, had then sold her to another planter, who having behav'd inhumanly to her, she fell ill and dy'd the 2d day of her illness" (177).

86. Certainly the text contains other embedded narratives of individuals Tom meets on his travels with Matthewson but Fanny is the primary character—and the only female—to speak in the first person.

87. Repeating the novel's pattern of human commodification, Barlow sells Tom to Matthewson, "an Indian trader" (88). Tom's relationship with Matthewson, although founded in an economic transaction, quickly becomes one of affection and mutual admiration. Matthewson adopts Tom and upon his death the renamed "Thomas Matthewson" inherits an estate totaling more than £10,000.

AFTERWORD

1. Jane Austen, *Pride and Prejudice*, ed. Pat Rogers (Cambridge: Cambridge University Press, 2006), 67.

2. Tim Fulford, "Sighing for a Soldier: Jane Austen and the Military *Pride and Prejudice*," *Nineteenth-Century Literature* 57, no. 2 (2002): 165.

3. Austen famously described herself as "much in love" with abolitionist writer Thomas Clarkson in her letter of Sunday, January 24, 1813. Devoney Looser points to the complex relationship with slavery of Austen specifically and the Austen family generally, pointing to the misinterpretations that have shaped both peer-reviewed scholarship and popular perceptions. See Devoney Looser, "Breaking the Silences: Exploring the Austen Family's Complex Entanglements with Slavery," *Times Literary Supplement*, May 21, 2021.

4. *Letters on Slavery, by William Dickson, Formerly Private Secretary to the Late Hon. Edward Hay, Governor of Barbadoes. To Which Are Added, Addresses to the Whites, and to the Free Negroes of Barbadoes; and Accounts of Some Negroes Eminent for Their Virtues and Abilities* (London, 1789), 14, 15. Dickson notes that in St. Kitt's, "they punish with a *cart-whip*." Both a cart-whip and a cowskin are substantially heavier and thicker than the cat-o-nine-tails, which generally weighted less than a pound.

5. I have briefly discussed this episode in "'A Private Had Been Flogged': Adaptation and the 'Invisible World' of Jane Austen," in *Adapting the Eighteenth Century: A Handbook of Pedagogies and Practices*, ed. Sharon Harrow and Kirsten Saxton (Rochester, N.Y.: University of Rochester Press, 2020), 141–57. Jo Baker also fictively expands upon this event in her novel *Longbourn* (New York: Random House, 2013), which presents the world of *Pride and Prejudice* from the perspective of the domestic servants.

6. Tandon suggests that that Austen's novels function "as a finely tuned seismograph, registering, however faintly, the echoes and rumbles coming

from the invisible world offstage." While Tandon does not extend his discussion to enslavement directly, the concept clearly applies. He also reminds us Austen "relied on the fact that once something's been mentioned, it can't be unmentioned," a particularly evocative conception in connection with the reference to flogging so early in the novel. Bharat Tandon, "'Labours Not Her Own': *Emma* and the Invisible World," *Persuasions* 38 (2016): 116–30.

7. Relevant information can be found in Sheila Johnson Kindred, *Jane Austen's Transatlantic Sister: The Life and Letters of Fanny Palmer Austen* (Montreal and Kingston: McGill-Queen's University Press, 2017).

· BIBLIOGRAPHY ·

PRIMARY SOURCES

Manuscripts

Bodleian Library, Oxford

Correspondence between Judith Cowper Madan and Martin Madan, 1723–50, MSS Eng. lett. c. 284–5.

Copies by Maria Cowper of letters and papers of Judith Madan, MS Eng. Misc. d. 637.

Other papers of the Madan family: MSS Eng. Misc. d. 286–9; Misc. c. 502, d. 636–8, 679–81, e. 588, 642–7; Eng. poet c. 62, d. 196.

British Library, London

Ashley Cowper's commonplace book, Add. MS 28101.

National Archives, Kew

Public Records Office (PRO).

Newspapers Consulted

British Journal

Daily Courant

Daily Journal

Daily Post

Daily Post Boy

Evening Post

The Gentleman's Journal, and Tradesman's Companion

London Gazette

London Journal

London News

The Post-Boy

The Post-Man and the Historical Account

St. James's Evening Post
Weekly Journal
Whitehall Journal

Books

Includes both eighteenth-century imprints and modern editions. Names of eighteenth-century publishers are omitted.

Acts of Assembly, Passed in the Island of Barbadoes from 1648 to 1718. London, 1721.

Adis, Henry. *A Letter Sent from Syrranam, to His Excellency, the Lord Willoughby of Parham General of the Western Islands, and of the Continent of Guianah, &c. Then Residing in Barbados* [. . .]. London, 1664.

Allestree, Richard. *The Ladies Calling.* Oxford, 1720.

Ashbridge, Elizabeth. *Some Account of the Early Part of the Life of Elizabeth Ashbridge.* Philadelphia, 1773.

The Assiento; or, Contract for Allowing to the Subjects of Great Britain the Liberty of Importing Negroes into Spanish America. London, 1712.

Astell, Mary. *Astell: Political Writings.* Edited by Patricia Springborg. Cambridge: Cambridge University Press, 1996.

——. *Reflections on Marriage.* 3rd ed. London, 1706.

Aubin, Penelope. *A Collection of Entertaining Histories and Novels.* 3 vols. London, 1739.

——. *The Life and Adventures of the Lady Lucy* [. . .]. London, 1726.

——. *The Life and Amorous Adventures of Lucinda, an English Lady.* London, 1722.

——. *The Life of Charlotta Du Pont, An English Lady; Taken from Her Own Memoirs.* London, 1723.

——. *The Noble Slaves.* London, 1722.

——. *The Strange Adventures of the Count de Vinevil and His Family* [. . .]. London, 1721.

——. *The Stuarts: A Pindarique Ode.* London, 1707.

Barber, Mary. *Poems on Several Occasions.* London, 1734.

——. "Verses said to be written by Mrs. Mary Barber. To a Friend desiring an Account of her Health in Verse." *Gentleman's Magazine* 7 (March 1737): 179.

Behn, Aphra. *The Cambridge Edition of the Works of Aphra Behn.* Vol. 4, *Plays 1685–1696.* General editors Claire Bowditch, Mel Evans, Elaine Hobby, and Gillian Wright. Cambridge: Cambridge University Press, 2021.

——. *To the Most Illustrious Prince Christopher, Duke of Albemarle, on His Voyage to His Government of Jamaica. A Pindarick.* London, 1687.

——. *The Works of Aphra Behn.* Edited by Janet Todd. 7 vols. Columbus: Ohio State University Press, 1992–96.

Berriman, William. *The Great Blessing of Redemption from Captivity. A Sermon Preached at the Cathedral Church of St. Paul, December 4, 1721. Before the Captives Redeem'd by the Late Treaty with the Emperor of Morocco* [. . .]. London, 1722.

Blackstone, William. *Commentaries on the Laws of England.* 4 vols. Oxford, 1765–69.

Bosman, Willem. *A New and Accurate Description of the Coast of Guinea, Divided into the Gold, the Slave, and the Ivory Coasts.* London, 1705.

Boyd, Elizabeth. *Altamira's Ghost; or, Justice Triumphant. A New Ballad. Occasion'd by a Certain Nobleman's Cruel Usage of His Nephew. Done Extempore.* London, 1744.

Britannia; or, A Chorographical Description of Great Britain and Ireland, Together with the Adjacent Islands. Written in Latin by William Camden. The Second Edition. Revised, Digested, and Published, with Large Additions, by Edmund Gibson, D.D., Rector of Lambeth; and Now Bishop of Lincoln, and Dean of His Majesty's Chapel-Royal. 2 vols. London, 1722.

Bullock, William. *Virginia Impartially Examined, and Left to Publick View, to Be Considered by All Iudicious and Honest Men.* London, 1649.

Byam, William. *The Most Execrable Attempts of John Allin, Committed on the Person of His Excellency Francis Lord Willoughby.* London, 1665.

Cary, John. *An Account of the Proceedings of the Corporation of Bristol.* London, 1700.

Certain Considerations Relating to the Royal African Company of England. In Which, the Original, Growth, and National Advantages of the Guiney Trade, Are Demonstrated: as Also That the Same Trade Cannot be Carried On, but by a Company and Joint-Stock. London, 1680.

The Character of a Town Miss. London, 1675.

Child, Josiah. *A New Discourse of Trade Wherein Is Recommended Several Weighty Points Relating to Companies of Merchants* [. . .] *Are Humbly Offered.* London, 1693.

A Christmas Box for a Certain Old Fox; or, A Sequel to the Children in the Wood. Dublin, 1744.

Chudleigh, Mary. *Poems on Several Occasions. Together with the Song of the Three Children Paraphras'd.* London, 1703.

Clarkson, Thomas. *Essay on the Impolicy of the African Slave Trade.* London, 1788.

Collier, Mary. *Poems on Several Occasions.* London, 1762.

———. *The Woman's Labour: An Epistle to Mr. Stephen Duck; in Answer to His Late Poem, Called The Thresher's Labour.* London, 1739.

The Cruel UNCLE; or, The Wronged NEPHEW: Being an Account of the Hardships, and 13 Year Slavery at Virginia, of That Unfortunate Young Nobleman James Annsly [sic] *Who Was Sent Abroad by His Uncle. In Five Parts.* Dublin, 1744.

Defoe, Daniel. *A General History of Discoveries and Improvements in the Useful Arts* [. . .]. London, 1725.

———. *Moll Flanders.* Edited by G. A. Starr. Oxford: Oxford University Press, 2011.

———. *Robinson Crusoe*. London, 1719.

de Frene, Marchioness. *The Unfortunate Marriage*. London, 1722.

Dibdin, Charles. *The Complete History of the English Stage*. 5 vols. London, 1800.

Dickson, William. *Letters on Slavery, by William Dickson, Formerly Private Secretary to the Late Hon. Edward Hay, Governor of Barbadoes. To Which Are Added, Addresses to the Whites, and to the Free Negroes of Barbadoes; and Accounts of Some Negroes Eminent for Their Virtues and Abilities*. London, 1789.

Drake, Judith. *An Essay in Defence of the Female Sex*. London, 1721.

Duck, Stephen. *Poems on Several Subjects: Written by Stephen Duck, Lately a Poor Thresher . . . Which Were Publickly Read by . . . the Earl of Macclesfield, . . . on Friday the 11th of September, 1730, to Her Majesty. Who Was Thereupon . . . Pleased to Take the Author into Her Royal Protection*. London, 1730.

Eyston, Charles. *The History and Antiquities of Glastonbury, To Which Are Added, (i.) The Endowment and Orders of Sherington's Chantry*. Oxford, 1722.

Great Newes from the Barbadoes; or, A True and Faithful Account of the Grand Conspiracy of the Negroes against the English. London, 1676.

Hale, Matthew. *A Discourse Touching on Provisions for the Poor*. London, 1683.

———. *The History of the Pleas of the Crown*. 2 vols. London, 1736.

Haywood, Eliza. *The Distressed Orphan; or, Love in a Madhouse*. London, 1726.

———. *Fantomina and Other Works*. Edited by Alexander Pettit, Margaret Case Croskery, and Anna C. Patchias. Peterborough, Canada: Broadview Press, 2004.

———. *The History of Miss Betsy Thoughtless*. Edited by Christine Blouch. Peterborough, Canada: Broadview Press, 1998.

———. *Memoirs of an Unfortunate Young Nobleman, Return'd from a Thirteen Years Slavery in America, Where He Had Been Sent by the Wicked Contrivances of His Cruel Uncle. A Story Founded on Truth, and Address'd Equally to the Head and Heart*. London, 1743.

———. *Mercenary Lover; or, The Unfortunate Heiresses*. London, 1726.

———. *The Selected Works of Eliza Haywood: Part II*. Vol. 2, *Epistles for the Ladies*, edited by Alexander Pettit and Kathryn R. King. London: Pickering & Chatto, 2001.

Jordon. Thomas. *London Triumphant*. London, 1672.

———. *The Triumphs of London*. London, 1675.

———. *The Triumphs of London*. London, 1678.

Kimber, Edward. "Itinerant Observations in America." *London Magazine*, July 1746, 326–27.

———. *Itinerant Observations in America*. Edited by Kevin J. Hayes. Newark: University of Delaware Press, 1998.

———. *The Life and Adventures of Mr. Anderson*. Edited by Matthew Mason and Nicholas Mason. Peterborough, Canada: Broadview Press, 2009.

La Motte, Philémon de. *Several Voyages to the Barbary. Containing an Historical and Geographical Account of the Country.* London, 1736.

A Letter to a Nobleman in the Country, on the Affair of Mr. Annesley, Containing a Full and Distinct Account of That Extraordinary Transaction and All Its Circumstances. Together with Some Particulars Not Hitherto Mentioned. London, 1744.

Ligon, Richard. *A True and Exact History of the Island of Barbados.* Edited by Karen Ordahl Kupperman. Indianapolis: Hackett Publishing, 2000.

A Manual of Prayers and Other Christian Devotion. London, 1720.

Marana, Giovanni Paolo. *Letters Writ by a Turkish Spy, Who Lived Five and Forty Years, Undiscover'd, at Paris.* London, 1687.

Marryott, Matthew. *An Account of Several Work-Houses for Employing and Maintaining the Poor [. . .].* London, 1725.

Moll, Herman. *A View of the Coasts, Countries and Islands within the Limits of the South-Sea Company.* London, 1711.

Moraley, William. *The Infortunate: The Voyage and Adventures of William Moraley, an Indentured Servant.* Edited by Susan E. Klepp and Bill G. Smith. University Park: Pennsylvania State University Press, 2005.

Pattison, William. *The Poetical Works of Mr. William Pattison.* London, 1728.

Pilkington, Laetitia. *Memoirs.* 3 vols. London, 1748–54.

Pinder, Richard. *The Captive (That Hath Long Been in Captivity) Visited with the Day-Spring from on High.* London, 1660.

Reasons Humbly Offer'd, Why a Duty Should Not Be Laid on Sugars. London, 1698.

The Richardiad. A Satire. Translated from a Greek Fragment of Petronius Arbiter, by Theodorus Gratian. With Notes Variorum. London, 1744.

Rogers, Woodes. *A Cruising Voyage round the World.* London, 1718.

Sanford, Robert. *Surinam Justice in the Case of Several Persons Proscribed by Certain Usurpers of Power in That Colony: Being a Publication of That Perfect Relation of the Beginning, Continuance, and End of the Late Disturbances in the Colony of Surinam [. . .].* London, 1662.

Saville, George. *The Lady's New-Year's Gift; or, Advice to a Daughter.* 7th ed. London, 1701.

The Several Declarations of the Company of Royal Adventurers of England Trading into Africa, Inviting All His Majesties Native Subjects in General to Subscribe, and Become Sharers in Their Joynt-Stock. London, 1667.

Steele, Richard. *An Account of the Fish-Pool: Consisting of a Description of the Vessel So Call'd, Lately Invented and Built for the Importation of Fish Alive, and in Good Health, from Parts However Distant.* London, 1718.

———. *The Correspondence of Richard Steele.* Edited by Rae Blanchard. Oxford: Clarendon Press, 1941.

————. *The Occasional Verse of Richard Steele.* Edited by Rae Blanchard. Oxford: Clarendon Press, 1952.

————. *The Plays of Richard Steele.* Edited by Shirley Strum Kenney. Oxford: Clarendon Press, 1971.

————. *The Spectator.* Edited by Donald Bond. 3 vols. Oxford: Clarendon Press, 1965.

————. *The Theatre.* Edited by John Loftis. Oxford: Oxford University Press, 1962.

Swift, Jonathan. *A Beautiful Young Nymph Going to Bed.* London, 1734.

————. *A Modest Proposal.* Dublin, 1729.

Tickell, Thomas. *Oxford. A Poem. Inscrib'd to the Right Honourable the Lord Lonsdale.* London, 1707.

The Voyage and the Several Declarations of the Company of Royal Adventurers of England Trading into Africa. London, 1667.

Ward, Edward. *A Trip to Jamaica: With a True Character of the People and Island.* London, 1698.

Warren, George. *An Impartial Description of Surinam upon the Continent of Guiana in America with a History of Several Strange Beasts, Birds, Fishes, Serpents, Insects and Customs of That Colony, etc. Worthy the Perusal of All, from Experience of George Warren.* London, 1667.

Wollestonecraft, Mary. *A Vindication of the Rights of Woman.* London, 1792.

SECONDARY SOURCES

Afroz, Sultana. "The Role of Islam in the Abolition of Slavery and in the Development of British Capitalism." *American Journal of Islamic Social Sciences* 29, no. 1 (2012): 1–29.

Airey, Jennifer L. *The Politics of Rape: Sexual Atrocity, Propaganda Wars, and the Restoration Stage.* Newark: University of Delaware Press, 2012.

Aitken, George A. *The Life of Richard Steele.* 2 vols. 1889. Reprint. New York: Greenwood Press, 1968.

Allderidge, Patricia. "Bedlam: Fact or Fantasy?" In *The Anatomy of Madness: Essays in History of Psychiatry.* Vol. 2, *Institutions and Society,* edited by W. F. Bynum, Roy Porter, and Michael Shepherd, 17–33. London: Tavistock Publications, 1985.

Alsop, J. D. "New Light on Richard Steele." *British Library Journal* 25, no. 1 (1999): 23–34.

Alsop, James. "Richard Steele and Barbados: Further Evidence," *Eighteenth-Century Life* 6, no. 1 (1981): 21–28.

Altick, Richard D. *The Shows of London.* Cambridge, Mass.: Belknap Press of Harvard University Press, 1978.

Amussen, Susan Dwyer. *Caribbean Exchanges: Slavery and the Transformation of English Society, 1640–1700.* Chapel Hill: University of North Carolina Press, 2007.

Anderson, Jennifer. "Recent Work in Early American Visual Culture." *Early American Literature* 50, no. 2 (2015): 555–60.

Andrews, Jonathan, Asa Briggs, Roy Porter, Penny Tucker, and Keir Waddington. *The History of Bethlehem.* London: Routledge, 1997.

Aravamudan, Srinivas. "Fiction/Translations/Transnation: The Secret History of the Eighteenth-Century Novel." In *A Companion to the Eighteenth-Century English Novel and Culture,* edited by Paula R. Backscheider and Catherine Ingrassia, 75–96. London: Blackwell, 2005.

Armstrong, Nancy. "Captivity and Cultural Capital in the English Novel." *Novel: A Forum on Fiction* 31, no. 3 (1998): 373–98.

Armstrong, Nancy, and Leonard Tennenhouse. *The Imaginary Puritan: Literature, Intellectual Labor, and the Origins of Personal Life.* Berkeley: University of California Press, 1992.

Averill, James H. "The Death of Stephen Clay and Richard Steele's *Spectators* of August 1711." *Review of English Studies* 28, no. 111 (1977): 305–10.

Backscheider, Paula R. *Daniel Defoe: His Life.* Baltimore: Johns Hopkins University Press, 1989.

———. "From *The Emperor of the Moon* to the Sultan's Prison." *Studies in Eighteenth-Century Culture* 43 (2014): 1–26.

———. *Spectacular Politics: Theatrical Power and Mass Culture in Early Modern England.* Baltimore: Johns Hopkins University Press, 1993.

———, ed. *Revising Women: Eighteenth-Century Women's Fiction and Social Engagement.* Baltimore: Johns Hopkins University Press, 2000.

Backscheider, Paula R., and Catherine E. Ingrassia, eds. *British Women Poets of the Long Eighteenth Century: An Anthology.* Baltimore: Johns Hopkins University Press, 2009.

Baer, Joel. "Penelope Aubin and the Pirates of Madagascar: Biographical Notes and Documents." In *Eighteenth-Century Women: Studies in Their Lives, Work, and Culture.* Vol. 1, edited by Linda V. Troost, 49–62. New York: AMS Press, 2001.

Bailyn, Bernard, and Philip D. Morgan. *Strangers within the Realm: Cultural Margins of the First British Empire.* Chapel Hill: University of North Carolina Press for the Omohundro Institute of Early American History and Culture, 1991.

Bannet, Eve Tavor. *Transatlantic Stories and the History of Reading, 1720–1810: Migrant Fictions.* Cambridge: Cambridge University Press, 2011.

Barber, Sarah. "Power in the English Caribbean: The Proprietorship of Lord Willoughby of Parham." In *Constructing Early Modern Empires: Proprietary Adventures in the Atlantic World, 1500–1700,* edited by L. H. Roper and B. Van Ruymbeke, 163–89. Boston: Brill, 2007.

———. *A Revolutionary Rogue: Henry Marten and the English Republic.* Stroud, UK: Sutton, 2000.

Barthelemy, Anthony Gerard. *Black Face, Maligned Race: The Representation of Blacks in English Drama, from Shakespeare to Southerne.* Baton Rouge: Louisiana State University Press, 1987.

Bartlett, Anne Clark. *Male Authors, Female Readers: Representation and Subjectivity in Middle English Devotional Literature.* Ithaca, N.Y.: Cornell University Press, 1995.

Beach, Adam R. "Aubin's *The Noble Slaves,* Montagu's *Spanish Lady,* and English Feminist Writing about Sexual Slavery in the Ottoman World." *Eighteenth-Century Fiction* 29, no. 4 (2017): 583–606.

——. "Global Slavery, Old World Bondage, and Aphra Behn's *Abdelazer.*" *Eighteenth Century: Theory and Interpretation* 53, no. 4 (2012): 413–43.

Beasley, Jerry. "Politics and Moral Idealism." In *Fetter'd or Free?: British Women Novelists, 1670–1851,* edited by Mary Anne Schofield and Cecilia Machesky, 216–37. Athens: Ohio University Press, 1986.

Beattie, John. *Crime and the Courts in England, 1660–1800.* Princeton, N.J.: Princeton University Press, 1986.

Beckles, Hilary. "Historicizing Slavery in West Indian Feminisms." *Feminist Review* 59 (1998): 34–56.

——. *White Servitude and Black Slavery in Barbados, 1627–1715.* Knoxville: University of Tennessee Press, 1989.

Bekkaoui, Khalid. "White Women and Moorish Fancy in Eighteenth-Century Literature." In *The Arabian Nights in Historical Context: Between East and West,* edited by Saree Makdisi and Felicity Nussbaum, 153–67. Oxford: Oxford University Press, 2008.

——. *White Women Captives in North Africa: Narratives of Enslavement, 1735–1830.* New York: Palgrave Macmillan, 2011.

Bennet, Herman Lee. *Africans in Colonial Mexico: Absolutism, Christianity, and Afro-Creole Consciousness, 1570–1640.* Bloomington: Indiana University Press, 2005.

Birnbaum, G. "Servants in England and America in the Eighteenth Century: The Beginning of Slavery." *Revue de la Société d'études anglo-américaines des XVIIe et XVIIIe siècles* (1985): 45–64.

Black, Jeremy. *British Foreign Policy in the Age of Walpole.* Edinburgh: John Donald Publishers, 1985.

Blanchard, Rae. "Richard Steele's Maryland Story." *American Quarterly* 10, no. 1 (1958): 78–82.

——. "Richard Steele's West Indian Plantation." *Modern Philology* 39, no. 3 (1942): 281–85.

Boggs, Colleen Glenny. "Transatlantic Romanticisms." In *Transatlantic Literary Studies, 1660–1830,* edited by Eve Tavor Bannet and Susan Manning, 219–38. Cambridge: Cambridge University Press, 2012.

Bohls, Elizabeth A. *Slavery and the Politics of Place: Representing the Colonial Caribbean, 1770–1833.* Cambridge: Cambridge University Press, 2014.

Boulton, Jeremy. "'It Is Extreme Necessity That Makes Me Do This': Some 'Surveillance Households' in London's West End during the Early Eighteenth Century." *International Review of Social History* 45, suppl. 8 (2000): 47–69.

———. "The Painter's Daughter and the Poor Law: Elizabeth Laroon (b. 1689–fl. 1736)." *London Journal* 42, no. 1 (2017): 13–33.

Boulukos, George E. "Daniel Defoe's 'Colonel Jack,' Grateful Slaves, and Racial Difference." *ELH* 68, no. 3 (2001): 615–31.

———. *The Grateful Slave: The Emergence of Race in Eighteenth-Century British and American Culture.* Cambridge: Cambridge University Press, 2008.

Brewer, Holly. "Slavery, Sovereignty, and 'Inheritable Blood': Reconsidering John Locke and the Origins of American Slavery." *American Historical Review* 122, no. 4 (2017): 1038–78.

Brown, Laura. *Ends of Empire: Women and Ideology in Early Eighteenth-Century English Literature.* Ithaca, N.Y.: Cornell University Press, 1993.

Brummett, Palmira Johnson. *Ottoman Seapower and Levantine Diplomacy in the Age of Discovery.* Albany: State University of New York Press, 1994.

Brundage, Anthony. *The English Poor Laws, 1700–1930.* Basingstoke, UK: Palgrave Macmillan, 2001.

Brunsman, Denver. *The Evil Necessity: British Naval Impressment in the Eighteenth-Century Atlantic World.* Charlottesville: University of Virginia Press, 2013.

Budd, Adam. "'Merit in Distress': The Troubled Success of Mary Barber." *Review of English Studies* 53, no. 210 (2002): 204–27.

Burham, Michelle. *Captivity and Sentiment: Cultural Exchange in American Literature.* Hanover, N.H.: University Press of New England, 1997.

Burnard, Trevor, and John Garrigus. *The Plantation Machine: Atlantic Capitalism in French Saint-Dominique and British Jamaica.* Philadelphia: University of Pennsylvania Press, 2016.

Burnard, Trevor, and Kenneth Morgan. "The Dynamics of the Slave Market and Slave Purchasing Patterns in Jamaica, 1655–1788." *William and Mary Quarterly* 58, no. 1 (2001): 205–28.

Burwick, Frederick, and Manushag N. Powell. *British Pirates in Print and Performance.* New York: Palgrave, 2015.

Cameron, William James. *New Light on Aphra Behn: An Investigation into the Facts and Fictions Surrounding Her Journey to Suriname in 1663, and Her Activities as a Spy in Flanders in 1666.* Auckland, New Zealand: University of Auckland, 1961.

Canny, Nicholas, ed. *The Oxford History of the British Empire.* Vol. 1, *The Origins of Empire: The British Overseas Enterprise to the Close of the Seventeenth Century.* New York: Oxford University Press, 1998.

Carey, Daniel. "Reading Contrapuntally: *Robinson Crusoe*, Slavery, and Postcolonial Theory." In *The Postcolonial Enlightenment: Eighteenth-Century Colonialism and Postcolonial Theory*, edited by Daniel Carey and Lynn Festa, 105–36. Oxford: Oxford University Press, 2009.

Chater, Kathleen. *Untold Histories: Black People in England and Wales during the Period of the British Slave Trade, c. 1660–1807*. Manchester: Manchester University Press, 2009.

Christian, Rachel. "Empire of Outcasts." *History Today* (September 2015): 41–48.

Christmas, William, ed. *Eighteenth-Century English Labouring-Class Poets*. Vol. 1, *1700–1740*. London: Pickering and Chatto, 2003.

Clark, J.C.D. *English Society, 1660–1832: Religion, Ideology, and Politics during the Ancien Régime*. Cambridge: Cambridge University Press, 2000.

Cockburn, J. S. "Punishment and Brutalization in the English Enlightenment." *Law and History Review* 12, no. 1 (1994): 155–79.

Coldham, Peter Wilson. *Emigrants in Chains: A Social History of Forced Emigration to the Americas of Felons, Destitute Children, Political and Religious Non-Conformists, Vagabonds, Beggars, and Other Undesirables, 1607–1776*. Baltimore: Genealogical Publishing Co., 1994.

Colley, Linda. *Britons: Forging the Nation, 1707–1837*. New Haven: Yale University Press, 2005.

———. *Captives: Britain, Empire, and the World, 1600–1850*. New York: Anchor Books, 2002.

Connely, Willard. *Sir Richard Steele*. Port Washington, N.Y.: Kennikat Press, 1967.

Connolly, Brian, and Marisa Fuentes. "From Archives of Slavery to Liberated Future?" *History of the Present* 6, no. 2 (2016): 105–16.

Conway, Stephen. "From Fellow-Nationals to Foreigners: British Perceptions of the Americans, circa 1739–1783." *William and Mary Quarterly* 59, no. 1 (2002): 65–100.

Coppola, Al. "Retraining the Virtuoso's Gaze: Behn's *Emperor of the Moon*, the Royal Society, and the Spectacles of Science and Politics." *Eighteenth-Century Studies* 41, no. 4 (2008): 481–506.

Cousins, Mel. "The Irish Parliament and Relief of the Poor: The 1772 Legislation Establishing Houses of Industry." *Eighteenth-Century Ireland* 28 (2013): 95–115.

Cowan, Brian. "Mr. Spectator and the Coffeehouse Public Sphere." *Eighteenth-Century Studies* 37, no. 3 (2004): 345–66.

Craft, Peter. "'The Doves Are Censured While the Crows Are Spared': Steele's 1711 Inkle and Yarico Adaptation." *Journal of Commonwealth and Postcolonial Studies* 1, no. 2 (2013): 3–16.

Craton, Michael. *Empire, Enslavement, and Freedom in the Caribbean*. Oxford: James Currey Publishers, 1997.

——. "Reluctant Creole: The Planter's World in the British West Indies." In *Strangers within the Realm: Cultural Margins of the First British Empire*, edited by Bernard Bailyn and Philip D. Morgan, 314–62. Chapel Hill: University of North Carolina Press, 2012.

Dailey, Anne. "To Have and to Hold: The Marital Rape Exemption and the Fourteenth Amendment." *Harvard Law Review* 99, no. 6 (1986): 1255–73.

Darby, Robert. "Captivity and Captivation: Gulliver in Brobdingnag." *Eighteenth-Century Life* 27, no. 3 (2003): 124–39.

Daunton, M. J. *Progress and Poverty: An Economic and Social History of Britain 1700–1850*. Oxford: Oxford University Press, 1995.

Davies, K. G. *The Royal African Company*. 1957. Reprint. New York: Octagon Books, 1975.

Davis, Robert C. *Christian Slaves, Muslim Masters: White Slavery in the Mediterranean, the Barbary Coast, and Italy, 1500–1800*. Houndmills, UK: Palgrave Macmillan, 2003.

——. "Counting European Slaves on the Barbary Coast." *Past & Present* 172 (2001): 87–124.

Dawson, Warren R. "The London Coffee Houses and the Beginnings of Lloyds." *Journal of the British Archaeological Association* 40 (1935): 104–34.

de la Torre, Lillian. "New Light on Smollett and the Annesley Case." *Review of English Studies* 22, no. 87 (1971): 274–81.

Dillon, Elizabeth Maddock. "By Design: Remapping the Colonial Archive." *Social Text* 125 (2015): 142–47.

——. *New World Drama: The Performative Commons in the Atlantic World, 1649–1849*. Durham, N.C.: Duke University Press, 2014.

Dillon, Patrick. *The Last Revolution: 1688 and the Creation of the Modern World*. London: Thistle Publishing, 2006.

Ditz, Toby L. "Shipwrecked; or, Masculinity Imperiled: Mercantile Representations of Failure and the Gendered Self in Eighteenth-Century Philadelphia." *Journal of American History* 81, no. 1 (1994): 51–80.

Donahue, Jennifer. "Bringing the Other into View: Confronting the West Indian Creole in *The Conscious Lovers* and *The West Indian*." *Restoration and Eighteenth-Century Theatre Research* 26, no. 1/2 (2011): 41–56.

Donoghue, John. "Indentured Servitude in the Seventeenth-Century English Atlantic: A Brief Survey of the Literature." *History Compass* 11, no. 10 (2013): 893–902.

——. "'Out of the Land of Bondage': The English Revolution and the Atlantic Origins of Abolition." *American Historical Review* 115, no. 4 (2019): 943–74.

Dresser, Madge. *Slavery Obscured: The Social History of the Slave Trade in an English Provincial Port*. 2001. Reprint, Bristol: Redcliffe Press, 2007.

Dresser, Madge, and Andrew Hann, eds. *Slavery and the British Country House*. Swindon, UK: English Heritage, 2013.

Dunn, Richard S. *Sugar and Slaves: The Rise of the Planter Class in the English West Indies, 1624–1713*. Chapel Hill: University of North Carolina Press, 1972.

Earle, Peter. *The Making of the English Middle Class: Business, Society, and Family Life in London 1660–1730*. Berkeley: University of California Press, 1989.

Ekirch, A. Roger. "Bound for America: A Profile of British Convicts Transported to the Colonies, 1718–1775." *William and Mary Quarterly* 42, no. 2 (1985): 184–200.

Ennis, Daniel James. *Enter the Press-Gang: Naval Impressment in Eighteenth-Century British Literature*. Newark: University of Delaware Press, 2002.

Eltis, David. "Labour and Coercion in the English Atlantic World from the Seventeenth Century to the Early Twentieth Century." In *The Wages of Slavery: From Chattel Slavery to Wage Labour in Africa, the Caribbean, and England*, edited by Michael Twaddle, 207–226. London: Frank Cass, 1993.

———. "Slavery and Freedom in the Early Modern World." In *Terms of Labor: Slavery, Serfdom, and Free Labor*, edited by. Stanley L. Engerman, 25–49. Stanford, Calif.: Stanford University Press, 1999.

Evans, Mel. "Style and Chronology: A Stylometric Investigation of Aphra Behn's Dramatic Style and the Dating of *The Young King*." *Language and Literature* 27, no. 2 (2018): 103–32.

Felsenstein, Frank. *English Trader, Indian Maid: Representing Gender, Race, and Slavery in the New World: An Inkle and Yarico Reader*. Baltimore: Johns Hopkins University Press, 1999.

Ferguson, Margaret. "The Authorial Ciphers of Aphra Behn." In *Cambridge Companion to English Literature 1650–1740*, edited by S. Zwicker, 227–49. Cambridge: Cambridge University Press, 2001.

Ferguson, Moira. "Seventeenth-Century Women." In *Culture and Society in the Stuart Restoration: Literature, Drama, History*, edited by Gerald Maclean, 221–40. Cambridge: Cambridge University Press, 1995.

———. *Subject to Others: British Women Writers and Colonial Slavery, 1670–1834*. New York: Routledge, 1992.

Festa, Lynn. *Fiction without Humanity: Person, Animal, Thing in Early Enlightenment Literature and Culture*. Philadelphia: University of Pennsylvania Press, 2019.

Figlerowicz, Marta. "'Frightful Spectacles of a Mangled King': Aphra Behn's 'Oroonoko' and Narration through Theater." *New Literary History* 38, no. 2 (2008): 321–34.

Finucane, Adrian. *The Temptations of Trade: Britain, Spain, and the Struggles for Empire*. Philadelphia: University of Pennsylvania Press, 2016.

Floud, Roderick, and Paul Johnson. *The Cambridge Economic History of Modern Britain*. Vol. 1, *Industrialization, 1700–1860*. Cambridge: Cambridge University Press, 2004.

Foyster, Elizabeth. *Marital Violence: An English Family History, 1660–1857*. Cambridge: Cambridge University Press, 2005.

———. "The 'New World of Children' Reconsidered: Child Abduction in Late Eighteenth- and Early Nineteenth-Century England." *Journal of British Studies* 52, no. 3 (2013): 669–92.

Freeman, Lisa A. *Character's Theatre: Genre and Identity on the Eighteenth-Century English Stage.* Philadelphia: University of Pennsylvania Press, 2002.

Friedman, Ellen G. *Spanish Captives in North Africa in the Early Modern Age.* Madison: University of Wisconsin Press, 1983.

Frohock, Richard. *Heroes of Empires: The British Imperial Protagonist in America, 1596–1764.* Newark: University of Delaware Press, 2004.

———. "John Gay's *Polly* (1729), Bernard Mandeville, and the Critique of Empire." *Studies in Eighteenth-Century Culture* 46 (2017): 147–62.

Fryer, Peter. *Staying Power: The History of Black People in Britain.* London: Pluto Press, 1984.

Fuentes, Marisa J. *Dispossessed Lives: Enslaved Women, Violence, and the Archive.* Philadelphia: University of Pennsylvania Press, 2016.

Galenson, David W. "Demographic Aspects of White Servitude in Colonial British America." *Annales de demographie historique* (1980): 239–52.

———. "Literacy and Age in Preindustrial England: Quantitative Evidence and Implications." *Economic Development and Cultural Change* 29, no. 4 (1981): 813–29.

———. "The Market Evaluation of Human Capital: The Case of Indentured Servitude." *Journal of Public Economy* 89, no. 3 (1981): 446–67.

———. *Traders, Planters, and Slaves: Market Behavior in Early English America.* Cambridge: Cambridge University Press, 1986.

Garcia, Humberto. *Islam and the English Enlightenment, 1670–1840.* Baltimore: Johns Hopkins University Press, 2011.

Gerrard, Christine. *The Patriot Opposition to Walpole: Politics, Poetry, and National Myth, 1725–1742.* Oxford: Clarendon Press, 1995.

Gerzina, Gretchen. *Black London: Life before Emancipation.* New Brunswick, N.J.: Rutgers University Press, 1995.

Gikandi, Simon. *Slavery and the Culture of Taste.* Princeton, N.J.: Princeton University Press, 2011.

Gollapudi, Aparna. "Virtuous Voyages in Penelope Aubin's Fiction." *SEL: Studies in English Literature 1500–1900* 45, no. 3 (2005): 669–90.

Greene, Jack P. *Evaluating Empire and Confronting Colonialism in Eighteenth-Century Britain.* Cambridge: Cambridge University Press, 2013.

Guasco, Michael. *Slaves and Englishmen: Human Bondage in the Early Modern Atlantic World.* Philadelphia: University of Pennsylvania Press, 2014.

Haagen, Paul. "Imprisonment for Debt in England and Wales." PhD diss., Princeton University, 1986.

Hall, Catherine. "Gendering Property, Racing Capital." *History Workshop Journal* 78 (2014): 22–38.

Hall, Catherine, Nicholas Draper, Keith McClelland, Katie Donington, and Rachel Lang. *Legacies of British Slave-ownership: Colonial Slavery and the Formation of Victorian Britain.* Cambridge: Cambridge University Press, 2014.

Hall, Kim F. *Things of Darkness: Economies of Race and Gender in Early Modern England.* Ithaca, N.Y.: Cornell University Press, 1995.

Harol, Corrinne. "The Passion of Oroonoko: Passive Obedience, the Royal Slave, and Aphra Behn's Baroque Realism." *ELH* 79, no. 2 (2012): 447–75.

Harper, Graeme, ed. *Colonial and Postcolonial Incarceration.* London: Continuum, 2001.

Harris, Tim, and Stephen Taylor, eds. *The Final Crisis of the Stuart Monarchy: The Revolutions of 1688–91 in Their British, Atlantic, and European Contexts.* Woodbridge, UK: Boydell Press, 2013.

Harris, Robert. *A Patriot Press: National Politics and the London Press in the 1740s.* Oxford: Clarendon Press, 1993.

Harvard Law Review Association. "To Have and to Hold: The Marital Rape Exemption and the Fourteenth Amendment." *Harvard Law Review* 99, no. 6 (1986): 1255–73.

Hay, Douglas, Peter Linebaugh, John Rule, E. P. Thompson, and Cal Winslow. *Albion's Fatal Tree: Crime and Society in Eighteenth-Century England.* New York: Pantheon, 1976.

Hayden, Judy A. "Harlequin Science: Aphra Behn's *Emperor of the Moon* and the Plurality of Worlds." *English: The Journal of the English Association* 64, no. 246 (2015): 167–82.

———. *Of Love and War: The Political Choice in the Early Plays of Aphra Behn.* Amsterdam: Rodopi, 2010.

———. "Representations of 'Times of Trouble': Aphra Behn's *The Young King; or, The Mistake* and Calderon's *Life Is a Dream.*" In *Aphra Behn: Identity, Alterity, Ambiguity,* edited by Guyonne Leduc, Bernard Dhuicq, and Mary Ann O'Donnell, 49–58. Paris: Harmattan, 2000.

Henderson, Diana. "Theatre and Controversy, 1572–1603." In *The Cambridge History of British Theatre.* Vol. 1, *Origins to 1660,* edited by Jane Milling and Peter Thomson, 242–63. Cambridge: Cambridge University Press, 2004.

Hitchcock, Tim. *Down and Out in Eighteenth-Century London.* London: Boomsbury Publishing, 2004.

———. Rev. "*Vagrancy in Law and Practice under the Old Poor Law,* by Audrey Eccles." *Social History* 38, no. 4 (2013): 518–20.

Hitchcock, Tim, Adam Crymble, and Louise Falcini. "Loose, Idle and Disorderly: Vagrant Removal in Late Eighteenth-Century Middlesex." *Social History* 39, no. 4 (2014): 509–27.

Holroyd, Ryan. "Whatever Happened to Those Villains of the Indian Seas? The Happy Retirement of the Madagascar Pirates, 1698–1721." *International Journal of Maritime History* 29, no. 4 (2017): 752–70.

Horejsi, Nicole. "'A Counterpart to the Ephesian Matron': Steele's 'Inkle and Yarico' and a Feminist Critique of the Classics." *Eighteenth-Century Studies* 39, no. 2 (2006): 201–26.

———. "(Re)Valuing the 'Foreign Trinket': Sentimentalizing the Language of Economics in Steele's *Conscious Lovers*." *Restoration and Eighteenth-Century Theatre Research* 18, no. 2 (2003): 11–36.

Hudson, Nicholas. "Britons Never Will Be Slaves: National Myth, Conservatism, and the Beginnings of British Antislavery." *Eighteenth-Century Studies* 34, no. 4 (2001): 559–76.

Hughes, Derek. "Rape on the Restoration Stage." *The Eighteenth-Century: Theory and Interpretation* 46, no. 3 (2005): 227–32.

———. *The Theater of Aphra Behn.* Cambridge: Cambridge University Press, 1979.

Hughes, Derek, and Janet Todd, eds. *The Cambridge Companion to Aphra Behn.* Cambridge: Cambridge University Press, 2004.

Hulme, Peter. *Colonial Encounters: Europe and the Native Caribbean, 1492–1797.* London: Methuen, 1986.

Hynes, Peter. "Richard Steele and the Genealogy of Sentimental Drama: A Reading of *The Conscious Lovers*." *Papers on Language and Literature* 40, no. 2 (2004): 142–66.

Ingrassia, Catherine. "Contesting 'Home' in Eighteenth-Century Women's Verse." In *Home and Nation in British Literature from the English to the French Revolutions,* edited by A. D. Cousins and Geoffrey Payne, 154–68. Cambridge: Cambridge University Press, 2015.

———. "*Emma,* Slavery, and Cultures of Captivity." *Persuasions* 38 (2017): 95–106.

———. "'A Private Had Been Flogged': Adaptation and the 'Invisible World' of Jane Austen." In *Adapting the Eighteenth Century: A Handbook of Pedagogies and Practices,* edited by Sharon Harrow and Kirsten Saxton, 141–57. Rochester, N.Y.: University of Rochester Press, 2020.

Jamieson, Alan G. *Lords of the Sea: A History of the Barbary Corsairs.* London: Reaktion Books, 2012.

Jarvis, Michael J. *In the Eye of All Trade: Bermuda, Bermudians, and the Maritime Atlantic World, 1680–1783.* Chapel Hill: University of North Carolina Press, 2010.

Jones, Jane. "New Light on the Background and Early Life of Aphra Behn." *Notes & Queries* 37, no. 3 (1990): 288–93.

Kaplan, Cora, and John Oldfield, eds. *Imagining Transatlantic Slavery.* Basingstoke, UK: Palgrave Macmillan, 2009.

Kaul, Suvir. *Poems of Nation, Anthems of Empire: English Verse in the Long Eighteenth Century.* Charlottesville: University of Virginia Press, 2000.

Kelly, James. "'This iniquitous traffic': The Kidnapping of Children for the American Colonies in Eighteenth-Century Ireland." *Journal of the History of Childhood and Youth* 9, no. 2 (2016): 233–46.

Kenny, Shirley Strum. "Richard Steele and the 'Pattern of Genteel Comedy.'" *Modern Philology* 70, no. 1 (1972): 22–37.

Kim, Elizabeth S. "Penelope Aubin's Novels Reconsidered: The Barbary Captivity Narrative and Christian Ecumenism in Early Eighteenth-Century Britain." *Eighteenth-Century Novel* 8 (2011): 1–29.

Klein, Herbert, and Ben Vinson. *African Slavery in Latin America.* Cambridge: Cambridge University Press, 2009.

Knapp, Lewis, and Lillian de la Torre. "Smollett, MacKercher, and the Annesley Claimant." *English Language Notes* 1 (1963): 28–33.

Kozaczka, Edward J. "Penelope Aubin and Narratives of Empire." *Eighteenth-Century Fiction* 25, no. 1 (2012): 199–225.

Krise, Thomas W. *Caribbeana: An Anthology of English Literature of the West Indies, 1657–1777.* Chicago: University of Chicago Press, 2009.

Landry, Donna. *Muses of Resistance: Laboring-Class Women's Poetry in Britain, 1739–1796.* Cambridge: Cambridge University Press, 1990.

Lanor, Andrew, ed. *The Annesley Case.* Edinburgh: William Hodge Company, 1912.

Latimer, John. *History of the Society of Merchant Venturers of the City of Bristol with Some Account of the Anterior Merchants' Guilds.* Bristol: J. W. Arrowsmith, 1903.

Latimer, Jon. *Buccaneers of the Caribbean: How Piracy Forged an Empire.* Cambridge, Mass.: Harvard University Press, 2009.

Latsch, Wolfram. "A Black Lord Mayor of London in the Eighteenth Century?" *Notes and Queries* 63, no. 4 (2016): 615–17.

Law, Robin. *The English in West Africa, 1681–1683: The Local Correspondence of the Royal African Company of England 1681–1699, Part 1.* Oxford: Oxford University Press, 1997.

———. "The First Scottish Guinea Company, 1634–9." *Scottish Historical Review* 76, no. 202, pt. 2 (1997): 185–202.

Lewis, Andrew. "'An Incendiary Press': British West Indian Newspapers during the Struggle for Abolition." *Slavery & Abolition* 16, no. 3 (1995): 346–61.

Linebaugh, Peter. *The London Hanged: Crime and Civil Society in the Eighteenth Century.* Cambridge: Cambridge University Press, 1992.

Linebaugh, Peter, and Marcus Rediker. *The Many-Headed Hydra: Sailors, Slaves, Commoners, and the Hidden History of the Revolutionary Atlantic.* Boston: Beacon Press, 2000.

Loftis, John. *Steele at Drury Lane.* Berkeley: University of California Press, 1952.

Looser, Devoney. "Breaking the Silences: Exploring the Austen Family's Complex Entanglements with Slavery." *Times Literary Supplement,* May 21, 2021.

MacSwiney, Marquis. "Two Distinguished Irishmen in the Spanish Service: Sir Toby Bourke and Dr. John Higgins." *Studies: An Irish Quarterly Review* 28, no. 109 (1939): 63–84.

Madan, Falconer. *The Madan Family and the Maddens in Ireland and England: A Historical Account.* Oxford: Oxford University Press, 1933.

Madar, Allison. "Servitude in the Eighteenth-Century British Atlantic World: Old Paradigms and New Directions." *History Compass* 15, no. 11 (2017). https://doi-org.proxy .library.vcu.edu/10.1111/hic3.12411.

Magra, Christopher Paul. *Poseidon's Curse: British Naval Impressment and Atlantic Origins of the American Revolution.* Cambridge: Cambridge University Press, 2016.

Makdisi, Saree, and Felicity Nussbaum, eds. *The Arabian Nights in Historical Context: Between East and West.* Oxford: Oxford University Press, 2008.

Mallipeddi, Ramesh. "'A Fixed Melancholy': Migration, Memory, and the Middle Passage." *Eighteenth Century: Theory and Interpretation* 55, no. 2/3 (2014): 235–53.

———. *Spectacular Suffering: Witnessing Slavery in the Eighteenth-Century British Atlantic.* Charlottesville: University of Virginia Press, 2016.

Mannheimer, Katherine. "Celestial Bodies: Gender and the Spectacle of Readerly Rapture in Aphra Behn's *Emperor of the Moon,*" *Restoration* 35, no. 1 (2001): 39–61.

Marshall, Alan. "'Memorialls for Mrs. Affora': Aphra Behn and the Restoration Intelligence World." *Women's Writing* 22, no. 1 (2015): 13–33.

Marshall, E. Gerald. "'Joy too Exquisite for Laughter': A Re-evaluation of Steele's *The Conscious Lovers.*" *Literature and Belief* 4 (1984): 33–48.

Martin, Laura. "'Servants Have the Worser Lives': The Poetics and Rhetorics of Servitude and Slavery in *Inkle and Yarico's* Barbados." In *Invoking Slavery in the Eighteenth-Century British Imagination,* edited by Srividhya Swaminathan and Adam R. Beach, 115–32. Farnham, UK: Ashgate, 2013.

Mason, Matthew. "Slavery, Servitude, and British Representations of Colonial North America." *Southern Quarterly* 43, no. 4 (2006): 109–25.

Matar, Nabil. *Britain and Barbary, 1589–1689.* Gainesville: University Press of Florida, 2005.

———. *Turks, Moors, and Englishmen in the Age of Discovery.* New York: Columbia University Press, 1999.

Mathias, Peter. Rev. *Politics and the Port of Bristol in the Eighteenth Century* (1963), by W. E. Minchinton. *Economic History Review* 20, no. 2 (1967): 400–401.

McBurney, William H. "Mrs. Penelope Aubin and the Early-Eighteenth-Century English Novel." *Huntington Library Quarterly* 20 (1956–57): 245–67.

McCusker, John J. *Essays in the Economic History of the Atlantic World.* New York: Routledge, 1997.

McCusker, John J., and Kenneth Morgan, eds. *The Early Modern Atlantic Economy.* Cambridge: Cambridge University Press, 2000.

McDade, Katie. "Bristol and Liverpool Port Improvements in the Latter Half of the Eighteenth Century: The Case for Liverpool's Entrepreneurial Success." *International Journal of Maritime History* 24, no. 2 (2012): 201–24.

McKeon, Michael. *The Secret History of Domesticity: Public, Private, and the Division of Knowledge.* Baltimore: Johns Hopkins University Press, 2005.

McLeod, Bruce. *The Geography of Empire in English Literature, 1580–1745.* Cambridge: Cambridge University Press, 1999.

Michals, Teresa. "'That Sole and Despotic Dominion': Slaves, Wives, and Game in Blackstone's *Commentaries.*" *Eighteenth-Century Studies* 27, no. 2 (1993/94): 195–216.

Milhous, Judith. "Multimedia Spectacular on the Restoration Stage." In *British Theatre and the Other Arts, 1600–1800,* edited by Shirley Strum Kenny, 41–66. Washington, D.C.: Folger Books, 1984.

Miller, Shannon. "Executing the Body Politic: Inscribing State Violence onto Aphra Behn's *Oroonoko.*" In *Violence, Politics, and Gender in Early Modern England,* edited by Joseph P. Ward, 173–206. New York: Palgrave Macmillan, 2008.

Mitchell, Matthew David. "'Legitimate Commerce' in the Eighteenth Century: The Royal African Company of England under the Duke of Chandos, 1720–1726." *Enterprise and Society* 14, no. 3 (2013): 544–78.

Mitsein, Rebekah. "Trans-Saharan Worlds and World Views in Aphra Behn's *Oroonoko.*" *Eighteenth-Century Fiction* 30, no. 3 (2018): 339–68.

Molineux, Catherine. *Faces of Perfect Ebony: Encountering Atlantic Slavery in Imperial Britain.* Cambridge, Mass.: Harvard University Press, 2012.

Montaño, John Patrick. "The Quest for Consensus: The Lord Mayor's Day Shows in the 1670s." In *Culture and Society in the Stuart Restoration,* edited by Gerald MacLean, 31–51. Cambridge: Cambridge University Press, 1995.

Moore, Sean. "Exorcising the Ghosts of Racial Capitalism from the South Sea Bubble: Pent-up Racist Liquidity and the Recent Four-Year Stock Surge." *Eighteenth-Century Studies* 54, no. 1 (2020): 1–13.

Morgan, Gwenda, and Peter Rushton. "Visible Bodies: Power, Subordination, and Identity in the Eighteenth-Century Atlantic World." *Journal of Social History* 39, no. 1 (2005): 39–64.

Morgan, Jennifer L. "Accounting for 'The Most Excruciating Torment': Gender, Slavery, and Trans-Atlantic Passages." *History of the Present* 6, no. 2 (2016): 184–207.

———. "Archives and Histories of Racial Capitalism." *Social Text* 33, no. 4 (2015): 153–61.

———. "Periodization Problems: Race and Gender in the History of the Early Republic." *Journal of the Early Republic* 36, no. 2 (2016): 351–357.

Morgan, Kenneth. "Bristol and the Atlantic Trade in the Eighteenth Century." *English Historical Review* 107, no. 424 (1992): 626–50.

———. *Bristol and the Atlantic Economy in the Eighteenth Century*. Cambridge: Cambridge University Press, 1993.

———. "Bristol West India Merchants in the Eighteenth Century." *Transactions of the Royal Historical Society* 3 (December 1993): 185–208.

———. "English and American Attitudes towards Convict Transportation 1718–1775." *History* 72, no. 236 (1987): 416–31.

Morrissey, Lee. "Transplanting English Plantations in Aphra Behn's *Oroonoko*." *Global South* 10, no. 2 (2016): 11–26.

Mounsey, Chris, and Caroline Gonda, eds. *Queer People: Negotiations and Expressions of Homosexuality, 1700–1800*. Lewisburg, Pa.: Bucknell University Press, 2007.

Navin, John J. "Intimidation, Violence, and Race in British America." *Historian* 77, no. 3 (2015): 464–97.

Nussbaum, Felicity. "Between 'Oriental' and 'Blacks So Called,' 1688–1788." In *The Postcolonial Enlightenment: Eighteenth-Century Colonialism and Postcolonial Theory*, edited by Daniel Carey and Lynn Festa, 137–66. Oxford: Oxford University Press, 2009.

———. *The Limits of the Human: Fictions of Anomaly, Race, and Gender in the Long Eighteenth Century*. Cambridge: Cambridge University Press, 2003.

O'Brien, John. *Literature Incorporated: The Cultural Unconscious of the Business Corporation, 1650–1850*. Chicago: University of Chicago Press, 2016.

Ogborn, Miles. *Global Lives: Britain and the World, 1550–1800*. Cambridge: Cambridge University Press, 2008.

———. *Spaces of Modernity: London's Geographies, 1680–1780*. New York: Guilford Press, 1998.

O'Malley, Gregory E. *Final Passages: The Intercolonial Slave Trade of British America, 1619–1807*. Chapel Hill: University of North Carolina Press for the Omohundro Institute of Early American History and Culture, 2014,

Orr, Bridget. *Empire on the English Stage, 1660–1714*. Cambridge: Cambridge University Press, 2001.

Orr, Leah. "Attribution Problems in the Fiction of Aphra Behn." *Modern Language Review* 108, no. 1 (2013): 30–51.

———. "The Basis for Attribution in the Canon of Eliza Haywood." *The Library: The Transactions of the Bibliographical Society* 12, no. 4 (2011): 335–75.

Osteen, Mark, and Martha Woodmansee. "Taking Account of the New Economic Criticism: An Historical Introduction." In *The New Economic Criticism: Studies at the Interface of Literature and Economics*, edited by Mark Osteen and Martha Woodmansee, 30–50. London: Routledge, 2005.

Overton, Bill, ed. *A Letter to My Love: Love Poems by Women First Published in the Bar-bardos Gazette, 1731–1737.* Newark: University of Delaware Press; London: Associ-ated University Presses, 2001.

Owen, Susan J. "Behn's Dramatic Response to Restoration Politics." In *The Cambridge Companion to Aphra Behn,* edited by Derek Hughes and Janet Todd, 68–82. Cam-bridge: Cambridge University Press, 2004.

———. *Restoration Theatre and Crisis.* Oxford: Clarendon Press, 1996.

Oxford Dictionary of National Biography (DNB). https://www.oxforddnb.com/.

Oxford English Dictionary (OED). https://www.oed.com/.

Pacheco, Anita. "'Where Lies This Power Divine?': The Representation of Kingship in Aphra Behn's Early Tragicomedies." *Journal for Eighteenth-Century Studies* 38, no. 3 (2015): 317–34.

Paisey, David. "Black English in Britain in the Eighteenth Century." *Electronic British Li-brary Journal* (2015), Article 12. http://www.bl.uk/eblj/2015articles/article12.html.

Palmer, Colin. *Human Cargoes: The British Slave Trade to Spanish America, 1700–1739.* Urbana: University of Illinois Press, 1981.

Parent, Anthony. *Foul Means: The Formation of a Slave Society in Virginia, 1660–1740.* Chapel Hill: University of North Carolina Press for the Omohundro Institute of Early American History and Culture, 2003.

Parker, Katherine. Rev. Abigail L. Swingen, *Competing Visions of Empire* and Adrian Fi-nucane, *The Temptations of Trade. Eighteenth-Century Studies* 51, no. 3 (2018): 375–77.

Parker, Matthew. *Willoughbyland: England's Lost Colony.* New York: St. Martin's Press, 2015.

Pearce, Edward. *The Great Man: Sir Robert Walpole.* London: Pimlico, 2008.

Pettigrew, William. *Freedom's Debt: The Royal African Company and the Politics of the At-lantic Slave Trade, 1672–1752.* Chapel Hill: University of North Carolina Press, 2013.

———. "Free to Enslave: Politics and the Escalation of Britain's Transatlantic Slave Trade, 1688–1714." *William and Mary Quarterly,* 3d ser. 64, no. 1 (2007): 3–38.

Pietsch, Roland. "Ship's Boys and Youth Culture in Eighteenth-Century Britain: The Navy Recruits of the London Marine Society." *Northern Mariner* 14, no. 4 (2004): 11–24.

Pincus, Stephen. *1688: The First Modern Revolution.* New Haven: Yale University Press, 2009.

Pitcher, E. W. "An Editor of *The London Magazine* (1732–85): Alexander Hogg." *Notes and Queries* (June 1997): 213–14.

Pollock, Anthony. "Neutering Addison and Steele: Aesthetic Failure and the Spectato-rial Public Sphere." *ELH* 74, no. 3 (2007): 707–34.

Porter, Roy. *The Penguin Social History of Britain: English Society in the Eighteenth Cen-tury.* London: Penguin, 1980.

Prescott, Sarah. "Penelope Aubin and the Doctrine of Morality: A Reassessment of the Pious Woman Novelist." *Women's Writing* 1, no. 1 (1994): 99–112.

Procter, Frank. *Damned Notions of Liberty: Slavery, Culture, and Power in Colonial Mexico.* Albuquerque: University of New Mexico Press, 2010.

Puckrein, Gary A. *Little England: Plantation Society and Anglo-Barbadian Politics, 1627–1700.* New York: New York University Press, 1984.

Rawley, James A., with Stephen D. Behrendt. *The Transatlantic Slave Trade: A History.* Rev. ed. Lincoln: University of Nebraska Press, 2005.

Razi, Alpen. "Narratives of Amelioration: Mental Slavery and the New World Slave Society in the Eighteenth-Century Didactic Imagination." PhD diss., University of Toronto, 2016.

Rediker, Marcus Buford. *Between the Devil and the Deep Blue Sea: Merchant Seaman, Pirates, and the Anglo-American Maritime World, 1700–1750.* Cambridge: Cambridge University Press, 1987.

Ressel, Magnus. "Protestant Slaves in Northern Africa during the Early Modern Era." In *Serfdom and Slavery in the European Economy, 11th-18th Centuries,* edited by Simonetta Cavaciocchi, 523–36. Florence, Italy: Firenze University Press, 2013.

Richardson, David. *Bristol, Africa, and the Eighteenth-Century Slave Trade to America.* 4 vols. Bristol: Bristol Record Society, 1986–96.

———. *The Bristol Slave Traders: A Collective Portrait.* Bristol: Bristol Historical Association, 1985.

Richardson, John A. *Slavery and Augustan Literature: Swift, Pope, Gay.* London: Routledge, 2004.

Richetti, John. *Popular Fiction before Richardson: Narrative Patterns 1700–1739.* Oxford: Clarendon Press, 1969.

Roach, Joseph. *Cities of the Dead: Circum-Atlantic Performance.* New York: Columbia University Press, 1996.

Roberts, David. "First Night in Bristol: Reflections on a 250th Anniversary." *New Theatre Quarterly* 32, no. 3 (2016): 203–9.

Roberts, Leonard A. "Bridewell: The World's First Attempt at Prisoner Rehabilitation through Education." *Journal of Correctional Education* 35, no. 3 (1984): 83–85.

Rodgers, Nini. *Ireland, Slavery, and Anti-Slavery: 1612–1865.* Houndmills, UK: Palgrave Macmillan, 2007.

Rodriguez, Jarbel. *Captives and the Saviors in the Medieval Crown of Aragon.* Washington, D.C.: Catholic University of America Press, 2007.

Rothschild, Emma. *The Inner Life of Empires: An Eighteenth-Century History.* Princeton, N.J.: Princeton University Press, 2011.

Rozbicki, Michal J. "A Barrier or a Bridge to American Identity? The Uses of European Taste among Eighteenth-Century Plantation Gentry in British America." *American Studies* 42, no. 3 (1998): 433–49.

——. "The Curse of Provincialism: Negative Perceptions of Colonial American Plantation Gentry." *Journal of Southern History* 63, no. 4 (1997): 727–52.

Rubin, Gayle. "Traffic in Women: Notes on the 'Political Economy' of Sex." In *Toward an Anthropology of Women*, edited by Rayna R. Reiter, 157–210. New York: Monthly Review Press, 1975.

Rudé, George. *Hanoverian London, 1714–1808*. Berkeley: University of California Press, 1971.

Ryan, Barbara. *Love, Wages, Slavery: The Literature of Servitude in the United States*. Urbana: University of Illinois Press, 2006.

Sacks, David Harris. *The Widening Gate: Bristol and the Atlantic Economy, 1450–1700*. Berkeley: University of California Press, 1991.

Salinger, Sharon V. *"To Serve Well and Faithfully": Labor and Indentured Servants in Pennsylvania, 1682–1800*. Cambridge: Cambridge University Press, 1987.

——. "Labor, Markets, and Opportunity: Indentured Servitude in Early America." *Labor History* 38, no. 2 (1997): 311–38.

Schama, Simon. *Rough Crossings: Britain, the Slaves, and the American Revolution*. New York: Ecco, 2006.

Schneider, Elena. "African Slavery and Spanish Empire: Imperial Imaginings and Bourbon Reform in Eighteenth-Century Cuba and Beyond." *Journal of Early American History* 5, no. 1 (2015): 3–29.

Schulenburg, Jane Tibbetts. "The Heroics of Virginity: Brides of Christ and Sacrificial Mutilation." In *Women in the Middle Ages and the Renaissance*, edited by Mary Beth Rose, 29–72. Syracuse, N.Y.: Syracuse University Press, 1986.

Sedgewich, Romney, ed. *The History of Parliament: The House of Commons, 1715–1754*. London: Her Majesty's Stationery Office, 1970.

Shaffer, Jason. *Performing Patriotism: National Identity in the Colonial and Revolutionary American Theatre*. Philadelphia: University of Pennsylvania Press, 2007.

Shepherd, Verene A., ed. *Slavery without Sugar: Diversity in Caribbean Economy and Society since the 17th Century*. Gainesville: University Press of Florida, 2002.

Shyllon, Folarin. *Black People in Britain, 1555–1833*. New York: Oxford University Press, 1977.

Sills, Adam. "Surveying the 'Map of Slavery' in Aphra Behn's *Oroonoko*." *Journal of Narrative Theory* 36, no. 3 (2006): 314–40.

Skinner, Patricia. "Marking the Face, Curing the Soul? Reading the Disfigurement of Women in the Later Middle Ages." In *Medicine, Religion, and Gender in Medieval Culture*, edited by Naoë Kukita Yoshikawa, 181–201. Suffolk, UK: Boydell & Brewer, 2015.

Smith, Clint. *How the Word is Passed: A Reckoning with the History of Slavery across America*. New York: Little, Brown and Company, 2021.

Smith, David Chan. "Useful Knowledge, Improvement, and the Logic of Capital in Richard Ligon's *True and Exact History of Barbados*." *Journal of the History of Ideas* 78, no. 4 (2017): 549–70.

Snader, Joe. *Caught between Worlds: British Captivity Narratives in Fact and Fiction*. Lexington: University Press of Kentucky, 2015.

Spedding, Patrick. *A Bibliography of Eliza Haywood*. London: Pickering and Chatto, 2004.

Staves, Susan. *A Literary History of Women's Writing in Britain, 1660–1789*. Cambridge: Cambridge University Press, 2006.

———. *Married Women's Separate Property in England, 1660–1833*. Cambridge, Mass.: Harvard University Press, 1990.

Steele, Ian K. *The English Atlantic 1675–1740: An Exploration of Communication and Community*. New York: Oxford University Press, 1986.

Stoler, Ann Laura, and Frederick Cooper. "Between Metropole and Colony: Rethinking a Research Agenda." In *Tensions of Empire: Colonial Cultures in a Bourgeois World*, edited by Ann Laura Stoler and Frederick Cooper, 1–56. Berkeley: University of California Press, 2007.

Stone, Lawrence. *The Road to Divorce: England, 1530–1987*. Oxford: Oxford University Press, 1990.

Sussman, Charlotte. *Consuming Anxieties: Consumer Protest, Gender, and British Slavery, 1713–1833*. Stanford, Calif.: Stanford University Press, 2000.

Swaminathan, Srividhya, and Adam R. Beach, eds. *Invoking Slavery in the Eighteenth-Century British Imagination*. Farnham, UK: Ashgate, 2013.

Swingen, Abigail L. *Competing Visions of Empire: Labor, Slavery, and the Origins of the British Atlantic Empire*. New Haven: Yale University Press, 2015.

Tandon, Bharat. "'Labours Not Her Own': *Emma* and the Invisible World." *Persuasions* 38 (2016): 116–30.

Thomson, Ann. *Barbary and Enlightenment: European Attitudes toward the Maghreb in the Eighteenth Century* Leiden: Brill, 1987.

Thornton, James. *Africa and Africans in the Making of the Atlantic World, 1400–1800*. Cambridge: Cambridge University Press, 1998.

Todd, Janet. *The Secret Life of Aphra Behn*. New Brunswick, N.J.: Rutgers University Press, 1997.

Todd, Janet, and Francis McKee. "The 'Shee Spy': Unpublished Letters on Aphra Behn, Secret Agent." *Times Literary Supplement*, September 10, 1993, 4–5.

Tomkins, Alannah. "Almshouse versus Workhouse: Residential Welfare in 18th-Century Oxford." *Family and Community History* 7, no. 1 (2004): 45–58.

Tomlins, Christopher. "Reconsidering Indentured Servitude: European Migration and the Early American Labor Force, 1600–1775." *Labor History* 42, no. 1 (2001): 5–43.

Tumbleson, Raymond D. "The Triumph of London: Lord Mayor's Day Pageants and the Rise of the City." In *The Witness of Times: Manifestations of Ideology in Seventeenth Century England*, edited by Katherine Z. Keller and Gerald J. Schiffhorst, 53–68. Pittsburgh: Duquesne University Press, 1993.

Vallance, Edward. *The Glorious Revolution: 1688, Britain's Fight for Liberty*. New York: Pegasus Books, 2008.

Vitkus, Daniel J. "The Circulation of Bodies: Slavery, Maritime Commerce, and English Captivity Narratives in the Early Modern Period." In *Colonial and Postcolonial Incarceration*, edited by Graeme Harber, 23–38. London: Bloomsbury, 2001.

———. *Turning Turk: English Theatre and The Multicultural Mediterranean, 1570–1630*. Houndmills: Palgrave Macmillan, 2003.

———, ed. *Piracy, Slavery, and Redemption: Barbary Captivity Narratives from Early Modern England*. New York: Columbia University Press, 2001.

Walmsley, Peter. "The African Artisan Meets the English Sailor: Technology and the Savage for Defoe." *The Eighteenth Century: Theory and Interpretation* 59, no. 3 (2018): 347–68.

Ward, J. R. *British West Indian Slavery, 1750–1834: The Process of Amelioration*. Oxford: Clarendon Press, 1988.

Ware, Stephen. "A 20th-Century Debate about Imprisonment for Debt." *American Journal of Legal History* 54, no. 3 (2014): 351–77.

Wareing, John. *Indentured Migration and the Servant Trade from London to America, 1618–1718: 'There Is Great Want of Servants.'* Oxford: Oxford University Press, 2016.

Warner, William B. "The Elevation of the Novel in England: Hegemony and Literary History." *ELH* 59, no. 3 (1992): 557–96.

———. *Licensing Entertainment: The Elevation of Novel Reading in Britain, 1684–1750*. Berkeley: University of California Press, 1998.

Wear, Jeremy. "Indentured Servitude, Material Identities, and Daniel Defoe in the Chesapeake Colonies." *The Eighteenth Century: Theory and Interpretation* 55, no. 4 (2014): 435–40.

Weiss, Gillian. *Captivity and Corsairs: France and Slavery in the Early Modern Mediterranean*. Stanford, Calif.: Stanford University Press, 2011.

Welch, Pedro L. V. *Slave Society in the City: Bridgetown, Barbados, 1680–1834*. Kingston: Ian Randle Publishers, 2003.

Welham, Deborah. "Delight and Instruction: Women's Political Engagement in the Works of Penelope Aubin." PhD diss., University of Winchester, 2009.

———. "The Particular Case of Penelope Aubin." *Journal for Eighteenth-Century Studies* 31, no. 1 (2008): 63–76.

Wells, Camille. "The Planter's Prospect: Houses, Outbuildings, and Rural Landscapes in Eighteenth-Century Virginia." *Winterthur Portfolio* 28, no. 1 (1993): 1–31.

Wennerlind, Carl. *Casualties of Credit: The English Financial Revolution, 1620–1720*. Cambridge, Mass.: Harvard University Press, 2011.

Williams, E. Carleton. "The Aldermaston Candle Auction." *Berkshire Archaeological Journal* 51 (1948–49): 35–40.

Williams, Raymond. *Marxism and Literature*. New York: Oxford University Press, 1977.

Williamson, Arthur H. "An Empire to End Empire: The Dynamic of Early Modern British Expansion." *Huntington Library Quarterly* 68, no. 1/2 (2005): 227–56.

Williamson, Karina. *Contrary Voices: Representations of West Indian Slavery, 1657–1834*. Mona, Jamaica: University of the West Indies Press, 2008.

Willis, James J. "Transportation versus Imprisonment in Eighteenth- and Nineteenth-Century Britain: Penal Power, Liberty, and the State." *Law & Society Review* 39, no. 1 (2005): 171–210.

Wilson, Brett D. "Bevil's Eyes: Or, How Crying at *The Conscious Lovers* Could Save Britain." *Eighteenth-Century Studies* 45, no. 4 (2012): 497–518.

Wilson, Kathleen. *The Island Race: Englishness, Empire, and Gender in the Eighteenth Century*. New York: Routledge, 2014.

———. *A Sense of the People: Politics, Culture, and Imperialism in England, 1715–1785*. Cambridge: Cambridge University Press, 1995.

———, ed. *A New Imperial History: Culture Identity and Modernity in Britain and Empire, 1660–1840*. Cambridge: Cambridge University Press, 2004.

Winton, Calhoun. *Captain Steele: The Early Career of Richard Steele*. Baltimore: Johns Hopkins University Press, 1964.

———. *Sir Richard Steele, M.P.: The Later Career*. Baltimore: Johns Hopkins University Press, 1970.

Wolfram, Nathalie. "'I Am My Master's Servant for Hire': Contract and Identity in Richard Steele's *The Conscious Lovers*." *Eighteenth Century: Theory and Interpretation* 53, no. 4 (2012): 455–72.

Wolfram, Sybil. "Divorce in England, 1700–1857." *Oxford Journal of Legal Studies* 5, no. 2 (1985): 155–86.

Woodfine, Philip. "Debtors, Prisons, and Petitions in Eighteenth-Century England." *Eighteenth-Century Life* 30, no. 2 (2006): 1–31.

Zilfi, Madeline. *Women and Slavery in the Late Ottoman Empire*. Cambridge: Cambridge University Press, 2010.

Zook, George Frederick. *The Company of Royal Adventurers Trading into Africa*. Lancaster, Pa.: Press of the New Era Printing Company, 1919; reprinted from *Journal of Negro History* 4, no. 2 (1919).